Rio de Janeiro Handbook
The travel guide

Footprint

Mick Day and Ben Box

Nothing that I have ever seen compares to the beauty of this bay. Naples, the Firth of Forth, Bombay and Trincomalee, each of which I have judged perfect in their beauty, all must concede their place to this bay, which surpasses each one in its peculiarities. Superb mountains, rocks piled into columns, luxurious vegetation, bright and flowered islands, verdant beaches and all this combined with white housing, each hill crowned with its church or fortress, ships anchored or about to set off and many boats sailing about in a delicious climate all combine to make Rio de Janeiro the most enchanting setting that the mind can imagine.

Maria Graham 1821

Rio de Janeiro Handbook
1st edition
© Footprint Handbooks Ltd 2000

Published by Footprint Handbooks
6 Riverside Court
Lower Bristol Road
Bath BA2 3DZ. England
T +44 (0)1225 469141
F +44 (0)1225 469461
Email discover@footprintbooks.com
Web www.footprintbooks.com

ISBN 1 900949 80 6
CIP DATA: A catalogue record for this book is available from the British Library.

In USA, published by
NTC/Contemporary Publishing Group
4255 West Touhy Avenue, Lincolnwood (Chicago), Illinois 60712-1975, USA
T 847 679 5500 F 847 679 24941
Email NTCPUB2@AOL.COM

ISBN 0-658-01458-7
Library of Congress Catalog Card number on file

Footprint Handbooks and the Footprint mark are a registered trademark of Footprint Handbooks Ltd.

All rights reserved. No part of this publication may be reproduced, stored in a retrieval system, or transmitted, in any form or by any means, electronic, mechanical, photocopying, recording, or otherwise, without the prior permission of Footprint Handbooks Ltd.

Neither the black and white nor coloured maps are intended to have any political significance.

Credits

Series editor
Patrick Dawson and Rachel Fielding
Editorial
Editor: Sarah Thorowgood
Maps: Sarah Sorensen
Production
Typesetting: Emma Bryers
Maps: Kevin Feeney (colour), Robert Lunn, Claire Benison
Cover design: Camilla Ford

Design
Mytton Williams

Photography
Front cover: Art Directors and Trip
Back cover: original painting by Fábio Sombra
Inside colour section: Beatrix Boscardin, Getty One Stone, Eye Ubiquitous, Robert Harding Picture Library, South American Pictures.

Illustrations
Fábio Sombra

Print
Manufactured in Italy by LEGOPRINT

Every effort has been made to ensure that the facts in this Handbook are accurate. However, travellers should still obtain advice from consulates, airlines etc about current travel and visa requirements before travelling. The authors and publishers cannot accept responsibility for any loss, injury or inconvenience however caused.

Rio de Janeiro state

Contents

1

3 A foot in the door

4 The 'Marvellous city'
7 Cultural Rio
9 Islands and mountains
10 Carnival

2

19 Essentials

21 Planning your trip
25 Before you travel
29 Money
31 Getting there
37 Touching down
47 Where to stay
50 Getting around
59 Keeping in touch
62 Food and drink
65 Entertainment
66 Shopping
67 Holidays and festivals
68 Sport and special interest travel
76 Health
84 Further reading

3

87 Rio de Janeiro city

90 **Rio de Janeiro**
90 Ins and outs
94 Central Rio
111 Northern Rio
118 Southern Rio
118 Glória, Catete and Flamengo
125 Santa Teresa
129 Corvocado and Cosme Velho
131 Botafogo, Urca and Pão de Açúcar
136 Copacabana and Leme
146 Ipanema and Leblon
152 Lagoa, Jardim Botânico and Gávea
155 Vidigal and São Conrado
157 Barra da Tijuca
158 Tijuca National Park
163 Western Rio
118 Guanabara Bay
167 Niterói

4

171 Excursions

174 **The Costa do Sol**
174 Maricá
175 Saquarema
176 Araruama
177 São Pedro da Aldeia
177 Arraial do Cabo
178 Cabo Frio
180 Búzios
183 Macaé
183 **Northeast of Rio de Janeiro**
184 Campos
186 **Inland resorts**
186 Petrópolis
191 Teresópolis
193 Serra dos Órgãos
194 Nova Friburgo
195 Três Rios
196 **Towns in the Coffee Zone**
197 Vassouras
200 Barra do Piraí
200 Valença
201 **West of Rio de Janeiro**
201 Volta Redonda
202 Penedo
203 Visconde de Mauá
204 Itatiaia
206 **The Costa Verde**
207 Angra dos Reis
209 Ilha Grande
211 Paraty

5

217 Background

219 History
224 Modern Rio de Janeiro
226 Land and environment
230 Arts and architecture
240 Culture
250 Useful words and phrases

252 **Index**
255 Map index
255 Will you help us?

Inside front cover
Hotel and restaurant price guide
Dialling codes
Emergency numbers
Useful numbers

Inside back cover
Map symbols
Useful websites

Right: mulatas from a samba school dance on top of a carro alegórico during the Rio carnival.

A foot in the door

The 'marvellous city'

It's said that when God created the world in six days he spent at least two on Rio de Janeiro and certainly few cities have such a privileged location squeezed in between the mountains and the sea. No wonder its inhabitants call it the *cidade maravilhosa* – the marvellous city – and it's just as popular with foreign visitors. For many its name alone signifies glamour, fantasy and a veritable tropical paradise.

Carnival fun The Rio carnival is probably the most famous party in the world. For the five days before Ash Wednesday the city erupts into hedonistic and sometimes even licentious behaviour. The spectacular parades of the *escolas de samba* are the centre of the festivities with colourful costumes and floats that are works of art limited only by the bounds of their designer's imagination. In the streets *blocos* and *bandas* are dancing to samba whilst masked balls are taking place in the steamy clubs. This is the time of year where the rules of daily life are turned on their head and almost anything goes. New Year's Eve is almost as big a party, when fireworks illuminate a Copacabana beach packed with revellers dressed in white.

Smooth jazz Maybe it's something to do with its laid back lifestyle but Rio has produced some outstanding music over the years. At the beginning of the 20th century it was capital of the samba, then regarded as slightly vulgar, which Carmen Miranda later took to Hollywood. In the late fifties and sixties it was Tom Jobim's *Girl from Ipanema* that mixed Brazilian bossa nova with American cool school jazz. From then on the city somewhat lost its place on the world musical stage although it is now beginning to reclaim this with the growing links between the European dance music scene and local DJs culminating in beach raves. However, much gentler sounds such as MPB and *choro* can be heard in the city's bars whilst innovative jazz can still be encountered in piano bars and other clubs.

Sports central Whether body-boarding on the Atlantic waves, hang-gliding on warm thermals over the city or scaling the sheer sides of the Sugar Loaf mountain, sport is an integral part of daily life in Rio. The beach is a natural stadium for volleyball, football and even has its own open-air gymnasiums. Many of today's highly paid football stars started their careers playing barefoot on the hot sands before graduating to the huge Maracanã stadium. Also located inside the city is the tranquil beauty of the Tijuca forest, its shaded trails, cool waterfalls and spectacular viewpoints offer perfect trekking opportunities for those not too tired after a hard night's partying.

Beaches & bohemians Cariocas (the people of Rio de Janeiro) are recognized for their warmth, beauty and their fun-loving attitude towards life. Rio is their playground but it is one that they are more than willing to share with visitors. Looking good is important and everyone seems to be searching for the perfect figure on which to display the skimpiest of swimsuits. The beach is the main meeting place and the daytime schedule at weekends is often divided into before and after the beach. Even during the working week many still find time to slip away for a few hours' bronzing. Once the sun goes down the evening begins to warm up in traditional dance halls and chic discos but it's at the impromptu samba sessions that you begin to see the Cariocas' true spirit, as they sing their witty and joyful tunes accompanied by drums and guitars that seem to appear from nowhere.

Left: *a colourful football shirt is a popular souvenir with many tourists.*
Below: *Cariocas often take their early morning exercise on the beach.*

Left: *the wide sands of Copacabana Beach are home to many beach bars and sunbathers.*
Above: *Rio's last tram is the best way to visit the bohemian Santa Teresa district.*

Right: *the city's poor live in favelas clinging to the hillsides, but some are also now part of the tourist circuit.*
Below: *the modern architecture of the New Cathedral dominates Rio's downtown business district.*

Above: *the UFO style design of the Museum of Contemporary Art in Niterói is a popular attraction with visitors.*
Right: *the neo-colonial Largo do Boticário gives a feeling of what early Rio de Janeiro must have looked like.*

Cultural Rio

Since the days when Rio was the capital of the Portuguese Empire with its attendant court, the upper level of Rio's society has looked towards Europe for ballet, opera, theatre and orchestras. Today the city is still an important destination for the top names in the arts world, whether performing in the Teatro Municipal or on stage on Ipanema beach. The more popular aspects of Brazilian culture such as carvings and ceramic miniatures of rural life can be found in the Museu do Folclore in Catete or in the Casa da Pontal at Recreio dos Bandeirantes, and the Museu Internacional de Arte Naif in Cosme Velho has an excellent collection of folk art.

Colonial Rio

The gold-rush in nearby Minas Gerais and the profits from the lucrative slave trade with Africa made Rio de Janeiro the obvious choice for the Vice-Royalty's new capital in 1763. The riches flowing through the busy port funded the building and lavish decoration of churches and buildings in the city centre that can still be seen today. A walk through today's commercial district can conjure up images of what the city might have been like 200 years ago. Climb the *morro* on which São Bento monastery sits and you will have the same views of ships in the bay as the early colonists must have had. Many of the sombre and powerful forts such as Fortaleza de Santa Cruz in Niterói, which guarded the entrance to Guanabara Bay, can also be visited.

Imperial Rio

It was the arrival of the Portuguese royal family, fleeing from Napoleon's invasion of Portugal in 1808, that heralded a new dawn for the already growing city. The patrimony of the arts and sciences by Dom João and his son Dom Pedro, the first Brazilian emperor, has left a legacy of well-stocked museums and art galleries. The royal family's imposing palace and park in São Cristóvão is a fine reminder of imperial glory as is the Candelária church dividing the traffic on the city's main thoroughfare. The Botanical Gardens, also introduced by the king, are an oasis of peace with wide avenues of imposing palm trees and birds swooping.

Republican Rio

The proclamation of the Republic in 1889 did not bring a halt to the development of the city. There was much influence from France at the beginning of the 20th century, as evidenced in the similiarities between the Teatro Municipal and the Opéra in Paris. The defining building of this period is the Palácio do Catete which saw coups, suicides and was the presidential residence until the capital moved to Brasília in 1960. The quaint hilltop neighbourhood of Santa Teresa with its old mansions is today the bohemian quarter of Rio, peopled by artists and musicians and housing the impressive collection of Brazilian art collector, Castro Maya, a well as the popular bars of Largo dos Guimarães.

Modern Rio

Modern architecture clothes the city now, notably with the 20th-century pyramid of the new cathedral and the enormous Maracanã sports stadium. Across the bay in Niterói is the flying-saucer design of the contemporary arts museum, an extraordinary project by Brazil's most famous architect, Oscar Niemeyer. The marriage of nature and architecture by landscape designer Burle Marx is to be seen all over the city, particularly in the Parque do Flamengo. His museum is just west of Barra da Tijuca, Rio's Miami Beach look-alike suburb with its American atmosphere and steak houses.

Right: inland from Rio near Petrópolis and Teresópolis are the striking mountain peaks of the Serra do Mar.
Below: the peaceful waterfront of the colonial town of Paraty, once a major port for exporting gold to Portugal.

Above: the natural beauty of the Serra dos Órgãos National Park is a beacon for both walkers and climbers.
Right: the endangered coastal forest environment of the Mata Atlântica can still be found within the city in Tijuca National Park.

Islands and mountains

Natural beauty is to be found in all directions from Rio without the need to travel more than a few hours from the city. This long coastline with its many islands is excellent for sailing and diving whilst inland are many national parks offering opportunities for horse riding and trekking, especially near the northern border with Minas Gerais.

The Green Coast

At the end of the old gold route is the colonial town of Paraty. Built by masons, sacked by pirates, today it is a popular resort for weekend breaks from the nearby metropolises of both Rio and São Paulo. Many distilleries in the area produce *cachaça*, a strong local sugar-cane spirit. The survivors of local indigenous tribes still live nearby in isolated reserves. The Rio-Santos coastal highway, bordered by lush mountains, sparkling sea and offshore islands, has to be one of the most beautiful in the world. The historic resort of Angra dos Reis is the stepping stone to Ilha Grande, once a prison and today a nature reserve with unspoilt tropical beaches.

Costa do Sol

East of Rio is a series of salt lakes and sand spits which form a windswept yet stunningly beautiful coastline. Cabo Frio was the landing point for the Portuguese in 1503 and today a magnet for Cariocas wishing to escape from the city. The nearby resort of Búzios was discovered by Bridget Bardot and the world's press in the early 1960s and is now a fairly cosmopolitan yet informal place to spend a relaxing weekend break. Despite being a small fishing village at heart its restaurants boast some of the state's best international cuisine. Surfers are to be found on the beaches of Saquarema whilst divers head for the quieter peninsular and clear water of Arraial do Cabo.

Imperial cities & mountain parks

The imperial summer capital of Petrópolis, once the royal family's retreat, is now just as popular with lesser mortals wishing to escape the heat of the city or experience the grandeur of the emperor's palace. Nearby is the Serra dos Órgãos, a national park which is extremely popular for trekking or climbing the *finger of god*. This area with its alpine conditions drew communities from Switzerland and other parts of Northern Europe to form towns such as Nova Friburgo and Teresópolis. Brewing was an important industry with some of the best beers in Rio being made from the mountain water also home to delicious trout which are served up in the region's restaurants.

Coffee plantations & wild water

Once the coffee belt north and west of the capital dominated the economy of the state with its slave plantations producing the golden beans for export. Many of the deserted *fazendas* in the vicinity of Vassouras and Valença have been restored and are popular for short breaks with today's lords of the manor such as the rock star Mick Jagger. In small towns such as Conservatória, along the Rio Paraíba do Sul, the traditional *seresta* is maintained with processions of serenading musicians in the street. The rapids around Três Rios in the north and Visconde de Mauá in the west are excellent for rafting and canoeing. In the westernmost corner of the state is the 2,787-metre Agulhas Negras, seventh highest in Brazil, and the other peaks and waterfalls of the Itatiaia national park as well as the Finnish immigrant community of Penedo with their traditional saunas.

Carnival (*Carnaval*)

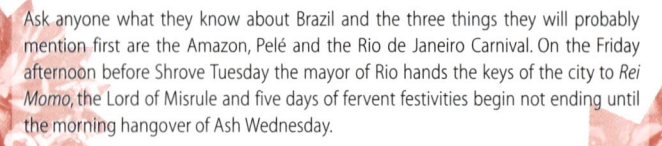

Ask anyone what they know about Brazil and the three things they will probably mention first are the Amazon, Pelé and the Rio de Janeiro Carnival. On the Friday afternoon before Shrove Tuesday the mayor of Rio hands the keys of the city to *Rei Momo*, the Lord of Misrule and five days of fervent festivities begin not ending until the morning hangover of Ash Wednesday.

Origins and history

Carnival has its roots in fertility festivals celebrated by the earliest human societies. With the coming of civilisations such as Rome these festivals became wilder as the strict rules of society and social classes were turned on their heads for the duration of the festivities. It was in cities such as Venice during the Middle Ages that Carnival first began to appear as we know it today, with masked balls, street processions and colourful floats.

The Brazilian carnival tradition originated in the early 18th century along with the *entrudo* (mock battle) and the arrival of immigrants from Portuguese islands such as Madeira and Cape Verde. During the festivities battles were fought with flour, soot, starch and water being thrown over anyone daring to come out in the streets. The battles later became more civilised, with *lança perfume* and confetti used as the weapons, but they were eventually banned although the tradition still survives in the water pistols popular with revellers today. The first parade was not held in Rio de Janeiro until March 1786 with floats designed by Lieutenant Antônio Francisco Soares.

The local rhythm played by Zé Pereira's group with drums, tambourines and other percussion instruments became popular in the late 1840s. The first carnival clubs called Grand Societies linked to civic groups were formed in 1855. Towards the end of the monarchy the themes of the carnival clubs 'Tenentes do Diabo' and the 'Clube dos Democráticos' predicted the abolition of slavery and the coming republic to general applause from the people.

The *Escolas de Samba* (Samba Schools) of today, however, trace their origins to the *blocos* and *cordões* of the old carnival tradition and the first school *Deixa Falar* was formed in 1928 in the Estácio neighbourhood in the north of Rio de Janeiro. The first unofficial parade was held in 1932 followed by an official one in 1935 held in Praça Onze. The first parade with seats sold to the public was held in Avenida Presidente Vargas in the centre of Rio taking place in 1963 and finally moved to its current location in the specially constructed Sambódromo in 1984.

For those with a reading ability in Portuguese, Dr Hiram Araújo's *Carnaval, Seis Milênios de História* (Gryphus: Rio de Janeiro, 2000) is a mine of information on the development of carnival from pre-history to its introduction to Brazil, as well as containing all the results of the Rio de Janeiro carnival since 1932.

Samba schools

It is the parades of the *Escolas de Samba* that are what most recognize as the face of Carnival in Brazil. Although there are samba schools through out the country it is in Rio de Janeiro that the tradition is strongest and most artistic. Carnival is serious stuff and the parades are the culmination of months of intense activity by community groups, mostly in the city's poorest districts. In Rio you're as likely to be asked which samba school you support as which football team.

The most important person in a *Grêmio Recreativo Escola de Samba* – as it is more formally known – is, of course, the president who will be a figure of respect and often authority in the community. Many presidents have also been organised crime figures such as *jogo do bicho* (numbers game) bankers who bankrolled the schools in a form of community relations. It is, however, probably this source of financial support that has helped develop the carnival tradition to its current artistic form due to the high costs of the luxurious parades from the seventies onwards. It is only in recent years that the vast sums to be made from television and recording rights, as well as the popularity of the parades with foreign tourists, have attracted mainstream attention. This has resulted in a new professionalism but also a commercialisation of carnival that is often at odds with the more traditional members.

Escola de Samba (the samba school)

After the president next in importance are the *velha guarda*, the most venerable school members often involved since the first half of last century: figures such as Dona Zica, wife of Cartola one of the founders of *Mangueira* in 1929, and one of the most respected personages in samba. Another very traditional school is *Portela* whose symbol is an eagle, which invariably opens their parade on the first float. Like *Mangueira* (green and pink), this school's distinctive colours (blue and white) will dominate the costumes and floats to create a striking effect in the Sambódromo.

These days the *carnavalesco* is rarely a permanent member of the school although some stay for many years. These are the visionaries who design the floats and costumes in accordance with the *enredo* (theme). The most famous is undoubtedly the charismatic Joãozinho Trinta who revolutionised the parades in the 1970s with first *Salgueiro* and later *Beija-Flor*. He won championships with both schools as well as with *Viradouro* in the 1990s. His recent move to *Grande Rio* can only bode well for this strong school. Others have been just as successful, particularly Rosa Magalhães of *Imperatriz Leopoldinse* whose fantastic creations always put the school in the running for another championship win.

The public face of the samba school is usually the *porta bandeira* (flag bearer) and *mestre sala* (her escort) who with the best *passistas* (individual dancers) will tour Brazil and often the world putting on samba shows to raise money and publicise the school. There are a number of *casais* (couples) in the school including children who are in training to take over the role of the flag bearer and her escort in the future. It is however the *primeira casal* (first couple) who are so important to the school's chances in the competition as the slightest flaw will result in heavy penalisation. The current star is Selma Rocha (known as Selminha Sorriso after her wide smile), flag bearer of *Beija-Flor*, regarded by critics, judges and the public as the epitome of elegance, grace and charm who consistently receives *nota 10* (top marks).

Sambódromo

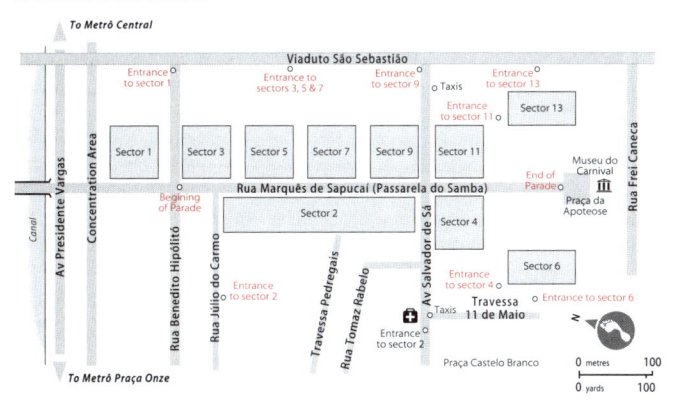

Samba Schools

Grupo Especial: Paraíso de Tuiuti, Tradição, Unidos da Tijuca, Acadêmicos do Salgueiro, Mocidade Independente de Padre Miguel, Portela, Beija Flor de Nilópolis, Império Serrano, Caprichosos de Pilares, Unidos da Viradouro, Imperatriz Leopoldinense, Primeira Estação de Mangueira, União da Ilha do Governador, Acadêmicos do Grande Rio.

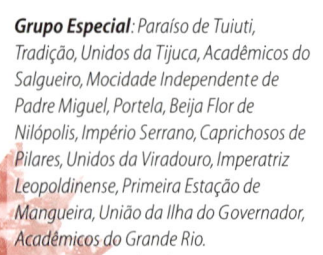

Grupo A: Unidos da Ponte, Leão de Nova Iguaçu, Em Cima da Hora, Unidos de Vila Isabel, Acadêmicos de Santa Cruz, Estácio de Sá, Inocentes de Belford Roxo, São Clemente, Unidos do Porto da Pedra, Império da Tijuca.

Grupo B: Renascer de Jacarepaguá, Unidos da Vila Kennedy, Lins Imperial, Unidos da Vila Rica, Unidos do Jacarezinho, União de Jacarepaguá, Unidos do Cabuçu, Arranco do Engenho de Dentro, Acadêmicos da Rocinha, Foliões de Botafogo, Boi da Ilha do Governador, Acadêmicos de Cubango.

Grupo C: Vizinha Faladeira, Alegria de Zona Sul, Unidos de Lucas, Acadêmicos do Engenho da Rainha, Mocidade Independente de Inhaúma, União do Parque Curicica, Mocidade Unida de Santa Marta, Difícil é o Nome, Unidos de Padre Miguel, Acadêmicos do Sossego, Arrastão de Cascadura, Canários de Laranjeiras.

Grupo D: Acadêmicos da Abolição, Acadêmicos da Barra da Tijuca, Unidos do Cabral, Serreno de Campo Grande, Unidos da Vila Santa Teresa, Boêmios de Inhaúma, Arrastão de São João, Unidos do Anil, Infantes da Piedade, Acadêmicos de Vigário Geral, Mocidade Unida de Jacarepaguá, Imperial de Morro Agudo.

Grupo E: Mocidade de Vicente de Carvalho, Unidos do Uraiti, Délirio da Zona Oeste, União de Vaz Lobo, Gato de Bonsucesso, Unidos de Manguinhos, Arame de Ricardo de Albuquerque, União de Guaritiba, Acadêmicos do Dendê, Unidos do Valéria.

Escolas Mirins: Ainda Existe Criança na Vila Kennedy, Aprendizes do Salgueiro, Corações Unidos do Ciep, Golfinhos de Guanabara, Herdeiros da Vila, Império do Futuro, Infantes do Lins, Inocentes do Caprichosos, Mangueira do Amanhã, Miúda da Cabuçu.

Ensaios (the rehearsals) The samba schools rehearse from around August until the parades in February or March and hold parties on Saturdays (usually) to raise money for the school. The best time to go is until Christmas and the standard improves every week. From the New Year onwards the sessions begin to be crowded with tourists and are hot and more expensive with fewer local people attending. At this time it's best to go to the technical rehearsals which are where the real practice is done. These usually happen during the week or on Sundays: there are no entrance fees and you will only find school members and the drum group attending.

Ensaios are a world away from the fake samba shows in Zona Sul but can be somewhat difficult to reach as the *quadras* are often in poorer communities a long way from the centre in Zona Norte. Two schools that are easier to reach are *Salgueiro*, a mostly white, middle-class school in Tijuca near the Maracanã stadium and *Mangueira*, one of the oldest and most traditional schools (although currently also the favoured school of the gay community) in a slum district not so far away. They're safe and it's easy to take a taxi there with plenty waiting outside all night long. Technical rehearsals are also often held in the streets near the docks close to Praça Mauá where many of the schools have their *barracão* (workshop). Although Saturday nights are essentially *pagode* (see page 247) parties, the *bateria* (percussion wing) will be there and the *porta bandeira* and *mestre sala* will perform. There are often competitions to choose the schools samba and all generations are represented with elderly *sambistas* bringing their grandchildren who will carry on the traditions.

Desfiles (the parades)

The samba schools of Rio are divided into the 14 schools of the *Grupo Especial* organised by the *Liga Independente das Escolas de Samba do Rio de Janeiro*, www.liesa.com.br whilst the *Associação das Escolas de Samba da Cidade do Rio de Janeiro*, www.rioarte.com/aescrj/ organises the schools of the *Grupos de Acesso A* to *E*.

During the next Carnival in February 2001 the Sambódromo parades will occur in the following order: The *mirins* (younger members of the established schools) parade will take place on Friday. The schools of Group A will parade on Saturday. The Special Group will parade on Sunday (first seven schools) and Monday (last seven schools). Finally the schools of Group B will parade on the Tuesday. The schools of Group C parade in Avenida Rio Branco on the Sunday whilst the schools of Group D and E parade in Rua Cardoso de Morais in the Bonsucesso neighbourhood on the Monday and Tuesday respectively.

Every school in the Special Group presents between 2500 and 6000 participants divided into *alas* (wings) each with a different costume and from 5 to 9 *carros alegóricos* which are beautifully designed floats. Each school chooses an *enredo* (theme) and composes a *samba* (song) that is a poetic, rhythmic and catchy expression of this theme. The *enredo* is further developed through the design of the floats and costumes. The *bateria* maintains a reverberating beat that must keep the entire school, and the audience, dancing throughout the parade.

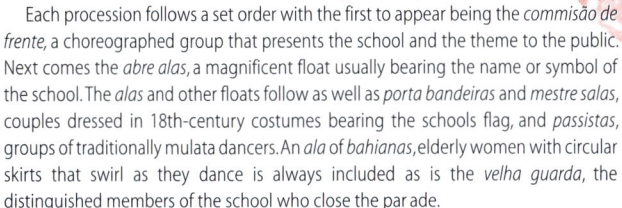

Each procession follows a set order with the first to appear being the *commisão de frente*, a choreographed group that presents the school and the theme to the public. Next comes the *abre alas*, a magnificent float usually bearing the name or symbol of the school. The *alas* and other floats follow as well as *porta bandeiras* and *mestre salas*, couples dressed in 18th-century costumes bearing the schools flag, and *passistas*, groups of traditionally mulata dancers. An *ala* of *bahianas*, elderly women with circular skirts that swirl as they dance is always included as is the *velha guarda*, the distinguished members of the school who close the par ade.

Schools are given between 65 and 85 minutes and lose points for failing to keep within this time. Judges award points to each school for components of their procession, such as costume, music and design, and make deductions for lack of energy, enthusiasm or discipline. The judging takes place on Wednesday afternoon and the winners of the *Grupos de Acesso* are promoted to the next higher group while their losers and those of the *Grupo Especial* are relegated to the next lowest group. Competition is intense and the results are disputed every year especially by those dropping a group. The winners gain a monetary prize funded by the entrance fees as well as the honour of taking part in the Champions' parade on the following Saturday. This is a cheaper option for spectators with ticket prices at a fraction of the main parade but be aware that it is no substitute for the night of the competition which is the true performance of carnival.

Puxador (samba singer)

It's not enough to have a good voice to be a *puxador do samba* but also the stamina to carry the rhythm at the correct tone continuously for the hour and a half of the school's *desfile*. This pivot of the school's performance is accompanied by about four to six backing singers as well as a *surdo de marcação* (drum to mark the beat) and some string instruments. The parade starts to the explosion of fireworks over the Sambódromo and the *grito de guerra* (war cry) of the *puxador* amplified by the *carro de som* (loud speaker truck). Two of the most famous singers currently are Neguinho de Beija Flor (the first to utter the *grito de guerra* in 1976) and Jamaleão the veteran *puxador* of Mangueira.

Bateria (the drum group)

One of the most traditional and important elements of the parade is the *bateria* formed by anything between 200 and 350 percussionists playing a variety of different instruments. The most important is the *surdo*, a huge drum played with a single beater and the sound that marks the rhythm. Other drums include the *repinique*, the *tarol*, similar to a small snare, the *caixa*, for the lighter beats, and the *tamborim*. Other percussion instruments used are the *pandeiro*, a tambourine played with a thin flexible beater, the *agogô*, a sort of cowbell struck by a stick and particularly favoured by *Império Serrano*, *Portela* and *Tradição*. The *chocalho* is similar to a rattle in a frame giving a metallic touch to the sound and is popular with female members. The *cuíca* resembles a small drum into which a hand is inserted to give a sound reminiscent of a laugh, an instrument pioneered by *Estácio de Sá*.

There has been some recent criticism that today the schools have a uniform sound and that innovation is stifled by the judging criteria. In 1998 *Viradouro* mixed in a little American funk only to be heavily penalized, yet in the 1960s it was *mestre* André of *Mocidade Independente de Padre Miguel* who introduced the *paradinha* to great success. In this move the drummers pause and then start again, an incredibly difficult task to do flawlessly. However, in the 1930s the schools would parade with only about 50 drummers and the large increase in numbers today has drowned out the more subtle instruments such as the *pandeiro*. Now few schools have their own individual and easily recognised sound although *Mangueira* is a notable exception by using to this day only *surdo de primeira*, a strong beat which marks the samba rhythm. Other schools may also use a *surdo de segunda* which beats in reply to the first and even a *surdo de terceira* falling in between the other beats as practised by *Mocidade*. The other instruments will add colour to this sound and the jurors are looking for a consistent rhythm, enthusiasm as well as an integration with the *samba-enredo*.

Rainhas & Madrinhas

Although not part of the judging requisites, the Queen or Godmother of the drum group has become one of the most talked about and controversial school members. Although the position requires no more than a senior *passista* who will encourage the audience to chant the school's samba, it was the adoption of famous actresses for the role by a few schools in the late 1980s that awoke media attention. *Rainhas* now fall into two categories, those like *Beija-Flor's* Sônia Capeta, who has come from within the school and community, and others like Luisa Brunet, a white TV actress placed in front of the *bateria* of *Imperatriz Leopoldinse*. No one can doubt her enthusiasm and loyalty to the school but it is incongruous, to say the least, for someone in such a prominent position to be unable to samba convincingly.

The famous guests however are now firmly part of the carnival and no school, even the most traditional, is immune to the lure of publicity from having a star strategically placed on a float to draw the TV cameras. Some like the footballer Edmundo (*Salgueiro*) grew up in the community and have remained loyal to it, whilst others drift from school to school wherever the exposure will be best for their careers. For many starlets this is the time to be noticed whatever it takes on the night.

Celebrities & gossip

Rio's large social circle of celebrities have their own festivities which are for the elite and their invited guests only. Known as the *carnival de camorotes*, special boxes in the Sambódromo are taken over by companies like the brewery Brahma looking to promote their brand in the full light of the cameras and viewing public. There is always a strong rivalry with different companies trying to get the most notable guest list for their box. To encourage them to attend millions of dollars are spent on food, drink and services such as hairdressers. A little bit of drama in the box always helps to keep the cameras focused on the logos and over the years a number of incidents have passed into carnival folklore. Moments after being honoured in Mangueira's parade, musician Caetano Veloso's failure to wear the compulsory Brahma T-shirt resulted in him and his wife being turned away by the doormen. Maradona's drunken antics and Grace Jones' overly amorous behaviour with her bodyguard are also notable. But the most remembered event of all was in 1994 when Itamar Franco, Brazil's president, found himself in the full glare of the cameras embracing a glamour model who was wearing only a short T-shirt and no panties, whilst in the box belonging to a notorious numbers game banker. "Scandal. What scandal?" was his only comment the next morning.

Street carnival

These can be found on the streets in all neighbourhoods of Rio during Carnival. They will have a small drum and musical section and always rehearse at some fixed point such as a bar. During the festivities they parade on the streets and people join in dressing in whatever costumes they want. They are reminiscent of what the samba schools were originally like before the official parades arrived and are a lot of fun. It is generally necessary to join a *bloco* in advance to receive their distinctive T-shirts but anyone can usually still join in.

Blocos
See also under entertainment on page 115

Some of the most popular and entertaining are *Cordão do Bola Preta*, *Simpatia é Quase Amor* and *Suvaco de Cristo*. Their names are usually an obscene or amusing play on words for example *Nem Muda Nem Sai de Cima*, which mixes the expression *nem trepa nem sai de cima* meaning someone who doesn't make up their mind with *Muda*, part of the Tijuca district but also the verb for change. Controversy is often courted and the *Carmelitas de Santa Teresa* encounter problems every year with the head of the Catholic Church in Rio because they parade with a huge doll of a nun. The police take the doll away the night before the parade but the lawyers who support the *bloco* always end up getting it back in time for the parade!

Bandas can often be even more anarchic than *blocos* and especially feature men in drag. There are a number of these transvestite bandas such as the *Banda de Carmen Miranda* and the *Banda da Ipanema* which are both extremely popular with foreign gay tourists. The *Banda da Ipanema* always has an original theme which is often a wry comment on current events. In 1998 many members turned out dressed as firemen. This was after the fire brigade had found a group of children who were lost in Tijuca forest and their father a Russian diplomat had thanked their rescuers with a kiss on both cheeks.

Bandas

The *bandas* came to prominence in the 1960s as a form of resistance to the military regime with the first being the *Banda da Ipanema* in 1965. They were later followed by the *Banda do Leme* and the *Banda Sá Ferreira* in Copacabana and soon the tradition of street carnival had been revived in the neighbourhoods of Zona Sul. There are still many active today and the presence of these costumed and riotous revellers in the streets is a common occurrence during carnival as well as a few weeks beforehand.

Carnaval de Salão (carnival parties)

The first carnival ball was held in January 1840 after the unusual arrival in Rio de Janeiro of a consignment of masks, false beards and moustaches but the first costume ball as such was held in 1846 in the Teatro São Januário in Rua Dom Manuel after the arrival of the *polca*.

Carnival balls

Today Rio´s *bailes* (fancy-dress balls) range from the sophisticated to the wild and the majority of clubs and hotels host at least one. The *Copacabana Palace* hotel's famous ball on Saturday is an elegant and expensive event. The *Scala* club used to have the most licentious parties but the *Help* disco in Copacabana appears to be recently challenging this reputation. Two of the most famous are the Red & Black Ball (held by Clube de Regatas do Flamengo) at the *ATL Hall* in Barra da Tijuca on Friday and the Gala Gay (drag queens costume ball) at *Scala* in Leblon on Tuesday, which are both televised. Gay balls are also held throughout Carnival at *Le Boy* in Copacabana and the *Elite Club* in Lapa. It is not necessary to wear fancy dress, just join in although you will feel more comfortable if you wear a minimum of clothing to the clubs which are crowded, hot and rowdy. All start at around 11pm but only really begin to heat up after midnight. Sunday and Monday are the quietest days as many people are watching the Grupo Especial parades in the Sambódromo.

The top hotels in Rio have special Carnival breakfasts from dawn onwards which are a popular way to end the evenings celebrations. The *Caesar Park* is highly recommended for a wonderful meal and a top-floor view of the sunrise over the beach.

Costumes There are many costume competitions during the run up to Carnival and this is where the beautifully designed outfits of the *destaques* who ride on top of the *carros alegóricos* can be seen. They are divided into the categories of most luxurious and most original for both male and female costumes. The official costume competition was traditionally held on the Monday of Carnival in the Teatro Municipal with the first taking place in 1936. Since 1972 it has generally taken place on Saturday at the Hotel Glória and over the years many stars have distinguished themselves, in particular Clóvis Bornay who would take part but not compete as his costumes were considered so superior to the other contestants.

Alternative Carnival Not everyone in Rio likes Carnival and many Cariocas use it as an excuse to escape the city for a few days of peace and quiet in the countryside or on the beach. For those who have little interest in samba there is also a strong programme of alternative parties and music. The X-Demente party at the *Fundição Progresso* club in Lapa, held on Saturday and Tuesday is reported to be very good whilst the main clubs such as *Club B.A.S.E.* and *Bunker 94* in Copacabana, *W* in Ipanema and many others are also good options throughout the Carnival period.

Carnival essentials

Carnival dates **2001** 25 Feb, **2002** 10 Feb. (This date refers to the Sunday before Shrove Tuesday – the first day of the special groups' parades.)

Tickets The Sambódromo parades start at 1900 and last about 12 hours. Gates (which are not clearly marked) open at 1800. There are *cadeiras* (seats) at ground level, *arquibancadas* (terraces) and *camarotes* (boxes). The best boxes are reserved for tourists and VIPs and are very expensive or by invitation only. Seats are closest to the parade, but you may have to fight your way to the front. Seats and boxes reserved for tourists have the best view, sectors 4, 7 and 11 are preferred (they house the judging points); 6 and 13 are least favoured, being at the end when dancers might be tired, but you will have more space. The terraces, while uncomfortable, house the most fervent fans, tightly packed; this is where to soak up the atmosphere but not take pictures (too crowded). Tickets start at US$40 for *arquibancadas* and are sold at travel agencies as well as the Maracanã Stadium box office (T5689962). Tickets are usually sold out before Carnival weekend but touts outside can generally sell you tickets at inflated prices. Samba schools have an allocation of tickets which members sometimes sell, if you are offered one of these, check its date. Tickets for the champions' parade on the Saturday following Carnival are much cheaper. Taxis to the Sambódromo are negotiable and the driver will find your gate, the nearest metrô is Praça Onze and this can be an enjoyable ride in the company of costumed samba school members. You can follow the participants to the *concentração*, the assembly and formation on Avenida Presidente Vargas, and mingle with them while they queue to enter the Sambódromo. Ask if you want to take photos.

Sleeping & security Visitors wishing to attend the Carnival are advised to reserve accommodation well in advance. Virtually all hotels raise their prices during Carnival, although it is usually possible to find a room. Your property should be safe inside the Sambódromo, but the crowds outside can attract pickpockets; as ever, don't brandish your camera, and only take the money you need for fares and refreshments (food and drink are sold in the Sambódromo.) It gets hot! Wear as little as possible.

Most samba schools will accept a number of foreigners and you will be charged upwards of US$125 for your costume as your money helps to fund poorer members of the school. You should be in Rio for at least two weeks before carnival. It is essential to attend fittings and rehersals on time, to show respect for your section leaders and to enter into the competitive spirit of the event. For those with the energy and the dedication, it will be an unforgettable experience.

Ensaios are held at the schools' *quadras* from August onwards and are well worth seeing. It is wise to go by taxi, as most schools are based in poorer districts. Tour agents sell tickets for glitzy samba shows, which are nothing like the real thing. When buying a Carnival video, make sure the format is compatible (Brazilian format matches the USA; VHS PAL for most of Europe).

Carnival week comprises an enormous range of official and unofficial contests and events which reach a peak on the Tuesday. *Riotur's* guide booklet gives concise information on these in English and Portuguese. The entertainment sections of newspapers and magazines such as *O Globo, Jornal do Brasil* and *Veja Rio* are worth checking. The book, *Rio Carnival Guide*, by Felipe Ferreira, has good explanations of the competition, rules, the schools, a map and other practical details in English and Portuguese.

Taking part

Rehearsals
See page 115 for addresses of samba schools with rehearsal times

Useful information

Essentials

2

Essentials

21	**Planning your trip**	51	Train
21	Where to go	52	Road networks
22	When to go	53	Bus
22	Tours and tour operators	54	Taxi
24	Finding out more	54	Car
24	Language	57	Motorcycling
25	**Before you travel**	58	Cycling
29	**Money**	59	Hitchhiking
31	**Getting there**	59	**Keeping in touch**
31	Air	59	Communications
36	Road	61	Media
36	Boat	62	**Food and drink**
37	**Touching down**	65	Entertainment
37	Airport information	66	**Shopping**
38	Tourist information	67	**Holidays and festivals**
40	Special interest groups	68	**Sport and special interest travel**
42	Rules, customs and etiquette	76	**Health**
45	Safety	76	Before travelling
47	**Where to stay**	79	Staying healthy
50	**Getting around**	82	Other risks and more serious diseases
50	Air	84	**Further reading**

Planning your trip

Where to go

The first port of call in Brazil for most visitors is Rio de Janeiro and so many journeys in South America also begin and end here. Although the city has had a poor reputation in the past regarding its tourist facilities, concerted efforts have been made now to improve the situation. Today both the city and state are an excellent place to spend a few relaxing (or active) weeks which could also include excursions to mountain resorts, national parks, colonial towns, coastal beaches and islands.

Rio de Janeiro, the state capital offers a good mix of history and hedonism. Although the city's colonial history has largely been built over, there are still remnants of all the periods of Rio's time as a capital city of both the Portuguese Empire and the Brazilian Republic. The 20th century has seen the construction of some fine modern buildings in Rio such as the work of architects **Burle Marx** and **Oscar Niemeyer**. The beaches of Zona Sul, especially the famous **Copacabana**, are the most popular with visitors but there are many other points within the city, such as **Santa Teresa**, well away from the tourist hot spots of Sugar Loaf and the Christ. It is here that you begin to see the side of the city that the Cariocas reserve for themselves and which few foreign visitors ever discover. **Rio de Janeiro**

As for having fun, Rio is one of the world's capitals of entertainment, with its famous annual carnival, its spirited and varied nightlife and beach lifestyle, with all the sports that go on there. Culturally, Rio is also rich with theatres, art galleries, libraries, museums and other shows. A recent development has been the movement to integrate *favelas* (shanty towns) into city life, including tourism. Within the city itself is the **Tijuca Forest**, one of the biggest urban forest parks anywhere in the world. Within easy driving distance west of the city there are the **mountains**, coastal *restinga* (marshland, see page 71) and unspoilt beaches around **Guaratiba** and **Grumari**. *See page 10 for special carnival section*

The city is an excellent base for making excursions into the state. There are many fine examples of colonial Portuguese towns, of which the most famous is the port of **Paraty** which grew rich during the gold rush. Later periods are represented by the Imperial cities of **Petrópolis** and **Teresópolis** and the *fazendas* and towns such as **Vassouras** which date from the coffee era. Good beaches can be found along the whole length of the Rio de Janeiro coastline which is divided into the **Costa do Sol** east of Rio and the popular resorts of **Búzios** and **Cabo Frio**. West of the city is the **Costa Verde** with its secluded beaches and islands. The once pirate haunt of **Ilha Grande** near Angra dos Reis is also worth visiting. **Excursions**

Unfortunately only a few tiny pockets of the **Mata Atlântica**, the coastal forest which covered the mountains of the seaboard are left in Rio de Janeiro. Although outsiders are not encouraged to visit the reserve at Poço das Antas, where experts are trying to save the golden lion tamarin from extinction, there are many other national parks which offer good opportunities to see natural habitats. The **Serra da Bocaina** contains Mata Atlântica, while other national parks such as **Serra dos Órgãos** and **Itatiaia** have fine mountain landscapes excellent for climbing, trekking and horse riding. Canoeing and rafting are popular at **Três Rios** and **Visconde de Mauá**.

The cooler mountains attracted immigrants from Scandinavia and Northern Europe during the 19th and early 20th century and their communities can be seen at **Penedo** and **Nova Friburgo**. In the north of the state are Campos and Macaé, both centres for the offshore oil industry but the northern coast around **São João da Barra** is being developed for tourism and is a good place to get off the beaten track.

In the city of Rio you could easily spend a week and not get bored. At one of the beach resorts like Búzios or Angra dos Reis you could spend a weekend (or the equivalent in midweek to avoid the crowds), while Paraty deserves a couple of days. Petrópolis and Teresópolis can be done together in a quick day trip, but an overnight stop is recommended, especially if you want to explore the Serra dos Órgãos. The same applies to the former coffee zone of the Rio Paraíba do Sul and Itatiaia national park.

When to go

Best time to visit The best time for a visit is from April to June, and August to October, inclusive. Business visitors should avoid the city from mid-December to the end of February, when it is hot and people are on holiday. In these months hotels, beaches and means of transport tend to be crowded. July is a school holiday month. If visiting Rio de Janeiro in the low season (ie April to June or August to December) be aware that some tourist sights may be closed for restoration.

Climate Rio, cooled by trade winds, has one of the healthiest climates in the tropics. Conditions during the winter (May to September) are like those of a North European summer (including periods of rain and overcast skies). June, July and August are the coolest months with temperatures ranging from 22°C (18° in a cold spell) to 32°C on a sunny day at noon. However, it can get surprisingly cold south and west of Rio, and on high ground at night, warm clothes are needed.

Summer conditions are tropical and December to March are the hottest months, with temperature ranging from 32°C to 42°C (although temperatures of 40°C are comparatively rare). Humidity is high. It is important, especially for children, to guard against dehydration in summer by drinking as much liquid as possible.

October to March is the rainy season and the annual rainfall is about 1,120 mm. On the coast there is a high degree of humidity. The luminosity is also very high; sunglasses are advisable.

Festivals The dates of the Rio de Janeiro Carnival change every year and can take place between February and early March (see page 16). New Year's Eve known as *Reveillon* is another popular party with beaches all along the coast becoming packed with revellers. June can also be a busy month with the São João festivities. Although the city is livelier at these times accommodation can be hard to find and prices are higher.

Tours and tour operators

Europe Many overland tour operators either start or finish their journeys through South America in Rio de Janeiro. Footprint's *South American Handbook* has their contact details. ***Austral tours***, 20 Upper Tachbrook St, London, SW1V 1SH, T020-72335384, F72335385. ***Cox & Kings Travel***, St James Court, 45 Buckingham Gate, London, T020-78735001, F76306038, Cox.Kings@coxkings.sprint.com ***Destination South America***, T01285-885333, www.destinationsouthamerica.co.uk ***Exodus***, 9 Weir Road, London, SW12 0LT, T020-87723822, F86730779, www.exodus.co.uk Nature trips in Brazil which can start or finish in Rio. ***Hayes & Jarvis***, 152 King St, London, W6 0QU, T020-82227844. Long-established operator offering tailor-made itineraries as well as packages. ***Journey Latin America***, 12 & 13 Heathfield Terrace, Chiswick, London, W4 4JE, T020-87478315, F87421312 and Suites 28-30 Barton Arcade (second floor), Deansgate, Manchester, M3 2BH, T0161-8321441, F8321551, www.journeylatinamerica.co.uk Long-established company running escorted tours throughout South America starting from Rio. They also offer a wide range of flight options and can book hotels in the city. ***Last Frontiers***, Fleet Marston Farm, Aylesbury, Buckinghamshire, HP18 0PZ, T01296-658650, F658651, www.lastfrontiers.co.uk Offer tours throughout Brazil from

Rio de Janeiro as well as excursions to Paraty and Búzios. *Scott Dunn*, Fovant Mews, 12 Noyna Rd, London, SW17 7PH, T020-87678989, F87672026, www.scottdunn.com *Sol e Vida*, Rugensasstr 7, 81479 München, Germany, T089-7917031, F798356, www.solevida.de Specialize in Brazil and South America. *South American Experience*, 47 Causton St, Pimlico, London, SW1P 4AT, T020-79765511, F79766908, www.sax.mcmail.com Good for flights, hotels and tailor-made trips. *STA Travel*, Priory House, 6 Wrights Lane, London, W8 6TA, T020-73616161, F73616262, www.statravel.co.uk Low cost student & under 26 travel. *Trailfinders*, 194 Kensington High St, London, W8 7RG, T020-79383939, 254-284 Sauchiehall Street, Glasgow, G2 3EH, T0141-3532224 and 4/5 Dawson Street, Dublin 2, T01-6777888, www.trailfinders.com Open seven days a week for flights and hotel bookings. *USIT Campus*, 52 Grosvenor Gardens, opposite Victoria underground station, London, T0870-2401010, www.usitcampus.co.uk Student and youth travel with many branches worldwide.

Brazil Nuts, 1854 Trade Center Way, Naples, Florida 34109, USA, T800-5539959, F941-5930267, www.brazilnuts.com Specializes in Brazil with an office in Rio de Janeiro. *BR Online Travel*, 1110 Brickell Avenue, Suite 502, Miami, Florida 33131, T888-5272745, F305-3799397, www.brol.com Specializes in Brazil. *eXito Travel*, 1212 Broadway Suite, Oakland, California 94612, USA, T800-6554053, F510-6554566, www.exitotravel.com Specialists in discount airfares from US or Canada as well as Latin American airpasses. *Field Guides*, 9433 Bee Cave Rd, Building 1, Suite 150, Austin, Texas 78733, T800-7284953, F512-2630117, www.fieldguides.com Specialists in birdwatching with regular tours to Brazil. *Focus Tours*, 103 Moya Road, Santa Fe, New Mexico 87505, USA, T505-4664688, F505-4664689, www.focustours.com Specialists in birdwatching and environmentally responsible travel. *Ladatco Tours*, 2220 Coral Way, Miami, Florida 33145, USA, T800-3276162, F2850504.

North America

sightseeing.

exodus.co.uk
The Different Holiday

Leaders in small group Walking & Trekking, Discovery & Adventure Holidays, Biking Adventures, European Destinations and Overland Expeditions Worldwide.

Tel 020 8772 3822 for brochure.
e-mail: sales@exodustravels.co.uk

Exodus Travels Ltd ATOL 2582/AITO

www.exodus.co.uk

Finding out more

Tourist information
See page 60 for an explanation of phone codes in Brazil

This is handled by the Brazilian Tourist Board, *Embratur*, Setor Comercial Norte, Quadra 2, Bloco G, Brasília, DF 70710-500, Brazil, T0xx61-3289100, F3283517, www.embratur.gov.br

Outside Brazil, tourist information can be obtained from Brazilian embassies and consulates (see box on page 26). Other sources of information are:

Riotur, Rio Tourist Office, 421a Finchley Road, London NW3 6HJ, UK, T0207-4310303, F0207-4317920, destinations@pwaxis.co.uk

South American Explorers, formerly the *South American Explorers Club*, is a non-profit educational organization functioning primarily as an information network for South America. It is a useful organization for travellers to Brazil and the rest of the continent. They can be contacted in the USA at 126 Indina Creek Rd, Ithaca, NY 14850, T607-2770488, F2776122, www.samexplo.org

The *Latin American Travel Advisor* is a complete travel information service offering up-to-date detailed and reliable information about Brazil and countries throughout South and Central America. Public safety, health, weather and natural phenomena, travel costs, economics and politics are highlighted for each nation. You can subscribe to this comprehensive quarterly newsletter (a free sample is available), obtain country reports by email or fax and choose from a wide selection of Latin American maps. Orders may be placed by mail, fax, or through the Web; credit cards accepted. Individual travel planning assistance is available for all customers. Contact PO Box 17-17-908, Quito, Ecuador, F593-2562566, USA and Canada toll free F1-800-3273573, www.amerispan.com/lata/

Language

See page 250 for useful words & phrases

No amount of dictionaries, phrase books or word lists will provide the same enjoyment of being able to converse directly with the people of Brazil. Learning Portuguese is an important part of the preparation for any trip there and you are encouraged to make the effort to grasp the basics before you go. As you travel you will pick up more of the language and the more you know, the more you will benefit from your stay. Efforts to speak Portuguese are greatly appreciated and for the low-budget traveller, Portuguese is essential. If you cannot lay your tongue to Portuguese, apologize for not being able to speak it and try Spanish, but note that the differences in the spoken languages are very much greater than appears likely from the printed page and you may not be understood: you will certainly have difficulty in understanding the answers.

There are Brazilian tutors in most cities (in London, see *Time Out* and *Leros*, the Brazilian magazine, for advertisements). Otherwise try a self study course orientated towards Brazilian Portuguese such as: Barbara McIntyre, João Sampaio & Esmenia Simões Osborne, *Colloquial Portuguese of Brazil* (Routledge, 1997). Language course with cassettes.

General pronunciation

There is no standard Portuguese and there are many differences between the Portuguese of Portugal and Brazil. If learning Portuguese before you go to Brazil, get lessons with a Brazilian, or from a language course which teaches Brazilian Portuguese. Within Brazil itself, there are variations in pronunciation, intonation, phraseology and slang. This makes for great richness and for the possibility of great enjoyment in the language. Describing the complex Portuguese vocalic system is best left to the experts; it would take up too much space here. A couple of points which the newcomer to the language will spot immediately, however, are the use of the til (~) over a and o. This makes the vowel a nasal vowel; vowels also become nasal when a word ends in 'm' or 'ns', when a vowel is followed by 'm' + consonant, or by 'n' + consonant. Another important point of spelling is that words ending in 'i' and 'u' are accented on the last syllable, though (unlike Spanish) no accent is used there. This is especially important in place names: Buriti, Guarapari, Caxambu, Iguaçu. Note also the use of ç, which changes the pronunciation of c from hard [k] to soft [s].

Instituto Brasil-Estados Unidos, Av NS de Copacabana 690, fifth floor, T0xx21-5488332. eight-week course, three classes a week, US$200, five-week intensive course US$260. Good English library at same address. *IVM Português Prático*, R do Catete 310, room 302, T0xx21-2857842, F2854979. US$20 per hr for individual lessons, cheaper for groups. Helpful staff. Recommended. *Cursos da UNE* (União Nacional de Estudantes), R do Catete 243. Include cultural studies and Portuguese classes for foreigners. *Curso Feedback*, branches in Botafogo, Centro, Barra and Ipanema, T0xx21-2211863.

Language courses

Before you travel

Consular visas are not required for stays of up to 90 days by tourists from Andorra, Argentina, Austria, Bahamas, Barbados, Belgium, Bermuda, Bolivia, Chile, Colombia, Costa Rica, Denmark, Ecuador, Finland, France, Germany, Greece, Iceland, Ireland, Italy, Liechtenstein, Luxembourg, Monaco, Morocco, Namibia, the Netherlands, Norway, Paraguay, Peru, Philippines, Portugal, San Marino, South Africa, Spain, Suriname, Sweden, Switzerland, Trinidad and Tobago, UK, Uruguay, the Vatican and Venezuela. For them, only the following documents are required at the port of disembarkation: a **passport** valid for at least 6 months (or *cédula de identidad* for nationals of Argentina, Chile, Paraguay and Uruguay); and a return or onward ticket, or adequate proof that you can purchase your return fare, subject to no remuneration being received in Brazil and no legally binding or contractual documents being signed. Venezuelan passport holders can stay in Brazil for 60 days on filling in a form at the border.

Visas
See box on page 26 for a list of Brazilian embassies & consulates worldwide

Extensions Foreign tourists may stay a maximum of 180 days in any one year. Ninety day renewals are easily obtainable, but only at least 15 days before the expiry of your 90-day permit, from the Polícia Federal, Praça Mauá (passport section), entrance in Av Venezuela. The procedure varies, but generally you have to do the following: fill out three copies of the tax form at the Polícia Federal, take them to a branch of Banco do Brasil, pay US$15 and bring two copies back. You will then be given the extension form to fill in and be asked for your passport to stamp in the extension. According to regulations (which should be on display) you should be able to show a return ticket, cash, cheques or a credit card, a personal reference and proof of an address of a person living in the same city as the office (in practice you simply write this in the space on the form). Some offices will only give you an extension within 10 days of the expiry of your permit.

If you overstay your visa, or extension, you will be fined US$7 per day, with no upper limit. After paying the fine to Polícia Federal, you will be issued with an exit visa and must leave within eight days. If you cannot pay the fine you must pay when you next return to Brazil.

NB Officially, if you leave Brazil within the 90-day permission to stay and then re-enter the country, you should only be allowed to stay until the 90-day permit expires. If, however, you are given another 90-day permit, this may lead to charges of overstaying if you apply for an extension. For UK citizens a joint agreement signed in 1998 allows visits for business or tourism of up to six months a year from the date of first entry into Brazil. However in practice, expect to have to follow the same procedure as detailed above.

US and **Canadian** citizens, **Australians** and **New Zealanders** and people of other nationalities, and those who cannot meet the requirements above such as those requiring to stay longer than 180 days, *must* get a visa before arrival, which may, if you ask, be granted for multiple entry. Visa fees vary from country to country, so apply to the Brazilian consulate in the home country of the applicant. The consular fee in the USA is around US$55. Students planning to study in Brazil or employees of foreign companies can apply for a one or two year visa. Two copies of the application form,

Brazilian embassies and consulates

Argentina C Cerrito 1350, 1010 Buenos Aires, T005411-48158737, F48144689.
Australia 19 Forster Crescent, Yarralumla, Canberra ACT 2600, T00612-62732372. Consulate: St Martins Tower L 17, 31 Market St, Sydney NSW 2000, T00612-92674414/4415, F92674419.
Austria Am Lugeck 1/5/15, A-1010 Wien, T00431-5120631, F5138374.
Belgium 350 Ave Louise, 6eme Étage, Boite 5-1050 Bruxelles, T00322-6402015/6402111, F6408134.
Bolivia C Capitán Ravelo 2334, Ed Metrobol, Sopocachi, La Paz, Casilla 429, T005912-8112233, F8112733.
Canada 450 Wilbrod St, Sandyhill, Ottawa, ON K1N 6M8, T001613-2371090, F2376144. Consulates: 2000 Mansfield, Suite 1700, Montreal, Quebec, H3A 3A5, T001514-4990968/4990969, F4993963. 77 Bloor St West, Suite 1109, Toronto, Ontario, M5S 1M2 T001416-9221058/9222503, F9221832. 1140 West Pender St, Suite 1300, Vancouver, BC V6E 4G1, T001604-6874589, F6816534.
Chile C Alonso Ovalle 1665, Santiago, T00562-6982347, F6715961.
Colombia C 93, No 14-20, 8th floor, Bogota 8, Aptdo Aéreo 90540, T00571-2180800, F2188393.
Denmark Ryvangs Alle, 24-2100 Kobenhavn, T00453-9206478, F9273607.
Finland Itainen Puisotie 4B 1/2-00140 Helsinki, Suomi, T003589-177922, F650084.
France 34 Cours Albert I, 75008 Paris, T00331-45616300, F42890345. Consulates: 11 Bis, Rue Saint-Ferreul, 4eme Étage, 13001 Marseille, T003391-543391/338837, F555176. 34 bis de Cour Albert, 1er Étage, 75008 Paris, T00331-44139030, F43590326.
French Guiana Consulate: 23 Chemin Saint Antoine (Troubiran), BP793, 97337 Cayenne Cedex, T00594-296010, F303885.
Germany Kennedyallee 74-53175 Bonn, T0049228-959230, F373696. Consulates: Esplanade 11, Berlin Pankow, 13187 Berlin, T00490-4459121/4459185, F4459184. Stephanstrasse 3, 4 Stock 60313 Frankfurt Am Main, T004969-9207420, F9207430. Grosse Theaterstrasse, 42-7 Stock 20354, Hamburg, T004940-351827, F351929. Widenmayerstrasse 47, 80538 Munchen, T004989-2103760, F29160768.
Guyana 308 Church St, Queenstown, Georgetown, PO Box 10.489, T005922-57970/57977, F69063.
Ireland Harcourt Centre, Europa House, 5th Floor, 41-54 Harcourt St, Dublin 2, T003531-4756000/4751338, F4751341.
Israel Beit Yachin, 2 Kaplin St, 8th Floor, Tel Aviv, T009723-6963934, F6916060.
Italy 14 Piazza Navona, 00186 Roma, T003906-683981, F6867858. Consulate: Via Santa Maria Dell'Anima 32, 00186 Roma, T003906-6889661/6877891, F68802883.
Japan 11-12 Kita-Aoyama 2-Chome, Minato-Ku, Tokyo 107, T00813-34045211,

---

two photos, a letter from the sponsoring company or educational institution in Brazil, a police form showing no criminal convictions and a fee of around US$80 is required.

Identification You must always carry identification when in Brazil. It is a good idea to take a photocopy of the personal details in your passport, plus your Brazilian immigration stamp, and leave your passport in the hotel safe deposit. This photocopy, when authorized in a *Cartório*, US$1.50, is then a legitimate copy of your documents (these are found all over the city and there is one at Avenida Nossa Senhora de Copacabana 895, look for *autenticação*). Be prepared, however, to present the originals when travelling in sensitive areas such as near the frontiers. Always keep an independent record of your passport details. It is a good idea to register with your consulate to expedite document replacement if yours gets lost or stolen.

Warning Do not lose the emigration permit they give you when you enter Brazil. Leaving the country without it, you may have to pay up to US$100 per person. It is

F34055846. Consulate: Gotanda Fuji Building, 2nd floor, 13-12 Higashi Gotanda, 1 Chome Shinagawa-Ku, Tokyo 141, T00813-54885451/54885452, F54885458.
Netherlands Mauritskade 19-2514 HD, The Hague, T003170-3023959, F3023950. Consulate: Stationsplein 45-3013 AK Rotterdam, T003110-4119656/4119657, F4110088.
New Zealand 19 Brandon St, level 9, Wellington 1, T00644-4733516, F4733517.
Norway Sigurd Syrs Gate 4, 1st floor, 0273 Oslo, T0047-22552029/22552070, F22443964.
Paraguay C Coronel Irrazabal esq Eligio Ayala, Casilla de Correo 22, 1521 Asunción, T0059521-214466/213450, F212693. Consulate: C Gen Díaz esq 14 de Mayo, N 521 Ed Faro Internacional, 3rd floor, Asunción, T0059521-448069/448084, F441719.
Peru Av José Pardo 850, Miraflores, Lima 100, T00511-4212759/4216102, F4452421.
Portugal Estrada das Laranjeiras, 144-1600 Lisboa, T003511-7267777, F7267623.
South Africa 201 Leyds St, Arcadia, Pretoria, Code 0007, T002712-3411712/3411720, F3417547.
Spain C Fernando El Santo, 6 DP 28010 Madrid, T00341-7004650, F7004660. Consulate: Carrer Consell de Cent, 357/1a Ed Brasilia, 08007 Barcelona, T0034-934-882288, F934-872645.
Sweden Sturgegatan 11, 2 Tr 114 36 Stockholm, T00468-234010, F234018.
Switzerland Monbijouster 68-3007 Berne, T004131-3718515, F3710525.
UK 32 Green St, London WIY 4AT, T004420-74990877, F74935105. Consulate: 6 St Albans St, London SW1Y 4SQ, T004420-79309055, F78398958.
USA 3006 Massachusetts Ave NW, Washington DC 20008-3699, T001202-2382700/2805, F2382827.
 Consulates: 401 North Michigan Ave, Suite 3050, Chicago, Illinois 60611, T001312-4640245, F4640299. 1700 West Loop South, Suite 1450, Houston, Texas 77027, T001713-9613063/9613064, F9613070. 8484 Wilshire Blvd, Suite 711/730 Beverley Hills, California 90211-3216, T001213-6512664, F6511274. 2601 South Bay Shore Drive, Suite 800, Miami, Florida 33133, T001305-2856200, F2856232. 630 Fifth Ave, 20th floor, New York 10020, T001212-4897930/9570624, F9563465. 300 Montgomery St, Suite 900, San Francisco, CA 94104-1913, T001415-9818170, F9813628.
Uruguay Blvd Artigas, 1328, Montevideo, Aptdo Postal 16022, T005982-7072119/7072115, F7072086.
Venezuela Centro Gerencial Mohedano, 6th floor, C Los Chaguaramos con Av Mohedano, La Castellana, 1060 Caracas, T00582-2616529/2615505, F2619601.

suggested that you photocopy this form and have it authenticated at a *cartório*, US$1.50, in case of loss or theft.

On arrival in Rio a ship's owner or master should present himself to the Capitania dos Portos (port authorities), in the Espaço Cultural da Marinha at Avenida Alfredo Agache, Centro, T0xx21-2165313, between 1315-1700 Monday – Friday. Local port authorities or their agents should be sought at the other possible entry points in the state such as Macaé, Cabo Frio, Mangaratiba (Itacuruçu), Angra dos Reis and Paraty. Passports and all necessary visas must be presented to the Federal Police at the passenger station in Armazém 1, Praça Mauá, Centro, T/F0xx21-2912122 extension 1106, from 1000-1900 Mon-Fri. Next stops are Serviço de Operações Aduaneiras (Customs) at Avenida Rodrigues Alves, next to the *Banerj* bank, T0xx21-5161715, from 1100-1630 Mon-Fri, and the Vigilância Sanitária (health authorities), Rua México 128, 6th floor, T0xx21-2403568, open daily 1000-1100 and 1400-1500. On leaving the country or sailing in Brazil outside of Rio de Janeiro then the process must be repeated apart from the visit to the health authorities.

Port formalities

Vaccinations
See also page 77

You should be protected by immunization against typhoid, polio, tetanus and hepatitis A. Vaccination against smallpox is no longer required for visitors. Poliomyelitis vaccination is required for children from three months to six years.

Proof of vaccination against **yellow fever** is only required if you are also visiting Amazônia and the Centre West, or are coming from countries with Amazonian territories, eg Bolivia, Colombia, Ecuador, or Peru. It is strongly recommended to have a yellow fever inoculation before visiting northern Brazil since those without a certificate will be inoculated on entering any of the northern and centre-western states. Although yellow fever vaccination is free it might be administered in unsanitary conditions.

Yellow fever and some other vaccinations can be obtained from the *Ministério da Saúde*, R Cais de Pharoux, Rio de Janeiro. Less common vaccinations can be obtained at Saúde de Portos, *Praça 15 de Novembro*, Rio de Janeiro.

What to take
A good principle: take half the clothes, & twice the money, that you think you will need

Everybody has his/her own list. Those most often mentioned include **air cushion**s for slatted seats, inflatable **travel pillow** for neck support, **strong shoes**, a small **first-aid kit** and handbook, fully **waterproof top clothing**, **waterproof treatment** for leather footwear, **wax earplugs** (which are almost impossible to find outside large cities) and an airline-type **eye mask** to help you sleep in noisy and poorly curtained hotel rooms, **sandals** (rubber-thong Japanese-type or other – can be worn in showers to avoid athlete's foot), a **polyethylene sheet** 2 x 1 m to cover possibly infested beds and shelter your luggage, **polyethylene bags** of varying sizes (up to heavy duty rubbish bag size) with ties, a **toilet bag** you can tie round your waist (if you use an **electric shaver**, take a rechargeable type), a **sheet sleeping bag** and pillowcase or separate pillowcase (a 1½-2 m piece of 100 cotton can be used as a towel, a bedsheet, beach towel, makeshift curtain and wrap), a **mosquito net** (or a hammock with a fitted net), a **straw hat** which can be rolled or flattened and reconstituted after 15 minutes soaking in water, a **clothes line**, a **nailbrush** (useful for scrubbing dirt off clothes as well as off oneself), a **vacuum flask**, a **water bottle**, a **small dual-voltage immersion heater**, a small dual-voltage (or battery-driven) **electric fan**, a light nylon waterproof **shopping bag**, a universal bath- and basin-plug of the flanged type that will fit any waste-pipe (or improvise one from a sheet of thick rubber), **string**, **velcro**, **electrical insulating tape**, large **penknife** preferably with tin and bottle openers, scissors and corkscrew – the famous Swiss Army range has been repeatedly recommended (for knife sharpening, go to a butcher's shop), **alarm clock** or watch, **candle**, **torch** (flashlight) – especially one that will clip on to a pocket or belt, **pocket mirror**, **pocket calculator**, an **adaptor and flex** to enable you to take power from an electric light socket (the Edison screw type is the most commonly used), a **padlock** (combination lock is best) for the doors of the cheapest and most casual hotels, spare **chain-lengths** and padlock for securing luggage to bed or bus/train seat. Remember not to throw away spent batteries containing mercury or cadmium; take them home to be disposed of, or recycled properly.

Useful medicaments are given in 'Health' (see page 76); to these might be added some lip salve with sun protection, and pre-moistened wipes (such as 'Wet Ones'). Always carry **toilet paper**. Natural fabric sticking plasters, as well as being long lasting, are much appreciated as gifts. Dental floss can be used for backpack repairs, in addition to its original purpose.

NB contact lens: major cities have a wide selection of products for the care of lenses, so you don't need to take kilos of lotions. Ask for products in a chemist/pharmacy, rather than an optician's.

Customs

Duty free allowance Clothing and personal articles are free of import duty. Such articles as cameras, movie cameras, portable radios, tape recorders, typewriters and binoculars are also admitted free if there is not more than one of each. Tourists may also bring in, duty-free, 24 alcoholic drinks (no more than 12 of any one type), 400 cigarettes, 25 cigars, 280 grams of perfume, up to 10 units of cosmetics, up to three each of any electronic item or watch, up to a total value of US$500 monthly. There is a limit of US$150 at land borders and a written declaration must be made to this effect. Duty free goods may only be purchased in foreign currency.

Money

The unit of currency is the *real*, R$ (plural *reais*) introduced on 1 July 1994 on a par with the US dollar. In June 2000, however, the official rate for the *real* had fallen to around R$1.75 = US$1. Any amount of foreign currency and 'a reasonable sum' in *reais* can be taken in, but sums over US$10,000 must be declared. Residents may only take out the equivalent of US$4,000. Notes in circulation are: 100, 50, 10, 5 and 1 *real*; coins: 1 *real*, 50, 25, 10, 5 and 1 centavo. A new plastic R$10 note has also been recently introduced. Carry low-value US dollar bills for changing into local currency if arriving in Rio de Janeiro when banks or *casas de câmbio* are closed (US$5 or US$10 bills) and take plenty of local currency, in small denominations, when making trips away from large cities.

Currency

Some banks in Rio de Janeiro and other tourist areas in the state will change cash and travellers' cheques. If you keep the exchange slips, you may convert back into foreign currency up to 50% of the amount you exchanged. This applies to the official markets only and there is no right of reconversion unless you have an official exchange slip. The parallel market, found in travel agencies, exchange houses and among hotel staff, was of marginal benefit compared with bank rates in June 2000. Many banks may only change US$300 minimum in cash, US$500 in travellers' cheques. Dollars cash are becoming more frequently used for tourist transactions and are also useful for those places where travellers' cheques cannot be changed and for when the banks go on strike. Damaged dollar notes may be rejected. Parallel market and official rates are quoted in the papers and on TV news programmes. Most large hotels and reputable travel agencies will change currency and TCs. Copacabana (where rates are generally worse than in the centre) abounds with *câmbios* and there are many also on Av Rio Branco. **NB** Some *câmbios* will change US$ cheques for US$ cash with a 4% commission. These transactions are not strictly legal, so you will have to look around for the *câmbios* that do them.

Exchange

Travellers' cheques (TCs) are a safer way to carry your money, but rates for cheques are usually lower than for cash and they are less easy to change, commission may be charged. The international airport is one of the few places to change TCs at weekends.

Tourists cannot change US dollars TCs into dollar notes, but US dollar TCs can be obtained on an American Express card (against official policy). It is a good idea to take two kinds of cheque: if large numbers of one kind have recently been forged or stolen, making people suspicious, it is unlikely to have happened simultaneously with the other kind.

Travellers' cheques

Credit cards are widely used; Diners Club, Mastercard, Visa and American Express are useful. Credit card fraud however is a problem in Rio de Janeiro. Try to avoid the card leaving your sight as duplicate copies could be made. Mastercard/Access is accepted by *Banco Real* and *Citibank*. Overseas credit cards need authorization from São Paulo, this can take up to two hours, allow plenty of time if buying air tickets. Mastercard and Diners are equivalent to Credicard, and Eurocheques can be cashed at Banco Alemão (major cities only). *Banco do Brasil* and *Bradesco Dia e Noite* handle the international Visa automatic teller machine (ATM) network, Visa cash advances up to US$600 can also be withdrawn at these banks. Some of Banco Itaú's. ATMs give cash withdrawals on Mastercard/Cirrus, but are not as common as Visa ATMs. *Banco do Brasil*, *Bradesco* and *Itaú* often have machines at airports, shopping centres and major thoroughfares;

Credit cards
See box on page 30 for a list of emergency telephone numbers to report card loss or theft

Credit card emergency numbers

Credicard: T0800-784411
Diners Club: T0800-784444
Mastercard: T000811-8870533
Visa: T000811-9335589

American Express: T011-2470966
Thomas Cook Visa: T000811-7840553
Thomas Cook refund service:
F+44-1733-502370

Banco 24 Horas machines, at similar locations, operate with Amex, Diners, Boston, Citibank, HSBC cards among others. Credit card transactions are charged at the tourist official rate. Mastercard hotline, 0800-784422 24 hrs a day. *American Express*, Toll-free number 0800-785050. *Visa*, T0xx21-2925394.

Cash advances on credit cards will only be paid in *reais* at the tourist rate, incurring a 1½% commission. Banks in small remote places may still refuse to give a cash advance: if you have run out of cash and TCs, try asking for the manager ('gerente'). Automatic cash dispensers are common in Brazil, but machines which accept foreign cards are harder to find than in some other South American countries. Mastercard is generally difficult to use outside large cities. It's worth remembering your PIN number since queues can be extremely long. In some instances, especially Visa, the card is swiped down a slot, not inserted into the machine, thus avoiding the possibility of the card not being returned.

There are two international **ATM** (automatic telling machine) acceptance systems, Plus and Cirrus. Many issuers of debit and credit cards are linked to one, or both (eg Visa is Plus, Mastercard is Cirrus). Look for the relevant symbol on an ATM and draw cash using your PIN. Frequently, the rates of exchange on ATM withdrawals are the best available. Find out before you leave what ATM coverage there is in Rio de Janeiro and what international 'functionality' your card has. Check if your bank or credit card company imposes handling charges. Obviously you must ensure that the account to which your debit card refers contains sufficient funds. With a credit card, obtain a credit limit sufficient for your needs, or pay money in to put the account in credit. If travelling for a long time, consider a direct debit to clear your account regularly. Do not rely on one card, in case of loss. If you do lose a card, immediately contact the 24-hour helpline of the issuer in your home country (keep this number in a safe place).

Money transfers Money can be transferred between banks. Money sent to Brazil is normally paid out in Brazilian currency, so do not have more money sent to Brazil than you need for your stay. Before leaving, find out which local bank is correspondent to your bank at home, then when you need funds, telex your own bank and ask them to telex the money to the local bank (confirming by fax). Give exact information to your bank of the routing number of the receiving bank. Funds can be received within 48 banking hours.

Professional advice from the specialists on South America

Destination South America

EXPLORE YOUR IMAGINATION

Tailor-Made Holidays
Antarctica, Atacama, Pantanal...

Escorted Group Tours
Andes, Inca Trail, Patagonia...

Special Interest
Fishing, Whale Watching, Wine Tasting...

Cruises & Boat Trips
Amazon, Galapagos, Orinoco...

Islands
Easter, Falkland, Galapagos, Tierra del Fuego...

Beaches
Caribbean, North East Brazil, Pacific Coast...

Tel: **01285 885333**
www.destinationsouthamerica.co.uk
E-mail: sales@dsatravel.co.uk

LATA ATOL 2914

In most large cities *Citibank* will hold US personal cheques for collection, paying the day's tourist dollar rate in *reais* with no charge. *Banco do Brasil* offers the same service with a small charge. From the UK the quickest method for having money sent is by *Swift Air*.

To open a bank account in Brazil, you need to have a visa valid for more than one year and have residency status.

Since the devaluation of the *real* in January 1999, prices for visitors have decreased. Eating in smart restaurants is still costly but hotel accommodation is much more affordable. Budget hotels have responded by cutting extras, cramming more beds into rooms etc. A cheap room will cost about US$10. Shopping prices are equivalent to Europe. Hotel price categories and transport fares in this book reflect the depreciation of the *real*, but travellers may find some variations as the *real* fluctuates against the dollar.

Cost of living

Getting there

Air

International flights to Rio de Janeiro land at Galeão-Antônio Carlos Jobim International Airport (GIG) north of the city. Check all flight details with the agencies concerned. Prices are more competitive during the low season but cheap flights can be very difficult to find during the high season (generally between 15 December and 15 January, the Thursday before Carnival to the Saturday after Carnival and 15 June to 15 August). Flight frequency changes regularly and you are advised to check current timetables.

Regulations state that you cannot buy an air ticket in Brazil for use abroad unless you first have a ticket out of Brazil

If buying a ticket to another country but with a stopover in Rio de Janeiro, check whether two tickets are cheaper than one. Airline tickets are expensive in Brazil, buy internal tickets with *reais* (you can pay by credit card). External tickets must be paid for in dollars.

Varig also has an extensive 'Stopover' programme which gives reduced rates on transfers and hotel rooms in Rio de Janeiro and many other cities in Latin America.

Rio de Janeiro is connected to the principal European cities direct by *Aerolíneas Argentinas* (Amsterdam and Madrid), *Air France* (Paris), *Alitalia* (Rome), *British Airways* (London), *Iberia* (Barcelona and Madrid), *KLM* (Amsterdam), *LanChile* (Frankfurt and Madrid), *Lufthansa* (Frankfurt), *Pluna* (Madrid), *Swissair* (Zurich), *TAM* (Paris), *TAP Air Portugal* (Lisbon), *Transbrasil* (Amsterdam, London and Vienna), *Varig* (Copenhagen, Frankfurt, London, Lisbon, Paris and Milan) and *Vasp* (Athens, Barcelona, Brussels, Frankfurt and Zurich). **NB** in May 2000 *Vasp* cancelled all its international flights for the foreseeable future.

From Europe

Rio de Janeiro is connected to the USA direct by *American Airlines* (Chicago, Dallas, Miami), *Continental* (New York), *Delta* (Atlanta), *TAM* (Miami), *Transbrasil* (Miami, New York, Orlando and Washington), *United Airlines* (Chicago, Miami), *Varig* (Los Angeles, Miami and New York). Other US gateways are Boston, Cincinnati, Denver, Detroit and San Francisco. The cheapest routes are generally from Miami.

From the USA & Canada

Most Latin American cities are connected by air to Rio de Janeiro. There are flights from Asunción with *American Airlines*, *TAM* and *Varig*; Bogotá with *Varig* and *Avianca*; Buenos Aires with *Aerolíneas Argentinas*, *TAM* and *Varig*; Caracas with *Varig*; Córdoba with *Varig*; Guayaquil with *Ecuatoriana*; La Paz with *Varig*; Lima with *Aero México*, *TAM* and *Varig*; Mexico City with *Aero México* and *Varig*; Montevideo with *TAM*, *Pluna* and *Varig*; Santa Cruz with *LAB*, *TAM* and *Varig*; San José, Costa Rica with *Lacsa*; Santiago with *LanChile*, *TAM* and *Varig*; Quito with *Ecuatoriana*.

From Latin America

Essentials

www.journeylatinamerica.co.uk
GO
JOURNEY LATIN AMERICA
BRITAIN'S FOREMOST LATIN AMERICAN SPECIALIST
20 YEARS
SINCE 1980
Flights only
Escorted Groups
Active Adventures
Cruises
Insurance
Brochures
Tailor-made Tours
Search
Favourites
Amazon
Brasilia
Iguassu
Lencois
Manaus
Ouro Preto
Pantanal
Recife
Rio
Salvador
Beaches
Carnival
Cities
History
Wildlife
Search
Regions
Argentina
Bolivia
Brazil
Caribbean
Central America
Chile
Colombia
Ecuador
Mexico
Peru
Uruguay
Venezuela
Fully Bonded
ATOL
ABTA
IATA
JOURNEY LATIN AMERICA
12-13 Heathfield Terrace, Chiswick
LONDON
W4 4JE
020 8747 8315
Fax 020 8742 1312
28-30 Barton Arcade
Deansgate
MANCHESTER
M3 2BH
0161 832 1441
Fax 0161 832 1551

Aerolíneas Argentinas, Austral, Lan Chile, Lapa, Líneas Aéreas Paraguayas, Pluna, Transbrasil and *Varig* operate the **Mercosur Airpass**. Valid for a minimum of seven and a maximum of 30 days, the pass is for a maximum of eight flight coupons with no more than two stops allowed per country. At least two Mercosur member countries must be included; rerouting is not permitted. The air pass is available to all international return ticket holders travelling by air into the participating countries. Passes are price-banded according to mileage flown and fares range from US$225 to US$870. Children pay 67 whilst infants pay 10 of the adult fare and some of the carriers operate a blackout period between 17 December and 10 January.

LAB and *Ecuatoriana* operate a **South American Airpass** valid for 90 days, available to non-residents of Brazil arriving in South America on longhaul flights. There is no child discount and infants pay 10% of the price which varies between US$560 for up to four flights and US$1,100 for the maximum of nine flights. Up to two transfers of less than five hours are permitted and coverage is from northern Argentina, Chile, Bolivia, Peru, Ecuador as well as Brazil.

Air passes

Airlines will only allow a certain weight of luggage without a surcharge; this is normally 30 kilos for first class and 20 kilos for business and economy classes, but these limits are often not strictly enforced when it is known that the plane is not going to be full. On some flights from the UK, special outbound concessions are offered (by *Iberia, Air France*) of a two-piece allowance up to 32 kilos, but you may need to request this. Passengers seeking a larger baggage allowance can route via the USA, but with certain exceptions, the fares are slightly higher using this route.

Baggage allowance
Weight limits for internal flights are often lower; enquire beforehand

---

South America

Tailor-made itineraries
Estancias and haciendas
Galapagos Islands
Riding, walking and fishing
Photographic & painting tours
Antarctic Cruises
Discounted scheduled flights
Brochure and sensible advice

Telephone: 01296-658650
Fax: 01296-658651
Email: info@lastfrontiers.co.uk
Internet: www.lastfrontiers.co.uk

Fleet Marston Farm
Aylesbury
Buckinghamshire
HP18 0QT
England

LAST FRONTIERS

Prices & discounts

1 Fares from Europe to Rio de Janeiro vary from airline to airline and according to time of year. Check with an agency for the best deal for when you wish to travel. There is a wide range of offers to choose from in a highly competitive environment in the UK.

2 Most airlines offer discounted fares of one sort or another on scheduled flights. These are not offered by the airlines direct to the public, but through agencies who specialize in this type of fare.

The very busy seasons are 7 December-15 January and 1 July-10 September. If you intend travelling during those times, book as far ahead as possible. Between February-May and September-November special offers may be available.

3 Other fares fall into three groups, and are all on scheduled services:

i) **Excursion (return) fares** (A) With restricted validity, eg 5-90 days. Carriers are introducing flexibility to these tickets, permitting a change of dates on payment of a fee.

ii) **Yearly fares** (B) These may be bought on a one-way or return basis. Some airlines require a specified return date, changeable upon payment of a fee. To leave the return completely open is possible for an extra fee. You must fix the route (some of the cheapest flexible fares now have six months validity).

iii) **Student (or under 26) fares** Some airlines are flexible on the age limit, others strict. One-way and returns available, or 'Open Jaws' (see below). Do not assume that student tickets are the cheapest; though they are often very flexible, they are usually more expensive than A or B above. On the other hand, there is a wider range of cheap one-way student fares originating in Latin America than can be bought outside the continent.

4 For people intending to travel a linear route and return from a different point from that which they entered, there are 'Open Jaws' fares, which are available on student, yearly, or excursion fares.

5 Many of these fares require a change of plane at an intermediate point, and a stopover may be permitted, or even obligatory, depending on schedules. Simply because a flight stops at a given airport does not mean you can break your journey there – the airline must have traffic rights to pick up or set down passengers between points A and B before it will be permitted. This is where dealing with a specialized agency will really pay dividends. There are dozens of agencies that offer the simple returns to Rio at roughly the same (discounted) fare. On multi-stop itineraries, the specialized agencies can often save clients hundreds of pounds.

Austral Tours
www.latinamerica.co.uk

20 Upper Tachbrook Street
London SW1V 1SH / UK
Tel. +44(0)20-7233 5384
Fax +44(0)20-7233 5385
E-mail: info@latinamerica.co.uk

From the samba rhythms of Rio de Janeiro to the hidden Colonial gems of the Green Coast, let our experts make your dreams of Brazil a reality

ATOL 3616 — LATA — IATA

- Tailor-Made Itineraries & Expert Advice
- Hotels and Low-cost flights
- Fully Bonded Tour Operator

6 Although it's a little more complicated, it's possible to sell tickets in London for travel originating in Latin America at substantially cheaper fares than those available locally. This is useful for the traveller who doesn't know where he/she will end up, or who plans to travel for more than a year. Because of high local taxes (see paragraph 7), a one-way ticket from Latin America is more expensive than a one-way in the other direction, so it's always best to buy a return (but see 'Student fares', above). Taxes are calculated as a percentage of the full IATA fare; on a discounted fare the tax can therefore make up as much as 30-50 of the price.
7 Brazil imposes a local tax on flights originating there. This often applies if you happen to have bought a ticket, say, London-Rio-Santiago-Lima-Los Angeles and then on to Australia.
8 Travellers starting their journey in continental Europe should make local enquiries about charters and agencies offering the best deals.
9 If you buy discounted air tickets *always* check the reservation with the airline concerned to make sure the flight still exists. Also remember the IATA airlines' schedules change in March and October each year, so if you're going to be away a long time it's best to leave return flight coupons open (but see NB under 'Student fares', above).

In addition, check whether you are entitled to any refund or re-issued ticket if you lose, or have stolen, a discounted air ticket. Some airlines require the repurchase of a ticket before you can apply for a refund, which will not be given until after the validity of the original ticket has expired. The Iberia group and Air France, eg, operate this costly system. Travel insurance in some cases covers lost tickets.
10 Note that some South American carriers change departure times of short-haul or domestic flights at short notice and, in some instances, schedules shown in the computers of transatlantic carriers differ from those actually flown by smaller, local carriers. If you book, and reconfirm, both your transatlantic and onward sectors through your transatlantic carrier, you may find that your travel plans have been based on out of date information. The surest solution is to reconfirm your outward flight in an office of the onward carrier itself.

Airline offices in Rio de Janeiro

Aerolíneas Argentinas, R São José 70, 8th floor, T2103121; airport, T33983520. *Air France*, Av Pres Antônio Carlos 58, 9th and 10th floors, T5323642; airport, T33983490. *Alitalia*, Av Pres Wilson 231, 21st floor, T5242544; airport, T33983663. *American*, Av Pres Wilson 165, fifth floor, T2103126; airport, T33984053. *Avianca*, Av Pres Wilson 165, offices 801-08, T2404413; airport, T33983778. *British Airways*, International airport, T3983889. 1300-1800, 1830-2130 Mon, Fri and Sun, 1300-1800, 2055-2355 Thu and Sat. *Canadian Airlines*, R Almte Barroso 63, office 208, T2205343; airport, T33983604. *Continental*, R da Assembléia 10, office 3710, T5311142. *Delta*, R do Ouvidor 161, 14th floor, 0800-221121; airport, T33983492. *Iberia*, Av Pres Antônio Carlos 51, 9th floor, T2102415; airport, T33983168. *Japan Airlines*, Av Rio Branco 156, office 2014, T2206414. *KLM*, Av Rio Branco 311A, T5443232; airport, T33983700. *LanChile*, R 7 de Setembro 111, office 701, T0800-554900; airport, T3983797. *Lloyd Aéreo Boliviano*, Av Calógeras 30A, T2209548; airport, T33983738. *Lufthansa*, Av Rio Branco 156D, T2176111; airport, T33983855. *Pluna*, Av Rio Branco 147, 11th floor, T2624466; airport, T33983851. *RioSul Nordeste*, Av Rio Branco 85, 11th floor, T2636171; domestic airport, T8145960 (has an advance check-in desk on first floor of Shopping Rio Sul). *South African*, Av Rio Branco 245, fourth floor, T2626252; airport, T33983665. *Spanair*, Av Marechal Câmara 160, office 1707, T5446779. *Swissair*, Av Rio Branco 108, 10th floor, T2975177; airport, T33984330. *Tam*, Praça Floriano 19, 28th floor, T5241717; airport, T33982000. *TAP*, Av Rio Branco 311B, T2101278; airport, T33983455. *Transbrasil*, R Santa Luzia 651, T2974477; Av Atlântica 1998, Copacabana, T2367475; airport, T3985485. *United*, Av Pres Antônio Carlos 51, fifth floor, T5321212; airport T33984050. *Varig*, Av Rio Branco 277G, T5340333; R Rodolfo Dantas 16A, Copacabana, T5416343; R Visconde de Pirajá 351C/D, Ipanema, T5231954; airport, T33983522. Most staff speak English in Varig offices. *Vasp*, R Santa Luzia 735, T0800-998277 (24 hours); R Visconde de Pirajá 444, Ipanema, T8148098.

Road

International buses
There are good road connections between Argentina, Paraguay, Uruguay and the southeast of Brazil. Rio de Janeiro can easily be reached by international buses from Asunción, Buenos Aires, Santiago & Montevideo. Asunción, 1,511 km via Foz do Iguaçu, 30 hrs (Pluma), US$70; Buenos Aires (Pluma), via Porto Alegre and Santa Fe, 48 hrs, US$100 (book two days in advance); to Uruguaiana, US$90, cheaper and quicker to get a through ticket; Santiago de Chile, with Pluma US$135, or Gen Urquiza, about 70 hrs.

Driving
According to Detran, the state transport department, foreign tourists driving in Brazil need an international driving licence and a passport, which must be presented to the police if requested. A national driving licence is acceptable as long as your home country is a signatory to the Vienna and Geneva conventions. If it is not a signatory, your home driving licence will only be accepted if it is translated into Portuguese by a public notary. Car hire companies say they will accept national driving licences, but this may not be acceptable to the traffic police. Detran in Rio de Janeiro is at Av Presidente Vargas 817, second floor, T0xx21-5509744.

There are agreements between Brazil and all South American countries (but check in the case of Bolivia) whereby a car can be taken into Brazil (or a Brazilian car out of Brazil) for a period of 90 days without any special documents; an extension of up to 90 days is granted by the customs authorities on presentation of the paper received at the border, which must be retained; this may be done at most customs posts and at the Serviço de Controle Aduaneiro, Ministério da Fazenda, Av Presidente Antônio Carlos, Sala 1129, Rio de Janeiro.

For cars registered in other countries, the requirements are proof of ownership and/or registration in the home country and valid driving licence (see above). A 90-day permit is given by customs and procedure is very straightforward. Nevertheless, it is better to cross the border into Brazil when it is officially open because an official who knows all about the entry of cars is then present. You must specify which border station you intend to leave by, but application can be made to the Customs to change this.

Boat

Passenger vessels
There is an 8% tax on international shipping line tickets bought in Brazil

Voyages on passenger-carrying cargo vessels between Brazilian ports and Europe, the USA, or elsewhere, are listed here: the *Grimaldi Line* sails from Tilbury to Brazil (Vitória, Santos, Paranaguá, Rio) and Buenos Aires via Hamburg, Amsterdam and Antwerp, Le Havre, Southampton and Bilbao, round trip about 51 days, US$3,040-5,400, also from Genoa to Paranaguá, Santos and Rio for US$1,100-1,400 (round trip or southbound only, no northbound only passages). A number of German container ships sail the year round to the east coast of South America: Felixstowe, Hamburg, Antwerp, Bilbao or Algeciras, Santos, Buenos Aires, Montevideo, Rio Grande do Sul, Itajaí, Santos, Rio de Janeiro, Rotterdam, Felixstowe (about 45 days, £3,100-3,500 per person round trip). Four German vessels make a 49-day round trip: Tilbury, Hamburg, Antwerp, Le Havre, Suape, Rio de Janeiro, Santos, Buenos Aires, Montevideo, São Francisco do Sul, Paranaguá, Santos, Suape, Rotterdam, Tilbury. There are also German sailings from Genoa or Livorno (Italy), or Spain to the east coast of South America.

From the USA, a German consortium has a 48-day round trip to New York, Savannah, Miami, Rio, Santos, Buenos Aires, Montevideo, Rio Grande do Sul, Santos, Salvador, Fortaleza, Norfolk, Philadelphia, New York, £4,020 per person (one-way to Rio, 15 days £1,395).

Enquiries regarding passages should be made through agencies in your own country, or through John Alton of **Strand Voyages**, Charing Cross Shopping Concourse, The Strand, London WC2N 4HZ, T020-78366363, F74970078. *Strand Voyages* are booking agents for all the above. Advice can also be obtained from **Cargo Ship Voyages Ltd**,

Hemley, Woodbridge, Suffolk, IP12 4QF, T/F01473-736265. Also in London: *The Cruise People*, 88 York St, W1H 1DP, T020-77232450 (reservations 0800-526313). In Europe, contact *Wagner Frachtschiffreisen*, Stadlerstrasse 48, CH-8404, Winterthur, Switzerland, T052-2421442, F2421487. In the **USA**, contact *Freighter World Cruises*, 180 South Lake Ave, Pasadena, CA 91101, T818-4493106, *Travltips Cruise and Freighter Travel Association*, 163-07 Depot Rd, PO Box 188, Flushing, NY 11358, T800-8728584, or *Maris Freighter Travel Inc*, 215 Main St, Westport, CT06880-3210, T1-800-9962747. Do not try to get a passage on a non-passenger carrying cargo ship to South America from a European port; it is not possible.

Rio is a popular destination for the yachting fraternity and there are a number of other ports and marinas along the coast both east and west of the city (see page 76). For the arrival procedure for private vessels see page 27. Cruise liners also visit the city docking off Praça Mauá near the city centre although their length of stay is often short. **Yachting & Cruise liners**

Touching down

Airport information

Your point of arrival will be Galeão – **Antônio Carlos Jobim International Airport** on the Ilha do Governador, some 16 km from the centre of Rio de Janeiro. There are now two terminals which are linked by a short walkway: Terminal 1 which handles most international and domestic flights and the new Terminal 2 which handles international and domestic flights for Varig, Rio Sul, TAM and Star Alliance members such as United and Lufthansa. The third floor of Terminal 1 is where most of the services are located such as restaurants, shops and hotels (see page 115). There are many *câmbios* and official porters (helpful but looking to change cash so may say there are no *câmbios* or banks), but all will generally give worse rates than the Banco do Brasil, on the third floor of Terminal 1, which has Visa ATMs and will give cash advances against Visa card. There are other cash machines including Banco 24 Horas from which you can withdraw money with Amex, Diners Card and MasterCard (although not all foreign cards are accepted). *Arrive 2 hrs before international flights & it is wise to reconfirm your flight in case departure times may have changed*

Duty-free shops are well-stocked, but not especially cheap. Duty free is open to arrivals as well as departures. Only US dollars or credit cards are accepted on the airside of the departure lounge. There is a wider choice of restaurants outside passport control.

Check at the *Riotur* counters in international and domestic arrivals before leaving, for guides, maps and advice. They will give help in booking hotels if required.

The **Santos Dumont** national airport on Guanabara Bay, situated right in the city centre, is used for the Rio-São Paulo shuttle flights, some other domestic routes, air taxis and private planes. The shuttle services operate every 30 minutes throughout the day from 0630 to 2230. Sit on the right-hand side for views to São Paulo, the other side coming back, you can just turn up at the airport but you will need to book in advance for particular flights at busy times. For airport information telephone toll free 0800-244646.

There are a/c **taxis**. *Cootramo* and *Transcopass* have fixed rates (around US$20 to Centro; US$25 to Copacabana; US$37.50 to Barra de Tijuca). Buy a ticket at the counters near the arrivals gate in both terminals before getting into the car. The hire is for the taxi, irrespective of the number of passengers. Make sure you keep the ticket, which carries the number to phone in case of difficulty. Ordinary taxis also operate with the normal meter reading (about US$30, but some may offer cheaper rates from Copacabana to the airport, US$15-20). Do not negotiate with a driver on arrival, unless you are a frequent visitor. Beware of unlicensed pirate taxis and it is better to pay extra for an official vehicle than run the risk of robbery. **Public transport to & from airport**

Touching down

Official time Brazil has four time zones: Brazilian standard time is three hours behind GMT; the Amazon time zone (Pará west of the Rio Xingu, Amazonas, Roraima, Rondônia, Mato Grosso and Mato Grosso do Sul) is four hours behind GMT, the State of Acre is five hours behind GMT; the Fernando de Noronha archipelago is two hours behind GMT. Clocks move forward one hour in summer for approximately five months (usually between October and February or March), but times of change vary. This does not apply to Acre.
IDD code 55. Equal tones with long pauses means the phone is ringing; equal tones with equal pauses indicates engaged.
Business hours Generally 0900-1800 Monday to Friday; closed for lunch some time between 1130 and 1400. **Shops** are open on Saturday till 1230 or 1300.
Government offices: 1100-1800 Monday to Friday. **Banks**: 1000-1600 or 1630, closed on Saturday.
Voltage Generally 110V 60 cycles AC, but in some cities and areas 220V 60 cycles AC is used.
Weights and measures The metric system is used by all.

The a/c '*Real*' **bus** runs very frequently from the first floor of the airport to Recreio dos Bandeirantes via the municipal rodoviária and city centre, Santos Dumont Airport, Flamengo, Copacabana, Ipanema and Leblon. Luggage is secured in the hold (receipted), passengers are given a ticket and fares are collected during the journey; to anywhere in Rio it costs R$3.50 (US$2) and there is also a shuttle bus to Santos Dumont domestic airport in central Rio, R$3 (US$1.75). The driver will stop at requested points (the bus runs along the seafront from Leme to Leblon), so it's worth checking a map beforehand so that you can specify your required junction. The bus returns by the same route. Town buses M94 and M95, *Bancários/Castelo*, take a circular route passing through the centre and the interstate bus station. They leave from the second floor of the airport but you are recommended to take the *Real* bus if you are carrying luggage.

Airport departure tax The amount of tax depends on the class of airport. All airports charge US$36 international departure tax. First class airports charge R$9.15 domestic tax; second class airports R$7; domestic rates are lower still in third and fourth class airports. Tax must be paid on checking in, in *reais* or US dollars. Tax is waived if you stay in Brazil less than 24 hours.

Tourist information

Tourist offices
For full details of the Brazilian Tourist Board, Embratur, & for on-line information see 'Finding out more' (page 24). Addresses of municipal tourist offices are given under their respective towns & cities. They are not usually too helpful regarding information on cheap hotels

Riotur, R da Assembléia 10, 9th floor, RJ 20119-900, T0xx21-2177575, F5311872, www.rio.rj.gov.br/riotur, for information on the city of Rio de Janeiro. Their main tourist information office is in Copacabana at Av Princesa Isabel 183, T0xx21-5417522, open 0800-2000, helpful with English and German spoken by some staff, has good city maps and a very useful free brochure *Rio Guide*, written in both Portuguese and English. More information stands can be found at the International airport and at Rodoviária Novo Rio (bus station), all open 0600-2400, very friendly and helpful in finding accommodation. **Alô Rio** is a tourist information service in English and Portuguese, T0xx21-5428080, open daily from 0800-2000.

TurisRio, R da Ajuda 5, sixth floor (information centre), 12th floor (administration), RJ20040-000, T0xx21-2150011, F5446558, www.turisrio.rj.gov.br, for information on the State of Rio de Janeiro.

Embratur, R Uruguaiana 174, 8th floor, RJ 20050-090, T0xx21-5096017, F5097381, rio@embratur.gov.br, for information on the whole of Brazil.

See 'Tours and tour operators' (page 22) for a list of specialist tour operators operating from outside of Brazil.

Guide books

The following are recommended guidebooks and relevant reading: *Rio de Janeiro* (Apa Publications, 1999) has good photos and articles on the city. *The Insider's Guide to Rio de Janeiro* (Rio de Janeiro: 1995), an excellent book by Christopher Pickard, but difficult to find now in Rio bookshops as is *Rio de Janeiro, Cidade e Estado* (Rio de Janeiro: Michelin, 1999), full of detailed historical and cultural information, maps and illustrations. *Trilhas do Rio*, by Pedro da Cunha e Meneses (Editora Salamandra, second edition), describes walking trips around Rio. For a light-hearted approach to living in Rio, see *How to be a Carioca* (Rio de Janeiro: 1991) by Priscilla Ann Goslin, available in most bookshops.

For more background reading see 'Further reading' page 84

Maps

A recommended map is *Rio de Janeiro* (1:20,000) published by International Travel Maps (ITM), 345 West Broadway, Vancouver BC, V5Y 1P8, Canada, T604-8793621, F8794521, compiled with historical notes, by the late Kevin Healey. Another map that has been mentioned is *Brasilien* (1:4M) of New World Edition, Bertelsmann, Neumarkter Strasse 18, 81673 München, Germany. *Guia Rex* street guide has been recommended. *Guia Schaeffer Rio de Janeiro* is a good map. Maps are also available from *Touring Clube do Brasil*, Av Pres Antônio Carlos 130 and Av Brasil 4294, news stands, touring agencies and hotels. The *Geomapas* tourist map is clear. Cia de Comunicaçao publishes a map of the city in perspective, which is good for orientation (US$2). Paulini, R Lélio Gama 75 (outside the entrance of the downtown tram station) sells topographical and other maps of Brazil and of South America.

Quatro Rodas, a motoring magazine, publishes an excellent series of maps and guides in Portuguese (some maps in English and Spanish) from about US$10. Its annual *Guia Brasil* is a type of Michelin Guide to hotels, restaurants (not the cheapest), sights, facilities and general information on hundreds of cities and towns in the country, including good country and street maps. Other recommended guides are *Guia Ruas Rio de Janeiro* a comprehensive street map of the city, and *Fim de Semana* covering destinations in Rio de Janeiro state. These can be purchased in most bookshops or from street newspaper stands throughout the country or direct from the publishers, Av das Nações Unidas 7221, 14° andar, Pinheiros, SP 05425-902, T0xx11-30376004, F30376270, www.publiabril.com.br Quatro Rodas Guides may be bought in Europe from: 33, rue de Miromesnil, 75008 Paris, T0033-1-42663118, F00331-42661399, abrilparis@wanadoo.fr; and *Deltapress-Sociedade Distribuidora de Publicaçõ*es, Capa Rota, Tapada Nova, Linhó, 2710 Sintra, Portugal, T003511-9249940, F9240429. In the USA: Lincoln Building, 60 East 42nd St, Suite 3403, New York, NY 10165/3403, T001212-5575990/3, F9830972, abril@walrus.com

Other useful local publications

Many of the more expensive hotels provide locally produced tourist information magazines for their guests such as *Rio de Janeiro this month* published in English and Portuguese. Travel information can sometimes be out of date though and it is wise to recheck details thoroughly. *Balcão*, an advertising newspaper, US$2, twice weekly, offers apartments in and around Rio, language lessons, discounted tickets, items for sale and advertises shops. There are similar advertisements in the classified sections of *O Globo* and *Jornal do Brasil*, daily. Both dailies have good entertainment pages. *O Globo* has a travel section on Thursdays. The *Jornal do Brasil's Programa* on Friday is an essential 'what's-on' magazine, as is the *Rio* supplement to *Veja*, a weekly news magazine. *Riotur's* bimonthly *Rio Guide* in English and Portuguese is very thorough and lists most attractions. *TurisRio's* free magazine about the State of Rio de Janeiro is interesting; if your hotel does not have these publications, just ask at the reception of one of the larger establishments. *Guia do Executivo* published by *Gazeta Mercantil* has a lot of useful information on the city in English, Portuguese and Spanish.

Information for business travellers

A useful guide is *Hints to Exporters Visiting Brazil*, available from DTI Publications Orderline, Admail 528, London, SW1W 8YT, T0870-1502500, F1502333. Furthermore, specific information for UK exporters can be obtained from the British Trade International's Brazil Desk, Bay 826, Kingsgate House, 66-74 Victoria St, London, SW1E 6SW, T020-72154262, F72158247, www.brittrade.com/brazil/

The *Rio Convention and Visitors Bureau* at R Visconde de Pirajá 547, 6th floor, RJ 22415-900, T0xx21-2596165, F5112592, www.rioconventionbureau.com.br can provide information on local conferences and trade shows.

Special interest groups

Student travellers

If you are in full time education you will be entitled to an **International Student Identity Card (ISIC)**, which is distributed by student travel offices and travel agencies in 77 countries. The ISIC card gives you special prices on all forms of transport (air, sea, rail etc), and access to a variety of other concessions and services. If you need to find the location of your nearest ISIC office contact: The ISIC Association, Box 15857, 1001 NJ Amsterdam, Holland, T+45-33939303. ISIC cards can be obtained in Rio de Janeiro from **Student Travel Bureau**, Av Nilo Peçanha 50, SL 2417, Centro, T/F5442627, and R Visconde de Pirajá 550, shop 201, Ipanema, T5128577, F511437, www.stb.com.br You can also find details of travel, discounts and cultural exchanges for ISIC holders here. Remember to take photographs when having a card issued.

In practice, however, the ISIC card is rarely recognized or accepted for discounts outside of the south and southeast of Brazil. It is nonetheless useful for obtaining half price entry to the cinema. Youth hostels will often accept it in lieu of a IYHA card or at least give a discount, and some university accommodation (and subsidized canteens) will allow very cheap short term stays to holders.

Disabled travellers

As in most Latin American countries, facilities for disabled travellers are severely lacking. Wheelchair ramps are a rare luxury and getting a wheelchair into a bathroom or toilet is practically impossible, except for some of the more modern hotels. Pavements are often in a poor state of repair or crowded with street vendors requiring passers-by to brave the passing traffic. Disabled Brazilians obviously have to cope with these problems mainly by relying on the help of others to get on and off public transport and generally move around. An exception, however, are the new *City Rio* tourist buses (see 'Getting around' page 53) which have easier access.

Gay & lesbian travellers

Brazil is a good country for gay and lesbian travellers as attitudes are fairly liberal, especially in the big cities. Opinions in the interior and rural areas are far more conservative and it is wise to adapt to this. There is a well developed scene in Rio de Janeiro and detailed information in English, German and Portuguese can be gleaned from the *Rio Gay Guide*, www.ipanema.com/rio/gay/ Carnival is extremely popular with foreign gay tourists, who come to take part in the transvestite *bandas* and the gay balls.

Travelling with children

Travel with children can bring you into closer contact with Brazilian families and, generally, presents no special problems – in fact the path is often smoother for family groups. Officials tend to be more amenable where children are concerned and they are pleased if your child knows a little Portuguese. Moreover, even thieves and pickpockets seem to have some of the traditional respect for families, and may leave you alone because of it!

People contemplating overland travel in Brazil with children should remember that a lot of time can be spent waiting for buses, trains, and especially for aeroplanes. On bus journeys, if the children are good at amusing themselves, or can readily sleep while travelling, the problems can be considerably lessened. If your child is of an early reading age, take reading material with you because it is difficult and expensive to find. Travel on trains, while not as fast or at times as comfortable as buses, allows more scope for moving about. Some trains provide tables between seats, so that games can be played. Beware of doors left open for ventilation, especially if air-conditioning is not working.

Food This can be a problem if the children are not adaptable. It is easier to take biscuits, drinks, bread etc with you on longer trips than to rely on meal stops where the food may not be to their taste. Avocados are safe, easy to eat and nutritious; they can be fed to babies as young as six months and most older children like them. A small immersion heater and jug for making hot drinks is invaluable, but remember that electric current varies. Try and get a dual-voltage one (110v and 220v).

Fares On all long distance buses you pay for each seat, and there are no half-fares if the children occupy a seat each. For shorter trips it is cheaper, if less comfortable, to seat small children on your knee. Often there are spare seats which children can occupy after tickets have been collected. In city and local excursion buses, small children generally do not pay a fare, but are not entitled to a seat when paying customers are standing. On sightseeing tours you should *always* bargain for a family rate – often children can go free. (In trains, reductions for children are general, but not universal.)

All civil airlines charge half for children under 12, but some military services don't have half-fares, or have younger age limits. Note that a child travelling free on a long excursion is not always covered by the operator's travel insurance; it is advisable to pay a small premium to arrange cover.

Hotels Try to negotiate family rates. If charges are per person, always insist that two children will occupy one bed only, therefore counting as one tariff. If rates are per bed, the same applies. In either case you can almost always get a reduced rate at cheaper hotels. Occasionally when travelling with a child you will be refused a room in a hotel that is 'unsuitable'. (In restaurants, you can normally buy children's helpings, or divide one full-size helping between two children.)

Women travellers

First-time exposure to countries where sections of the population live in extreme poverty or squalor and may even be starving can cause odd psychological reactions in visitors. So can the exceptional curiosity extended to visitors, especially women. Simply be prepared for this and try not to over-react. These additional hints have mainly been supplied by women, but most apply to any single traveller. When you set out, err on the side of caution until your instincts have adjusted to the customs of a new culture. If, as a single woman, you can befriend a local woman, you will learn much more about the country you are visiting. Unless actively avoiding foreigners like yourself, don't go too far from the beaten track; there is a very definite 'gringo trail' which you can join, or follow, if seeking company. This can be helpful when looking for safe accommodation, especially if arriving after dark (which is best avoided). Remember that for a single woman a taxi at night can be as dangerous as wandering around on her own. At borders dress as smartly as possible. It is easier for men to take the friendliness of locals at face value; women may be subject to much unwanted attention. To help minimize this, do not wear suggestive clothing and do not flirt. By wearing a wedding ring, carrying a photograph of your 'husband' and 'children', and saying that your 'husband' is close at hand, you may dissuade an aspiring suitor. If politeness fails, do not feel bad about showing offence and departing. When accepting a social invitation, make sure that someone knows the address and the time you left. Ask if you can bring a friend (even if you do not intend to do so). A good rule is always to act with confidence, as though you know where you are going, even if you do not. Someone who looks lost is more likely to attract unwanted attention. Do not disclose to strangers where you are staying.

Jeitinho: How to get your own way

The sensual side of life in Brazil has a positive benefit for women in many situations encountered in daily life. A little bit of charm can resolve small problems or perhaps allow exceptions such as for example entering a shop that has just closed. In Brazil a woman never takes a refusal or a no as a final reply. It's always worth insisting a little bit more. This little act can generally take care of small problems in airports, bus stations, restaurants or in the street. It's all part of the Brazilian jeitinho, the little ways to get around certain barriers as quickly as possible.

If the other person is also a woman, forget any ideas of seduction. After receiving a refusal, still insist in your request but straight away tell a sad story. Say you missed your bus and spent the whole night awake in the bus station or you missed your plane, took the wrong bus or that you're extremely tired. For men the technique is the same but you could also make some compliments about the woman in front of you but make sure you are subtle in these.

Compliment the friendliness, the hospitality of the people as well as the local cuisine. Comment on the beautiful colour of a Brazilian woman's tanned skin. Praise Brazil (never criticise the country as then you will have all doors closed immediately). Never be curt, offhand or overbearing because this means you will have to wait a week for something that could be resolved in an hour. Never offer money but if this is required, let the other person suggest it first.

Rules, customs and etiquette

Clothing In general, clothing requirements in Brazil are less formal than in the Hispanic countries. It is, however, advisable for men visiting restaurants and cinemas to wear long trousers (women in shorts may also be refused entry). As a general rule, it is better not to wear shorts in official buildings, cinemas, interstate buses and on flights. Brazillian female fashions are often provocative, and while women are advised to dress in the local style, this can have unnerving effects!

Conduct Men should avoid arguments or insults (care is needed even when overtaking on the road); pride may be defended with a gun. Gay men, while still enjoying greater freedom than in many countries, should exercise reasonable discretion. It is normal to stare and comment on a woman's appearance, and if you happen to look different or to be travelling alone, you will undoubtedly attract attention. You are very unlikely to be groped or otherwise molested: this is disrespectful, and merits a suitable reaction. Be aware that Brazilian men can be extraordinarily persistent, and very easily encouraged; it is safest to err on the side of caution until you are accustomed to this.

Colour The people of Brazil represent a unique racial mix: it is not uncommon for the children of one family to be of several different colours. Individuals are often described by the colour of their skin (ranging through several shades of brown), and 'white' can refer to people who would not necessarily be thought white in Europe or North America. Generally speaking, the emphasis is on colour rather than racial origins.

Racial discrimination is illegal in Brazil. There is, however, a complex class system which is informed both by heritage and by economic status. This effectively discriminates against the poor, who are chiefly (but by no means exclusively) black due to the lack of inherited wealth among those whose ancestors were servants and slaves. Some Brazilians might assume that a black person is poor and therefore of low status. Black visitors to the country may encounter racial prejudice. We have also received a report from a black North American woman who was the subject of sexual advances by non-Brazilian, white tourists. Black women travelling with a white man may experience some problems, which should disappear with the realization that your partnership is not a commercial arrangement. A surprising number of Brazilians are unaware that black Europeans exist, so you could become the focus of some curiosity.

Prohibitions

Despite the wide distribution and use of drugs such as marijuana and cocaine, they are still illegal and you will face a heavy sentence if you are caught with them. A campaign against the exploitation of minors for sexual purposes gained wide publicity in 1997(in Brazilian law a minor is considered to be under the age of 18). Although the local bikinis leave little to the imagination you will be prosecuted for nude bathing except on an official nudist beach of which there are very few. **Never** carry firearms. Their possession could land you in serious trouble.

Time-keeping

Brazilians have a very 'relaxed' attitude towards time. It is quite normal for them to arrive an hour or so late even for business appointments. If you expect to meet someone more or less at an exact time, you can add 'em punto' or 'a hora inglesa' (English time) but be prepared to wait anyway.

Tipping

Tipping is usual, but less costly than in most other countries, except for porters. In restaurants, tip 10 of bill if no service charge is added, but give a small tip if there is. Taxi drivers are not tipped. To cloakroom attendants give a small tip; cinema usherettes, none; hairdressers, 10-15; porters, fixed charges but tips as well; airport porters, about US$0.50 per item.

Responsible tourism

See also 'Ecotourism', page 72

Travel to the furthest corners of the globe is now commonplace and the mass movement of people for leisure and business is a major source of foreign exchange and economic development in many parts of South America. In some regions (eg the Galapagos Islands and Machu Picchu) it is probably the most significant economic activity.

The benefits of international travel are self-evident for both hosts and travellers – employment, increased understanding of different cultures, business and leisure opportunities. At the same time there is clearly a downside to the industry. Where visitor pressure is high and/or poorly regulated, adverse impacts to society and the natural environment may be apparent. Paradoxically, this is as true in undeveloped and pristine areas (where culture and the natural environment are less 'prepared' for even small numbers of visitors) as in major resort destinations.

The travel industry is growing rapidly and increasingly the impacts of this supposedly 'smokeless' industry are becoming apparent. These impacts can seem remote and unrelated to an individual trip or holiday (eg air travel is clearly implicated in global warming and damage to the ozone layer, resort location and construction can destroy natural habitats and restrict traditional rights and activities), but individual choice and awareness can make a difference in many instances (see box), and collectively, travellers are having a significant effect in shaping a more responsible and sustainable industry.

In an attempt to promote awareness of and credibility for responsible tourism, organizations such as *Green Globe*, greenglobe@compuserve.com, T020-79308333 and the *Centre for Environmentally Sustainable Tourism (CERT)*, T01268-795772 in the UK now offer advice on destinations and sites that have achieved certain commitments to conservation and sustainable development. Generally these are larger mainstream destinations and resorts, but they are still a useful guide and increasingly aim to provide information on smaller operations.

Of course travel can have beneficial impacts and this is something to which every traveller can contribute – many national parks are part funded by receipts from visitors. Similarly, travellers can promote patronage and protection of important archaeological sites and heritage through their interest and contributions via

A few ideas

Where possible choose a destination, tour operator or hotel with a proven ethical and environmental commitment – if in doubt ask;

Spend money on locally produced (rather than imported) goods and services and use common sense when bargaining – your few dollars saved may be a week's salary to others;

Use water and electricity carefully – travellers may receive preferential supply while the needs of local communities are overlooked;

Learn about local etiquette and culture – consider local norms and behaviour and dress appropriately for local cultures and situations;

Protect wildlife and other natural resources – don't buy souvenirs or goods made from wildlife unless they are clearly sustainably produced and are not protected under CITES legislation (CITES controls trade in endangered species);

Don't give money or sweets to children – it encourages begging – instead give to a recognized project, charity or school;

Always ask before taking photographs or videos of people;

Consider staying in local accommodation rather than foreign owned hotels – the economic benefits for host communities are far greater – and there are far greater opportunities to learn about local culture.

---

entrance and performance fees. They can also support small-scale enterprises by staying in locally run hotels and hostels, eating in local restaurants and by purchasing local goods, supplies and arts and crafts.

In fact, since the Responsible Travel section was first introduced in Footprint's *South American Handbook* in 1992 there has been a phenomenal growth in *tourism that promotes and supports the conservation of natural environments and is also fair and equitable to local communities*. This ecotourism segment is probably the fastest growing sector of the travel industry and provides a vast and growing range of destinations and activities such as visits and experiences in Brazil's Atlantic forest (one of the most endangered ecosystems in the world).

While the authenticity of some ecotourism operators' claims need to be interpreted with care, there is clearly both a huge demand for this type of activity and also significant opportunities to support worthwhile conservation and social development initiatives.

Organizations such as **Conservation International**, T202-4295660, www.ecotour.org, the **Eco-Tourism Society**, T802-4472121, http://ecotourism.org, **Planeta**, www2.planeta.com/mader, and the UK-based **Tourism Concern**, T020-77533330, www.gn.apc.org/tourismconcern, have begun to develop and/or promote ecotourism projects and destinations and their web sites are an excellent source of information and details for sites and initiatives throughout South America. Additionally, UK organizations such as **Earthwatch**, T01865-311601, www.earthwatch.org and **Discovery International**, T020-72299881, www.discoveryinitiatives.com, offer opportunities to participate directly in scientific research and development projects throughout the region.

South America offers unique and unforgettable experiences – often based on the natural environment, cultural heritage and local society. These are the reasons many of us choose to travel and why many more will want to do so in the future. Shouldn't we provide an opportunity for future travellers and hosts to enjoy the quality of experience and interaction that we take for granted?

Safety

Personal safety in Brazil has deteriorated in recent years, largely because of economic hardship, and crime is increasing. Some recommend avoiding all large cities, but efforts are being made to improve the situation in major tourist centres like Rio de Janeiro. The situation is far less insecure in smaller towns and in the country. Where you need to take most care is in crowded places, eg bus stations, markets, because this is where opportunistic crime occurs. If you are aware of the dangers, act confidently and use your common sense, you will lessen many of the risks.

See 'Women travellers', page 41 for additional advice on safety

Apart from the obvious precautions of not wearing jewellery (wear a cheap, plastic digital watch), do not camp or sleep out in isolated places and if you are hitchhiking, never accept a lift in a car with two people in it.

Protecting money & valuables

Consider buying clothing locally to avoid looking like a gringo. Take only your towel and lotion to the beach, tuck enough money for cold drinks into your trunks/bikini bottom. A few belongings can safely be left at a bar. If you are held up and robbed, it is worth asking for the fare back to where you are staying. It is not uncommon for thieves to oblige. Do carry some cash, to hand over if you are held up. Never trust anyone telling 'sob stories' or offering 'safe rooms', when looking for a hotel, always choose the room yourself. Ted Stroll of San Francisco advises, "remember that economic privation has many Brazilians close to the edge, and that they are probably as ashamed of exploiting you as you are angry at being exploited". The corollary is be generous to those who give you a good deal.

Always photocopy your passport, air ticket and other documents, make a record of travellers' cheque and credit card numbers and keep them separately from the originals. Leave another set of records at home. Keep all documents secure; hide your main cash supply in different places or under your clothes: extra pockets sewn inside shirts and trousers, pockets closed with a zip or safety pin, moneybelts (best worn below the waist rather than outside or at it or around the neck), neck or leg pouches, a thin chain for attaching a purse to your bag or under your clothes and elasticated support bandages for keeping money and cheques above the elbow or below the knee have been repeatedly recommended (the last by John Hatt in *The Tropical Traveller*). Keep cameras in bags or briefcases; take spare spectacles (eyeglasses). If you wear a shoulder bag in a market, carry it in front of you.

If someone follows you when you're in the street, let him catch up with you and 'give him the eye'. While you should take local advice about being out at night, do not assume that daytime is safer than night-time. If walking after dark, walk in the road, not on the pavement/sidewalk.

Be wary of 'plainclothes policemen'; insist on seeing identification and on going to the police station by main roads. Do not hand over your identification (or money – which he should not need to see anyway) until you are at the station. On no account take them directly back to your lodgings. Be even more suspicious if he seeks confirmation of his status from a passer-by. If someone tries to obtain a bribe from you, insist on a receipt.

Avoiding con tricks

Do not leave valuables in hotel rooms, except where a safe is provided. Hotel safe deposits are generally (but not always) secure. If you cannot get a receipt for valuables in a hotel safe, seal the contents in a plastic bag and sign across the seal. Always keep an inventory of what you have deposited. If you can trust your hotel, leave any valuables you don't need in safe-deposit when sightseeing locally. If you don't trust the hotel, lock everything in your pack and secure that in your room (some people take eyelet-screws for padlocking cupboards or drawers). If you lose valuables, always report to the police and note details of the report – for insurance purposes.

Hotel security

Dangerous places Visitors should not enter *favelas* except when accompanied by workers for NGOs, tour groups or other people who know the local residents well and are accepted by the community. Walking around the city centre of Rio is best avoided at night and weekends when it is deserted. Zona Norte and the Baixada Fluminense are some of the poorest parts of the city with a higher crime rate as a result.

Public transport When you have all your luggage with you at a bus or railway station, be especially careful. Take a taxi between airport/bus station/railway station and hotel, if you can possibly afford it. Keep your bags with you in the taxi and pay only when you and your luggage are safely out of the vehicle. Make sure the taxi has inner door handles, in case a quick exit is needed. Avoid night buses; never arrive at your destination at night. Major bus lines often issue a luggage ticket when bags are stored in the bus' hold. When getting on a bus, keep your ticket handy; someone sitting in your seat may be a distraction for an accomplice to rob you while you are sorting out the problem. If travelling alone, first-class *frescão* buses are a safe option as they always have an attendant who screens people who get on.

Drugs As mentioned above under 'Prohibitions', illegal drugs should be avoided. Not only will you be entering the criminal underground with all the associated risks, but you are also opening yourself up to extortion.

Red-light districts should also be given a wide berth as there are reports of drinks being drugged with a substance popularly known as 'Good night Cinderella'. This leaves the victim easily amenable to having their possessions stolen, or worse.

Rape This can happen anywhere in the world. If you are the victim of a sexual assault, you are advised in the first instance to contact a doctor (this can be your home doctor if you prefer). You will need tests to determine whether you have contracted any sexually transmitted diseases; you may also need advice on post-coital contraception. You should also contact your embassy, where consular staff are very willing to help in cases of assault.

Violent crime The main areas where violent crime occurs are places that no visitor should go anyway. If the worst does happen and you are threatened with a firearm, don't panic, hand over your valuables and the incident should pass quickly. Do not resist, but report the crime to the local tourist police later.

It is extremely rare for a tourist to be hurt during a robbery in Brazil

Police There are several types of police: Polícia Federal, civilian dressed, who handle all federal law duties, including immigration. A subdivision is the Polícia Federal Rodoviária, uniformed, who are the traffic police on federal highways. Polícia Militar are the uniformed, street police force, under the control of the state governor, handling all state laws. They are not the same as the Armed Forces' internal police. Polícia Civil, also state-controlled, handle local laws and investigations. They are usually in civilian dress, unless in the traffic division. Polícia Civil are to merge with Polícia Militar in the near future. In cities like Rio, the Prefeitura controls the Guarda Municipal, who handle local security. Tourist police operate in places with a strong tourist presence such as Copacabana. In case of difficulty, visitors should seek them out in the first instance.

Foreign embassies & consulates in Rio *Argentina*, Praia de Botafogo 228, office 201, T5531646. 1000-1300, 1330-1530 Mon-Fri. *Australia*, Av Rio Branco 1, room 810, T5183351. 1000-1200 Mon-Fri. *Austria*, Av Atlântica 3804, T5222286. 0900-1300 Mon-Fri. *Belgium*, R Lauro Müller 116, office 3904, T5438558. 0900-1300, 1400-1700 Mon-Fri. *Canada*, R Lauro Müller 116, office 2707, T5427593. 0900-1300 Mon-Fri. *Denmark*, Praia do Flamengo 66, Bloco B, office 1318, T5586050. 0900-1700 Mon-Thu; 0900-1400 Fri. *Finland, Norway and Sweden*, Praia do Flamengo 344, 9th floor, T5535505. 0900-1400 Mon-Fri. *France*, Av Pres

Antônio Carlos, 58, 6th floor, T2101272. 0830-1200 Mon-Fri. *Germany*, R Pres Carlos de Campos 417, Laranjeiras, T5536777. 0830-1130 Mon-Fri. *Greece*, Praia do Flamengo 344, office 201, T5526849. 0900-1300 Mon-Fri. *Israel*, Av NS de Copacabana 680, roof, T5485432. 0900-1230 Mon-Thu, 0900-1430 Fri. *Italy*, Av Pres Antônio Carlos, 40, 7th floor, T2821315. 0900-1200 Mon-Fri. *Japan*, Praia do Flamengo 200, 10th floor, T2655252. 0900-1200, 1430-1700 Mon-Fri. *Luxembourg*, R Francisco Otaviano 87, office 203, T/F5217835. 0900-1200 Mon-Fri. *Netherlands*, Praia de Botafogo 242, 7th floor, T5529028. 1000-1200 Mon-Fri, Dutch newspapers here and at KLM office on Av Rio Branco. *Paraguay*, Praia de Botafogo, second floor, T5532294. 0900-1300 Mon-Fri, visas US$5. *Portugal*, Av Marechal Câmara 160, office 1809, T5442444. 0800-1200 Mon-Fri. *Spain*, R Lauro Müller 116, office 1601, T5433200. 0830-1400 Mon-Fri. *Switzerland*, R Cândido Mendes 157, 11th floor, T2211867. 0900-1200 Mon-Fri. *UK*, Praia do Flamengo 284, second floor, Metrô Flamengo, or bus 170. T5533223 (0830-1700 Mon-Fri), Cell96966665 (Duty officer after 1700 and at weekends), consular section, T5335976 (Mon-Fri 0930-1230). The consulate issues a useful 'Guidance for Tourists' pamphlet. *Uruguay*, Praia de Botafogo 242, 6th floor, T5536030. 0900-1300 Mon-Fri. *USA*, Av Pres Wilson 147, T2927117. 0830-1100 (1330-1500 Passport) Mon-Fri. *Venezuela*, Praia de Botafogo 242, fifth floor, T5526699. 0900-1300 Mon-Fri.

Where to stay

The best guide to hotels in Rio de Janeiro state is the *Quatro Rodas Guia Brasil*, which has good maps of towns. Motels are specifically intended for very short-stay couples: there is no stigma attached and they usually offer good value (the rate for a full night is called the *pernoite*), though the décor can be a little unsettling. The type known as *hotel familiar*, to be found in the interior – large meals, communal washing, hammocks for children – is much cheaper, but only for the enterprising. *Pousadas* are the equivalent of bed and breakfast, often small and family run, although some are very sophisticated and correspondingly priced. Usually hotel prices include breakfast; there is no reduction if you don't eat it. In the better hotels (our category A and upwards), the breakfast is well worth eating: rolls, ham, eggs, cheese, cakes, fruit. Normally the *apartamento* is a room with a bath; a *quarto* is a room without a bath. Leave rooms in good time so frigobar bills can be checked.

Hotels
For a quick reference price guide to our hotel categories, see inside the front cover

The star rating system for hotels (five-star hotels are not price-controlled) was not the standard used in North America or Europe. The only five-star hotels according to a new system introduced in 1997 were the **Sheraton**, **Caesar Park** and **Inter-Continental**. Others previously rated as five-star were expected to upgrade their services to meet the new standards. All hotels of two-stars and above are a/c. A 10 service charge is usually added to the bill and tax of 5% or 10% may be added (if not already included). Note that not all higher-class hotels include breakfast in their room rates. Economy hotels are found mainly in three districts of Rio: Flamengo/Botafogo (best), Lapa/Fátima and Saúde/Mauá.

Business visitors are strongly recommended to book accommodation in advance, and this can be easily done for Rio hotels with representation abroad. *Varig* has a good hotel reservation service, with discounts of up to 50% for its passengers.

It's also a good idea to book accommodation in advance in small towns near Rio de Janeiro which are popular at weekends with city dwellers eg Paraty and Búzios.

Roteiros de Charme In many locations throughout Rio de Janeiro state, this is an association of hotels and *pousadas* which aims to give a high standard of accommodation in establishments which represent the town they are in. It is a private initiative. If you are travelling in the appropriate budget range (our A price range

Hotel prices and facilities

*Prices include taxes and service charges, but are without meals unless otherwise stated. They are based on a double room, except in the **E** and **F** ranges, where prices are almost always per person.*

***LL** (over US$150) to **AL** (US$66-99)* Hotels in these categories can be found in most of the large cities in Brazil, but especially so in areas with a strong concentration of tourists or business travellers. They should offer pool, sauna, gym, jacuzzi, all business facilities (including email), several restaurants and bars. A safe box is usually provided in each room. In cities such as Rio de Janeiro the top hotels compare with the highest standards in the world, although service can sometimes still be very Brazilian.

***A** (US$46-65) and **B** (US$31-45)* Hotels in these categories should provide more than the standard facilities and a fair degree of comfort. Most include a good breakfast and many offer extras such as colour TV, minibar, a/c and a swimming pool. They may also provide tourist information and their own transport for airport pickups. Service is generally good and most accept credit cards, although a lower rate for cash is often offered.

***C** (US$21-30) and **D** (US$12-20)* Hotels in these categories range from very comfortable to functional and there are some real bargains to be had. You should expect your own bathroom, constant hot water, a towel, soap and toilet paper. There is sometimes a restaurant and a communal sitting area. In tropical regions rooms are usually equipped with a/c, although this may be rather old. Hotels used to catering for foreign tourists and backpackers often have luggage storage, money exchange and kitchen facilities.

***E** (US$7-11) and **F** (US$6 and under)* Hotels in these categories are often extremely simple with bedside or ceiling fans, shared bathrooms and little in the way of furniture. Breakfast when included is very simple, usually no more than a bread roll and coffee. The best accommodation and facilities for under US$10 per night is generally found in the Youth Hostels (see below), although tourist areas with high quantities of bed spaces, such as Búzios, often have good quality rooms at this price during low season.

---

upwards), you can plan an itinerary which takes in these high class hotels, with a reputation for comfort and good food, and some fine places of historical and leisure interest. Roteiros de Charme hotels are listed in the text and any one of them can provide information on the group. Alternatively, contact the office in the *Caesar Park Hotel* in Rio de Janeiro (Av Vieira Souto 460, Ipanema, F0xx21-2871592, or www.roteirosdecharme.com.br).

Advice & suggestions

The service stations (*postos*) and hostels (*dormitórios*) along the main roads provide excellent value in room and food, akin to truck-driver type accommodation in Europe, for those on a tight budget.

Most sizeable towns have laundromats with self service machines. *Lavanderias* do the washing for you but are very expensive.

The electric showers used in innumerable hotels should be checked for obvious flaws in the wiring; try not to touch the rose while it is producing hot water.

Some taxi drivers will try to take you to the expensive hotels, who pay them commission for bringing in custom. Beware!

The city is noisy. An inside room is cheaper and much quieter.

Cockroaches are ubiquitous and unpleasant, but not dangerous. Take some insecticide powder if staying in cheap hotels; Baygon (Bayer) has been recommended. Stuff toilet paper in any holes in walls that you may suspect of being parts of cockroach runs.

Away from the main commercial centres, many hotels, restaurants and bars have inadequate water supplies. Almost without exception, used toilet paper should not be flushed down the pan, but placed in the receptacle provided. This applies even in quite expensive hotels. Failing to observe this custom will block the pan or drain, a considerable health risk.

Self-catering apartments A popular form of accommodation in Rio, available at all price levels: eg furnished apartments for short-term let, accommodating up to six, cost about US$300 per month in Maracanã, about US$400 per month in Saúde, Cinelândia, Flamengo. In Copacabana, Ipanema and Leblon prices range from about US$25 a day for a simple studio, starting at US$500-600 a month up to US$2,000 a month for a luxurious residence sleeping 4-6. Heading south past Barra da Tijuca, virtually all the accommodation available is self-catering. Renting a small flat, or sharing a larger one, can be much better value than a hotel room. Blocks consisting entirely of short-let apartments can attract thieves, so check the (usually excellent) security arrangements; residential buildings are called *prédio familial*. Higher floors (*alto andar*) are considered quieter.

'Apart-Hotels' are listed in the *Guia 4 Rodas* and Riotur's booklet. Agents and private owners advertise in *Balcão* (like *Exchange and Mart*), twice weekly, *O Globo* or *Jornal do Brasil* (daily); under 'Apartamentos – Temporada'; advertisements are classified by district and size of apartment: 'vagas e quartos' means shared accommodation; 'conjugado' (or 'conj') is a studio with limited cooking facilities; '3 Quartos' is a three-bedroom flat. There should always be a written agreement when renting.

Youth hostels For information about Youth Hostels in Rio de Janeiro contact **Federação Brasileira dos Albergues da Juventude (FBAJ)**, R General Dionísio 63, Botafogo, RJ 22271-050, T0xx21-2860303, F2865652, www.hostels.org.br Their annual book provides a full list of good value accommodation. The regional representatives are **Associação de Albergues da Juventude do Rio de Janeiro (ALBERJ)**, R da Assembleia 10, room 1616, T0xx21-5312234, F5311943, albergue@microlink.com.br Youth hostels are fully booked between Christmas and Carnival so if intending to stay at this time reserve well in advance.

Low-budget travellers with student cards (photograph needed) can sometimes use the **Casa dos Estudantes (CEU)** network but this usually depends on the policy of each individual residence and canteen.

Camping Members of the **Camping Clube do Brasil** or those with an international campers' card pay only half the rate of a non-member, which is US$10-15 per person. The Club has 43 sites in 13 states and 80,000 members. For enquiries, *Camping Clube do Brasil*, Divisão de Campings, R Senador Dantas 75, 29th floor, Centro, Rio de Janeiro, RJ 20037-900, T0xx21-2103171, F2623143, ccb@ax.ibase.org.br. They have two beach sites at Barra da Tijuca however during high season (Jan-Feb) these sites are often full and sometimes restricted to club members. Private campsites charge about US$8 per person. For those on a very low budget and in isolated areas where there is no campsite, service stations can be used as camping sites (Shell stations recommended); they have shower facilities, watchmen and food; some have dormitories; truck drivers are a mine of information. There are also various municipal sites. Campsites often tend to be some distance from public transport routes and are better suited to those with their own transport. Never camp at the side of a road; wild camping is generally not possible.

Good camping equipment may be purchased in Brazil and there are several rental companies. Camping gas cartridges are easy to buy in sizeable towns in Rio de Janeiro state eg in HM shops. *Guia de Camping* is produced by Artpress, R Araçatuba 487, São Paulo SP 05058. It lists most sites and is available in bookshops in most cities. Quatro Rodas' *Guia Brasil* lists the main campsites.

Getting around

Air

Because of the great distances, flying is often the most practical option. Internal air services are highly developed, but expensive. The larger cities are linked with each other several times a day. A monthly magazine, *Panrotas*, gives all the timetables and fares. All national airlines offer excellent service on their internal flights. The largest airlines are *TAM*, *Transbrasil*, *Varig* and *Vasp*. Two other airlines, *Rio-Sul* and *Nordeste* (both allied to Varig), have extensive networks.

Between 2200 and 0600, internal flights cost 30% less than daytime flights. (Ask for the *vôo coruja*.) On some flights couples can fly for the price of 1½. A 30% discount is offered on flights booked seven days or more in advance. Discounts on flights are available at airports a few hours before a domestic flight. It is well worth enquiring in detail. Double check all bookings (reconfirm frequently) and information given by ground staff as economic cutbacks have led to pressure on ground service (but not to flight service). Toll free numbers for the major airlines are given under domestic airlines.

Domestic airlines
Internal flights often have many stops & are therefore quite slow

Nordeste Av Tancredo Neves 1672, 1o andar, Pituba, Salvador, BA 41820-020, T0800-992004, www.nordeste.com **Rio-Sul** Av Rio Branco 85, 10° andar, Rio de Janeiro, RJ 20040-004, T0800-992004, www.rio-sul.com **TAM** R Gen Pantaleão Teles 210, São Paulo, SP 04355-900, T0800-123100, www.tam.com.br **Transbrasil** R Gen Pantaleão Teles 40, São Paulo, SP 04355-900, T0800-151151, www.transbrasil.com.br **Varig** Av Almte Silvio de Noronha 365, Rio de Janeiro, RJ 20021-010, T0800-997000, www.varig.com.br **Vasp** Edif VASP, Aeroporto Congonhas, Praça Comandante Lineu Gomes, São Paulo, SP 04626-910, T0800-998277, www.vasp.com.br

Domestic air routes

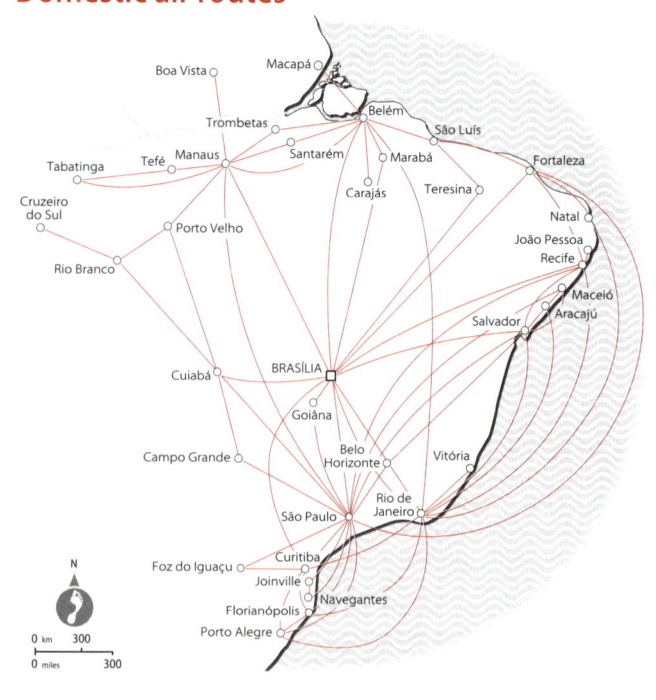

TAM, *Transbrasil*, *Varig* and *Vasp* offer good value 21-day air passes for people resident outside Brazil. There are no discounts for children and infants pay 10% of the price. The **Varig airpass** covers three zones: All Brazil US$540 high season (490 low) for five flights (six if Santarém is included), with a maximum of four extra coupons available for US$100 each; Central and South Brazil US$400 (350 low season) with a maximum of four coupons; and North East Brazil US$340 (290 low season) with a maximum of four coupons (Varig sells 'linking' flights from São Paulo or Rio to the North East for US$150 return). Routes must be specified before arrival. High season is 10 Dec-29 Feb, 25 Jun-25 Jul. Amendments may be made once prior to commencement of travel at US$30 per change. The *Varig* pass is only available to travellers arriving in Brazil from the UK with *Varig* or *British Airways*. A new **Airpass 500** costing US$450, is valid for 30 days with unlimited coupons only during the year 2000.

The **Transbrasil airpass**, also divided into three zones, is available to individuals arriving on the services of other carriers as well as their own. Unlike the *Varig* pass, it does not have the facility to start the North East pass in São Paulo or Rio and it has no Santarém connection. Both *Varig* and *Transbrasil* require an itinerary to be specified and reserved at time of purchase. It is essential to check all arrangements very carefully.

The All Brazil **Vasp airpass** costs US$440 for five flights with a maximum of four extra coupons available for US$100 each (must be purchased with the air pass). A maximum of two connections can be made, but there is no high or low season and it is only available to non-residents of Brazil arriving in Brazil on a *Vasp* flight (but see note above).

The **TAM airpass** is similar to the *Varig* airpass except that you can arrive in Brazil on any airline; two connections are permitted at specified hubs, but these must not exceed four hours and re-routing is permitted for US$50.

All airpasses must be purchased outside Brazil, no journey may be repeated and none may be used on the Rio-São Paulo shuttle. Make sure you have two copies of the airpass invoice when you arrive in Brazil; otherwise you will have to select all your flights when you book the first one. Remember that domestic airport tax has to be paid at each departure. Hotels in the Tropical and Othon chains, and others, offer discounts of 10% to Varig airpass travellers; check with *Varig*, who have a hotel reservation service (Av Paulista 1765, first floor, São Paulo, SP 01311-200, T0xx11-2532003, F2533510). Promotions on certain destinations offer a free flight, hotel room etc; enquire when buying the airpass. We have been told that it is advisable for users of the airpasses to book all their intended flights in advance or on arrival in Brazil, especially around summer holiday and Carnival time. Converting the voucher can take some hours, do not plan an onward flight immediately, check at terminals that the airpass is still registered, faulty cancellations have been reported. Cost and restrictions on the airpass are subject to change. An alternative is to buy an internal flight ticket which includes several stops.

Small scheduled domestic airlines operate Brazilian-built *Bandeirante* 16-seater prop-jets into virtually every city and town with any semblance of an airstrip. Most airports have left-luggage lockers (US$2 for 24 hours). Seats are often unallocated on internal flights; board in good time.

Train

There are 30,379 km of railways which are not combined into a unified system. Brazil has two gauges and there is little transfer between them. There are passenger services in the state of Rio de Janeiro but more and more services are being withdrawn. There are suburban trains to Nova Iguaçu, Nilópolis, Campo Grande and elsewhere. Buses marked 'E Ferro' go to the railway station.

Metrô The Metrô provides good service – it is clean, air conditioned and fast. Line 1 operates between the inner suburb of Tijuca (station Saens Peña) and Arcoverde (Copacabana), via the railway station (Central), Glória and Botafogo. Line 2 runs from Pavuna, passing Engenho da Rainha and the Maracanã stadium, to Estácio. It operates 0600-2300, Sun 1400-2000; closed holidays. The fare is R$1 (US$0.55) single; multi-tickets and integrated bus/Metrô tickets are available. Substantial changes in bus operations are taking place because of the extended Metrô system; buses connecting with the Metrô have a blue-and-white symbol in the windscreen.

Trams The last remaining tram runs from near the Largo da Carioca (there is a museum, open only Fri 0830-1700) across the old aqueduct (Arcos) to Dois Irmãos or Paula Mattos in Santa Teresa – historical and interesting, R$0.60 (US$0.35). For more details see under Santa Teresa page 128.

Road network

Though the best paved highways are heavily concentrated in the southeast, those serving the interior are being improved to all-weather status and many are paved. Most main roads between principal cities are paved. Some are narrow and therefore dangerous whilst many are in poor condition.

Routes Distances in km to some nearby major cities with approximate journey time in brackets: Juiz de Fora, 184 (2¾ hours); Belo Horizonte, 434 (seven hours); São Paulo, 429 (six hours); Vitória, 521 (eight hours).

Rio de Janeiro Metrô

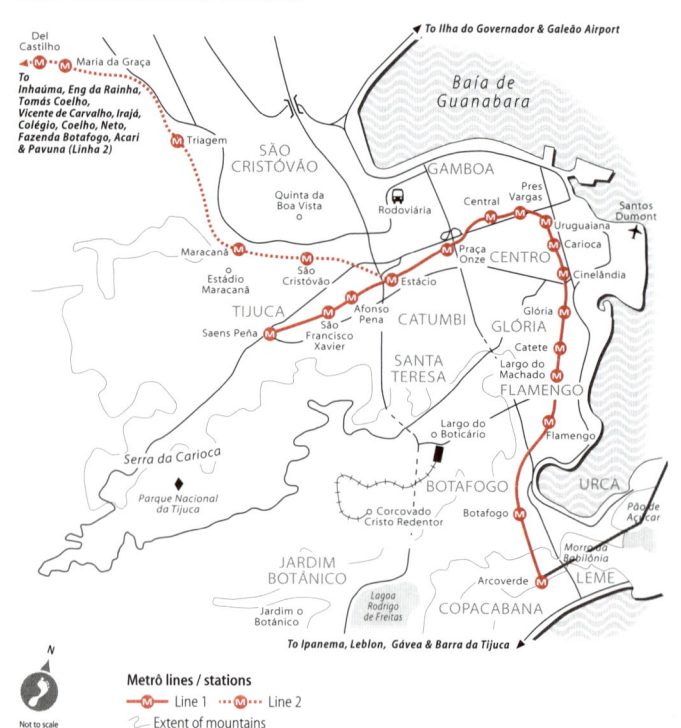

Bus

There are good local services to all parts of Rio de Janeiro (including airports), but buses are very crowded and not for the aged and infirm during rush hours. Town buses have turnstiles which are awkward if you are carrying luggage or a large pack. At busy times allow about 45 mins to get from Copacabana to the centre by bus. The fare on city buses is R$0.90 (US$0.50) whilst suburban bus fares are around US$0.75. Bus stops are often not marked. The route is written on the side of the bus, which is hard to see until the bus has actually pulled up at the stop.

Local
Hang on tight on Rio's buses: drivers live out Grand Prix fantasies

Private companies such as *Real*, *Pegaso* and *Anatur* operate air-conditioned *frescão* buses which can be flagged down practically anywhere. They run from all points in Zona Sul to the city centre, Rodoviária and the airports. Fares are around US$1.50 (US$2 to the international airport).

City Rio is an a/c bus service with recorded tourist information, running every 30 minutes between all the major parts of the city. You can buy tickets valid for 24 (US$9), 48 (US$15) or 72 hrs (US$22) and use the bus as often as you want within that period. There are three routes which you can change between: **Linha 1** Blue which starts at Sugar Loaf and runs via the City Centre and Glória to Rio Sul Shopping Centre. **Linha 2** Orange starting at Sugar Loaf and returning via Corvocado, Jardim Botânico, Hotel Inter-Continental, Ipanema, Copacabana, Leme and Rio Sul Shopping Centre. **Linha 3** Lilac which starts at Hotel Inter-Continental and returns there after passing throughout Barra da Tijuca. Good maps show what sites of interest are close to each bus stop. T0800-258060 for further information, tickets can be bought at the main hotels or on the buses.

There is no lack of road transport between Rio de Janeiro and the principal towns of the state. There are three standards of bus: *comum*, or *convencional* (conventional), which are quite slow, not very comfortable and fill up quickly; *executivo* (executive), which are a few reais more expensive, comfortable (many have reclining seats), but don't stop to pick up passengers *en route* and are therefore safer; and *leito* (literally, bed), which run at night between the main centres, offering reclining seats with foot and leg rests, toilets, and sometimes refreshments, at double the normal fare. For journeys over 100 km, most buses have chemical toilets. Air conditioning can make *leito* buses cold at night, so take a blanket or sweater (and plenty of toilet paper); on some services blankets are supplied. Some companies have hostess service. Ask for window seats (*janela*), or odd numbers if you want the view.

Long distance

Brazilian bus services have a top speed limit of 80 kph (buses are supposed to have governors fitted). They stop fairly frequently (every 2-4 hrs) for snacks. The cleanliness of these *postos* is generally good, though may be less so in the poorer regions. Standards of comfort on buses and in *postos* vary from line to line, which can be important on long journeys. Take something to drink on buses in the north.

Bus stations for interstate services and other long distance routes are usually called *rodoviárias*. They are frequently outside the city centres and offer fair facilities in the way of snack bars, lavatories, left-luggage stores ('*guarda volume*'), local bus services and information centres. Buy bus tickets at *rodoviárias* (most now take credit cards), not from travel agents who add on surcharges. Reliable bus information is hard to come by, other than from companies themselves. It is not easy to sell back unused bus tickets. Some bus companies have introduced a system enabling passengers to purchase return tickets at the point of departure, rather than individual tickets for each leg. Buses usually arrive and depart in very good time; you cannot assume departure will be delayed.

Taxi

Taxis have red number plates with white digits (yellow for private cars, with black digits) and have meters. Smaller ones (mostly Volkswagen) are marked 'TAXI' on the windscreen or roof. Only use taxis with an official identification sticker on the windscreen. Rates vary from city to city, but are consistent within each city. At the outset, make sure the meter is cleared and shows tariff 1, except 2300-0600, Sun, and in December when 2 is permitted. Check that the meter is working; if not, fix the price in advance. The fare between Copacabana and the centre is about US$7. Don't hesitate to argue if the route is too long or the fare too much. Radio Taxis are safer but about 50% more expensive, eg **Cootramo**, T0xx21-5605442, **Coopertramo**, T0xx21-2602022, **Centro de Táxi**, T0xx21-5932598, **Transcoopass**, T0xx21-5604888. Luxury cab services offered by smartly dressed individuals outside larger hotels usually cost twice as much as ordinary taxis. If you are seriously cheated note the number of the taxi and insist on a signed bill, threatening to go to the police which can work. Inácio de Oliveira, T0xx21-2254110, is a reliable taxi driver for excursions, he only speaks Portuguese. Recommended. Grimalde, T0xx21-2679812, has been recommended for talkative daytime and evening tours, English and Italian spoken, negotiate a price.

A new service in the last year or so is the **Moto-Taxi**, which is much more economical for the majority of the population. This is not a recommended form of travel because, apart from the unreliability of Brazilian roads, many Moto-Taxis are unlicensed and there have been a number of robberies of passengers.

Car

Any foreigner with a passport can purchase a Brazilian car and travel outside Brazil if it is fully paid for, or if permission is obtained from the financing body in Brazil. Foreigners do not need the CPF tax document (needed by Brazilians – you only have to say you are a tourist) to purchase a car, and the official purchase receipt is accepted as proof of ownership. Sunday papers carry car advertisements and there are second-hand car markets on Sunday mornings in most cities – but don't buy an alcohol-driven car if you propose to drive outside Brazil. It is essential to have an external intake filter fitted, or dust can rapidly destroy an engine. VW Combi vans are cheapest in Brazil where they are made, they are equivalent to the pre-1979 model in Europe. Be sure to travel with a car manual and good quality tools, a VW dealer will advise. There are VW garages throughout the continent, but parts (German or Latin American) are not always interchangeable. In the main, though, there should be no problems with large components (eg gears). If a lot of time is to be spent on dirt roads, the Ford Chevrolet pickup is more robust. A letter in Spanish from your consul explaining your aims and that you will return the vehicle to Brazil can make life much easier at borders and check points. Brazilian cars may not meet safety regulations in North America and Europe, but they can be easily resold in Brazil.

In 1998 new driving laws were introduced which impose severe fines for many infringements of traffic regulations. Driving licences will be endorsed with points for infringements; 20 points = loss of licence.

Motoring Remember service stations are closed in many places on Saturday and Sunday. Road signs are notoriously misleading in Rio and you can end up in a *favela*. Take care if driving along the Estr da Gávea to São Conrado as it is possible to enter Rocinha unwittingly, Rio's biggest slum.

Car repairs *Kyoso Team Mecânico Siqueira Campos*, at the entrance to the old tunnel, T0xx21-2550506. A good mechanic who enjoys the challenge of an unusual car. Recommended. **Land Rio**, Estr da Barra da Tijuca 75, T0xx21-4942316, landrio@bridge.com.br Land Rover and BMW motorcycle parts and repairs.

Fuel

It is virtually impossible to buy premium grades of petrol/gasoline anywhere. With alcohol fuel you need about 50% more alcohol than regular gasoline. Larger cars have a small extra tank for 'gasolina' to get the engine started; remember to keep this topped up. Fuel is only 85% octane (owing to high methanol content), so be prepared for bad consumption and poor performance and starting difficulties in non-Brazilian cars in winter. Diesel fuel is cheap and a diesel engine may provide fewer maintenance problems. Service stations are free to open when they like. Very few open during Carnival week. Fuel prices vary from week to week, but as a rough guide: *alcool comun* US$0.40-0.50 per litre; *gasolina comun* US$0.70-0.80 per litre; *gasolina maxi* US$0.80-0.90 per litre; *maxigold* US$0.90 per litre. There is no unleaded fuel. Diesel is sold for commercial and public service vehicles and costs around US$0.35 per litre, the same price as oil.

The machine

What kind of motoring you do will depend on what kind of car you set out with. While a normal car will reach most places of interest, high ground clearance is useful for badly surfaced or unsurfaced roads and for fording rivers. Four-wheel drive vehicles are recommended for greater flexibility in mountain territory. Wherever you travel you should expect from time to time to find roads that are badly maintained, damaged or closed during the wet season, and delays because of floods, landslides and huge potholes. There is also the possibility of hold-ups from major roadworks. Do not plan your schedules too tightly.

Preparation

Preparing your own car for the journey is largely a matter of common sense: obviously any part that is not in first class condition should be replaced. It's well worth installing extra heavy-duty shock-absorbers (such as Spax or Koni) before starting out, because a long trip on rough roads in a heavily laden car will give heavy wear. Fit tubes on 'tubeless' tyres, since air plugs for tubeless tyres are hard to find, and if you bend the rim on a pothole, the tyre will not hold air. Take spare tubes, and an extra spare tyre. Also take spare plugs, fan-belts, radiator hoses and headlamp bulbs; even though local equivalents can easily be found in cities, it is wise to take spares for those occasions late at night or in remote areas when you might need them. You can also change the fanbelt after a stretch of long, hot driving to prevent wear (eg after 15,000 km/10,000 miles). If your vehicle has more than one fanbelt, always replace them all at the same time (make sure you have the necessary tools if doing it yourself). Find out about your car's electrics and filters and what spares may be required. Similarly, know how to handle problems arising from dirty fuel. It is wise to carry a spade, jump leads, tow rope and an air pump. Fit tow hooks to both sides of the vehicle frame. A 12 volt neon light for camping and repairs will be invaluable. Spare fuel containers should be steel and not plastic, and a siphon pipe is essential for those places where fuel is sold out of the drum. Take a 10 litre water container for self and vehicle. Note that in some areas gas stations are few and far between. Fill up when you see one: the next one may be out of fuel.

Security

Spare no ingenuity in making your car secure. Your model should be the Brink's armoured van: anything less secure can be broken into by the determined and skilled thief. Use heavy chain and padlocks to chain doors shut, fit security catches on windows, remove interior window winders (so that a hand reaching in from a forced vent cannot open the window). All these will help, but none is foolproof. Anything on the outside – wing mirrors, spot lamps, motifs etc – is likely to be stolen too. So are wheels if not secured by locking nuts. Try never to leave the car unattended except in a locked garage or guarded parking space. Remove all belongings and leave the empty glove compartment open when the car is unattended. Also lock the clutch or accelerator to the steering wheel with a heavy, obvious chain or lock. Adult minders or street children will generally protect your car fiercely in exchange for a tip. Be sure to note down key numbers and carry spares of the most important ones (but don't keep all spares inside the vehicle).

Documents Be very careful to keep **all** the papers you are given when you enter, to produce when you leave. Bringing a car in by sea or air is much more complicated and expensive: generally you will have to hire an agent to clear it through customs, expensive and slow.

See 'Driving', page 36, for required documents

Insurance for the vehicle against accident, damage or theft is best arranged in the country of origin, but it is getting increasingly difficult to find agencies who offer this service. In Latin American countries it is very expensive to insure against accident and theft, especially as you should take into account the value of the car increased by duties calculated in real (ie non devaluing) terms. If the car is stolen or written off you will be required to pay very high import duty on its value. Get the legally required minimum cover for third party insurance, not expensive, as soon as you can, because if you should be involved in an accident and are uninsured, your car could be confiscated. If anyone is hurt, do not pick them up (you may become liable). Seek assistance from the nearest police station or hospital if you are able to do so.

Car hire It is essential to have a credit card in order to hire in Brazil; very few agencies accept travellers' cheques, dollars cash may not be accepted, but *reais* cash may qualify for a discount. Renting a car in Brazil is expensive: the cheapest rate for unlimited mileage for a small car is about US$50 per day. Minimum age for renting a car is 21. Companies operate under the names *aluguel de automóveis* or *autolocadores*. Avis is found only in the major cities and has only a time-and-mileage tariff. *National* (or *Localiza*) is represented in many places, often through licencees; it is connected with *InterRent/Europcar* in Europe, will accept credit cards from *InterRent/Europcar* and offers unlimited mileage if booked in advance from Europe on a fixed US$ rate. Compare prices of renting from abroad and in Brazil. If you intend to hire a car for a long time, buying and reselling a vehicle within Brazil may be a reasonable alternative. Toll free numbers for nationwide firms are *Avis*, T0800-558066 and *Localiza*, T0800-992000, www.localiza.com.br A credit card is virtually essential for hiring a car. Recent reports suggest it is cheaper to hire outside Brazil, you may also obtain fuller insurance this way.

There are many agencies on Av Princesa Isabel, Copacabana

Golden Car, R Ronald de Carvalho 154C, Copacabana, T2754748, F5428647. **Hertz**, International airport T33984338, F33984337; Domestic airport, T2620612; Av Princesa Isabel 334B, Copacabana, T2757440. **Interlocadora**, International airport T33983181; Domestic airport, T2400754. **LocaBarra**, Av das Américas 15000, office 209, Recreio dos Bandeirantes, T4371209, www.locabarra.com.br **Localiza**, International airport T3985445; Domestic airport, T5332677, F533215; Av Princesa Isabel 214, Copacabana, T2753340; Av das Américas 676, Barra da Tijuca, T4934477. **Mega**, International airport, T33983361; Av Princesa Isabel 150A and B, Copacabana, T2958197, F2959656. **Nobre**, R da Passagem, Botafogo, T2959494. **Telecar**, R Figueiredo Magalhães 701, Copacabana, T5486778, F2356985. **Unidas**, International airport, T33983452, F33983844; Domestic airport, T/F2406715; Av Princesa Isabel 350, shop A, Copacabana, T2758299.

Scooter hire Funny Frog, R Felipe de Oliveira 4, close to Praça Demétrio Ribeiro, Copacabana, T54366064. No driving licence required.

Car hire insurance Check exactly what the hirer's insurance policy covers. In many cases it will only protect you against minor bumps and scrapes, not major accidents, nor 'natural' damage (eg flooding). Ask if extra cover is available. Also find out, if using a credit card, whether the card automatically includes insurance. Beware of being billed for scratches which were on the vehicle before you hired it.

Motorcycling

The machine It should be off-road capable, eg the BMW R80/100/GS for its rugged and simple design and reliable shaft drive, but a Kawasaki KLR 650s, Honda Transalp, XR600, or XR250, or the ubiquitous Yamaha XT600 Tenere would also be suitable. A road bike can go most places an off-road bike can go at the cost of greater effort.

Preparations Many roads are rough. Fit heavy duty front fork springs and the best quality rebuildable shock absorber you can afford (Ohlins, White Power). Fit lockable luggage such as Krausers (reinforce luggage frames) or make some detachable aluminium panniers. Fit a tank bag and tank panniers for better weight distribution. A large capacity fuel tank (Acerbis), +300 mile/480 km range is essential if going off the beaten track. A washable air filter is a good idea (K&N), also fuel filters and fueltap rubber seals. A good set of trails-type tyres, as well as a high mudguard, are useful. Get to know the bike before you go, ask the dealers in your country what goes wrong with it and arrange a link whereby you can get parts flown out to you. If using a fully enclosed chaincase on a chain driven bike, an automatic chain oiler, to stop it getting it, is a good idea. The Scott-Oiler (106 Clober Road, Milngavie, Glasgow G62 7SS, Scotland) has been recommended. Fill it with Sae 90 oil. A hefty bash plate/sump guard is invaluable.

Spares Reduce service intervals by half if driving in severe conditions. A spare rear tyre is useful but you can buy modern tyres in most capital cities. Take oil filters, fork and shock seals, tubes, a good manual, spare cables (taped into position), a plug cap and spare plug lead. A spare electronic ignition is a good idea, try and buy a second-hand one and make arrangements to have parts sent out to you. A first-class tool kit is a must and if riding a bike with a chain then a spare set of sprockets and an 'o' ring chain should be carried. Spare brake and clutch levers should also be taken as these break easily in a fall. Parts are few and far between, but mechanics are skilled at making do and can usually repair things.

Take a puncture repair kit and tyre levers. Find out about any weak spots on the bike and improve them. Get the book for international dealer coverage from your manufacturer, but don't rely on it. They frequently have few or no parts for modern, large machinery.

Clothes & equipment A tough waterproof jacket, comfortable strong boots, gloves and a helmet with which you can use glass goggles (Halycon) which will not scratch and wear out like a plastic visor. The best quality tent and camping gear that you can afford and a petrol stove which runs on bike fuel is helpful.

Security This is not a problem in most parts of the country. Try not to leave a fully laden bike on its own. An Abus D or chain will keep the bike secure. A cheap alarm gives you peace of mind if you leave the bike outside a hotel at night. Most hotels will allow you to bring the bike inside. Look for hotels that have a courtyard or more secure parking and never leave luggage on the bike overnight or whilst unattended.

Documents Passport, International Driving Licence, bike registration document are necessary. Temporary import papers are given on entry, to be surrendered on leaving the country.

Shipping You must drain the fuel, oil and battery acid, or remove the battery, but it is easier to disconnect and seal the overflow tube. Tape cardboard over fragile bits and insist on loading the bike yourself.

Cycling

A bicycle may not appear to be the most obvious vehicle for a major journey, but if you have time and a reasonable amount of energy it is probably one of the best. It can be ridden, carried by almost every form of transport from an aeroplane to a canoe, and can even be carried for short distances. Cyclists have many advantages over travellers using other forms of transport, since they can travel at their own pace, explore more remote regions and often meet people who are not normally in contact with tourists.

Choosing a bicycle Unless you are planning a journey almost exclusively on paved roads – when a high quality touring bike such as a Dawes Super Galaxy would probably suffice – a mountain bike is strongly recommended. The good quality ones (and the cast iron rule is **never** to skimp on quality) are incredibly tough and rugged, with low gear ratios for difficult terrain, wide tyres with plenty of tread for good road-holding, cantilever brakes, and a low centre of gravity for improved stability. Although touring bikes – and to a lesser extent mountain bikes – and spares are available in the larger cities, remember that most locally manufactured goods are shoddy and rarely last. Buy everything you possibly can before you leave home.

Bicycle equipment A small but comprehensive tool kit (to include chain rivet and crank removers, a spoke key and possibly a block remover), a spare tyre and inner tubes, a puncture repair kit with plenty of extra patches and glue, a set of brake blocks, brake and gear cables and all types of nuts and bolts, at least 12 spokes (best taped to the chain stay), a light oil for the chain (eg Finish-Line Teflon Dry-Lube), tube of waterproof grease, a pump secured by a pump lock, a Blackburn parking block (a most invaluable accessory, cheap and virtually weightless), a cyclometer, a loud bell, and a secure lock and chain. *Richard's Bicycle Book* makes useful reading for even the most mechanically minded.

Luggage and equipment Strong and waterproof front and back panniers are a must. When packed these are likely to be heavy and should be carried on the strongest racks available. Poor quality racks have ruined many a journey for they take incredible strain on unpaved roads. A top bag cum rucksack (eg Carradice) makes a good addition for use on and off the bike. A Cannondale front bag is good for maps, camera, compass etc. (Other recommended panniers are Ortlieb – front and back – which is waterproof and almost 'sandproof', *Mac-Pac*, *Madden* and *Karimoor*.) Gaffer tape is excellent for protecting vulnerable parts of panniers and for carrying out all manner of repairs.

All equipment and clothes should be packed in plastic bags to give extra protection against dust and rain. (Also protect all documents etc, carried close to the body, from sweat.) Always take the minimum clothing. It's better to buy extra items en route when you find you need them. Naturally the choice will depend on the terrain you are planning to cover, and whether rain is to be expected.

Useful tips Wind, not hills, is the enemy of the cyclist. Try to make the best use of the times of day when there is little; mornings tend to be best but there is no steadfast rule. Take care to avoid dehydration, by drinking regularly. In hot, dry areas with limited supplies of water, be sure to carry an ample supply. For food, carry the staples (sugar, salt, dried milk, tea, coffee, porridge oats, raisins, dried soups etc) and supplement these with whatever local foods can be found in the markets. Give your bicycle a thorough daily check for loose nuts or bolts or bearings. See that all parts run smoothly. A good chain should last 3,200 km or more but be sure to keep it as clean as possible – an old toothbrush is good for this – and to oil it lightly from time to time. Remember that thieves are attracted to towns and cities, so when sight-seeing, try to leave your bicycle with someone such as a café owner or a priest. Country people tend to be more honest and are usually friendly and very inquisitive. However, don't take unnecessary risks; always see that your bicycle is secure (most hotels will allow bikes to be kept in rooms). In more remote regions dogs can be vicious; carry a stick or some small stones to frighten them off. Traffic on main roads can be a nightmare; it is usually far more rewarding to keep to the smaller roads or to paths if they exist. Most cyclists agree that the main danger comes from other traffic. A rearview mirror has been frequently recommended to forewarn you of vehicles which are too close behind. You also need to watch out for oncoming, overtaking vehicles, unstable loads on trucks, protruding loads etc. Make yourself conspicuous by wearing bright clothing and a helmet. Most towns have a bicycle shop of some description, but it is best to do your own repairs and adjustments whenever possible. In an emergency it is amazing how one can improvise with wire, string, dental floss, nuts and bolts, odd pieces of tin or electrical Gaffer tape!

The *Expedition Advisory Centre*, administered by the *Royal Geographical Society*, 1, Kensington Gore, London, SW7 2AR, has published a useful monograph entitled *Bicycle Expeditions*, by Paul Vickers. Published in March 1990, it is available direct from the Centre, price £6.50 (postage extra if outside the UK). (In the UK there is also the **Cyclist's Touring Club (CTC)**, Cotterell House, 69 Meadrow, Godalming, Surrey, GU7 3HS, T01483-417217, cycling@ctc.org.uk, for touring and technical information.)

Hitchhiking

Hitchhiking (*carona* in Portuguese) is rather difficult everywhere in Brazil as drivers are reluctant to give lifts because passengers are their responsibility. Try at the highway police check points on the main roads (but make sure your documents are in order) or at the service stations (*postos*).

Keeping in touch

Communications

It is estimated that some three million people in Brazil are now on-line. Email is becoming more common and public access to the internet is growing in Rio de Janeiro with cybercafés also opening in most large towns in the state. There is usually a charge for every 15 minutes and the longer you stay on the cheaper this will be. There is a regularly updated list of locations around the world at www.netcafeguide.com

Internet & email
For cybercafé locations & other places offering internet access see Communications, in the individual area Directories

Letters & postcards To send a standard letter or postcard to the USA costs around US$0.45, to Europe US$0.55, to Australia or South Africa US$0.60. Air mail takes four to seven days to or from Britain or the US, whilst surface mail takes some four weeks. 'Caixa Postal' addresses should be used when possible. All places and streets in Brazil have a post code, *CEP*; these can be obtained from a book displayed in most post offices. You can buy charge collected stamps, Compraventa de Francamento (CF), for letters only, to be paid on delivery.

Postal services
The website www.addresses.com.br is a comprehensive guide to addresses in the city & there is a companion book as well

Franked and registered (insured) letters are normally secure, but check that the amount franked is what you have paid, or the item will not arrive. Aerogrammes are most reliable. It may be easier to avoid queues and obtain higher denomination stamps by buying at the philatelic desk at the main post office.

Parcels The post office sells cardboard boxes for sending packages internally and abroad (they must be submitted open); pay by the kilo; you must fill in a list of contents; string and official sellotape are provided in all post offices. Courier services such as **DHL**, **Federal Express** and **UPS** (recommended) are useful, but note that they may not necessarily operate under those names.

Receiving mail Postes restantes usually only hold letters for 30 days. Identification is required and it's a good idea to write your name on a piece of paper to help the attendant find your letters. Charge is usually minimal but often involves queuing at another counter to buy stamps which are attached to your letter and franked before it is given to you. Poste Restante for Amex customers is efficiently dealt with by the Amex agents in most large towns.

Telephone services

For the area codes see the inside front cover, or look in the telephone directory

There is a trunk dialling system (DDD) linking all parts of Brazil. Recent privatization of the telephone system has led to increased competition. The consumer must now choose a telephone company for long distance and international calls by inserting a two-digit code between the zero and the area code. Phone numbers in Brazil are now often printed thus: 0xx21 (0 for a national call, xx for the code of the phone company chosen, 21 for Rio de Janeiro, for example), followed by the seven-digit number of the subscriber. To phone Brazil from abroad dial 0055 followed by the appropriate DDD code eg 21 for Rio de Janeiro or 24 for some areas in the state.

Nationwide and international telephone operators and their codes are: *Embratel*, 21 and *Intelig*, 23. For calls to towns in Rio de Janeiro state with the 0xx24 code the choice of telephone operator widens to include: *Telemar*, 31 and *Vésper*, 85.

National calls There are telephone boxes at airports, post offices, railway stations, hotels, most bars, restaurants and cafés, and in the main cities there are telephone kiosks, for local and intercity calls, in the shape of large blue shells; in Rio they are known as *orelhões* (big ears). Local phone calls and telegrams are quite cheap.

Phone cards are available from telephone and post offices which are the cheapest places to buy them. They cost US$0.75 for 10 units up to US$3 for 90 and can also be obtained from newstands, some chemists or from street vendors at a higher cost. To use the telephone office, tell the operator which city or country you wish to call, go to the booth whose number you are given; make your call and you will be billed on exit. Not all offices accept credit cards. Collect calls within Brazil can be made from any telephone – dial 9, followed by the number, and announce your name and city. Local calls from a private phone are normally free.

Telephone numbers often change in Rio de Janeiro. If in doubt, phone 102, *Auxílio à Lista*, which is the current daily updated directory of telephone numbers. This number can be used all over the country, but if you want to find out a Rio phone number from outside Rio, dial the city code 0xx21, then 121. If you do not understand Portuguese, you should seek assistence from a hotel receptionist or similar because the numbers are only spoken in Portuguese.

International calls At the moment it is possible to call abroad from public telephones only in areas with large numbers of foreign tourists such as Copacabana in Rio. There are, however, boxes within most telephone offices for international calls. Make sure you buy at least one 90-unit card or pay at the desk after making your call from a booth. Calls are priced on normal and cheaper rates, depending on time of day. Check with the local phone company. Peak rate to Europe is around US$4 per minute, to USA US$3. There is a 40% tax added to the cost of all telephonic and telegraphic communications, which makes international service extremely expensive.

See also the inside front cover for international phone codes

NB Brazil is linked to North America, Japan and most of Europe by trunk dialling (DDI). Codes are listed in the telephone directories. Home Country Direct is available from hotels, private phones or blue public phones to the following countries (prefix all numbers with 00080); Argentina 54, Australia 61, Belgium 03211, Bolivia 13, Canada 14, Chile 56 (Entel), 36 (Chile Sat), 37 (CTC Mundo), Colombia 57, Costa Rica 50, Denmark 45, France 33, Germany 49, Holland 31, Hong Kong 85212, Israel 97, Italy 39, Japan 81 (KDD), 83 (ITJ), 89 (Super Japan), Norway 47, Paraguay 18, Peru 51, Portugal 35, Singapore 65,

Spain 34, Sweden 46, Switzerland 04112, UK 44 (BT Direct), USA 10 (AT&T), 12 (MCI), 16 (Sprint), 11 (Worldcom), Uruguay 59, Venezuela 58. For collect calls from phone boxes (in Portuguese: 'a cobrar'), dial 107 and ask for the *telefonista internacional*.

Mobile phones These have made a big impact in Brazil owing to past difficulties in getting fixed lines, especially outside the main towns. When using a *celular* telephone you do not drop the zero from the area code as you now have to when dialling from a fixed line. There are two different companies *ATL* and *Telefônica Celular* in Rio de Janeiro which work on different wavelengths. Due to occasional difficulties getting through to a mobile phone in the city some people carry two mobile phones, one from each system. In Rio de Janeiro mobile phones, or even a line for your own phone, can be hired. Try **Presscell**, Estr da Gávea 847, office 118, São Conrado, T/F0xx21-33222692, International airport, T0xx21-33984932. **Fast Cell/Star Coast**, R Bolivar 42, office 302, Copacabana, T0xx21-2567607, F2359955. Pay-as-you-go phones are now available, which is another option for travellers. **NB** The systems in Rio de Janeiro are AMPS analog and CDMA or TDMA digital. There are no GSM systems yet.

Fax services These operate in main post offices in major cities, at telephone offices, or from private lines. In the last case the international fax rates are as for phone calls; from the post office the rates are US$3-4 per page within Brazil, US$10.50 to Europe and US$9 to the USA. To receive a fax costs US$1.40.

Media

Television Nationwide TV channels are Globo based in Rio de Janeiro and SBT, Record, Bandeirantes based in São Paulo. TVE is an educational channel showing documentaries and original language films. Programming revolves around light entertainment, soap operas, foreign films dubbed in Portuguese and football.

Newspapers There is no national newspaper although the news magazines (see below) are distributed nationally. The main Rio papers are *Jornal do Brasil* (www.jb.com.br), *O Globo* (www.oglobo.com.br), *O Dia* (www.uol.com.br/odia) and *Jornal do Commércio* (www.jornaldocommercio.com.br).

There are a number of local community newspapers in the city such as *Posto Seis* (www.nemesis.com.br/posto6) from Copacabana, *Folha de Ipanema* (www.nemesis.com.br/ipanema), and *Folha do Centro* which can be good guides to local events and news.

Foreign language newspapers include *The Brazilian Post* and *Sunday News* in English, and *Deutsche Zeitung* in German. In Europe, the *Euro-Brasil Press* is available in most capitals; it prints Brazilian and some international news in Portuguese. London office 23 Kings Exchange, Tileyard Rd, London N7 9AH, T020-77004033, F77003540, eurobrasilpress@compuserve.com

Magazines There are a number of good, informative weekly news magazines which are widely read: *Veja* (www.uol.com.br/veja) which has a Rio de Janeiro section included (www.veja-rio.com.br), *Istoé* (www.uol.com.br/istoe), *Epoca* and *Exame*.

Radio South America has more local and community radio stations than practically anywhere else in the world; a shortwave (world band) radio offers a practical means to brush up on the language, sample popular culture and absorb some of the richly varied regional music. International broadcasters such as the BBC World Service, the Voice of America and Boston (Mass)-based Monitor Radio International (operated by *Christian Science Monitor*) keep the traveller abreast of news and events, in English, Portuguese and Spanish.

Compact or miniature portables are recommended, with digital tuning and a full range of shortwave bands, as well as FM, long and medium wave. Detailed advice on radio models (around US$240 for a decent one) and wavelengths can be found in the annual publication, *Passport to World Band Radio* (Box 300, Penn's Park, PA 18943, USA), £14.99. Details of local stations is listed in *World TV and Radio Handbook* (WTRH), PO Box 9027, 1006 AA Amsterdam, The Netherlands, £19.99. Both of these, free wavelength guides and selected radio sets are available from the BBC World Service Bookshop, Bush House Arcade, Bush House, Strand, London WC2B 4PH, UK, T020-75572576.

English-language radio broadcasts daily at 15290 kHz, 19 m Short Wave (Rádio Bras, Caixa Postal 04/0340, DF-70 323 Brasília).

Food and drink

Eating out

Meals are extremely large by European standards; if your appetites are small, you can order, say, one portion and one empty plate, and divide the portion. However, if you are in a position to do so tactfully, you may choose to offer the rest to a person with no food (many Brazilians do – observe the correct etiquette), alternatively you could ask for an *embalagem* (doggy bag) or get a takeaway called a *marmita* or *quentinha*. Most restaurants have this service but it is not always on the menu. Many restaurants now serve *comida por kilo* where you serve yourself and pay for the weight of food on your plate. Unless you specify to the contrary many restaurants will lay a *couvert (coberto opcional)*, olives, carrots etc, costing US$0.50-0.75.

Cariocas usually have dinner at 1900 or 2000, occasionally later at weekends after going out to the cinema, theatre or a concert or show

The main meal is usually taken in the middle of the day; cheap restaurants tend not to be open in the evening. In a restaurant, always ask the price of a dish before ordering.

With the devaluation of the *real*, the cost of eating out in Rio has come down, but you can still expect to pay US$20-40 per person in the first-class places, more in the very best restaurants. You can, however, eat well for an average US$10-20 per person, less if you choose the *prato feito* at lunchtime (US$1.50-2), or eat in a place that serves food by weight (starting at about US$0.65 per gram). While many of Rio's quality hotels offer world-class food and service, they may lack atmosphere and close at midnight. There are much livelier and cheaper places to eat if going out for an evening meal. There are many juice bars in Rio with a wide selection (eg the *Rei dos Sucos* chain). Most restaurants are closed on 24 and 25 Dec.

The guide Restaurantes do Rio, by Danusia Bárbara, published annually by Record (in Portuguese only), is worth looking at for ideas on where to eat; also on the Internet www.brazilweb.com/rio/contents.htm

If travelling on a tight budget, remember to ask in restaurants for the *prato feito* or *sortido*, a money saving, excellent value *table-d'hôte* meal. The *prato comercial* is similar but rather better and a bit more expensive. *Lanchonetes* are cheap eating places where you generally pay before eating. *Salgados* (savoury pastries), *coxinha* (a pyramid of manioc filled with meat or fish and deep fried), *esfiha* (spicey hamburger inside an onion bread envelope), *empadão* (a filling – eg chicken – in sauce in a pastry case), *empadas* and *empadinhas* (smaller fritters of the same type), are the usual fare. *Pão de queijo* is a hot roll made with cheese. A *bauru* is a toasted sandwich either filled with steak or with a tomato, ham and cheese filling. *Cocada* is a coconut and sugar biscuit.

Warning Avoid mussels, marsh crabs and other shellfish caught near Rio as they are likely to have lived in a highly polluted environment.

Fast food

There are plentiful hamburger stands (literally 'stands' as you stand & eat the hamburger) & lunch counters all over the city

McDonalds and *Bob's* (similar) can be found at about 20 locations each (Big Mac US$3). *Galetos* are lunch counters specializing in chicken and grilled meat, very reasonable. In the shopping centres there is usually a variety of restaurants and snack bars grouped around a central plaza where you can shop around for a good meal. Most less-expensive restaurants in Rio have basically the same type of food (based on steak, fried potatoes and rice) and serve large portions; those with small appetites,

Food and drink

Drinks Bebidas
beer cerveja
coffee café
fruit juice suco
hot chocolate chocolate quente
milk leite
mineral water água mineral
soft drink refrigerante
tea chá
tonic water água tónica
whisky uísque
wine vinho

Fruit Frutas
apple maçã
banana banana
coconut coco
grape uva
lime limão
mango manga
orange laranja
papaya mamão
passion fruit maracujá
pineapple abacaxi
strawberry morango
watermelon melancia

Meat Carne
beef bife
chicken frango/galinha
fish peixe
ham presunto
hot dog cachorro quente
kid cabrito
pork porco
toasted cheese and ham sandwich misto quente
sausages salsichas
steak filé
turkey peru

Vegetables Legumes
carrot cenoura
lettuce alface
onion cebola
potato batata
rice arroz
salad salada
sweetcorn milho
tomato tomate

Others
bread pão
butter manteiga
cake bolo
cheese queijo
egg ovo
ice cream sorvete
mustard mostarda
peanut amendoim
pepper pimenta
pie pastel
salt sal
sandwich sanduiche
sugar açúcar
yoghurt iogurte

---

especially families with children, can ask for a spare plate and split helpings. *La Mole*, at 11 locations, serves good, cheap Italian food, very popular.

There are very few public toilets in Rio de Janeiro, but many bars and restaurants (eg Macdonalds) offer facilities. Just ask for the 'banheiro' (banyairoo). Good toilets are to be found in the Shopping Centres.

For vegetarians, there is a growing network of restaurants in the main cities. In smaller places where food may be monotonous, try vegetarian for greater variety. We list several. Most also serve fish. Alternatives in smaller towns are the Arab and Chinese restaurants.

Vegetarians

The most common dish in Rio de Janeiro is *bife (ou frango) com arroz e feijão*, steak (or chicken) with rice and the excellent Brazilian black beans. However, due to Brazil's rich cultural mix many other regional cuisines are found in the city. Rio de Janeiro has a number of good French, Italian and Japanese restaurants as well as other foreign cuisines from Arabic to Polish.

Different cuisines

Feijoada The most famous dish with beans is the *feijoada completa*: several meat ingredients (jerked beef, smoked sausage, smoked tongue, salt pork, along with spices, herbs and vegetables) are cooked with the beans. Manioc flour is sprinkled over it, and it is eaten with kale (*couve*) and slices of orange, and accompanied by glasses of *aguardente* (unmatured rum), usually known as *cachaça* (booze), though *pinga* (drop) is a politer term. Most restaurants serve the *feijoada completa* for Saturday lunch (up to about 1630).

Comida Mineira comes from the nearby state of Minas Gerais and is quite distinctive and very wholesome and you can often find restaurants serving this type of food in Rio. There are two splendid special dishes involving pork, black beans, *farofa* and kale; they are *tutu á mineira* and *feijão tropeiro*. A white hard cheese (*queijo prata*) or a slightly softer one (*queijo Minas*) is often served for dessert with bananas, or guava or quince paste.

Bahian cuisine has some excellent fish dishes and many restaurants in Rio specialize in them. *Vatapá* is a good dish containing shrimp or fish sauced with palm oil, or coconut milk. *Empadinhas de camarão* are worth trying; they are shrimp patties, with olives and heart of palm.

Churrasco This is a mixed grill, including excellent steak, served with roasted manioc flour (*farofa*; raw manioc flour is known as *farinha*), known as *churrasco* (it came originally from the cattlemen of Rio Grande do Sul), normally served in specialized restaurants known as *churrascarias* or *rodízios* (or *espeto corrido*). In the latter, waiters ask you in advance what types of meat you want and then bring them round to you until you tell them to stop. Each *rodízio* has its own variation on the red light/green light system for communicating to the staff that you are full. *Churrascarias* usually have a self-service salad bar; they are good places for large appetites and are relatively cheap, especially by European standards. There are many at São Conrado and Joá, on the road out to Barra da Tijuca (see page 157).

Desserts & fruits

There is fruit all the year round, ranging from banana and orange to mango, pawpaw, custard-apple (*fruta do conde*) and guava. One should try the *manga de Ubá*, a non-fibrous small mango. Also good are *amora* (a raspberry that looks like a strawberry), *jaboticaba*, a small black damson-like fruit, and *jaca* (jackfruit), a large yellow/green fruit.

The exotic flavours of Brazilian ice creams should be experienced. Try *açaí, bacuri, biribá, buruti, cupuaçu* (not eveyone's favourite), *mari-mari, mucajá, murici, pajurá, pariri, patuá, piquiá, pupunha, sorva, tucumá, uxi* and others mentioned below under 'drinks'.

Drinks

Tap water in Brazil is not suitable to drink unless it has been passed through a filter. Bottled mineral water is the safest option

Imported drinks are expensive, but there are some fair local wines. Among the better ones are Château d'Argent, Château Duvalier, Almadén, Dreher, Preciosa and Bernard Taillan. The red Marjolet from Cabernet grapes, and the Moselle-type white Zahringer, have been well spoken of. Also reckoned to be good is Anticuário from Caxias do Sul; its Vinho Velho do Museu and Vinho Fino Branco do Museu sell for about US$12.50 a bottle and its Reserva Especial red at US$10. It has often been noticed that a new *adega* starts off well, but the quality gradually deteriorates with time; many vintners have switched to American Concorde grapes, producing a rougher wine. Greville Brut champagne-type is inexpensive and very drinkable. A white wine *Sangria*, containing tropical fruits such as pineapple and papaya, is worth looking out for. Chilean and Portuguese wines are sometimes available at little more than the cost of local wines.

Some genuine Scotch whisky brands are bottled in Brazil; they are very popular because of the high price of Scotch imported in the bottle; Teacher's is the most highly regarded brand. Locally made gin, vermouth and campari are very good. The local firewater, *aguardente* (known as *cachaça* or *pinga*), made from sugar-cane, is cheap and wholesome, but visitors should seek local advice on the best brands; São Francisco, Praianinha, Nega Fulô, '51' and Pitu are recommended makes. Mixed with fruit juices of various sorts, sugar and crushed ice, *cachaça* becomes the principal element in a *batida*, a delicious and powerful drink; the commonest is a lime batida or *batida de limão*; a variant of this is the *caipirinha*, a *cachaça* with several slices of lime in it, a *caipiroska* is made with vodka. *Cachaça* with Coca-Cola is a *cuba*, while rum with Coca-Cola is a *cuba libre*.

The beers are good and there are plenty of brands: *Antarctica, Brahma, Bohemia, Cerpa, Skol* and *Xingu* black beer. Beers are cheaper by the bottle than on draught. The best known of many local soft drinks is *Guaraná*, which is a very popular carbonated fruit drink. Buying bottled drinks in supermarkets, you may be asked for empties in return.

There is an excellent range of non-alcoholic fruit juices, known as *sucos: açai, acerola, caju* (cashew), *pitanga, goiaba* (guava), *genipapo, graviola* (= *chirimoya*), *maracujá* (passion fruit), *sapoti* and *tamarindo* are recommended. *Vitaminas* are thick fruit or vegetable drinks with milk. *Caldo de cana* is sugar-cane juice, sometimes mixed with ice. *Água de côco* or *côco verde* (coconut water from chilled, fresh green coconut) cannot be missed. Remember that *água mineral*, available in many varieties at bars and restaurants, is a cheap, safe thirst-quencher (cheaper still in supermarkets). Apart from the ubiquitous coffee, good tea is grown and sold. **NB** If you don't want sugar in your coffee or *suco*, you must ask when you order it.

These can vary from basic neighbourhood bars open to the street, often known as *pé sujos* or *botequins*, to sophisticated places with waiter service. Food and snacks are often served and there is usually some form of music, whether a live band or the customers providing their own in an improvised samba session with guitars and drums.

Bars
Wherever you are, there's one near you

See the books *O Guia dos Botequins do Rio de Janeiro*, or *Rio Botequim*, published annually by the Prefeitura da Cidade do Rio de Janeiro which describe Rio's best, most traditional bars and their history (in Portuguese), US$20. A beer costs around US$1.50, but up to US$5 in expensive hotel bars. A cover charge of US$3-7 may be made for live music. Snack food is always available. Single drinkers/diners are usually welcome, though you may not remain alone for long unless you stick your nose in a book. Copacabana, Ipanema and Leblon have many beach *barracas*, several open all night.

Entertainment

Rio nightlife is rich and infinitely varied, one of the main attractions for most visitors. If you are not in Rio for Carnival, it's worth seeing a samba show. Organized trips cost around US$50 including dinner and are good, but it's cheaper to pay at the door. Most notable is **Plataforma I** in Leblon. There are dozens of other good clubs for all tastes and styles of music, most open Wed-Sun, action starts around midnight, lone women and male-only groups may have trouble getting in.

Nightclubs
See also 'Tourist information', above, for guides to what's on

The usual system in nightclubs is to pay an entrance fee (about US$10) and then you are given a card onto which your drinks are entered. There is often a minimum consumption of US$10-15 on top of the entry charge. Do not lose your card or they may charge you more than you could possibly drink, sometimes US$200-300. Most places will serve reasonable snack food and some have restaurants attached.

New American releases (with original soundtrack), plus Brazilian and worldwide films and classics are all shown. Many of the cultural centres also have cinemas and there are a few screens dedicated to art house films. See the local press for details. The normal seat price is US$4, discounts on Wed and Thu (students pay half price any day of the week).

Cinemas

Salsa is in fashion at the moment, after the popularity of the film *Buena Vista Social Club*, and has followed on from Tango. There are often samba classes for foreigners at carnival time. **Casa de Dança Carlinhos de Jesus**, Rua da Passagem 145, Botafogo, T0xx21-5416186. Classes in ballroom, Salsa, Forró and Samba no Pé. **Escola de Dança de Salão Maria Antonieta**, Rua do Catete 112, second floor, next to Catete Metrô, T5558589. Most styles of ballroom and Latin dance, beginners on Tue and Thu at 2030, dances on Fri and Sun.

Dance classes

There are free concerts throughout the summer, along the Copacabana and Ipanema beaches, in Botafogo and at the parks: mostly samba, reggae, rock and MPB (Brazilian pop): there is no advance schedule, information is given in the local press. **Canecão** in Botafogo and **ATL Hall** in Barra de Tijuca are big venues for live concerts, most nights, see press for what's on during your visit. Rio's famous jazz, in all its forms, is performed in lots of enjoyable venues especially in Ipanema and Lagoa.

Music

There are about 40 theatres in Rio, presenting a variety of classical and modern performances in Portuguese. Seat prices start at about US$15 however some children's theatre is free. See the directory sections for addresses and telephone numbers.

Theatre

Shopping

Tips/Trends — **Prices & bargaining** As a rule, shopping is easier, quality more reliable and prices higher in the shopping centres (mostly excellent) and in the wealthier suburbs such as Ipanema and Leblon. Better prices are posted at the small shops and street traders. Shopping is most entertaining at markets and on the beach. Bargaining (with good humour) is expected in the latter.

Rio has an excellent selection of markets of which the **Feira do Nordeste** held at Campo de São Cristóvão and the **Feira Hippy** held in Ipanema are probably the most popular with tourists. Souvenirs and typical food can also be found at the many markets in Copacabana and there are some interesting antiques markets in the centre. Shopping centres are also excellent places to find services such as telephone offices, cyber cafés, restaurants and nightclubs as well as a wide variety of shops. There are many places where both photos and slides can be quickly processed. Kodachrome slide film can be difficult to get in Rio.

What to buy — **Clothing** Design in clothing is impressive, though unfortunately not equalled by manufacturing quality. Buy your beachwear in Rio de Janeiro: it is matchless. *Saara* is a multitude of little shops along Rua da Alfândega and Rua Senhor dos Passos (between city centre and Campo Santana), where clothes bargains can be found (especially jeans and bikinis); it is known popularly as 'Shopping a Céu Aberto'. Little shops on Rua Aires Saldanha, Copacabana (one block back from beach), are good for bikinis and cheaper than in shopping centres.

Jewellery There are two high-class stores selling precious stones and jewellery which contains them, *H Stern* and *Amsterdam Sauer*. They both have their headquarters in Rio de Janeiro (see page 147) and both provide lots of information in booklets or their museum/displays on the process of turning mined stones into desirable objects. In Rio de Janeiro there are many other reputable dealers from whom gold, diamonds and gemstones can be bought. There are also jewellery stores selling both traditional styles and innovative designs incorporating Brazilian gems. Some of the nicest pieces contain a combination of different stones, selected for their hues to make gradations of colour in a single setting. Cheap, fun pieces can also be bought from street traders.

Many people come to Brazil looking for bargains in gemstones. Because so many different types of stone are mined and sold here, it is logical to assume that prices will be better than elsewhere. However, if you want good quality, you have to pay for it, especially if you are just looking for a special gift and are not a trained assessor of gemstones. If you decide to buy on the street, you need to beware of imitations, particularly of emeralds, which can easily be manufactured in a laboratory, and of aquamarines. In a shop, you should ask to see the owner's qualification (*título*) as well as the guarantee that the stone is genuine. It is not possible to quantify the cost of a gemstone because, even though its weight, brilliance and cut can be determined, outlets will put their own price on it. You should therefore buy from a reputable retailer, or investigate the market thoroughly. Note that the distinction between 'precious' and 'semi-precious' is no longer used; the demand for rare and interesting stones is such that some types of what used to be called 'semi-precious' are now more valuable than the old 'precious stones'. Similarly, a good quality 'semi-precious stone' will command a higher price than a poor quality 'precious stone'.

Souvenirs There are interesting furnishings made with gemstones, and marble. Clay figurines from the northeast, lace from Ceará, leatherwork, strange pottery from Amazônia, carvings in soapstone and in bone, tiles and other ceramic work,

African-type pottery and basketwork from Bahia, are all worth seeking out. Many large hotel gift shops stock a good selection of handicrafts at reasonable prices. Brazilian cigars are excellent for those who like the mild flavours popular in Germany, the Netherlands and Switzerland. Other recommended purchases are musical instruments, eg guitars and other stringed and percussion instruments. In Rio de Janeiro many contemporary artists work in wood.

There are excellent textiles: good hammocks from the Northeast (ironmongers sell hooks *ganchos para rede* for hanging your hammock at home); other fabrics.

For those who know how to use them, medicinal herbs, barks and spices can be bought from street markets; coconut oil and local skin and haircare products (fantastic conditioners) are better and cheaper than in Europe, but known brands of toiletries are exorbitant. Other bad buys are film (including processing), cameras and any electrical goods (including batteries). Sunscreen, sold in all department stores and large supermarkets, is expensive.

Holidays and festivals

January On the 1st, the New Year begins with a procession of decorated boats from Praia das Flechas, Angra dos Reis. On the 6th, Folia dos Reis (Epiphany) is celebrated especially in Paraty. On the 15th the Afro-Brazilian ceremony of Lavagem do Bonfim is held in front of the Igreja do Senhor do Bonfim on the corner of Rua Monsenhor Manuel Gomes and Avenida Brasil in São Cristóvão. The festival of **São Sebastião**, patron saint of Rio, is celebrated by an evening procession on the 20th, leaving Capuchinhos Church, Tijuca and arriving at the cathedral of São Sebastião. On the same evening, an *umbanda festival* is celebrated at the Caboclo Monument in Santa Teresa.

February
See page 10 for more details on carnaval

The major festival is **Carnaval**, which is held in either February or March for the six days up to and including Ash Wednesday and is celebrated all over the state (see page 10). On the 2nd the Afro-Brazilian ceremony of **Presente de Yemanjá** is held with flowers and gifts being thrown into the bay after a maritime procession from Praça XV. The 9th is **Carmen Miranda's birthday** with an exhibition and film shows at her museum in Flamengo.

March The 1st is the city's **foundation day** which is celebrated with a mass in the Igreja de São Sebastião.

April **Semana Santa**, which ends on Easter Sunday in either March or April, is celebrated with parades in many cities and towns. The 21st is **Tiradentes Day** when civic ceremonies are held in front of the Palácio Tiradentes in Central Rio.

May The 1st, is **Labour Day** celebrated with cultural and sporting events throughout Rio. At the end of the month, the **Festa do Divino Espírito Santo** (Whitsun) is celebrated throughout the state but particularly in Paraty.

June **Corpus Christi** can be held this month or in May. In Rio the **Festas Juninas** start with the festival of **Santo Antônio** on 13th, whose main event is a mass, followed by celebrations at the Convento do Santo Antônio and the Largo da Carioca. Throughout the state, the festival of **São João** is a major event, marked by huge bonfires on the night of 23-24th. It is traditional to dance the *quadrilha* and drink *quentão*, cachaça and sugar, spiced with ginger and cinnamon, served hot. The Festas Juninas close with the festival of **São Pedro** on 29th. Being the patron saint of fishermen, his feast is normally accompanied by processions of boats.

July This is a school holiday month when many people are travelling and prices in resorts are often higher.

August A *Festa do Peixe* is held in Angra dos Reis.

September The 7th is **Independence Day** celebrated with military parades. During this month a *film festival* is often held in Rio de Janeiro.

October The 12th is *Nossa Senhora Aparecida*. The feast of **Nossa Senhora da Penha** (see page 114) is also held during this month.

November The 1st is **All Saint's Day** (Todos os Santos) and the 2nd **All Souls' Day** (Finados). 15th is **Proclamation of the Republic** as well as the day elections are held.

December The 25th is **Christmas Day**. The festival year ends with the atmospheric festival of *Iemanjá* (see 'Religion', page 241) held on the night of 31st, when devotees of the *orixá* of the sea dress in white and gather on Copacabana, Ipanema and Leblon beaches, singing and dancing around open fires and making offerings. The elected Queen of the Sea is rowed along the seashore. At midnight small boats are launched as offerings to Iemanjá. The religious event is dwarfed, however, by a massive New Year's Eve party, called **Reveillon** at Copacabana. The beach is packed as thousands of revellers enjoy free outdoor concerts by big-name pop stars, topped with a lavish midnight firework display. It is most crowded in front of *Copacabana Palace Hotel*. Another good place to see the fireworks is in front of *Le Meridien*, famous for its fireworks waterfall at about 10 minutes past midnight.

NB Many followers of Iemanjá are now making their offerings on 29 or 30 December and at Barra da Tijuca or Recreio dos Bandeirantes to avoid the crowds and noise of Reveillon.

Other holidays Four religious or traditional holidays (Good Friday must be one; other usual days: 1 November, All Saints Day; 24 December, Christmas Eve) must be fixed by the municipalities. Other holidays are usually celebrated on the Monday prior to the date.

Sport and special interest travel

Adventure sports To some extent there is a mingling of ecotourism and adventure tourism in Brazil. This is partly because the adventurous activities nearly always take place in unspoilt parts of the country, but also because the term 'ecotourism' is applied to almost any outdoor activity. This section will deal specifically with participation sports, but that should not rule out the awareness of keeping the impact of one's activities to a minimum. This applies as much on land as in the sea or on rivers. The main adventure sports in the state of Rio de Janeiro are **climbing**, **trekking**, **mountain biking** and **horse riding** although **rafting** and **canoeing** are gaining in popularity.

Climbing As Brazil has no mountain ranges of Alpine or Andean proportions, the most popular form of climbing (*escalada*) is rock-face climbing. In the heart of Rio, you can see, or join, climbers scaling the rocks at the base of Pão de Açúcar and on the Sugar Loaf itself. Not too far away, the Serra dos Órgãos provides plenty of challenges, not least the Dedo de Deus (God's Finger – see page 193). Another popular activity is abseiling (*rappel*).

Information *União de Caminhantes e Escaladores do Rio de Janeiro*, Rua do Catete 228, shop 205, Catete, T0xx21-5579079.

Tour operators *Companhia Escalada*, Rua Doutor Satamini 171, room 701, Tijuca, T0xx21-5673058. *Escalada Café*, Rua Capitão Salomão 55, Botafogo, RJ 22271-040, T0xx21-5379131. Mountaineering. *Escola de Alpinismo Cabeça Verde*, Rua Alice 1512A, Laranjeiras, T/F0xx21-5576093 (Marco Vidon). Basic climbing course. *Parede – Esportes de Montanha*, Rua Senador Pedro Velho 219, Cosme Velho, Cell0xx21-91657577, F5578045, www.parede.net Climbing and trekking in Serra dos Órgãos, Serra da Bocaina and Itatiaia. *Rapel Radical*, Cell0xx21-99995095 (Felipe). For climbing on Pão de Açúcar.

Trekking This sport is becoming very popular in Rio de Janeiro. There are plenty of hiking shops and agencies which handle hiking tours. Trails are frequently graded according to difficulty; this is noticeably the case in areas where *trilhas ecológicas* have been laid out in forests or other sites close to busy tourist areas. Many national parks and other protected areas provide good opportunities for trekking and local information can easily be found to get you on the right track. Close to the city there are a number of options in Tijuca national park and Pedra Branca state park.

There are some basic rules you should follow: never hike on your own and it is best to go with a guide who knows the trails; take water and food with you in a small day sack as well as sun cream, hat, torch and a rubbish sack; wear suitable footwear and light cotton clothing; it is best to start your walk in the morning and let someone know where you are going and when you expect to return.

Information *Centro Excursionista Brasileiro (CEB)*, Avenida Almirante Barroso 2, 8th floor, Centro, RJ 20031-000, T0xx21-2529844, F2626360, www.ceb.org.br Climbing and trekking, book hikes in advance between 1400-2200 Mon-Fri. *Clube Excursionista Carioca*, Rua Hilário Gouveia 71, room 206, Copacabana, RJ 22040-020, T0xx21-2551348. Meets Wed and Fri, recommended for enthusiasts. *Clube Excursionista Guanabara*, Rua Washington Luís 9, cobertura, Centro, T0xx21-2320569. *Clube Excursionista Light*, Av Marechal Floriano 199, room 501, Centro, T0xx21-2535052.

Tour operators *Arzeatur*, T0xx21-5443851, Cell99617038. Walking in national and state parks. *ECA*, Av Erasmo Braga 217, room 305, Centro, T0xx21-2426857. Personal guide US$100 per day, owner Ralph speaks English. *Paulo Miranda*, R Campos Sales 64, room 801, RJ 20270-210, T/F0xx21-2644501. See also **Tijuca National Park** tour operators page 159.

Horse riding Some of the best trails for horse riding are the routes that used to be taken by the mule trains that transported goods between the coast and the interior. The Serra da Bocaina near Paraty is a particularly good area as is the mountain region around Penedo (see page 202) and Visconde de Mauá.

Information *Sociedade Hípica Brasileira*, Av Borges de Medeiros 2248, T5278090, Lagoa.

Canoeing Canoeing is supervised by the Confederação Brasileira de Canoagem (CBCa – Brazilian Canoeing Federation), founded in 1989. It covers all aspects of the sport, speed racing, slalom, downriver, surfing and ocean kayaking. For downriver canoeing, go to **Visconde de Mauá** (see page 203 where the Rio Preto is famous for the sport). For kayak surfing the best places are in Rio while ocean kayaking is popular in both Rio and Búzios.

Tour operators *Águas Brancas – Rafting e Montanhismo*, T0xx24-2423797. Canoeing and kayaking near Itaipava and Petrópolis. Also offer trekking, waterfall abseiling and rafting on the Paraibuna and Paraíba do Sul rivers.

Caving There are cave systems in the Tijuca forest near the city as well as many others in Rio de Janeiro state such as Grutas do Espa near Niterói. Ibama (see 'National Parks' page 228) has a programme for the protection of the national speleological heritage.

Tour operators *Ar Livre*, T0xx21-2083029. Organizes trekking throughout the state with some canyoning and caving trips.

Mountain biking and cycling Rio de Janeiro is well-suited to cycling, both on and off-road and the city has some 74 km of cycle paths which run from Centro through Zona Sul to Barra da Tijuca. On main roads it is important to obey the general advice of being on the look out for motor vehicles as cyclists are very much second-class citizens. Also note that when cycling on the coast you may encounter strong winds which will hamper your progress. There are endless roads and tracks suitable for mountain biking, and there are many clubs which organize group rides, activities and competitions. Cycling tours are run at weekends along the city's cycle paths conducted by bilingual guides. (For information and booking T0xx21-4910718.)

Information *Federação de Ciclismo*, T0xx21-2699994.

Tour operators Tours (hire available) with *Rio Bikers*, R Domingos Ferreira 81, room 201, T0xx21-2745872, and *Rio by Bike*, T0xx21-2595532, Cell99857540, riobybike@travelrio.com, who will deliver and pick your bike up. *Ypê Amarelo Ecoturismo*, Rua Senador Dantas 117, office 1224, Centro, T0xx21-5324395, F5246778, ypeamarelo@uol.com.br Cycling, motocycling, trekking and radical sports such as waterfall abseiling.

Parachuting There are several clubs for skydiving and tandem jumping (*salto duplo*) at the Aeroporto de Jacarepaguá, Avenida Ayrton Senna 2541. *Barra Jumping*, T0xx21-33252494, Cell9881566. *Aero Club do Brasil*, T/F0xx21-33255301. Several other people offer tandem jumping; check that they are accredited with the Associação Brasileira de Vôo Livre (see below). For ultralight flying enquire at the Autodrómo de Jacarepaguá, Avenida Embaixador Abelardo Bueno 671. *Clube Esportivo Ultraleves (CEU)*, in front of gate 7, T/F0xx21-2216489.

Parapenting and hang gliding Hang gliding and paragliding are both covered by the Associação Brasileira de Vôo Livre (ABVL – Brazilian Hangliding Association, Rio de Janeiro, T0xx21-33220266). There are state associations affiliated with ABVL and there are a number of operators who offer tandem flights for those without experience. Launch sites (called *rampas*) are growing in number. Among the best known are: Pedra Bonita at Gávea in Rio and Parque da Cidade in Niterói. Also; *Just Fly*, Cell99857540, T/F0xx21-2680565, flycelani@ax.apc.org, www.travelrio.com US$80 for tandem flights with Paulo Celani (licensed by Brazilian Hang Gliding Association, over 15 years of experience and 5.000 flights with tourists), pick-up and drop-off at hotel included, in-flight pictures US$15 extra, flights all year round, best time of day 1000-1500 even on cloudy days which can be better for flying.

Information For more details, contact names and addresses for most of the these *rampas*, see www.iis.com.br/~afett for *Brazil Paragliding Hang-Gliding*.

Tour operators *Just Fly*, T/F0xx21-2680565, Cell99857540, flycelani@ax.apc.org US$80 for tandem flights with Paulo Celani (licensed by Brazilian Hang Gliding Association), pick-up and drop-off at hotel included, in-flight pictures US$15 extra, flights all year, best time of day 1000-1500 (5% discount for *South American* and *Brazil Handbook* readers on presentation of book at time of reservation). *Paulo Falcão*, T0xx21-33225187, Cell99663416, pefalcao@prolink.com.br Hotel transfer and photos or video available, licenced by ABVL. *Ultra Força Ltda*, Av Sernambetiba 8100, Barra da Tijuca, T0xx21-33993114; 15 minutes. From Leblon beach with Sr Ruy Marra, Brazilian paragliding champion (US$75), T0xx21-33222286, or find him at the beach: "Just fantastic!" **NB** Beware of people offering cheap flights on the beach as they may be unlicensed and spend much less time in the air.

Rafting Whitewater rafting started in Brazil in 1992. There are companies offering trips on the Rio Paraibuna at Três Rios in the north of Rio de Janeiro state. Another popular local sport is *Bóia-cross* (rafting with rubber tubes). Rafting can be a dangerous sport and you should check safety arrangements with any tour company.
   Tour operators *Aventur*, T0xx21-2783651, aventur@aventur.com.br Descents on the Rio Paraibuna rapids. See also **Três Rios** page 195 and 'Canoeing' above.

Birdwatching There are many good opportunities for birdwatching in Rio de Janeiro state due to the availability of large areas of unspoilt wilderness which are still little visited. There are also popular and accessible tourist destinations in the city such as Tijuca Forest or the Botanical Gardens that are excellent for viewing many species. Some of the specialist tour agencies listed above such as *Focus Tours* and *Field Guides* offer packages to the many good areas in the state.

Guide books A good field guide for light travelling is *South American Land Birds: A Photographic Aid to Identification* by John S Dunning (1987, Harrowood Books). Other comprehensive (but heavier) guides are *Birds of South America Volumes 1 & 2* by Robert S Ridgely and Guy Tudor (1989 and 1994, University of Texas Press), or *Birds in Brazil* by Helmut Sick (1993, Princeton University Press). Also recommended is *Where to Watch Birds in South America* by Nigel Wheatley (1994, Christopher Helm/A & C Black: London – pages 101-154 on Brazil).

Key sites Details of the following sites are given in the main travelling text.

Serra do Mar This mountain range runs parallel to the coast throughout the state and still has some remains of the once mighty Atlantic rainforest. It is an excellent site for birds of prey including three types of eagles and the *acuuān* or laughing falcon. Turkey-like *Guans* are frequently seen, as are hummingbirds and parrots. Other common species are the pigeon-like *araponga* and the colourful varieties of *tanager*. Itatiaia National Park is a good starting point for this range but there are many others.
Restinga These areas of coastal lagoons, sand spits, mangroves and other vegetation found all along the state's Atlantic coastline are refuges for many marine and land birds. The Restinga de Marambaia near Guaritiba, west of the city is a good area as is the Restinga de Jurubatiba national park near Campos in the north east of the state.

Cultural tourism Rio de Janeiro has many historical sites and other points of cultural interest from its many art galleries and museums to its forts and churches. A number of local tour guides such as Professor Carlos Roquette (see page 144), and Fábio Sombra (see page 136) specialize in these particular aspects of the city and state.
   Many people look for *umbanda* religious ceremonies. Those offered on the night tours sold at hotels are usually not genuine and a disappointment. You need a local contact to see the real ones, which are usually held in *favelas* and are none too safe for unaccompanied tourists. There are also a number of umbandista and candomblé *terreiros* in Northern Rio and the Baixada Fluminense (see page 117) but you are advised to obtain permission before attending.

Favela tourism An increasingly popular tour in Rio de Janeiro is to the many favelas that occupy so much of the city and house the majority of its population. The most popular destinations such as Dona Marta near Botafogo and Rocinha near São Conrado are orientating themselves more and more towards receiving foreign visitors. You are however advised to visit only on an organized tour such as those run by Marcelo Armstrong (see page 157) or with people who are known and accepted by the local residents.

Diving The Atlantic coast offers many possibilities for scuba diving (*mergulho*). In some areas in Brazil, diving includes underwater sport fishing; if you like this sort of thing, contact a company which specializes in fishing.

In Rio de Janeiro state, **Búzios**, **Arraial do Cabo**, visibility of 8 m to 15 m, depths of 7 m to 70 m, grottoes, ridges and the greatest number of wrecks in the country, and **Cabo Frio** are sites to the north of Rio. South of the state capital, the island filled bay of **Angra dos Reis**, together with **Ilha Grande**, and **Paraty**, best from December-April with calm seas, visibility from 5 m to 20 m and an average depth of 15 m, are all recommended sites.

The further south you go, the lower the water temperatures become in winter (15-20°C). Visibility can also be affected by currents and weather. Many resorts have dive shops. Whether you are already a qualified diver or a beginner seeking tuition, get local advice on which companies provide the level of expertise and knowledge of local waters that you need.

Dive shops *Calypso*, Rua da Alfândega 98, third floor, Centro, T0xx21-5091176. Equipment hire, diving courses and boat trips. *Centro de Instrutores de Mergulho Autônomo (CIMA)*, Rua Muniz Barreto 356, Botafogo, T0xx21-5391377. Diving couses and underwater tours. *Deep Blue*, Rua Marquês de Olinda 18, Botafogo, T0xx21-5532615. Diving courses and boat trips. *Dive Point*, Avenida Ataulfo de Paiva 1174, basement, Leblon, T0xx21-8130312, Cell96999633, www.divepoint.com.br Diving and boat tours to Rio's beaches, Cagarras Islands as well as Búzios, Arraial do Cabo and Angra dos Reis. *Diver's Quest*, Rua Maria Angélica 171, shop 110, Jardim Botânico, T0xx21-5391268. *Portão do Mar*, Marina de Glória, Cell0xx21-99952466. *Squalo Dive Shop*, Avenida Armando Lombardi 949D, Barra de Tijuca, T/F0xx21-4933022, squalo1@hotmail.com Offers courses at all levels, NAUI and PDIC training facilities, also snorkelling and equipment rental as well as daily diving trips. *Turbarão Rio*, Marina de Glória, box 29, T0xx21-2655342, Cell99632632. Diving courses and boat trips.

Information *Confederação Brasileira de Pesca e Desportes Subaquáticos*, Rua Buenos Aires 93, office 1203, Centro, T0xx21-2212110, divingbrasil@antares.com.br There is a diving magazine called *Mergulho*. *Océan* is a dive shop and tour operator based in Rio de Janeiro state (Rio, Angra dos Reis, Ilha Grande, Arraial do Cabo) which has a *Diving in Brasil* website, www.ocean.com.br

Ecotourism This is becoming important in Rio de Janeiro as a form of sustainable development and as a means of alleviating local unemployment in a way that doesn't harm the environment. Many efforts are also being made to save what is left of the Atlantic forest cover in the state and the areas of Restinga along the coast. The Pedra Branca state park (see page 164) and the Tijuca national park (see page 158) are both close to the city whilst there are many options for excursions to other reserves and parks in the state such as Serra dos Órgãos (see page 193).

Information *Instituto Brasileiro de Meio Ambiente (Ibama)*, Praça XV de Novembro 42, 8th floor, Centro, RJ 21610-490, T0xx21-2246124, F2246190. *Secretaria Estadual do Meio Ambiente*, Av 13 de Maio 33, 24th floor, Centro, T0xx21-5525296. *Secretaria Municipal do Meio Ambiente*, Rua Afonso Cavalcanti 455, Estácio, T0xx21-5032793.

Tour operators *Igarapé Ecoturismo*, Avenida Nossa Senhora de Copacabana 861, office 505, Copacabana, T0xx21-5768690, F5789645, e-garape@terra.com.br Trekking, rafting, off road, expeditions and observation of wild animals. *São Conrado Eco-Aventura*, T0xx21-5225586, Cell99667010. Jeep rides and trekking to Pedra da Gávea, Pedra Bonita, Morro de Agulinha.

Fishing

Rio de Janeiro has enormous potential for angling given the number and variety of the state's rivers, lakes and reservoirs. Add to this the scope for sea angling along the Atlantic coast and it is not difficult to see why the sport is gaining in popularity (but see under 'Diving' above). Officially, all fish stocks are under the control of Ibama (see 'National Parks', page 228) and a license is required for fishing in any waters. All details on prices, duration and regulations concerning catches can be obtained from Ibama; the paperwork can be found at Ibama offices, some branches of the Banco do Brasil and some agencies which specialize in fishing. There are a number of fishing tournaments and trophies in the state such as that held in Guanabara Bay by *Clube Barracuda*, R Cândido Gafrée, Urca. Good places in Rio for shore fishing are the Paredão da Urca, Av João Luis Alves and from the Morro do Leme.

Information Freshwater fishing can be practiced in so many places that the best bet is to make local enquiries in the part of the state that you are visiting. You can then find out about the rivers, lakes and reservoirs, which fish you are likely to find and what types of angling are most suited to the conditions. Many agencies can arrange fishing trips and there are several local magazines on the subject. **Universidade da Pesca**, R México 111, office 502, Centro, T/F0xx21-2408117, Cell99492363, www.upesca.com.br, has fishing tours with instructors and multilingual guides to the Ilhas Cagarras, offshore of Ipanema, Guanabara Bay as well as Angra dos Reis, Ilha Grande Búzios and Cabo Frio.

The fishing magazine *Aruanã* has a website with lots of information in English or Portuguese, www.wfc.com.br/aruana/index1.htm, while *Fishing World's* website, http://wfc.com.br/fishing, is in Portuguese, but is also informative. The latter is not exclusively about Brazil and also includes diving.

Football

The most die-hard fan of the game will certainly not be disappointed by the talent on display whether in the stadium or on the beach. The most important teams in Rio de Janeiro are *Botafogo* (white star on black), *Flamengo* (red and black hoops), *Fluminense* (tricolour stripes) and *Vasco de Gama* (white with black diagonal stripe). All have long histories and the number of championships won by each are proudly displayed by their supporters.

The season starts in mid-January with the hotly contested *Rio-São Paulo* tournament whose final is generally held at the beginning of March. Next begins the *Campeonato Carioca* (Rio de Janeiro championship) which is held in two parts, *Taça Rio* and *Taça Guanabara* with the winners playing each other for the title. Rio teams also take part in the *Copa do Brazil* and in the *Copa Libertadores da América* involving Brazilian and other South American teams. The year culminates in the *Campeonato Brasileiro* (Brazilian championship) which begins in August with the final being held in December. The most important games are played in the famous Maracanã stadium see page 111.

Information The schedule of games to be played in the Rio de Janeiro stadiums can be obtained from the *CBF* (*Confederação Brasileira de Futebol*), R da Alfândega 70, 7th floor, Centro, T0xx21-5095937.

Golf

There are both 18-hole and nine-hole courses at the *Itanhangá Golf Club*, Estr da Barra da Tijuca 2005, T0xx21-4942507, visiting cards from Av Rio Branco 26, 16th floor. The *Gávea Golf Club*, Estr da Gávea 800, São Conrado, T0xx21-33224141, and the *Teresópolis Golf Club*, Estr Imbuí (Várzea), both have 18 holes. Nine holes at *Petrópolis Country Club*, Nogueira. Six holes at *Golden Green Golf Club*, Av Canal de Marapendi 2901, Barra de Tijuca, T/F0xx21-4340696.

Gyms

There are hundreds of excellent gyms and sports clubs but most will not grant temporary (less than one month) membership. Big hotels may allow use of their facilities for a small deposit. **Estação do Corpo**, Avenida Borges de Medeiros 1426,

Lagoa, T0xx21-2193131. Large gym also equipped for outdoor sports. *Equipe 1*, Av NS de Copacabana 702, first and third floors, T0xx21-2552554. Weights, aerobics, open 0600-2300 Mon-Fri, 0800-1200, 1600-2000. *Paissandu Athletic Club*, Av Afrânio de Melo Franco 330, Leblon. Tennis, bowls, swimming, Scottish dancing, Tue, Apr-Oct, 2000-2230, may admit non-members.

Horse racing *Jockey Club Racecourse*, by Jardím Botânico and Gávea, meetings on Mon 1830-2245, Fri 1600-2100, Sat and Sun 1300-1900, entrance US$2, long trousers required, a table may be booked. Take any bus marked 'via Jóquei'. Betting is by totalizator only.

Motor sport Although the Brazilian Grand Prix is now held in São Paulo there are still many car and motorbike events held at the *Autódromo Internacional Nelson Piquet*, Av Embaixador Abelardo Bueno, Jacarepaguá, T0xx21-4412158. These include the *Brazil-Rio 200 GP* which is the fifth stage of the World Formula Championships, www.rio200.com.br and the *Rio GP* which is part of the World Motospeed motorcycle competition with 125cc, 250cc, 500cc and sidecar categories.

Surfing This can be enjoyed in just about every part of the state's coast. It does not require permits; all you need is a board and the right type of wave.

Brazilians took up surfing in the 1930s and have been practicing ever since: in this beach-obsessed country, with 8,000 km of coastline, all shore and watersports are taken seriously. Many Brazilian surf spots are firmly on the international championship circuit: best known is **Saquarema**, in Rio de Janeiro state.

There are many other good surf spots in Rio de Janeiro state. Most of the coastline faces south, head-on to the powerful swell, and is freshened by an early morning north-northeast offshore wind blowing off the mountains which run parallel to the coast. It receives a consistent winter swell, although in summer it stays flat for long periods. The urban beaches have good surf, and are friendly, but beware of thieves. Don't leave your board unattended: get straight in the water.

The beautiful, mountainous coast along the BR-101 between Paraty and Rio de Janeiro, with its many beaches and forested coves, is well worth a visit for its scenery, its historic villages and peaceful resorts. Scattered with small islands, it is great for sailing and diving, but there is no surf except to the ocean side of Ilha Grande, which protects the mainland coast.

Surf decoder The following run-down of Rio de Janeiro's surf spots uses the following codes: **BB**: Beach break; **PB**: Point break; **RB**: Reef break; **SB**: Shore break; **R&L**: Right and left. Wave heights are given in feet: 1 ft = 0.3 m approximately. The survey deals with the surf spots by state, in the same order in which they appear in the book.

In Rio de Janeiro city: **Barra de Guaratiba**: river mouth, perfect and powerful waves in the right conditions, B, L, 2-5 ft. **Grumari**: BB, R&L, 1-7 ft. **Prainha**: wild and good, BB, R&L, 1-8 ft. **Macumba**: small waves, BB, R&L, 1-4 ft. **Recreio dos Bandeirantes**: breaks by a rock a few metres from shore, on both sides and in different directions, can handle some size when other spots close out, BB, R&L, 2-8 ft. **Barra da Tijuca**, 18 km long, good sand banks, close out when big, BB, R&L, 1-5 ft. **Quebra Mar**: next to the breakwater, hollow in the right conditions, BB, L, 1-7 ft. **Pepino**: sometimes a good hollow left can break next to the rocks on the L side of the beach, hang gliders land here, BB, R&L, 1-6 ft. **São Conrado**: BB, R&L, 1-5 ft. **Canto de Leblon**: on a big swell a wave breaks next to the rocks, BB, R, 3-8 ft. **Leblon**: hollow next to the breakwater, BB, R&L, 1-5 ft. **Ipanema**: hollow, not much shape, BB, R&L, 1-5 ft. **Arpoador**: breaks next to the rocks, gets good, the beach is illuminated making night surfing possible, BB, L, 1-8 ft. **Forte**: BB, R&L, 1-4 ft. **Copacabana**, posto 5: needs a big swell, SB, R&L, 1-4 ft. **Leme**: BB, L, 1-5 ft.

In Rio de Janeiro state: Niterói, **Itaipu**: BB, R&L, 1-5 ft. **Itacoatiara**: BB, R&L, 1-6 ft. Maricá, 60 km from Rio, on RJ-102, great for surfers, with mostly pounding shore breaks: **Ponta Negra**: BB, R&L, 1-6 ft: **Jacone**: breaks on submerged rocks outside the shore break, powerful, short and shallow, RB, R&L, 1-5 ft. Saquarema, the home of surfing in Brazil. Its cold, open seas provide consistent, crashing waves of up to 3 m. Frequent national and international surfing championships take place here: **Vila**: next to the rocks in town, BB, L, 1-8 ft. **Itaúna**: 2 km north of town, consistent, one of the best wave spots in Brazil, breaks up to 6-8 ft, when big it breaks L behind the rocks, can get heavy, BB, R&L, 1-12 ft. **Massambaba**: a long stretch of deserted beach between Saquarema and Arraial do Cabo, BB, R&L, 1-6 ft. Arraial do Cabo, on the point south of Cabo Frio, where the coast turns to the east, Arraial is the northernmost spot with a big, head-on south swell: **Praia Grande**, at the eastern end of Massambaba, 2 km out of Arraial town, BB, R&L, 1-6 ft. **Brava**: the small beach between the rocks on the point, go up Atalaia hill and walk down to the water, BB, R&L, 1-5 ft. Cabo Frio, **Fogete**: 4 km south, BB, R&L, 1-5 ft. **Brava**: 15 minutes walk north of town, a naturist beach, surf naked (cold water!), BB, R&L, 1-5 ft. **Pero**: 7 km north, BB, R&L, 1-5 ft. Búzios, **Geribá**: 3.5 km south, BB, R&L, 1-5 ft. **Brava**: 2 km east, BB, R&L, 1-5 ft. Campos, close to the border with Espírito Santo, marks a change in the waves which, from here northwards, don't have as much power or consistency as further south: **Farol de São Tomé**: 38 km southeast of town, BB, R&L, 1-5 ft. Ilha Grande, **Lopes Mendes**: walk from Praia dos Mangues. **Aventureiro**: 4 km from Provetá by a leafy trail, in the Reserva Biológica: apply here for permission to use *Leste* and *Sul* beaches, backing onto lakes, waterfalls and protected woodlands; all BB, R&L, 1-4

Information *Associação Brasileira de Bodyboard*, T0xx21-2590669. *Organização dos Surfistas Profissionais do Rio de Janeiro*, T0xx21-4932472. *Federação de Surf do Estado do Rio de Janeiro*, R Visconde de Pirajá 437/407, Ipanema, T/F0xx21-2872385, feser@highway.com.br *Federação de Bodyboard do Estado do Rio de Janeiro*, Rua Barata Ribeiro 348, room 602, T0xx21-2565653.

Surfing information was compiled with the help of Piet Hein Snel, a surfboard shaper and builder who has surfed the coast of Brazil extensively.

Swimming

With an extensive coastline and the beach being an integral part of Brazilian culture, there are plenty of opportunities for good bathing. Do, however, observe local warnings as strong undertows and currents can make it extremely dangerous to swim in places. A number of people are drowned every year from recklessness on Rio de Janeiro's beaches. Triathlon has become a popular sport in the southeast of Brazil with many organized competitions.

Information *Confederação Brasileira de Desportes Aquáticos*, Gate 18, Maracanãzinho, T0xx21-5689962, extension 289. *Federação de Triathlon*, R Pres Carlos de Campos 286, room 402, Laranjeiras, T0xx21-5530521, www.triathlon.com.br *Swim Center*, R So Clemente 180, Botafogo, T0xx21-5399682. Adults and childrens classes, open 0600-2200 Mon-Fri.

Tennis & squash

There are tennis courts in the Parque do Flamengo and Parque Brigadeiro Faria Lima beside the Lagoa as well as in some hotels. *Akxe Sport Club*, Av Canal de Marapendi 2900, Barra da Tijuca, T0xx21-33253232. Tennis courts and many other facilities, open 0700-2300 Mon-Fri, 0900-2000 Sat-Sun. *LOB Academia de Tênis*, Rua Stefan Zewig 290, Laranjeiras, T0xx21-2250239. Largest tennis club in Rio with courts that can be rented on the same day, open 0600-Midnight Mon-Fri, 0700-1900 Sat, 0800-1800 Sun. *Rio Sport Center*, Av Ayrton Senna 2541, Barra da Tijuca, T33256644. Also has a gym and pool as well as tennis and squash courts, open 0615-2200 Mon-Fri, 0700-1300, 1600-2000 Sat. *Rio Squash Club*, Rua Cândido Mendes 581, Glória, T2420642, F2427562. *Smash Squash*, Rua Couto Fernandes 210, Laranjeiras, T0xx21-55/3758.

Windsurfing The best places for this sport are the beach and Lagoa de Marapendi in Barra da Tijuca. *Fisilabor*, Condomínio Mandala, Avenida Prefeito Dulcídio Cardoso 400, Barra da Tijuca, T0xx21-4384882. For board and other equipment hire. *Hi Winds Brasil*, R Olegário Maciel 130, shop F, Barra da Tijuca, T0xx21-4938668, F4927088. For both beginners and experienced windsurfers.

Yachting & sailing A popular sport along Rio de Janeiro's Atlantic coastline. There are marinas and yacht clubs in Rio (Marina da Glória), Niterói (Jurujuba Bay, 4 nm), Cabo Frio (Arraial do Cabo, 65 nm), Armação dos Búzios (Ossos beach, 85 nm), Macaé (Ilha de Santana, 108 nm), Mangaratiba (Itacuruçá), Ilha Grande (Palmas Bay, 60 nm), Angra dos Reis (Gipóia, 76 nm and Port of Bracuhy, 83 nm), and Paraty (98 nm). Almost all are connected to VHF channels 16 and 68 with the weather forecast being passed daily around 1500. For information on general sea conditions see 'Climate' on page 227. Most clubs have ramps for light craft, technical assistance and generally welcome visitors when there is space for docking. *Guanabara Regatta Club*, Av Repórter Nestor Moreira 42, Botafogo, T0xx21-2751796 (VHF 68, HF 4431.8, callsign E25). Amateur club welcoming boats from abroad but fee required, water depth at dock is 1.5 m. *late Clube do Rio de Janeiro*, Av Pasteur 333, Urca (22° 52.500' S, 042° 01.000 W), T0xx21-5431244 (VHF 16, 68, HF 4431.8, 8291.1, callsign E21). Welcomes vessels from abroad with three day courtesy docking, boating basin is 3 m deep with 5 m depth at buoy anchors. For Marina da Glória see page 118. Clubs and ports outside of Rio are mentioned in the text under their respective sections. Much of the sailing information has been kindly provided by *Riotur*.

Information *Federação Brasileira de Vela e Motor*, R Alcindo Guanabara 15, upstairs room 801, Centro, T0xx21-2203738. *Federação de Vela do Rio de Janeiro (FEVEJ)*, Praça Mahatma Gandhi 2, 12th floor, T0xx21-2208785. Sailing federation.

Health

With the following advice and precautions you should keep as healthy as you do at home. Most visitors return home having experienced no problems at all apart from some travellers' diarrhoea. In Rio de Janeiro rather than other parts of Brazil the health risks with some exceptions are not so different from those encountered in Europe or the USA. This of course depends on where and how you travel. There are clear differences in health risks for the business traveller, who stays in international class hotels in large cities, the backpacker trekking in the mountains and the tourist who heads for the beach. There are no hard and fast rules to follow; you will often have to make your own judgement on the healthiness or otherwise of your surroundings. There are English (or other foreign language) speaking doctors in most major cities who have particular experience in dealing with locally occurring diseases. Your embassy representative will often be able to give you the name of local reputable doctors and most of the better hotels have a doctor on standby. If you do fall ill and cannot find a recommended doctor, try the Outpatient Department of a hospital – private hospitals are usually less crowded and offer a more acceptable standard of care to foreigners. Take note of local advice on water pollution. Air pollution also occurs.

Before travelling

Take out medical insurance. Make sure it covers all eventualities, especially evacuation to your home country by a medically equipped plane, if necessary. You should have a dental check up, obtain a spare glasses prescription, a spare oral contraceptive prescription (or enough pills to last) and, if you suffer from a chronic illness (such as diabetes, high blood pressure, ear or sinus troubles, cardio-pulmonary disease or nervous disorder), arrange for a check up with your doctor, who can at the same time provide you with a letter explaining the details of your condition in English and if possible Portuguese. Check the current practice in countries you are visiting for malaria prophylaxis (prevention). If you are on regular medication, make sure you have enough to cover the period of your travel.

Children

More preparation is probably necessary for babies and children than for an adult, and perhaps a little more care should be taken when travelling to remote areas where health services are primitive. This is because children can become more rapidly ill than adults (on the other hand they often recover more quickly). Diarrhoea and vomiting are the most common problems, so take the usual precautions, but more intensively. Breastfeeding is best and most convenient for babies, but powdered milk is generally available and so are baby foods in most countries. Papaya, bananas and avocados are all nutritious and can be cleanly prepared. The treatment of diarrhoea is the same for adults, except that it should start earlier and be continued with more persistence. Children get dehydrated very quickly in hot countries and can become drowsy and unco-operative unless cajoled to drink water or juice plus salts. Upper respiratory infections, such as colds, catarrh and middle ear infections are also common, and if your child suffers from these normally take some antibiotics against the possibility. Outer ear infections after swimming are also common and antibiotic eardrops will help. Wet wipes are always useful and sometimes difficult to find in South America, as, in some places, are disposable nappies.

Medical facilities

There is very little control on the sale of drugs and medicines in South America. You can buy any and every drug in pharmacies without a prescription. Be wary of this because pharmacists can be poorly trained and might sell you drugs that are unsuitable, dangerous or old. Many drugs and medicines are manufactured under license from American or European companies, so the trade names may be familiar to you. This means you do not have to carry a whole chest of medicines with you, but remember that the shelflife of some items, especially vaccines and antibiotics, is markedly reduced in hot conditions. Buy your supplies at the better outlets where there are refrigerators, even though they are more expensive and check the expiry date of all preparations you buy. Immigration officials occasionally confiscate scheduled drugs (Lomotil is an example) if they are not accompanied by a doctor's prescription.

What to take

Self-medication may be forced on you by circumstances, so make sure you carry a **first aid kit**, a small pack containing a few sterile syringes and needles and disposable gloves. The risk of catching hepatitis etc from a dirty needle used for injection is now negligible in Brazil, but some may be reassured by carrying their own supplies – available from camping shops and airport shops. The following is a list of further items which you may also find useful in an emergency or in out-of-the-way places:

Sunglasses ones designed for intense sunlight; **earplugs** for sleeping on aeroplanes and in noisy hotels; **suntan cream** with a high protection factor; **insect repellent** containing DET for preference; **mosquito net** lightweight, permethrin-impregnated for choice; **travel sickness tablets**; **tampons** can be expensive; **condoms**; **contraceptives**; **water sterilizing tablets**; **antimalarial tablets**; **anti-infective ointment** eg Cetrimide; **dusting powder** for feet etc containing fungicide; **antacid tablets** for indigestion; **sachets of rehydration salts** plus anti-diarrhoea preparations; **painkillers** such as Paracetamol or Aspirin; **antibiotics** for diarrhoea etc; **hydrocare contact lens products** are available, but are expensive.

Vaccination & immunization

Smallpox vaccination is no longer required anywhere in the world. Neither is cholera vaccination recognized as necessary for international travel by the World Health Organisation – it is not very effective either. Nevertheless, some immigration officials are demanding proof of vaccination against cholera in Brazil and in some countries outside Latin America, following the outbreak of the disease which originated in Peru in 1990-91 and subsequently affected most surrounding countries. Although very unlikely to affect visitors to Brazil, the cholera epidemic continues making its greatest impact in poor areas where water supplies are polluted and food hygiene practices are insanitary.

Vaccination against the following diseases are recommended:

Yellow Fever This is a live vaccination not to be given to children under nine months of age or persons allergic to eggs. Immunity lasts for 10 years, an International Certificate of Yellow Fever Vaccination will be given and should be kept because it is sometimes asked for. Yellow fever is very rare in Brazil, but the vaccination is practically without side effects and almost totally protective.

Typhoid A disease spread by the insanitary preparation of food. A number of new vaccines against this condition are now available; the older TAB and monovalent typhoid vaccines are being phased out. The newer, eg Typhim Vi, cause fewer side effects, but are more expensive. For those who do not like injections, there are now oral vaccines.

Poliomyelitis Despite its decline in the world this remains a serious disease if caught and is easy to protect against. There are live oral vaccines and in some countries injected vaccines. Whichever one you choose it is a good idea to have a booster every 3-5 years if visiting developing countries regularly.

Tetanus One dose should be given with a booster at six weeks and another at six months, and 10 yearly boosters thereafter are recommended. Children should already be properly protected against diphtheria, poliomyelitis and pertussis (whooping cough), measles and HIB, all of which can be more serious infections in Brazil than at home. Measles, mumps and rubella vaccine is also given to children throughout the world, but those teenage girls who have not had rubella (German measles) should be tested and vaccinated. Hepatitis B vaccination for babies is now routine in some countries. Consult your doctor for advice on tuberculosis inoculation: the disease is still widespread in Brazil.

Infectious Hepatitis is less of a problem for travellers than it used to be because of the development of two extremely effective vaccines against the A and B form of the disease. It remains common, however, in Brazil. A combined hepatitis A & B vaccine is now licensed and available – one jab covers both diseases.

Other vaccinations might be considered in the case of epidemics, eg meningitis. There is an effective vaccination against rabies which should be considered by all travellers, especially those going through remote areas or if there is a particular occupational risk, eg for zoologists or veterinarians.

Further information Further information on health risks abroad, vaccinations etc may be available from a local travel clinic. If you wish to take specific drugs with you such as antibiotics these are best prescribed by your own doctor. Beware, however, that not all doctors can be experts on the health problems of remote countries. More detailed or more up-to-date information than local doctors can provide are available from various sources. In the UK there are hospital departments specializing in tropical diseases in London, Liverpool, Birmingham and Glasgow, and the Malaria Reference Laboratory at the London School of Hygiene and Tropical Medicine provides free advice about malaria, T0891-600350. In the USA the local Public Health Services can give such information and information is available centrally from the Centre for Disease Control (CDC) in Atlanta, T404-3324559.

There are additional computerized databases which can be accessed for destination-specific up-to-the-minute information. In the UK there is *MASTA* (Medical Advisory Service to Travellers Abroad), T0020-76314408, F020-74365389, and *Travax* (Glasgow, T0141-9467120, ext 247). Other information on medical problems overseas can be obtained from the book by Dawood, Richard (Editor) (1992) *Travellers' Health: How to stay healthy abroad*, Oxford University Press 1992, £7.99. We strongly recommend this revised and updated edition, especially to the intrepid traveller heading for the more out of the way places. General advice is also available in the UK in *Health Information for Overseas Travel* published by the Department of Health and available from HMSO, and *International Travel and Health* published by WHO, Geneva.

Staying healthy

The thought of catching a stomach bug worries visitors to Brazil but there have been great improvements in food hygiene and most such infections are preventable. Travellers' diarrhoea and vomiting is due, most of the time, to food poisoning, usually passed on by the insanitary habits of food handlers. As a general rule the cleaner your surroundings and the smarter the restaurant, the less likely you are to suffer.

Intestinal upsets

Foods to avoid: uncooked, undercooked, partially cooked or reheated meat, fish, eggs, raw vegetables and salads, especially when they have been left out exposed to flies. Stick to fresh food that has been cooked from raw just before eating and make sure you peel fruit yourself. Wash and dry your hands before eating – disposable wet-wipe tissues are useful for this.

Shellfish eaten raw are risky and at certain times of the year some fish and shellfish concentrate toxins from their environment and cause various kinds of food poisoning. The local authorities notify the public not to eat these foods. Do not ignore the warning.

Heat treated milk (UHT), pasteurized or sterilized, is becoming more available in Brazil as is pasteurized cheese. On the whole, matured or processed cheeses are safer than the fresh varieties and fresh unpasteurized milk from whatever animal can be a source of food poisoning germs, tuberculosis and brucellosis. This applies equally to ice cream, yoghurt and cheese made from unpasteurized milk, so avoid these homemade products – the factory made ones are probably safer.

Tap water is rarely safe outside the major cities, especially in the rainy season. Streamwater, if you are in the countryside, is often contaminated by communities living surprisingly high in the mountains. Filtered or bottled water is usually available and safe, although you must make sure that somebody is not filling bottles from the tap and hammering on a new crown cap. If your hotel has a central hot water supply, this water is safe to drink after cooling. Ice for drinks should be made from boiled water, but rarely is so stand your glass on the ice cubes, rather than putting them in the drink. The better hotels have water purifying systems.

Travellers' diarrhoea This is usually caused by eating food which has been contaminated by food poisoning germs. Drinking water is rarely the culprit. Sea water or river water is more likely to be contaminated by sewage and so swimming in such dilute effluent can also be a cause.

Infection with various organisms can give rise to travellers' diarrhoea. They may be viruses, bacteria, eg Escherichia coli (probably the most common cause worldwide), protozoal (such as amoebas and giardia), salmonella and cholera. The diarrhoea may come on suddenly or rather slowly. It may or may not be accompanied by vomiting or by severe abdominal pain and the passage of blood or mucus when it is called dysentery. How do you know which type you have caught and how to treat it?

If you can time the onset of the diarrhoea to the minute ('acute') then it is probably due to a virus or a bacterium and/or the onset of dysentery. The treatment in addition to rehydration is Ciprofloxacin 500 mg every 12 hours; the drug is now widely available and there are many similar ones.

If the diarrhoea comes on slowly or intermittently ('sub-acute') then it is more likely to be protozoal, ie caused by an amoeba or giardia. Antibiotics such a Ciprofloxacin will have little effect. These cases are best treated by a doctor, as is any outbreak of diarrhoea continuing for more than three days. Sometimes blood is passed in amoebic dysentery and for this you should certainly seek medical help. If this is not available then the best treatment is probably Tinidazole (Fasigyn), one tablet four times a day for three days. If there are severe stomach cramps, the following drugs may help but are not very useful in the management of acute diarrhoea: Loperamide (Imodium) and Diphenoxylate with Atropine (Lomotil). They should not be given to children.

Any kind of diarrhoea, whether or not accompanied by vomiting, responds well to the replacement of water and salts, taken as frequent small sips, of some kind of rehydration solution. There are proprietary preparations consisting of sachets of powder which you dissolve in boiled water, or you can make your own by adding half a teaspoonful of salt (3.5 gms) and four tablespoonfuls of sugar (40 gms) to a litre of boiled water.

Thus the linchpins of treatment for diarrhoea are rest, fluid and salt replacement, antibiotics such as Ciprofloxacin for the bacterial types and special diagnostic tests and medical treatment for the amoeba and giardia infections. Salmonella infections and cholera, although rare, can be devastating diseases and it would be wise to get to a hospital as soon as possible if these were suspected.

Fasting, peculiar diets and the consumption of large quantities of yoghurt have not been found useful in calming travellers' diarrhoea or in rehabilitating inflamed bowels. Oral rehydration has on the other hand, especially in children, been a lifesaving technique and should always be practised, whatever other treatment you use. As there is some evidence that alcohol and milk might prolong diarrhoea they should be avoided during and immediately after an attack.

Diarrhoea occurring day after day for long periods of time (chronic diarrhoea) is notoriously resistant to amateur attempts at treatment and again warrants proper diagnostic tests (most towns with reasonable sized hospitals have laboratories for stool samples). There are ways of preventing travellers' diarrhoea for short periods of time by taking antibiotics, but this is not a foolproof technique and should not be used other than in exceptional circumstances. Doxycycline is possibly the best drug. Some preventatives such as Enterovioform can have serious side effects if taken for long periods. Paradoxically **constipation** is also common, probably induced by dietary change, inadequate fluid intake in hot places and long bus journeys. Simple laxatives are useful in the short term and bulky foods such as maize, beans and plenty of fruit are also useful.

Heat & cold Full acclimatization to high temperatures takes about two weeks. During this period it is normal to feel a bit apathetic, especially if the relative humidity is high. Drink plenty of water (up to 15 litres a day are required when working physically hard in the tropics), use salt on your food and avoid extreme exertion. Tepid showers are more cooling than hot or cold ones. Large hats do not cool you down, but do prevent sunburn. Remember that, especially in the highlands, there can be a large and sudden drop in temperature between sun and shade and between night and day, so dress accordingly. Warm jackets or woollens are essential after dark at high altitude. Loose cotton is still the best material when the weather is hot.

Insects These are mostly more of a nuisance than a serious hazard and if you try, you can prevent yourself entirely from being bitten. Some, such as mosquitoes are, of course, carriers of potentially serious diseases, so it is sensible to avoid being bitten as much as possible.

Sleep off the ground and use a mosquito net or some kind of insecticide. Preparations containing Pyrethrum or synthetic pyrethroids are safe. They are available as aerosols or pumps and the best way to use these is to spray the room thoroughly in all areas (follow the instructions rather than the insects) and then shut the door for a while, re-entering when the smell has dispersed. Mosquito coils release insecticide as they burn slowly. They are widely available and useful out of doors. Tablets of insecticide which are placed on a heated mat plugged into a wall socket are probably the most effective. They fill the room with insecticidal fumes in the same way as aerosols or coils.

You can also use insect repellents, most of which are effective against a wide range of pests. The most common and effective is diethyl metatoluamide (DET). DET liquid is best for arms and face (care around eyes and with spectacles – DET dissolves plastic). Aerosol spray is good for clothes and ankles and liquid DET can be dissolved in water and used to impregnate cotton clothes and mosquito nets. Some repellents now contain DET and Permethrin, insecticide. Impregnated wrist and ankle bands can also be useful.

If you are bitten or stung, itching may be relieved by cool baths, antihistamine tablets (care with alcohol or driving) or mild corticosteroid creams, eg hydrocortisone (great care: never use if any hint of infection). Careful scratching of all your bites once a day can be surprisingly effective. Calamine lotion and cream have limited effectiveness and antihistamine creams are not recommended – they can cause allergies themselves. Bites which become infected should be treated with a local antiseptic or antibiotic cream such as Cetrimide, as should any infected sores or scratches.

When living rough, skin infestations with body lice (crabs) and scabies are easy to pick up. Use whatever local commercial preparation is recommended for lice and scabies. Crotamiton cream (Eurax) alleviates itching and also kills a number of skin parasites. Malathion lotion 5 (Prioderm) kills lice effectively, but avoid the use of the toxic agricultural preparation of Malathion, more often used to commit suicide.

Be very careful about bathing in lakes or slow rivers anywhere in Brazil: harmful parasites abound (including the snails that carry schistosomiasis). Dengue fever (see below) is now endemic in Brazil, and Rio is one of the problem places: protect yourself against mosquitoes. Also beware of *borrachudos*, small flies with a sharp bite that attack ankles and calves; coconut oil deters them.

Ticks They attach themselves usually to the lower parts of the body often after walking in areas where cattle have grazed. They take a while to attach themselves strongly, but swell up as they start to suck blood. The important thing is to remove them gently, so that they do not leave their head parts in your skin because this can cause a nasty allergic reaction some days later. Do not use petrol, vaseline, lighted cigarettes etc to remove the tick, but, with a pair of tweezers remove the beast gently by gripping it at the attached (head) end and rock it out in very much the same way that a tooth is extracted.

Certain tropical flies which lay their eggs under the skin of sheep and cattle also occasionally do the same thing to humans with the unpleasant result that a maggot grows under the skin and pops up as a boil or pimple. The best way to remove these is to cover the boil with oil, vaseline or nail varnish so as to stop the maggot breathing, then to squeeze it out gently the next day.

Sunburn The burning power of the tropical sun, especially at high altitude, is phenomenal. Always wear a wide brimmed hat and use some form of suncream lotion on untanned skin. Normal temperate zone suntan lotions (protection factor up to 7) are not much good; you need to use the types designed specifically for the tropics or for mountaineers or skiers with protection factors up to 15 or above. These are often not available in Brazil. Glare from the sun can cause conjunctivitis, so wear sunglasses especially on tropical beaches, where high protection factor sunscreen should also be used.

Prickly heat A very common intensely itchy rash is avoided by frequent washing and by wearing loose clothing. Cured by allowing skin to dry off through use of powder and spending two nights in an a/c hotel!

Athlete's foot This and other fungal skin infections are best treated with Tolnaftate or Clotrimazole.

Other risks and more serious diseases

Rabies Remember that rabies is endemic throughout Brazil, so avoid dogs that are behaving strangely and cover your toes at night from the vampire bats, which also carry the disease. If you are bitten by a domestic or wild animal, do not leave things to chance: scrub the wound with soap and water and/or disinfectant, try to have the animal captured (within limits) or at least determine its ownership, where possible, and seek medical assistance at once.

The course of treatment depends on whether you have already been satisfactorily vaccinated against rabies. If you have (this is worthwile if you are spending lengths of time in developing countries) then some further doses of vaccine are all that is required. Human diploid vaccine is the best, but expensive: other, older kinds of vaccine, such as that derived from duck embryos may be the only types available. These are effective, much cheaper and interchangeable generally with the human derived types. If not already vaccinated, then anti rabies serum (immunoglobulin) may be required in addition. It is important to finish the course of treatment whether the animal survives or not.

AIDS In South America, AIDS is increasing but is not wholly confined to the well known high risk sections of the population, ie homosexual men, intravenous drug abusers and children of infected mothers. Heterosexual transmission is now the dominant mode and so the main risk to travellers is from casual sex. The same precautions should be taken as with any sexually transmitted disease. The AIDS virus (HIV) can be passed by unsterilized needles which have been previously used to inject an HIV positive patient, but the risk of this is negligible. It would, however, be sensible to check that needles have been properly sterilized or disposable needles have been used. If you wish to take your own disposable needles, be prepared to explain what they are for. The risk of receiving a blood transfusion with blood infected with the HIV virus is greater than from dirty needles because of the amount of fluid exchanged. Supplies of blood for transfusion should now be screened for HIV in all reputable hospitals, so again the risk is very small indeed. Catching the AIDS virus does not always produce an illness in itself (although it may do). The only way to be sure if you feel you have been put at risk is to have a blood test for HIV antibodies on your return to a place where there are reliable laboratory facilities. The test does not become positive for some weeks.

Sexual infections Brazilians are famous for their open sexuality: appearances can be deceptive, however, and attitudes vary widely. To generalize, the coastal cities are very easy-going, while in smaller towns and the interior, traditional morals are strictly enforced. AIDS is widespread, commonly transmitted by heterosexual sex, and tolerance of male homosexuality is diminishing. You should take reliable condoms with you, even if you are sure you won't be needing them. The primary means of HIV infection in Brazil is now heterosexual sex. Local condoms are reported not to be reliable.

Infectious hepatitis (jaundice) The main symptoms are pains in the stomach, lack of appetite, lassitude and yellowness of the eyes and skin. Medically speaking there are two main types. The less serious, but more common is Hepatitis A for which the best protection is the careful preparation of food, the avoidance of contaminated drinking water and scrupulous attention to toilet hygiene. The other, more serious, version is Hepatitis B which is acquired usually as a sexually transmitted disease or by blood transfusions. It can less commonly be transmitted by injections with unclean needles and possibly by insect bites. The symptoms are the same as for Hepatitis A. The incubation period is much longer (up to six months compared with six weeks) and there are more likely to be complications.

Hepatitis A can be protected against with gamma globulin. It should be obtained from a reputable source and is certainly useful for travellers who intend to live rough.

You should have a shot before leaving and have it repeated every six months. The dose of gamma globulin depends on the concentration of the particular preparation used, so the manufacturer's advice should be taken. The injection should be given as close as possible to your departure and as the dose depends on the likely time you are to spend in potentially affected areas, the manufacturer's instructions should be followed.

Gamma globulin has really been superseded now by a proper vaccination against Hepatitis A (Havrix), which gives immunity lasting up to 10 years. After that boosters are required. Havrix monodose is now widely available as is Junior Havrix. The vaccination has negligible side effects and is extremely effective. Gamma globulin injections can be a bit painful, but it is much cheaper than Havrix and may be more available in some places.

Hepatitis B can be effectively prevented by a specific vaccine (Engerix) – three shots over six months before travelling. If you have had jaundice in the past it would be worthwhile having a blood test to see if you are immune to either of these two types, because this might avoid the necessity and costs of vaccination or gamma globulin. There are other kinds of viral hepatitis (C, E etc) which are fairly similar to A and B, but vaccines are not available as yet.

Typhus

This can still occur and is carried by ticks. There is usually a reaction at the site of the bite and a fever. Seek medical advice.

Intestinal worms

These are common and the more serious ones such as hookworm can be contracted from walking barefoot on infested earth or beaches.

Various other tropical diseases can be caught in jungle areas, usually transmitted by biting insects. They are often related to African diseases and were probably introduced by the slave labour trade. Leishmaniasis (Espundia) is carried by sandflies and causes a sore that will not heal or a severe nasal infection. Wearing long trousers and a long sleeved shirt in infected areas protects against these flies. DET is also effective. Epidemics of meningitis occur from time-to-time. Be careful about swimming in caribe infested rivers. It is a good idea not to swim naked: the Candiru fish can follow urine currents and become lodged in body orifices. Swimwear offers some protection.

Leptospirosis

Various forms of leptospirosis occur throughout Brazil, transmitted by a bacterium which is excreted in rodent urine. Freshwater and moist soil harbour the organisms which enter the body through cuts and scratches. If you suffer from any form of prolonged fever consult a doctor.

Snake bites

This is a very rare event indeed for travellers. If you are unlucky (or careless) enough to be bitten by a venomous snake, spider, scorpion or sea creature, try to identify the creature, but do not put yourself in further danger. Snake bites in particular are very frightening, but in fact rarely poisonous – even venomous snakes bite without injecting venom.

What you might expect if bitten are: fright, swelling, pain and bruising around the bite and soreness of the regional lymph glands, perhaps nausea, vomiting and a fever. Signs of serious poisoning would be the following symptoms: numbness and tingling of the face, muscular spasms, convulsions, shortness of breath and bleeding. Victims should be got to a hospital or a doctor without delay.

Commercial snake bite and scorpion kits are available, but usually only useful for the specific type of snake or scorpion for which they are designed. Most serum has to be given intravenously so it is not much good equipping yourself with it unless you are used to making injections into veins. It is best to rely on local practice in these cases, because the particular creatures will be known about locally and appropriate treatment can be given.

Treatment Reassure and comfort the victim frequently. Immobilize the limb by a bandage or a splint or by getting the person to lie still. Do not slash the bite area and try to suck out the poison because this sort of heroism does more harm than good. If you know how to use a tourniquet in these circumstances, you will not need this advice. If you are not experienced do not apply a tourniquet.

Precautions Avoid walking in snake territory in bare feet or sandals – wear proper shoes or boots. If you encounter a snake, stay put until it slithers away, and do not investigate a wounded snake. Spiders and scorpions may be found in the more basic hotels. If stung, rest and take plenty of fluids and call a doctor. The best precaution is to keep beds away from the walls and look inside your shoes and under the toilet seat every morning.

Certain tropical sea fish when trodden upon inject venom into bathers' feet. This can be exceptionally painful. Wear plastic shoes when you go bathing if such creatures are reported. The pain can be relieved by immersing the foot in extremely hot water for as long as the pain persists.

Dengue fever This is increasing worldwide including in South American countries and there are occasional cases in Rio de Janeiro. It can be completely prevented by avoiding mosquito bites in the same way as malaria. No vaccine is available. Dengue is an unpleasant and painful disease, presenting with a high temperature and body pains, but at least visitors are spared the more serious forms (haemorrhagic types), which are more of a problem for local people who have been exposed to the disease more than once. There is no specific treatment for dengue – just pain killers and rest.

Chagas' disease (S American Trypanosomiasis) This is a chronic disease and difficult to treat. It is, however, very rarely caught by travellers. It is transmitted by the simultaneous biting and excreting of the Reduvid bug, also known as the Vinchuca or Barbeiro. Somewhat resembling a small cockroach, this nocturnal bug lives in poor adobe houses with dirt floors often frequented by opossums. If you cannot avoid such accommodation, sleep off the floor with a candle lit, use a mosquito net, keep as much of your skin covered as possible, use DET repellent or a spray insecticide. If you are bitten overnight (the bites are painless) do not scratch them, but wash thoroughly with soap and water.

Dangerous animals Apart from mosquitoes the most dangerous animals are men, be they bandits or behind steering wheels. Think carefully about violent confrontations and wear a seat belt if you are lucky enough to have one available to you.

When you get home If you have had attacks of diarrhoea it is worth having a stool specimen tested in case you have picked up amoebas. If you have been living rough, blood tests may be worthwhile to detect worms and other parasites. If you have been exposed to bilharzia (schistosomiasis) by swimming in lakes etc, check by means of a blood test when you get home, but leave it for six weeks because the test is slow to become positive. Report any untoward symptoms to your doctor and tell the doctor exactly where you have been and, if you know, what the likelihood of disease is to which you were exposed.

Further reading

For information on maps & guidebooks, see page 39

A number of books are referred to in the text; see especially 'Literature', page 236 where a list of Brazilian works in English translation is given. What follows is a selection of books by topic which may be of interest to travellers. For a full list of books on Brazil see Footprint's ***Brazil Handbook***.

Agassiz, Louis and Elizabeth *A Journey in Brazil* (New York: Praeger, 1969), describes a journey in 1868 through Rio de Janeiro, Juiz da Fora, up the coast to Pará, to Manaus, the Amazon, then back to Rio; illustrated. Alcock, Frederick *Trade and Travel in South America* (London: George Philip, 1907). Debret, Jean Baptiste *Viagem Pitoresca e Histórica ao Brasil* (São Paulo: Livraria Martins, 1954), translated by Sérgio Milliet, two volumes of text and black and white reproductions of Debret's wonderful illustrations. Fleming, Peter *Brazilian Adventure* (London: Pimlico, first published in 1933). The search for Colonel Fawcett by Ian Fleming's father begins in Rio. de Sainte-Hilaire, Auguste *Viagem pelo Distrito dos Diamantes e Litoral do Brasil*, translated by Leonam de Azeredo Penna (São Paulo: Livraria Itatiaia, 1974), from the original *Voyage dans le District de Diamants et sur le Littoral du Brésil*, two volumes (Paris 1833); *Segunda Viagem do Rio de Janeiro a Minas Gerais e a São Paulo*, translated by Vivaldi Moreira (same publisher and date as above), from the original *Livre du Voyage que j'ai entrepris de faire de Rio de Janeiro a Villa-Rica et de Villa-Rica a Saint-Paul pour aller chercher les 20 caisses que j'ai laissées dans cette dernière ville* (Orléans, 1887). Williams-Ellis, Annabel *H.M.S. 'Beagle' in South America*, adapted from the narratives of Charles Darwin and Captain Fitz Roy (London: Watts 1930).

Historical travellers

Berkoff, Steven *Prisoner of Rio* (London: Hutchison, 1989). The actor's observations of Rio whilst filming in the city. Biggs, Ronnie *Odd Man Out* (Pan, 1995). Also covers his life in Rio after the train robbery and the many attempts to bring him back to justice. Haddad, Annette and Doggett, Scott (collected and edited) *Travelers' Tales, Brazil*, by (San Francisco, CA: Traveler's Tales, 1997). Contains some interesting pieces on Rio de Janeiro.

Modern travellers

Wilson, Jason *Traveller's Literary Companion, South & Central America* (Brighton: In Print, 1993, pages 287-335 on Brazil).

Literature

Clarkson, Wensley *Ronaldo* (Blake Publishing Ltd, 1998). The famous international footballer's rise to fame and fortune from a small league Rio side.

Sport

McGowan, Chris and Pessanha, Ricardo, *The Brazilian Sound* (Temple University Press, 1997). Covers all Brazilian music and has interviews with the main musicians. Perrone, Charles A. *Masters of Contemporary Brazilian Song: MPB 1965-1985* (University of Texas Press, 1993). Woodall, James *A Simple Brazilian Song* (Abacus, 1998). Conversations with Chico Buarque and other Brazilian musicians as well as impressions of Rio.

Music

Guillermoprieto, Alma *Samba* (London: Bloomsbury, 1991). An account of the Rio de Janeiro carnival with the Mangueira samba school. Teissl, Helmut *Carnival in Rio* (New York: Abbeville Press, 2000). A book of good photographs of samba schools with accompanying CD.

Carnival

Bethel, Leslie (ed), *Colonial Brazil* (Cambridge: Cambridge University Press, 1987); *Brazil, Empire and Republic, 1822-1930* (Cambridge: Cambridge University Press, 1989), both in the Cambridge History of Latin America series. Gay, Robert *Popular Organization and Democracy in Rio de Janeiro* (Philadelphia, PA: Temple University Press 1994). Karasch, Mary J *Slave Life in Rio de Janeiro, 1808-1850* (Princeton University Press, 1987). Levine, Robert M and Crocitti, John J (eds), *The Brazil Reader* (London: Latin American Bureau; Durham: Duke University Press, 1999). Excellent collection of historical and modern writing on Brazil. Meade, Teresa A *Civilising Rio* (Penn State University Press, 1996). Covers the popular resistance to the renovation of the city at the beginning of the 20th century. Stein, Stanley J *Vassouras, A Brazilian*

History & politics

Coffee County, 1850-1900 (Princeton: Princeton University Press, 1985). Tomlinson, Regina Johnson *The Struggle for Brazil. Portugal and 'The French Interlopers' (1500-1550)* (New York: Las Americas, 1970).

Social & environmental issues
de Carvalho, Sarah *The Street Children of Brazil* (London: Hodder & Stoughton, 1996). An English woman's experience of life in Rio's favelas. Hanchard, Michael George *Orpheus and Power: The Movimento Negro of Rio de Janeiro and São Paulo, Brazil, 1945-1988* (Princeton University Press, 1994). Benjamin, Medea and Mendonça, Maisa *Benedita da Silva* (London: Latin American Bureau, 1998). Her journey from a Rio favela to become Brazil's first black woman senator.

Geography
Antunes, Celso *Geografia e Participação 2. Regiões do Brasil* (São Paulo: Scipione, 1996). Robinson, Roger *Brazil* (Heinemann Library, 1998). Educational geography text with good illustrations.

Sexuality
Trevisan, João *Perverts in Paradise* (CMP, 1986). See also the *Spartacus Guide*.

Reference
Brazil A/Z. Larousse Cultural (São Paulo: Editora Universo, 1988). Davies, Vitoria Harland, Mike and Whitlam, John *Collins Portuguese Dictionary* (HarperCollins, 1991). Good English-Portuguese, Portuguese-English dictionary which covers Brazilian Portuguese. Their pocket size *Collins Gem* (HarperCollins, 1993) is excellent for travelling.

Films
Barreto, Bruno *Four Days in September/O Que é Isso, Companheiro?* (1997). Oscar nominated film based on the book by Fernando Gabeira, one of the guerrillas involved in the 1969 kidnap of the US ambassador in Rio de Janeiro. Camus, Marcel *Black Orpheus/Orfeu Negro* (1959). Beautiful recreation of the Greek legend with Rio and its carnival as a backdrop. Donen, Stanley *Blame it on Rio* (1984). Enjoyable comedy set in the city starring Michael Caine and Demi Moore. Werneck, Sandra *Little Book of Love/Pequeno Dicionário Amoroso* (1997). Romantic comedy set in the city. Salles, Walter *Central Station/Central do Brasil* (1998). Oscar nominated and moving film about the people living around the railway station in Rio. Swartman, Rosane *How to be Single in Rio de Janeiro/Como Ser Solteiro* (1998). Romantic comedy about the lives of young Cariocas.

Useful websites
See also under individual sections in this & other chapters for more websites

Some useful websites with good links in English include: **Brazilian embassies** Canberra: http://brazil.org.au/, London: www.brazil.org.uk/, Washington: www.brasil emb.org/ **Brazilian Foreign Ministry** www.mre.gov.br **Brazilinfo** www.brazilinfo.com/

Destinations **Rio de Janeiro**: www.ipanema.com Information on the city in English and German. www.rio-off-rio.com.br Information on both the city and state. There are many other web guides to the city but the information given may not have been recently updated. **Búzios**: www.buziosonline.com, background and tourist information. **Petrópolis**: www.petropolisweb.com.br, photographs of the city.

Other information News and culture: www.brazil-brasil.com, many good articles on Brazilian culture as well as a number of useful links. **Music**: www.thebraziliansound.com, good information on Brazilian music in particular Bossa Nova, MPB and Jazz.

For newspaper and magazine websites, see page 61.

3

Rio de Janeiro city

Rio de Janeiro city

- **90 Rio de Janeiro**
- 90 Ins and outs
- 94 Central Rio
- 111 Northern Rio
- 118 Southern Rio
- 118 Glória, Catete and Flamengo
- 125 Santa Teresa
- 129 Corvocado and Cosme Velho
- 131 Botafogo, Urca and Pão de Açúcar
- 136 Copacabana and Leme
- 146 Ipanema and Leblon
- 152 Lagoa, Jardim Botânico and Gávea
- 155 Vidigal and São Conrado
- 157 Barra da Tijuca
- 158 Tijuca National Park
- 163 Western Rio
- 118 Guanabara Bay
- 167 Niterói

Rio has a glorious theatrical backdrop of tumbling wooded mountains, stark expanses of bare rock and a deep blue sea studded with rocky islands. Up in the gods, from the statue of Christ on the hunchbacked peak of Corcovado or from the conical Pão de Açúcar (Sugar Loaf), you can experience the beauty of a bird's-eye view over the city which sweeps 20 km along a narrow alluvial strip on the southwestern shore of the Baía de Guanabara. Although best known for the curving Copacabana beach, for Ipanema - home to the Girl and beautiful sunsets, and for its swirling, reverberating, joyous Carnival, Rio also has a fine artistic, architectural and cultural heritage from its time as capital of both imperial and republican Brazil. But this is first and foremost a city dedicated to leisure: sport and music rule, and a day spent hang-gliding or surfing is easily followed by an evening of jazz or samba.

Ins and outs

Getting there

Air
See also Essentials, Getting there, page 31

International flights land at the Aeroporto Internacional Tom Jobim (formerly Galeão) on the Ilha do Governador. The air bridge from São Paulo ends at the Santos Dumont domestic airport in the city centre. Taxis from here are cheaper than from the international airport. There are also frequent buses between the two airports and to the bus station, city centre and Copacabana (see page 37).

Bus
See also Transport, Northern Rio, page 117

International and buses from other parts of Brazil arrive at the Rodoviária Novo Rio near the docks. There are buses and taxis from here to all parts of Rio.

Getting around

Population: 6,000,000
Phone code: 0xx21
See Essentials page 52 for Metrô map

In four days you can see a lot of Rio, but you should build into your itinerary time for finding your bearings and time for relaxing. Because the city is a series of separate districts connected by urban highways and tunnels heavy with traffic, you will need to take some form of public transport to get around. Walking is only an option once you are in the district you want to explore (for example, Central Rio, Copacabana). An underground railway, the Metrô, runs under some of the centre and the south zone (and is being extended). Buses run to all parts, but should be treated with caution at night when taxis are a safer choice. There is also a tram that runs from the Largo da Carioca to Dois Irmãos or Paula Mattos in Santa Teresa. For newcomers the advice in the box on page 92 will be helpful.

Orientation & safety
See also boxes on next 2 pages

The city is divided into north, south and east zones, Zona Norte, Zona Sul and Zona Oeste, with the centre, Centro, in between. The Zona Norte is the part of the city which stretches through São Cristóvão and Penha, passing the international airport on Ilha do Governador. The main entry and exit routes to São Paulo, Petrópolis, Belo

Rio de Janeiro orientation

Related maps:
A *Rio De Janeiro centre, page 94*
B *Lapa, page 104*
C *Northwest Rio, west of centre, page 112*
D *Glória, Santa Teresa, Catete, Flamengo, page 120*
E *Barra da Tijuca & National Park, page 160*
F *Urca, Botafogo, Cosme Velho, page 132*
G *Copacabana, page 138*
H *Ipanema, Leblon, page 146*
I *Arpoador, page 149*
J *Niterói, page 167*

24 hours in Rio

After **breakfast** at your hotel or at a juice bar in the street, start with a trip to Sugar Loaf, the Christ or preferably both, for **spectacular views** of Rio and Guanabara Bay. Then consider resting at Copacabana or Ipanema **beaches** where you can surf, play volleyball or sunbathe to your heart's content. Both of these neighbourhoods have excellent shops, restaurants, bars and nightlife for when you tire of the hot sands. If you're looking for a beach **away from the crowds**, hire a car or take a tour west of the city to unspoilt Prainha or Grumari. There are lots of great restaurants in this area near Guaratiba, such as Tia Palmira, as well as the fascinating folklore collection at Museu Casa do Pontal near Recreio dos Bandeirantes.

If you are feeling a little more active and adventurous, consider a walk in the Tijuca Forest, trekking up Pedra da Gávea or even a **tandem hang-gliding** flight down to São Conrado beach from Pedra Bonita. A cultural stroll around downtown could take in colonial and imperial churches such as the **imposing Candelária** and Mosteiro de São Bento, the excellent museum collections in the **Quinta da Boa Vista** in São Cristóvão and the Palácio da República in Catete, or some fine examples of modern architecture such as the **Museu de Arte Contemporânea** across Guanabara Bay in Niterói.

Lunch is an important meal in Rio and you can find many good places to eat particularly in Centro: try Alba Mar with its view of the bay or Bar do Arnaudo in the **bohemian** Santa Teresa district, a short and scenic ride on the city's last surviving tram service. If you don't feel like returning to the beach straightaway, you might want to relax under the towering palm trees of the peaceful **botanical gardens** instead. Sports fans should not miss a visit to the famous **Maracanã stadium** either for a tour or better still to soak up the atmosphere of a match.

Dinner is generally taken late leaving you time to rest before throwing yourself into the evening's activities. Churrascarias such as Porcão in Ipanema and Marius in Leme, with their large selection of meat, or one of the many seafront restaurants such as Don Camillo or Gallo Nero in Copacabana are all good choices. For those worn out by a busy day a quiet walk along the calçadão beside the beach or people-watching at the many open-air bars and kiosks along Avenida Atlântica, listening to MPB and **sipping caipirinhas** is probably an ideal end to the evening. But if your feet are still tapping, head for the city's discos, clubs or dancehalls for a great variety of sounds and dance well into the early hours: Semente and Bar Emporium in Lapa for choro and samba; Mistura Fina in Lagoa and Vinícius Piano Bar in Ipanema for jazz and bossa nova; Bunker 94 and Club B.A.S.E in Copacabana for techno, or Estudantina in Centro for gafiera **dancing to a live band**.

Horizonte and the north of the country run through here. The areas that tend to interest visitors most are the city centre itself and the Zona Sul. The historic part of the city is mainly to be found in Centro, the business and commercial area near the docks. Ferries leave from here to Niterói, on the other side of the bay, with its impressive forts and modern art museum. South of the city centre are the mainly leisure and residential suburbs of Zona Sul including the famous Copacabana with its popular curved beach and Ipanema. Santa Teresa, famous for its artists, is a pleasant and pretty district best reached by Rio's last surviving tram. Also in the southern zone is the Lagoa Rodrigo de Freitas and the Jardim Botânico. The Pão de Açúcar is right on the coast, above Urca and Corcovado is west of Cosme Velho. Further west are the walking trails and peaks of the Tijuca National Park as well as Barra da Tijuca, a Miami Beach-style suburb on the way to the unspoilt beaches and wild mountain scenery of Zona Oeste.

The majority of visitors enjoy Rio's glamour and the rich variety of experience it has to offer without any problems. It is worth remembering that, despite its beach culture,

Chill out, you're in Rio

When I first flew into Rio de Janeiro, I was not an inexperienced traveller, but the city's reputation preceded it: I was scared. A few weeks after that nervous landing at Galeão airport, Brazil got the better of me. I've been back countless times, and it's still not enough. I know Rio as well as I know my home town (London), and I feel a sense of elation arriving there that, as much as I love London, I've never felt at Heathrow.

Nobody can tell you how to enjoy Rio: each person is different, and this marvellous city has plenty to satisfy everyone. What I can do is to share with first-time visitors my arrival routine in the belief that, if you're a little more confident than I was seven years ago, you'll get the best out of the place sooner than I did.

Head for the Zona Sul. Copacabana and Ipanema are tourist traps for the good reason that they are breathtakingly beautiful beaches, in the city's social centre, with many shops and hotels.

If you are arriving from another South American country, remember that Brazilians speak Portuguese, not Spanish. The bus station (Rodoviária) is in a rough district. Do not use the taxis waiting outside; Cariocas don't, for good reason. Use the regulated taxi service (pre-paid, see page 54), or catch the blue air-conditioned bus which waits in front of the bus station. If you tell the conductor/conductress where you want to get off, the bus will stop near your required street.

Arriving by plane, you will walk down a short corridor which has the tropical, damp-concrete smell that you are going to get used to during your stay here. You will have to queue for an entry visa. Apply for the maximum, 90 days. Keep your visa in your passport and make a mental note to photocopy both as soon as you can (leaving the country without your paperwork can be a nightmare). The airport is a pleasant three-storey building with one of everything: not at all primitive, but neither confusingly big. There is a duty free shop in arrivals: useful if you need presents for Brazilian friends because it sells fashionable brands at discount prices. Otherwise, don't bother. Customs operate a push-button system. Each passenger gets either a red or green light; red-light passengers are automatically searched.

The restaurant at Galeão's expensive hotel stays open 24 hours a day, but there is only one hour, early in the morning, when no other refreshments are available in the building. The airport chapel is next to the hotel. A bit further on, in the main area, is a lanchonete (pay first, ordering from the cashier, collect a ticket which you give to the server) and a smart restaurant which does an enormous tropical breakfast for US$10. Don't pay for any tourist information at Galeão: you can get basic maps free if Riotur is open, otherwise wait until you get into town.

The most expensive, and safest, way to get to the Zona Sul is by the pre-paid radio taxis. Most will drive you around for a while, if you haven't booked a hotel, without extra charge, but they are not chauffeurs. If you are in this situation try to have a list of addresses ready, so the driver can plan a sensible route around Copacabana's intricate one-way system - and smile! He's doing you a favour. The Real bus (see page 38) will drop you on the nearest corner to your hotel and your luggage is secured. The taxis outside Galeão are fairly reliable, but probably best kept for your next visit.

The 16 km drive into town cuts past some of the city's least attractive areas, through Rio's smelly industrialized Zona Norte. The six-lane highway that makes up most of the route then curves alongside the bay, giving a fabulous impression both of a glittering ocean framed by mountains and of Brazilian driving techniques: if you had been in any doubt, you will see why motor racing is a national passion. A whole range of Brazilian housing nestles among the forested hills to your right, from favelas to ordinary middle-class estates, and several impressively ornate colonial buildings. You are now approaching the Rio you will be getting to know during your stay.

Cherry Austin

Safety in Rio

The following are risky places: the tunnels are not safe to walk through; the city centre on Sunday when it is deserted; quiet alleyways; jostling crowds; dark corners. Locals don't walk on the beaches at night: if you must, do not go out of sight of the pavement. The Tijuca forest is best explored with a group of six or more, except the stretch between Afonso Vizeu square and Cascatinha which is well policed during the day; the tram to Santa Teresa attracts pickpockets, but a note on security in this area is given below; robberies sometimes happen in city buses: don't use them if guarding your property is essential (private frescão buses are more secure). The main bus station is patrolled inside, but uncomfortable outside. If you go to the Zona Norte at night, use a taxi; wandering around favelas alone at any time of day is both ill-advised and in questionable taste. Street vendors and children working the tables at your bar or restaurant will have been permitted by the management and there is little risk, though children can be light-fingered, so watch your wallet. It seems that far too many crimes against tourists are the result of thoughtlessness: remember that you are in a busy city and that the beaches are a pivot of daily life; leaving things unattended on the sand is equivalent to leaving them on Times Square while you go for a walk.

All the usual risks apply if hiring prostitutes of either sex (police may well take your companion's side in a dispute over prices – don't argue). The 'red light' districts of the Zona Sul are unlikely to offend anyone walking about at night, even children or unaccompanied women. Do, however, be suspicious of any club that you are invited into by a stranger (have your drink opened in front of you) and of anyone offering drugs. When ordering drinks in red-light bars, check prices first. Some girls may ask for a bottle of imported champagne, a little extravagance that may set you back US$300. You have the most to lose when carrying all your belongings and as you go in and out of banks, exchange houses and expensive shops, so take extra care at these times. At otherwise, put your passport, travellers' cheques etc in the hotel safe. Don't take too much out with you, have some sense and relax.

carefree atmosphere and friendly people, Rio is one of the world's most densely populated cities. If you live in London, Paris, New York or Los Angeles and behave with the same caution in Rio that you do at home, you will be unlucky to encounter any crime. There is extreme poverty in Rio: most robberies that occur are committed out of desperation. Overseas visitors are an obvious target: simply by having been able to afford the ticket, you are comparatively wealthy. Brazilians can usually tell you are foreign just by the way you carry yourself, but there is no sense in looking as if you have something worth stealing by wearing expensive clothes, valuable jewellery, a large daypack, or your camera – put it in your shoulder bag, worn in front of you, or buy disposable cameras as often as you need them. If you are unfortunate enough to be threatened, try to remember that the assailant is probably as scared as you are and will not hurt you if you give him what he's asking for (keep some money easily accessible, just in case). If you see someone having trouble, don't interfere, but try making a lot of noise to frighten the attacker away; if you think you are being followed, go up to a policeman. The streets are not excessively dangerous at night, but if you're going out in your best clothes, don't know the way, or are drunk, it's wisest to get a taxi. All the above advice comes from the **Tourist Police**, Avenida Afrânio de Melo Franco 159, Leblon (in front of the Casa Grande theatre), T5115112/33997170, who publish a sensible advice leaflet (available from hotels and consulates: consulates also issue safety guidelines). Tourist police officers are helpful, efficient and multilingual. All the main tourist areas are patrolled. If you have any problems, **contact the tourist police first**.

Central Rio

Known as 'Centro', this is the historical part of the city, and dates from 1567 when the Portuguese moved their settlement from the area now known as Urca to the Morro de São Januário. Today the centre stretches from the Mosteiro de São Bento to the Santos Dumont airport and inland to the Campo de Santana park.

The hill on which the original city was located was removed in the 1920s, so the historical centre effectively ends at the São José church. The 400 years following the founding of the city saw so many changes in architectural design and fashion that, today, the centre appears to be an incoherent collection of buildings, with the ultra-modern towering over the neo-classical, which in turn sits uneasily beside the colonial. Add to this the crowded streets and the constant traffic and it may seem a daunting place to explore. Don't give up! There is much to discover and it will repay your perseverance.

Rio de Janeiro centre

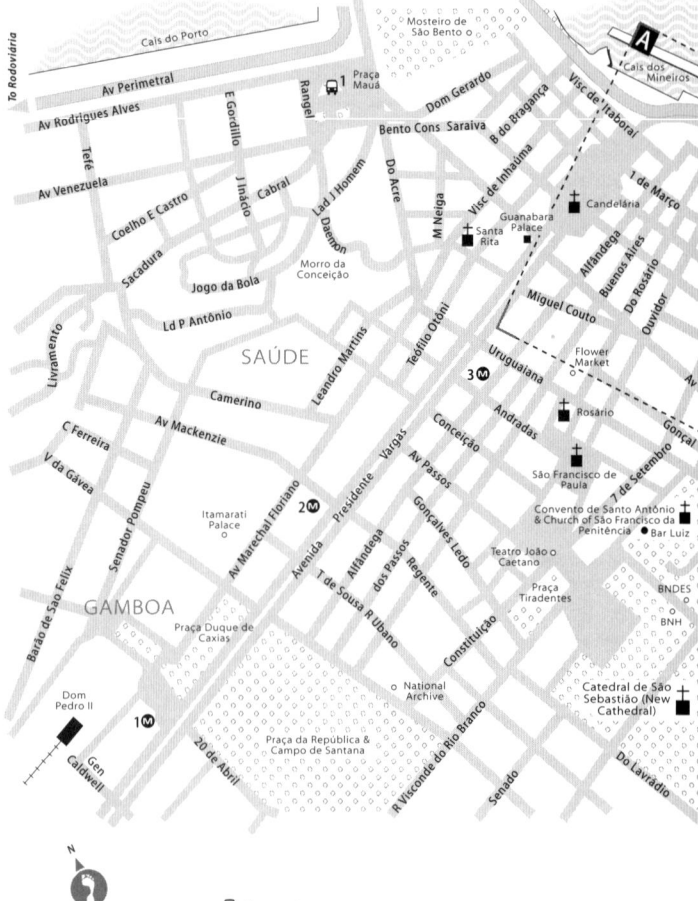

Related maps
A *Praça 15 de Novembre, page 96*

Transport
1 Mariano Procópio Bus Terminal (for Greater Rio de Janeiro)
2 Menezes Cortes Bus Terminal (Castelo - a/c buses to Zona sul)

Sights

An example of the juxtaposition of so many elements in close surroundings is the **Travessa do Comércio**, which runs between the Praça 15 de Novembro and the Rua do Ouvidor. On the northwest side of Praça 15 de Novembro (see below) is the Arco do Teles, all that remains of an 18th-century construction, now incorporated into a modern building. Through the arch is the Travessa do Comércio, a narrow, twisting street with neoclassical houses and wrought iron arches over the street lamps. This is how the whole city was in the 19th century. The Travessa, now dwarfed by 20th-century office blocks, leads to the church of Nossa Senhora da Lapa dos Mercadores, another 18th-century construction sandwiched between the concrete and glass. On Friday nights the Travessa is very lively; along it are several restaurants, including the *Arco Imperial*, where Carmen Miranda lived between 1925-30 (her mother kept a boarding house).

Check the opening times in advance of all churches, museums & other public buildings; they change frequently. All museums & the Jardim Botânico are closed over Carnival. When visiting churches & other religious buildings you should not wear shorts as it is likely that you will be refused entry

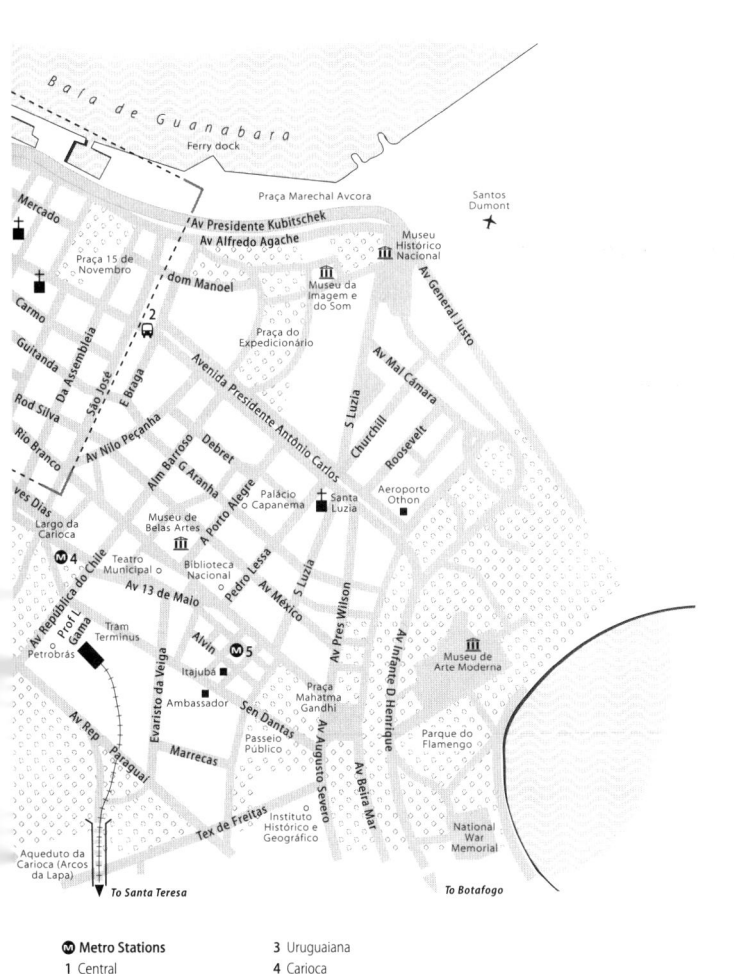

Metro Stations
1 Central
2 Pres Vargas
3 Uruguaiana
4 Carioca
5 Cinelândia

Two of the main streets are particularly impressive. The **Avenida Rio Branco**, nearly 2 km long, is intersected by the city's main artery, the **Avenida Presidente Vargas**, 4½ km long and over 90 m wide, which starts at the waterfront, divides to embrace the famous Candelária church, then crosses the Avenida Rio Branco in a magnificent straight stretch past the Central do Brasil railway station, with its imposing clock tower, until finally it incorporates a palm-lined, canal-divided avenue. Most of the Avenida Rio Branco's ornate buildings have been replaced by modern blocks; a few remain in the Cinelândia area such as the Biblioteca Nacional. Some of the finest modern architecture is to be found along the **Avenida República do Chile**, such as the Petrobrás, the Banco Nacional de Desenvolvimento Econômico and the former Banco Nacional de Habitação buildings and the new Cathedral.

Praça 15 de Novembro Originally an open space at the foot of the Morro do Castelo, the Praça 15 de Novembro (often called Praça XV) has always been one of the focal points in Rio de Janeiro. Today it has one of the greatest concentrations of historic buildings in the city. Having been through various phases of development in its history, it has undergone major remodelling (completed in 1997). The last vestiges of the original harbour, at the seaward end of the Praça, have been restored. The steps no longer lead to the water, but whereas in recent years the Praça was cut off by the Avenida Alfredo Agache, this road now goes through an underpass, creating an open space between the Praça and the seafront, beneath the Avenida Presidente Kubitschek flyover. This space now gives easy access to the ferry dock for Niterói. The area is well illuminated and clean and the municipality has started to stage shows, music and dancing here. ■ *At weekends an antiques, crafts, stamp and coin fair (Feirarte II) is held from 0900-1900.*

Praça 15 de Novembro

On **Rua 1 de Março**, across from Praça 15 de Novembro, there are two buildings related to the Carmelite order. The first is the **Convento do Carmo**, started in 1611, which is now used as the Faculdade Cândido Mendes. This convent was appropriated by the royal family in the early 19th century as a residence for the queen, Dona Maria I (nicknamed *A Louca* because of her mental illness). Such buildings were called PR, that is, taken over by the Príncipe Regente (or, in popular terminology, *prédio roubado* – stolen building). To prevent the members of the Imperial family sullying their feet on streets used by all and sundry, a covered bridge was built between the ex-Convento and the Cathedral when the Rua 7 de Setembro was driven between them in 1857.

Between this former convent and the Igreja da Ordem Terceira do Carmo (see below) is the old cathedral, the **Igreja de Nossa Senhora do Carmo da Antiga Sé**, separated from the other church by a passageway. It was the chapel of the Convento do Carmo from 1590 until 1754. A new church was built in 1761, which became the Capela Real with the arrival of the Portuguese royal family in 1808 and subsequently the city's cathedral. In the crypt are the alleged remains of Pedro Alvares Cabral, the Portuguese explorer (though Santarém, Portugal, also claims to be his last resting place).

The **Igreja da Ordem Terceira do Carmo**, is also in Rua Primeiro de Março on the other side of the old cathedral (see above) from the convent. The church was built in 1754, consecrated in 1770 and rebuilt between 1797 and 1826. It has strikingly beautiful portals by Mestre Valentim (see 'Fine Art and Sculpture', page 230), the son of a Portuguese nobleman and a slave girl. He also created the main altar of fine moulded silver, the throne and its chair and much else besides. ■ *Mon-Fri 0800-1400, Sat 0800-1200.* A fountain designed by Mestre Valentim stands in the Praça: the Chafariz do Mestre Valentim, or Chafariz do Pirâmide. (**NB** The Ordem Terceira do Carmo was created and administered by local tradesmen and wealthy families. It was not linked to the Carmelite orders in Europe and these neighbouring churches although united in their praise of Nossa Senhora do Carmo did not enjoy good relations.)

At the rear of the old cathedral and the Carmo Church (see above), on Rua do Carmo, is the **Oratório de Nossa Senhora do Cabo da Boa Esperança**, one of the few remaining public oratory from the colonial period in Rio.

The **Paço Imperial** (former Royal Palace) is on the southeast corner of the Praça 15 de Novembro. This beautiful colonial building was built in 1743 as the residence of the governor of the Capitania. It later became the king's storehouse and armoury (Armazens), then the Casa da Moeda, before being made into the Paço Real when the Portuguese court moved to Brazil. After Independence it became the Imperial Palace. During the Republic it was used as the post and telegraph office and fell into decline. In the 1980s it was completely restored as a cultural centre. It has several exhibition spaces, one theatre, one cinema for art films, a library, a section showing the original construction, a superb model of the city and the *Bistro* and the *Atrium* restaurants. ■ *T5334407. Tue-Sun 1200-1830.*

Beside the Paço Imperial, across Rua da Assembléia, is the **Palácio**

Ancient water fountain at Praça XV

☞ Favelas, a numberless existence

Rio de Janeiro's favelas, the slums which creep up the city's hillsides and spread out across the flat lands, have been the source of much of the city's bad press for many years. They have been represented in the press as no-go areas, where drug lords rule and fight for dominance, and out of which the city's criminals came. No sensible visitor would venture within their radius until favela *tours were started in the mid-1990s. One such tour is to Vila Canoas, see page 156.* The tours have the same motivation as a major scheme, Favela-Bairro, *designed to rehabilitate the favelas, to show that the* favelados *are hardworking, simple people, and that their communities deserve the same facilities and rights as elsewhere in the city.*

The name favela *was first used at the end of the 19th century after soldiers on the Canudos campaign in Bahia set up their guns on a hill called the Morro das Favelas. The hill was so-called because of a type of nettle that grew there. The soldiers became known as* favelados. *When they returned to Rio after the campaign, the soldiers built their homes on the Morro da Providência, but the* favela *nickname stuck. In time, any temporary settlement acquired the name* favela *and, as urban and rural poor alike strove to make it in the city, many people stayed initially in the shanties before moving to better accommodation. Many, of course, were unable to better themselves. In the 1970s and 1980s, there were some attempts to improve conditions in the* favelas *and residents, given assurances that they would not be forcibly removed, began to make their dwellings more permanent. Electricity and water supplies can be tapped into, usually illegally, but waste disposal and other basic facilities are rare. One of Rio's problems is that the* favelas *are in the middle of the city, not on the outskirts as in other metropolises. Almost a million people live in these conditions. The huge number of entries and exits make them difficult to police. Because the shanties rub shoulders with wealthier districts, it is easy for the young* favelados *to see the lifestyle of the young rich, and even mix with them on the beach. This can lead to envy which, for some, leads to criminality. Most of the leading criminals are in their late teens, and they die young. Their motto is: live life to the maximum as fast as possible.*

Since 1993, an ambitious project has been underway to upgrade the majority of the city's favelas *by 2004. A US$350m programme, aided by the Inter-American Development Bank, is providing the shanties with streets in place of alleys, sewerage, lighting, day-care centres, recreational areas, rubbish collection and transport. The* favelas *will be integrated with the surrounding neighbourhoods. The work also includes reforestation and the prevention of hill slides. Residents are given a say in how their district should be improved and no family will be rehoused in a part of the city which is alien to it. Having accepted that the* favelas *are permanent, not transitory, the city's authorities' task is to incorporate them into the whole, not leave them marginalized. An IADB special report on the project quoted* O Globo: *"Every citizen ought to have the right to live on a street in a house with a number".*

The **Secretaria Municipal da Habitação** and **IplanRio**, *the Empresa Municipal de Informática e Planejamento, produce a magazine on* Favela-Bairro, *available from Avenida Afonso Cavalcanti 455, bloco B, 4 andar, CEP 20.211-110, Rio de Janeiro, T2732345, or R Gago Coutinho 52, Largo do Machado, CEP 22.221-070, Rio de Janeiro, T5563399.
With thanks to Marcelo N Armstrong.*

Tiradentes, built between 1922 and 1926. It is now the legislative assembly of the State of Rio de Janeiro, but the building was closed twice in the 1930s as different administrations did not feel the need for a Chamber of Federal Deputies. The palace is in eclectic style (see 'Architecture', page 232), with a façade displaying heavy Greek influence. In front stands a statue of the Independence fighter, Tiradentes, by Francisco de Andrade; the palace was given his name because it was on this spot, the site of the old prison, that the national hero was held prisoner while awaiting execution. ■ *T5881411. Tue-Fri 1400-1800, Sat 1000- 1800, Sun 1200-1700 by prior appointment*

In the next block southeast is the **Igreja de São José**, Rua São José and Avenida Presidente Antônio Carlos, considerably altered since its construction in the 17th century. The current building dates from 1824 but it was remodelled in 1969. ■ *Mon-Fri 0900-1200, 1400-1700, Sun 0900-1100.*

One block further southeast again, at Rua Dom Manoel 15, is the **Museu Naval e Oceanográfico**. It had a collection of paintings and prints, as well as a display of weapons and figureheads, but most of the exhibits have been moved to the Espaço Cultural da Marinha.

Turning to the northwest side of Praça 15 de Novembro, you go through the Arco do Teles and the Travessa do Comércio (see above) to Rua do Ouvidor. The **Igreja Nossa Senhora da Lapa dos Mercadores**, Rua do Ouvidor 35, was consecrated in 1750 and remodelled in 1869-72. Restoration has been completed and it is worth visiting. ■ *Mon-Fri 0800-1400*. Across the street, with its entrance at Rua 1 de Março 36, is the church of **Santa Cruz dos Militares**, built 1780-1811. It is large, stately and beautiful and has inside been well renovated in a 'light' baroque style.

In the corner of the centre bounded by Praça 15 de Novembro and the Esplanada do Castelo is an area (between the ferry dock and Av Presidente Kubitschek) which has changed significantly since colonial times. Most alterations were made in the 20th century, first with the removal of the old municipal fish market, for health reasons, then with the levelling of the Morro do Castelo in the 1920s. There are two squares here, Praça Marechal Âncora, or Praça Rui Barbosa and Praça do Expedicionário. The only remnant of the Morro do Castelo is a short stretch of the Ladeira da Misericórdia, at the foot of which is the church of Nossa Senhora de Bonsucesso, also known as the church of the Santa Casa da Misericórdia. The Santa Casa itself is behind the church. The colonial hospital made way for a neo-classical building in the mid-19th century and contains a pharmacy museum. ■ *Mon-Fri, 0900-1600.* **Praça Marechal Âncora (Praça Rui Barbosa)**

Museu Histórico Nacional, Praça Marechal Âncora, contains a collection of historical treasures, colonial sculpture and furniture, maps, paintings, arms and armour, silver and porcelain. The building was once the old War Arsenal of the Empire, part of which was built in 1762 (this part is called the Casa do Trem). Two years later the Pátio de Minerva was added and significant expansion was done in 1808. Further changes were made in 1922 when the museum was inaugurated. ■ *T5509224, www.visualnet.com.br/mhn Tue-Fri, 1000-1730; Sat-Sun 1400-1800. US$1.*

Museu da Imagem e do Som, also on Praça Rui Barbosa, has many photographs of Brazil and modern Brazilian paintings; also collections and recordings of Brazilian classical and popular music and a non-commercial cinema Friday-Sunday. ■ *T2620309. Mon-Fri, 1300-1900. Free.*

The Church of **Nossa Senhora da Candelária** (1775-1810), on Praça Pio X (Dez), at the city end of Avenida Presidente Vargas where it meets Rua 1 de Março, has beautiful ceiling decorations and romantic paintings. It is on the site of a chapel founded in 1610 by Antônio da Palma after he had survived a shipwreck, an event depicted by paintings inside the present dome. ■ *Mon-Fri 0800-1600, Sun 0900-1300.* **Avenida Presidente Vargas**

In this part of the city a number of cultural centres have opened in recent years. The **Espaço Cultural dos Correios**, Rua Visconde de Itaboraí 20, holds temporary art exhibitions, theatre, music, videos and a postage stamp fair on Saturdays. ■ *T5038770. Tue-Sun 1200-2000.*

Opposite, with entrances on Avenida Presidente Vargas and Rua 1 de Março 66, is the **Centro Cultural Banco do Brasil (CCBB)**, which is highly recommended for good exhibitions and has a library, multimedia facilities, a cinema, concerts (about US$6 at lunchtime) and a restaurant. ■ *T38082000. Tue-Sun 1200-2000.* The **Museu Banco do Brasil** is at the same address and has an exhibition showing antique coins and notes from the bank's collection. ■ *T38082620. Mon-Fri 1100-2000. Free entry.*

At the corner of Rua Visconde de Itaboraí (No 253) and Avenida Presidente Vargas is the **Casa França-Brasil**. This building holds temporary exhibitions and is dedicated to cultural exchanges between the two countries, but is much more important for its history. Its construction dates from the first French Artistic Mission to Brazil (see 'Architecture' and 'Fine Art and Sculpture', pages 232 and 230 respectively) and it was the first neo-classical building in Rio. The interior is entirely neo-classical, although the pillars and mouldings are made of wood. The roof, though, is a hybrid between the colonial Brazilian style and the newly-introduced European fashion. It was built as a customs house and the strong-room can still be seen. ■ *T2535366. Tue-Sun 1200-2000.*

The newest cultural centre here is the **Espaço Cultural da Marinha**, on Avenida Alfredo Agache at Avenida Presidente Kubitschek. This former naval establishment now contains museums of underwater archaeology, historical shipping and navigation as well as the *Galeota*, the boat used by the Portuguese royal family for sailing around the Baía de Guanabara. Moored outside are the World War II torpedo boat *Bauru* and the modern submarine *Riachuelo* which can also be visited. ■ *T2166025. Tue-Sun 1200-1700.*

Offshore, but connected to the mainland by a causeway to Ilha das Cobras, is the **Ilha Fiscal**. It was built as a customs house at the emperor's request, but he deemed it too beautiful, so he said that it should be used only for official parties. Only one was ever held, five days before the Republic began. It is now a museum, linked with the Naval Cultural Centre. ■ *T2339165. Boats leave Fri, Sat and Sun at 1300, 1430 and 1600 (30 mins later Oct-Mar). The island is passed by the ferry to Niterói.*

Praça Mauá At the northern end of Avenida Rio Branco, Praça Mauá marks the end of Centro and the beginning of the port zone. Many of the empty warehouses are used as workshops by the samba schools and their beautiful floats are built here before being taken the short distance to the Sambódromo.

Rehearsal sessions are often held in this area in the months before carnival

Just north of Candelária, on a promontory overlooking the bay, is the **Mosteiro de São Bento**. The monastery's church, dedicated to Nossa Senhora de Monserrate (but usually referred to as the Igreja do Mosteiro de São Bento) contains much of what is best in the 17th- and 18th-century art of Brazil. Monks of the Benedictine order arrived in Rio de Janeiro in 1586, five years after their installation in Salvador.

São Bento is reached either by a narrow road from Rua Dom Gerardo 68, or by a lift whose entrance is at Rua Dom Gerardo 40 (taxi to the monastery from centre US$5). Both routes lead to a praça with tall trees, but stepping out of the lift into this oasis increases the sense of escape from the city below. The church's façade is in the mannerist style; plain and undecorated. You go throught the *galilé*, the antechamber for the unbaptized with its fine tiles, and enter the main body of the church. *Corta ventos*, doors which keep out the draughts so that the candles inside are not extinguished, are the last obstacle to the sight of the interior. Not an inch is unadorned in gold and red. The carving and gilding is remarkable, much of it by Frei Domingos da Conceição (see

'Fine Art and Sculpture', page 230). The paintings, too, should be seen; *O Salvador*, the masterpiece of Brazil's first painter, Frei Ricardo do Pilar, hangs in the sacristy. The lamps (*lampadarios* – two of which are attributed to Mestre Valentim) are of solid silver which, coming from Peru and Bolivia, was of greater value than Brazil's own gold. See also the two *anjos tocheiros*, angels carrying torches, common in many baroque churches. On top of the main altar is a statue of Nossa Senhora de Monserrate, made by Frei Domingos da Conceição; the eyes of both the Virgin and her Child are made from painted birds' eggs. The **Chapels of the Immaculate Conception** (Nossa Senhora da Conceição) and of the **Most Holy Sacrament** (Santíssimo Sacramento) are masterpieces of colonial art. The organ, dating from the end of the 18th century, is very interesting.

Every Sunday at 1000, mass is sung with Gregorian chant and music, which is free, but you should arrive an hour early to get a seat. On other days, mass is at 0715. At other times you may be lucky enough to hear the monks singing. There is a bookshop. The monastery is a few minutes' walk from Praça Mauá, turning left off Avenida Rio Branco; Rua Dom Gerardo 68 is behind the massive, new RBI building. ■ *Daily 0800-1100, 1430-1800, shorts not allowed.*

Also easily reached from Praça Mauá and requiring a climb is the **Morro da Conceição**, another hill from which the early Portuguese settlers could survey the bay. The first constructions on the hill were religious and a bishop's palace was built in 1702, the Palácio da Conceição. This and the subsequently built Fortaleza da Conceição are currently in the hands of the military. The Palácio has a small military museum dedicated to the history of map making in Brazil. The area is perfectly safe to visit and is another remnant of colonial Rio. Above the door of the Fortaleza is another of the few remaining public oratories; it is lit at night. ■ *Mon-Fri 0800-1700, T2232177.*

Largo da Carioca

The **Largo da Carioca**, a remarkable ensemble of old and new plus the muddle of the street vendors who have occupied the praça beween Rua da Carioca and the Metrô station, is another good location for seeing a variety of sites within a small area.

The second oldest convent in the city is the 17th-century **Convento de Santo Antônio**, on a hill off the Largo da Carioca, built between 1608 and 1615. Its church has a marvellous sacristy adorned with blue tiles and paintings illustrating the life of St Anthony. In the church itself, the baroque decoration is concentrated in the chancel, the main altar and the two lateral altars. Santo Antônio is a particular object of devotion for women who want to find husbands and many will be seen in the precincts. ■ *Mon-Fri 1400-1700.*

See also box, next page

Separated from this church only by some iron railings is the charming church of the Ordem Terceira de **São Francisco da Penitência**, built in 1773. Currently closed for renovation, it contains much more carving and gilding of walls and altar than its neighbour. The workmanship is superb. In the ceiling over the nave is a fine panel. There is a museum attached to the church. The church is due to reopen in 2000 when a new Museu de Arte Sacra will be inaugurated. This group of buildings is called officially the Conjunto Arquetetônico do Morro de Santo Antônio.

Across Ruas da Carioca and 7 de Setembro is the Church of **São Francisco de Paula**, at the upper end of the Rua do Ouvidor. The first stone

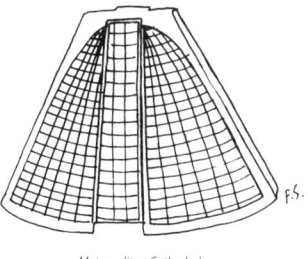

Metropolitan Cathedral

> ### 👉 Wild Jock of Skelater
>
> The crypt of Convento de Santo Antônio contains the tomb of a Scottish soldier of fortune known as 'Wild Jock of Skelater'. He was in the service of the Portuguese Government during the Napoleonic War, and had the distinction of being appointed the first Commander-in-Chief of the Army in Brazil. The statue of Santo Antônio was made a captain in the Portuguese army after his help had been sought to drive out the French in 1710, and his salary paid to the monastery. In 1810 the statue became a major, in 1814 a lieutenant-colonel, and was granted the Grand Cross of the Order of Christ. He was retired without pay in 1914.

was laid in 1759 and construction was completed in 1801. It contains some of Mestre Valentim's work – the carvings in the main chapel and the lovely Capela da Nossa Senhora das Vitórias (Our Lady of Victories). The beautiful fountain at the back of the church works only at night. ■ *Mon-Fri 0900-1300.*

One long block behind the Largo da Carioca and São Francisco de Paula is the **Praça Tiradentes**, old and shady, with a statue to Dom Pedro I. Erected in 1862, it is the work of Luís Rochet and shows the Emperor on horseback, declaring Independence. At the northeast corner of the praça is the **Teatro João Caetano**, named after a famous 19th-century actor. It was most recently restored in 1979. Shops in nearby streets specialize in selling goods for *umbanda*, the Afro-Brazilian religion.

South of the Largo da Carioca are the modern buildings on Avenida República do Chile mentioned above. The **New Cathedral**, the **Catedral Metropolitana**, was dedicated in November 1976. It is a bucket shaped building with an internal height of 68 m, diameter 104 m and external height 83 m; its capacity is 5,000 seated, 20,000 standing. The most striking feature is four enormous 60 m-high stained-glass windows, which are still incomplete. ■ *0800-1800.*

Crossing Avenida República do Paraguai from the east side of the Catedral Metropolitana, you come to an open area with the Petrobrás building and the station for the tram to Santa Teresa (entrance on Rua Senador Dantas – see below). Soon after leaving the station the tram traverses the **Arcos da Lapa**, which were built as an aqueduct to take water from the Rio Carioca to the Largo da Carioca and the rest of the city centre.

Nearby in Lapa and accessed via Rua Joaquim Silva is a **staircase** giving access to the Convent of Santa Teresa which has had most of its steps covered in a mosaic of coloured tiles by the Chilean artist Selarón. The effect is strikingly beautiful and there are larger tiles from various parts of the world on the sides of the staircase. The artist constantly changes the others whenever he manages to obtain new and interesting examples.

Avenida Rio Branco

Here are the last vestiges of the early 20th-century project of the grand Avenida Central. Facing Praça Marechal Floriano is the **Teatro Municipal**, one of the most magnificent buildings in Brazil in the Eclectic style (see 'Architecture', page 232). It was built in 1905-09, in imitation of the Opéra in Paris. On either side of the colonnaded façade are rotundas, surmounted by cupolas. Above the columns are statues of two women representing, Poetry and Music. The decorative features inside and out represent many styles, all lavishly executed. Opera and orchestral performances are given here. ■ *To book a tour of the theatre, T5442900, Mon-Fri 0900-1700, US$2 per person. The tour is worth it to see front and back stage, the decorations and the machine rooms. The box office is at the right hand side of the building; ticket prices start at about US$15.*

Across the avenue is the **Biblioteca Nacional**, at Avenida Rio Branco 219. This building also dates from the first decade of the 20th century. The monumental staircase leads to a hall, off which lead the fine internal staircases of Carrara marble. The first national library was brought to Brazil by the Prince Regent, Dom João, in 1808, the collection coming from the Ajuda Palace in Lisbon. Today it houses over three million volumes and documents, among which are many rare manuscripts. ■ *T2628255. Mon-Fri 0900-2000, Sat 0900-1500.*

The third major building in this group, opposite the Teatro Municipal, is the **Museu Nacional de Belas Artes**, Avenida Rio Branco 199. It was built between 1906 and 1908, also in Eclectic style. It has about 800 original paintings and sculptures and some thousand direct reproductions from the 17th to the 20th centuries. There is a gallery dedicated to works by Brazilian artists from the 17th century onwards, including paintings by Frans Janszoon Post (Dutch 1612-80), who painted Brazilian landscapes in classical Dutch style and the Frenchmen Debret and Taunay (see 'Fine Art and Sculpture', page 230, for these and other painters represented). Another gallery charts the development of Brazilian art in 20th century, including works by Cândido Portinari, Alberto da Veiga Guignard and others. A third gallery contains work by foreign artists. There is also a hall for temporary exhibitions. ■ *T2400068. Tue-Fri 1000-1800; Sat, Sun and holidays 1400-1800. US$1, free on Sun.*

Those interested in contemporary art should also visit the **Palácio Capanema**, which was first the former Ministry of Education and Health building then the Palácio da Cultura. It is on the Esplanada do Castelo, at the junction of Avenida Graça Aranha and Rua Araújo Porto Alegre, and dates from 1937-45 (Unesco has declared it an International Monument). A team of architects led by Lúcio Costa and under the guidance of Le Corbusier designed it; Oscar Niemeyer and Affonso Reidy were in the group (see 'Architecture', page 232). Inside are the great murals of Cândido Portinari, paintings and tiles, as well as other works by renowned artists. The gardens were laid out by Roberto Burle Marx (see page 163).

In the Rua de Santa Luzia, close by the Palácio Capanema and overwhelmed by tall office buildings, is the attractive little church of **Santa Luzia**. When built in 1752 it had only one tower; the other was added late in the 19th century. Feast day is 13 December, when devotees bathe their eyes with holy water, which is considered miraculous.

Museu Judaico, Rua México 90, first floor, has documents, photos and videos detailing the history of the Jewish immigrants to Rio de Janeiro. ■ *T2401598, guided visits, www.museujudaico.org.br Mon-Thu 1000-1600.*

Teatro Municipal
Rio's Opera House

The **Academia Brasileira de Letras**, Avenida Presidente Wilson 231, is housed in a replica of the Trianon of Versailles dating from 1922, and was later donated by the French government to the Brazilian Academy of Letters. There is a café open during the week for tea and snacks. ■ *T5248230, www.academia.org.br Guided tours on Mon and Thu 1400-1500 and 1600-1700, book in advance as there are few vacancies.*

Cinelândia **Praça Mahatma Gandhi**, at the end of Avenida Rio Branco, is flanked on one side by the old cinema and amusement centre of the city, known as Cinelândia. The cast iron fountain in the ornamental garden was moved here from Praça 15 de Novembro.

Next to the praça is the **Passeio Público**, a garden planted between 1779-83 and planned by the artist Mestre Valentim, whose bust is near the old former gateway. A coin and stamp market is held here on Sunday mornings. ■ *Open daily 0730-1900.*

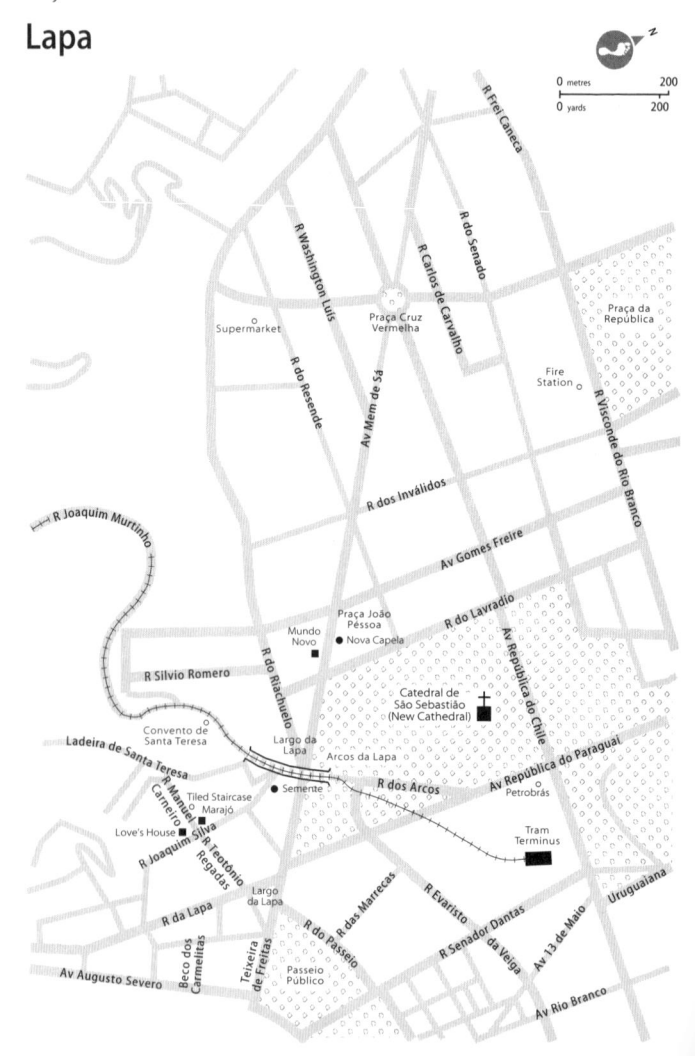

Lapa

Museu do Instituto Histórico e Geográfico, Avenida Augusto Severo 8 (10th-12th floors), just off Avenida Beira Mar, is across the street from the Passeio Público. It has an interesting collection of historical objects, Brazilian products and the artefacts of its peoples. ■ *T2321312. Mon-Fri 1200-1700 (library open from 0900).*

Museu da Força Expedicionária Brasileira, Rua das Marrecas 35, near the Passeio Público, has weapons, medals, photos and documents detailing the Brazilian Expeditionary Force's involvement in the Italian campaign during World War II. ■ *Mon-Fri 1200-1730. Free entry.*

Campo de Santana, Praça da República, is an extensive and picturesque public garden close to the Pedro II railway station popularly known as Central do Brasil. The Parque Júlio Furtado in the middle of the square is populated by agoutis (or gophers), best seen at dusk; there is also an artificial grotto, with swans. ■ *Daily 0900-1700.*

Praça da República

At Praça da República 197 lived Marechal Deodoro da Fonseca, who proclaimed Brazil a republic in 1889 (plaque). On the same side of the Praça is the Arquivo Nacional in the neo-classical former Casa da Moeda, Praça da República and Rua Azeredo Coutinho and the Faculdade de Direito, Rua Moncorvo Filho 8, in the Solar do Conde dos Arcos.

On the opposite side of Avenida Presidente Vargas from the Praça are the Palácio and **Panteão do Duque de Caxias**. The pantheon has the remains of the duke, who is the patron of the Brazilian army, and a military museum dedicated to his life. ■ *Mon-Thu 1000-1600, Fri 1000-1200.*

Palácio do Itamaraty (**Museu Histórico e Diplomático**, Historical and Diplomatic Museum), Avenida Marechal Floriano 196, is in the next block east from the Palácio do Duque de Caxias. Built in neo-classical style in the 1850s for the coffee baron Francisco José da Rocha, it became the president's residence between 1889 and 1897 and then the Ministry of Foreign Affairs until the opening of Brasília. ■ *T2537691, www.trip.com.br/mhd Free guided tours on Mon, Wed and Fri hourly between 1315 and 1615. Recommended.*

Centro Cultural Light, Av Marechal Floriano 168, is a cultural centre for shows and exhibitions. The building dates from 1911 and was formerly the headquarters and garage for the Tramway Light and Power company. There is a museum portraying the history of electricity in the city as well as a theatre and a covered space for musical shows, in particular new MPB artists. ■ *T2114822. Mon-Fri 1000-1900, Sat-Sun 1400-1800.*

Essentials

Sleeping

Near Cinelândia Metrô station and Central do Brasil railway station are a lot of cheap hotels, but many are short stay. This is not an area really recommended for tourists to stay as it is not very safe and the nearby sites of interest should only be visited in daylight. Business travellers, however, may prefer to stay nearer the centre and budget travellers may find the only affordable hotels in this area during carnival and New Year when it can be difficult to find a room.

A *Aeroporto Othon*, Av Beira-Mar 280, near Santos Dumont airport, T5441231, F2103253. Convenient for flights, bar, restaurant, breakfast not included. **A** *Ambassador*, R Senador Dantas 25, Cinelândia, T2977181, F2402439, ambassot@rural.rj.com.br Comfortable rooms, restaurant, parking. **A** *Guanabara Palace*, Av Pres Vargas 392, near Candelária church, T5180333, F5161582. Central location, meeting room, restaurant, sauna, pool, gym, parking, popular with business visitors.

B *Itajubá*, R Álvaro Alvim 23, Cinelândia, T2103163, F2407461, itahotel@openlink.com.br With breakfast, a/c, private bathroom, telephone, business center with fax and internet, laundry, quiet location, friendly staff, no credit cards accepted, very convenient for the centre and cinemas.

D *Estadual*, R Resende 31, near Praça Tiradentes, T2521481. Good. **D** *Marajó*, R Joaquim Silva 99, near the Arches in Lapa just beyond Passeio Público, T2244134. With breakfast, a/c, telephone, varied rooms, good beds and showers, some cheaper single rooms. **D** *Marialva*, Av Gomes Freire 430, near New Cathedral. 2-star, a/c, breakfast in room, some cheaper single rooms, convenient for Av Rio Branco and buses. Recommended. **D** *Mundo Novo*, Av Mem de Sá 85, pass under the Arches in Lapa (bus 127 from bus terminal), T2343805. Clean with a/c. **D** *Pouso Real*, R Resende 35, T2242757, F2325721. Good but in dubious area. Recommended. **D** *Rio Hotel*, R Silva Jardim 3, T2821213. Clean, noisy rooms on Praça Tiradentes, quieter overlooking São Sebastião cathedral, with breakfast (only served in rooms).

E *Love's House*, R Joaquim Silva 87, Lapa, T5095655. **F** without private bathroom, no breakfast, fan, ask for room with window, respectable and good value.

Eating

Many restaurants in Centro are open only for lunch during the week

Expensive *Le Champs Élysées*, Av Pres Antônio Carlos 58, Edif Maison de France, 12th floor, T2400300. French restaurant with good view popular for business lunches, open 1100-1600 Mon-Fri.

Mid-range *Café do Teatro*, ground floor of Teatro Municipal, Av Rio Branco. The Assyrian room is very interesting although it has a formal atmosphere (no one in shorts is admitted), open during the week for lunch only. *Confeitaria Colombo*, R Gonçalves Dias 32/36, near Largo da Carioca, T2322300. A Rio institution with its atmospheric and original Belle Epoque décor, open during the week in the afternoon only for teas and snacks, no service charge so tip the excellent waiters. The Feijoada Colonial on Sat from 1200 is accompanied by live *choro*. *Miako*, R do Ouvidor 45, T2222397. Long-established Japanese restaurant, open for lunch and dinner during the week and lunch only on Sat.

Cheap *Adega Flor de Coimbra*, R Teotônio Regadas 34, Lapa. Founded 1938, very good Portuguese food and wines, speciality *bacalhau*, open 1130-Midnight Mon-Sat. *Alba Mar*, Praça Marechal Âncora 184-186, T2408428, www.albamar.com.br Fish and seafood with good views of Guanabara Bay, open 1130-1600 Mon, 1130-2200 Tue-Sat. *Atrium* and *Bistro do Paço*, in Paço Imperial, Praça 15 de Novembro 48. Good food in nice surroundings, open 1130-2000 Mon-Fri, 1200-1830 Sat-Sun (*Bistro* only). *A Cabeça Grande*, R do Ouvidor 12. Traditional Portuguese seafood since 1903, open 1130-1600 Mon-Fri. *Mala e Cuia*, R Candelária 92, T2534032 and Av Rio Branco 120, 4th floor, T2427097. Good restaurant for *comida mineira*. *Mosteiro*, R São Bento 13. Portuguese food, 1100-1600 Mon-Fri. *Mr Ôpi*, R da Quitanda 51. Smart and well organised pay by weight buffet popular with office workers, good food including diet options, open 1100-1600. Recommended. *Nova Capela*, Av Mem de Sá 96, just past the Arches in Lapa. Bohemian bar and restaurant with good food and *chopp*, try the *cabrito* (kid goat). Open daily from 1100-0500 and frequented by a varied mix of people. Recommended. *Penafiel*, R Senhor dos Passos 121. Good traditional Portuguese, open 1100-1530 Mon-Fri. *Rio Minho*, R do Ouvidor 10. Good seafood in historic building.

Very cheap There are many *lanchonetes* for good, cheap meals in the business sector. Good areas to look are Trav do Comércio (see page 95), R das Marrecas and R Miguel Couto (opposite Santa Rita church) called the *Beco das Sardinhas* because on Wed and Fri especially it is full of people eating sardines and drinking beer (see box).

Sea Chicken and Ghosts?

If you should be in Rio's city centre at around 1800 to 1900 a good tip is to visit the Beco da Sardinha, just in front of the Santa Rita church in Rua Marechal Floriano. It is a small narrow street full of bars with outside tables where you will find ice cold draught beer and the best fried sardines you will ever taste in your life.

This tradition started about 40 years ago when a Portuguese bar owner decided to sell fried sardines cut in a different way. They were served open as if they were a chicken breast. He called his invention "sea chicken" and many curious customers soon arrived. Business boomed due to the success of this delicious snack and he opened other bars in the area that had now become a meeting point for happy hour. Nowadays the Beco is just as popular, especially on Friday nights when the place is crowded with workers resting after the long week. Musicians can be seen playing samba and passing their hats along the tables for pay.

Yet probably few of the revellers realise that underneath this alley with its nice, happy atmosphere, lies a 19th century slaves' cemetery! However it's a fact that many Africans were buried in front of Santa Rita church soon after their arrival in Rio, exhausted and ill from the long ocean crossing.

Fábio Sombra

There are also several Arab restaurants on Av Senhor dos Passos, which are also open Sat and Sun. **Luciano**, R das Marrecas 44. All you can eat buffet. **Nova Republica**, R Ubaldino do Amaral 41A. Good cheap pizza. **Pensão Nutricentro**, R 7 de Setembro 235, near Praça Tiradentes. Cheap *prato feito*, 2nd floor with balcony, open 1100-1500 week days, good value and pleasant surroundings. **Salad Market**, R 13 de Maio 33C, upstairs. Pay by weight, weekday lunches only.

Bars & nightclubs

There are a number of good bars and clubs in the centre with a varied mix of lively people but it's best to take a taxi at night as the area is not very safe. Although still currently popular with younger people even after the closing of Circo Voador, Lapa in particular has many tranvestites and prostitution as does Praça Mauá. There are many gay clubs also around Lapa and Cinelândia but good ones exist all over the city.

Bars **Amarelinho**, Praça Floriano 55. Popular bar with outside tables, good *chopp* and *frango à passarinho*. **Bico Doce Uisqueria**, Beco das Cancelas between R do Rosário and R Buenos Aires. Small bar with German food and a wide range of whiskey, 1200-2200 Mon-Fri. **Bar Brasil**, Av Mem de Sá 90, Lapa. Classic bohemian bar with German food and good beer founded in 1907, 1130-2300 Mon-Fri, 1130-1600 Sat. **Carlitos**, R Álvaro Alvim, 36, Cinelândia, in front of Teatro Rival. One of the last old-style bars in this area, which specializes in *batidas* of ginger, kiwi and other tropical fruits, 0600-1300 daily. **Casa da Cachaça**, Av Mem de Sá 110, Lapa. Tiny bar with more than 2500 brands of *aguardiente*, 1000-2200 Mon-Fri. **Cosmopolita**, Trav do Mosqueira 4, Lapa. Good *chopp* and food in this traditional *boteco*, 1100-Midnight Mon-Fri, 1100-1700 Sat. **Bar Luiz**, Rua da Carioca 39, www.barluiz.com.br Traditional bar that opened in 1887 and is still a popular meeting place, excellent beer and German food, 1100-Midnight Mon-Sat, 1100-1800 Sun. **Manuel & Juaquim**, Praça João Pessoa 7, Lapa. Good draught beer. **Paladino**, R Uruguaiana 224 corner of R Marechal Floriano. Entrance to the *art deco* back bar is through the liquor store, good beer and omelettes, 0700-2100 Mon-Fri, 0700-1200 Sat.

Nightclubs **Asa Branca**, Av Mem de Sá 17, Lapa. Dance hall with forró and pagode open most evenings until late, entry US$4.50. **By Marius**, Av Almte Barroso 139, 2nd floor. Buffet with dance and varied music from 1800 Mon-Thu and from 2200 Fri-Sat, entry and minimum consumption, US$15. *Cine Iris*, R da Carioca 53. Alternative parties and raves, entry US$6. *Cordão da Bola Preta*, Av 13 de Maio 13, 3rd floor. Samba club open Wed-Fri from 1800. *Elite Club*, R Frei Caneca 4, 1st floor, T2323217. *Gafieira* with forró, pagode and sometimes reggae or dance. *Estudantina*, Praça Tiradentes 79, T2321149. Traditional *gafieira* for samba dancing to a live band, open Thu-Sat from 1100-0400. *Bar do Ernesto*, Largo da Lapa 41. *Big Noise* rock party every other Sat from midnight, US$4.50. *Federação dos Afro Blocos do Rio de Janeiro (Febarj)*, Av Mem de Sá 31. Good forró on Sun from 1800, US$3. *Fundição Progresso*, R dos Arcos 24-50, Lapa. Casual disco with varied music from techno to forró, open from 2300 Fri-Sat, entry US$5. *Sinuca da Lapa*, R do Riachuelo 19. *Zoeira* hiphop party on Sat from 2300, US$5, gets packed.

Entertainment

Art galleries *Sociedade Brasileira de Belas Artes*, R do Lavradio 84. Brazilian Fine Arts Society. *Instituto de Pesquisa das Culturas Negras (IPCN)*, Av Mem de Sá 108. Minatures of old Rio created from scrap materials by Sérgio Luiz Cézar, 0800-2200 Mon-Fri.

Carnival blocos *Bloco Cacique de Ramos*, parades from 1800 on Sun, Mon and Tue during carnival at the corner of Av Pres Vargas and Av Rio Branco. Traditional bloco whose participants must be dressed as indians. *Cordão da Bola Preta*, meets at 1000 on Sat during carnival in front of the club (see above). The oldest carnival association still active in the city. No T-shirt but costumes are welcome especially if they have black spots.

Cinema Cinelândia has many cinemas showing Hollywood films such as *Odeon*, Praça Mahatma Gandhi 2, and *Palácio*, R do Passeio 40. Two screens. For art cinema try the cultural centres eg. *Centro Cultural Banco do Brasil*, R Primeiro de Março 66 (see above), *Centro Cultural Light*, Praça Marechal Floriano 168 (see above), mainly classic films and documentaries, and *Estação Paço*, Praça XV 48.

Music *Avenida Club*, Av Almte Barroso 139, T5330292. Jazz and blues, 2000-2300 Mon-Fri, 2300-0100 Sat. *Centro Cultural Light*, Av Marechal Floriano 168 (see above). Musical shows especially MPB. *Bar Emporium*, R do Lavradio 100. Sophisticated bar in antiques store with samba, choro and bossa nova from 2100 Wed-Sat, US$3. *Semente*, R Joaquim Silva 138, Lapa, T2425165. Popular botequim for samba, choro and salsa from 2200 Mon-Sat, US$5, best to reserve a table in advance at weekends. Gets full quickly but good atmosphere both inside and in the street outside. *Teatro Rival*, R Álvaro Alvim, 39, Cinelândia, T2404469. Many famous MPB singers perform here. Classical music can be heard at *Teatro Municipal* (see above) and *Sala Ceclia Meirelles*, Largo da Lapa 47, Lapa, T2243913.

Theatre *Centro Cultural Banco do Brasil*, R Primeiro de Março 66 (see above), T8082020. Three auditoriums. *Teatro João Caetano*, Praça Tiradentes, T2210305 (see above). *Teatro Municipal*, Praça Marechal Floriano (see above), T2623935. Ballet and opera.

Shopping

Bookshops There are many second-hand bookshops known as *sebos* on Av Marechal Floriano, near Av Rio Branco, especially at No 63. *Livraria Antiquário*, 7 de Setembro 207 and in R Pedro I. Second-hand books. *Casa dos Artistas*, south side of Praça Tiradentes. Second-hand paperbacks. *Livraria Brasileira*, Av Rio Branco 156, upstairs 229. Second-hand and rare books specializing in history. *Leonardo da Vinci*, Av Rio Branco 185, shop 2, www.leonardodavinci.com.br Traditional bookstore with all types of foreign books. *Aimée Gilbert*, R da Carioca 38. Second-hand books some in English. *Livraria Kosmos*, R do Rosário 155, www.kosmos.com.br Good shop with international stock. *Livraria São José*, R do Carmo 61. Many second-hand books (only a few in

Street Bazaar

If you want to see something completely different from the fancy fashion boutiques of Ipanema or those immaculately clean shopping malls, then make sure you visit the Saara, an enormous street bazaar located in the middle of Rio's downtown between Avenida Presidente Vargas and Praça Tiradentes.

In the streets of Avenida Passos, Rua Senhor dos Passos, Rua Buenos Aires and Rua da Alfândega you'll find hundreds of small shops selling everything from clothes to electronics and toys to carnival costumes. Renowned as a "popular market", prices tend to be very low and for things like touristy T-shirts, a real bargain. This is where street vendors buy before reselling them in Copacabana and Ipanema. You can also find jeans and bikinis without brand names at very attractive prices.

Most of the shop owners are of Arab or Jewish descent and recently some Koreans have also arrived. Regardless of national or religious differences they all seem to live together in reletive harmony. It is amazing to see the crowds and merchandise displayed outside the shops and to hear the vendors advertizing their goods. There are also some interesting restaurants in the area, many of which specialize in Arabic food such as the Restaurant Cedro do Líbano at Rua Senhor dos Passos 231. You will also find hundreds of small stalls in the streets offering delicious Middle Eastern snacks such as kibe (fried meat ball) or a sfiha (pastry filled with meat, cheese or spinach) for around US$1 with soft drink included! Go ahead and try them as this is one of the few places in Rio where eating street food is relatively safe.

There's also no need to worry about robberies as the association of shop owners have their own private security guards and thefts are extremely rare in this area.

To get there from Copacabana and Ipanema, take bus number 474, 415 or 455 and get out at Avenida Presidente Vargas, close to Avenida Passos. If using the Metro, get off at the Presidente Vargas station. The market is open daily Monday to Friday from 0900-1830 and on Saturday from 0900-1400.

Fábio Sombra

English). *Saraiva*, R do Ouvidor 98, T5079500, www.saraiva.com.br Megastore with books, magazines, music, videos and a café. *Livrarias Siciliano*, Av Rio Branco 156, shop 26. European books. *Sodiler*, R São José 35, shop V, and Santos Dumont airport. *Livros Técnicos*, R Miguel Couto 35. Wide selection. *Livraria da Travessa*, Trav do Ouvidor 11, www.travessa.com.br Good bookshop with branch in Ipanema.

Camping equipment On R 1 de Março, north of Av Pres Vargas, are military shops which sell jungle equipment, such as hammocks, mosquito nets and clothing. *Casa do Militar*, R 1 de Março 145. *London*, R 1 de Março 155. You can also buy the Brazilian flag in any size you want here. *Malamada*, R da Carioca 13. Recommended for rucksacks.

Clothing The centre is good for cheap clothing especially in the area called Saara around R da Alfândega and R Senhor dos Passos (see box 'Street Bazaar'). *Casa Turuna*, R Senhor dos Passos 122-124. Fancy dress shop and a good place to get your carnival costume.

Handicrafts *Arqueologia Urbana*, Av Rio Branco 44. Historical crafts and ornaments.

Markets Antiques market on the waterfront near Praça 15 de Novembro, 0900-1800 Sat. Also in Praça 15 de Novembro is *Feirarte II*, with arts and crafts, Thu-Fri 0800-1800. A stamp and coin market is held in the Passeio Público, Sun. *Feira do Livro*, Cinelândia, selling books at 20% discount. An antiques fair is held on the first Sat of each month in R do Lavradio, Lapa.

Photography For processing: *T Tanaka Cia Ltda*, Av Franklin Roosevelt 39, of 516, T2201127. *Mecánica de Precisão*, R da Conceição 31, shop 202.

Tour operators *Calypso*, R da Alfândega 98, 3rd floor, T5091176, F2212776. Boat trips to the Costa do Sol, Arraial do Cabo and Cabo Frio. *Hanseatic*, R 7 de Setembro 111, 20th floor, T2246672, F2245487. German-run (English, French, Portuguese spoken). Recommended. *Metropol*, R São José 46, T5335010, F5337160, metropol@arras.com.br Eco, adventure and culture tours to all parts of Brazil. *Roxy*, Av Franklin Roosevelt, 71, office 601, RJ 20021-120, T5320141, F5323165, www.roxytravel.com.br Established 1948, ask for Michael or Ricardo Werwie who speak English. Recommended. *Victor Hummel*, Av Pres Vargas 290, T2231262, F2537426. Swiss-run. Recommended.

Directory **Banks** *Banerj*, Av Nilo Peçanha 175. Changes TCs only. *Bank of Boston*, Av Rio Branco 110. Changes Amex TCs only, good rate and service. *Banco do Brasil*, R Sen Dantas 105, 4th floor and R do Acre 15. Changes US$ cash and TCs, minimum US$500, good rates, also changes Argentine pesos, US$20 per transaction, Mon-Fri 1000-1630. Also many ATMs for Visa card withdrawals to avoid queues. *Citibank*, R da Assembléia 100. Changes large US$ TCs into smaller ones, no commission, and advances cash on Eurocard/Mastercard. *Banco Francês e Brasileiro*, Av Rio Branco 193. Cash and TCs. *Itaú*, at Santos Dumont airport. Mastercard and Cirrus cash machines. *Lloyds Bank*, R da Alfândega 332, 7th floor. *Banco Holandês Unido*, R do Ouvidor 101. *Banco Internacional* (*Bank of America* and *Royal Bank of Canada*), R do Ouvidor 90. **Money changers** There are many *câmbios* on Av Rio Branco. *American Express*, Av Pres Wilson 231, 18th floor, Centro, T2921212.

Communications Post office: R 1 de Março 64, at the corner of R do Rosário, the central post office which handles international post and is the main location for poste restante. Another branch at Av Pres Vargas 3077. *Federal Express*, Av Calógeras 23, near Santa Luzia church, T2628565. Reliable service. **Telephone**: International calls can be made at Santos Dumont airport, mezzanine (0530-2300). Also *Telemar*, Praça Tiradentes 41, a few mins' walk from Metrô Carioca, and at R do Ouvidor 60. **Internet**: *CompRio*, R da Assembléia 10, basement shop 114. US$10 per hr, open 0900-1830 Mon-Fri. *Cybercafé Internet Center*, R da Alfândega 80, room 401. US$3 per hr, 0800-2100 Mon-Fri, 0800-1500 Sat. *Internet Café*, R da Assembléia 10, basement shop 112. US$5.50 per hr, 0900-1900 Mon-Fri, 0900-1300 Sat. *SR Café*, Av Rio Branco 156, room 315. US$1.50 per ¼ hr.

Cultural centres *American Chamber of Commerce for Brazil*, Praça Pio X 15, 5th floor. *American Society and American Club*, Av Rio Branco 123, 21st floor. *Marc Apoio Cultural Contact Center*, Av Pres Vargas 446, 1101, T/F2758605. *German Cultur-Institut* (Goethe), Av Graça Aranha 416, 9th floor. Open Mon-Thu 1200-1900, Wed-Thu 1000-1100. *Sociedade Brasileira de Cultura Inglesa*, Av Graça Aranha 327. *USICA Reference Library*, US Consulate General, Av Pres Wilson 147.

Laundry *Lavanderia Fênix*, R do Riachuelo 241A, shop 13.

Medical services Vaccinations at *Saúde de Portos*, Praça Mcal Âncora, T2408628, Mon-Fri 1000-1100, 1500-1800 (international vaccination book and ID required). *Policlínica*, Av Nilo Peçanha 38. Recommended for diagnosis and investigation. **Eye doctors** can be found at *Hospital Souza Aguiar*, Praça da República 111, T2964114. Free casualty ward. **Dentist**: Amílcar Werneck de Carvalho Vianna, Av Pres Wilson 165, room 811. Speaks English.

Places of worship *First Church of Christ Scientist*, Av Mcal Câmara 271, room 301. *Sociedaded Beneficiente Muçulmana*, Av Gomes Freire 176, rooms 205-206, T2241079. 1400-2200 daily, communal prayer 1300 Fri.

Northern Rio

The Zona Norte begins north and west of the Central do Brasil railway station and stretches northwards to the satellite towns of the Baixada Fluminense. This is a mainly residential area with large areas of deprivation such as the Jacarezinho favela. Both Zona Norte and the Baixada include some of the poorest areas in Rio and you should take care at all times. Of particular interest to tourists are the Feira do Nordeste held on Sundays in Campo de São Cristóvão, the Emperor's former residence in the Quinta da Boa Vista as well as the Sambódromo and the famous Maracanã Stadium. Further north is the church of Nossa Senhora da Penha, which hosts a popular pilgrimage in October and the International airport on the Ilha do Governador. There are also a number of interesting museums including the Museu Aeroespacial.

Sights

Rua da Gamboa

Over the Morro da Providência, which is between the Estação Dom Pedro II and the bay, is the **Cemitério dos Ingleses**, Rua da Gamboa 181. The cemetery was granted to the British community by Dom João, Regent of Portugal, in 1810. It is the oldest cemetery in Rio. Catholics who could afford a burial were laid to rest inside their churches (see the numbers on the church floors, marking the graves), but the British in Rio, being non-Catholic, were not allowed to be buried in the religious establishments.

Also in Gamboa, the **Centro Cultural José Bonifácio**, Rua Pedro Ernesto 80, was created in 1983 to preserve and promote Afro Brazilian culture through seminars, films, theatre and dance. The neo-classical building dates from 1877 and was once a school. ■ *T/F2536255.*

Sambódromo
See also Carnival section & map page 10

It is in the Sambódromo, a permanent site at R Marquês de Sapucai, Cidade Nova, 600 m long with seating for 43,000 people, that the parades of the samba schools take place during carnival. Designed by Oscar Niemeyer and built between 1983-84, it handles sporting events, conferences and concerts during the rest of the year. To understand the traditions of the schools, the meanings of the different parts of the parade, and canival as a whole, you should visit the **Museu do Carnaval** in the Sambódromo. Although small, it has lots of photographs and the English-speaking staff are very informative. ■ *T5026996. Mon-Fri 1100-1700. Free. Entrance in R Frei Caneca.*

The **Museu da Polícia Civil** in the Academia de Polícia Sílvio Terra, Rua Frei Caneca 162, next to the Sambódromo, was founded in 1912 and has a collection of firearms, propaganda confiscated during the Estado Novo, gaming tables from mobile casinos, and various other interesting items about the history of policing in the state. ■ *T6903261 to arrange a visit. Wed-Thu, 1500-1700.*

Maracanã Stadium

Maracanã Stadium, officially called Estádio Mário Filho, is one of the largest sports centres in the world. The football ground has seating capacity for 200,000 spectators. Matches are worth going to if only for the spectators' samba bands. There are three types of ticket: *cadeiras* (individual chairs), the most expensive; *arquibancadas* (terraces), good for watching the game, but don't sit at the edge of two rival groups of fans; *geral* (standing), the cheapest, not recommended, not safe. Prices vary according to the game, but note that agencies charge much more for tickets than at the gate. It is cheaper to buy tickets from club sites on the day before the match.

Maracanã is now used only for major games; Rio teams play most matches at their home grounds (still a memorable experience). Hotels can arrange visits to football matches: a good idea on Sunday when the metrô is closed and buses are very full. ■ *A guided tour of the stadium (in Portuguese) from Gate 16 costs US$2 and of the museum, US$0.50. T5689962. Highly recommended to football fans, look out for charismatic Isaías Ambrósio, Maracanã's longest serving employee who will do a fantastic rendition of the 1950 World Cup final (remember to tip him).*

Safety Don't take valuables or wear a watch; take special care when entering and leaving the stadium. The rivalry between the local clubs Flamengo and Vasco da Gama is intense, often leading to violence, so it is advisable to avoid their encounters. Don't be tempted to buy a club shirt or favour on match day: if you find yourself in the wrong place, you could be in trouble.

Transport Metrô station Maracanã is on Linha 2, one stop beyond São Cristóvão. Buses: 238 and 239 from the centre; 434 and 464 from Glória, Flamengo and Botafogo; 455 from Copacabana; 433 and 464 from Ipanema and Leblon.

Quinta da Boa Vista About 3 km west of the Praça da República (beyond the Sambódromo) is the Quinta da Boa Vista, formerly the Emperor's private park, from 1809 to 1889. The Palace in which the Imperial family lived now houses the Museu Nacional. In recent years the Quinta da Boa Vista has had the problem of thieves operating by the park entrance and in the park itself. The safest way to reach the museum is by taking a taxi to the main door but it can also be reached by Metrô to São Cristóvão, then cross the railway line and walk a few metres to the park.

Northern Rio: west of centre

Related map:
Sambódromo,
page 11

This is safer than taking a bus. If you are comfortable in crowds, perhaps the best time to visit the Quinta da Boa Vista is Saturday or better still Sunday afternoon. There are more people and therefore more police because it is full of Cariocas looking for fun and relaxation. It is a good time for people watching (but don't take an expensive camera to do so). The park becomes a noisy mixture of colours, smells of hot dogs and corn, people playing football, preachers warning of the end of the world, street sellers and so on.

Nearest Metrô: São Cristóvão on Linha 2. By bus: 472 or 474 from the centre; 472 from Glória, Flamengo, Botafogo or Leme; 474 from Copacabana, Ipanema or Leblon

The **Museu Nacional** in the Quinta da Boa Vista has many important collections. The building was the principal palace of the Emperors of Brazil, but only the unfurnished Throne Room and ambassadorial reception room on the second floor reflect past glories. In the entrance hall is the famous Bendegó meteorite, found in the State of Bahia in 1888; its original weight, before some of it was chipped, was 5,360 kilograms. Besides several foreign collections of note (for example, of Peruvian and Mexican archaeology, graeco-roman ceramics, Egyptian mummies), the Museum contains collections of Brazilian Indian weapons, dresses, utensils etc, of minerals and of historical documents. There are also collections of birds, beasts, fishes and butterflies. Despite the need for conservation work, the museum is still worth visiting. ■ *T5681149. www.acd.ufrj.br/museu Tue-Sun 1000-1600. US$2. Some of the collections are open to qualified research students only.*

Museu de Fauna, also in the Quinta da Boa Vista, contains a most interesting collection of Brazilian fauna. ■ *Tue-Sun 1200-1700.*

The **Jardim Zoológico** in the Quinta da Boa Vista contains Brazilian and imported wild animals and a comprehensive collection of tropical birds. Many 'visitors' come to the gardens, so it is a good place for birdwatchers. The gateway is a replica of Robert Adam's famous gateway to Syon House, near London. The zoo is maintained by a special foundation, the Fundação Rio Zoo, which is making efforts to provide the animals with good conditions. ■ *T5692024. Tue-Sun 0900-1630, best in the morning. US$2.*

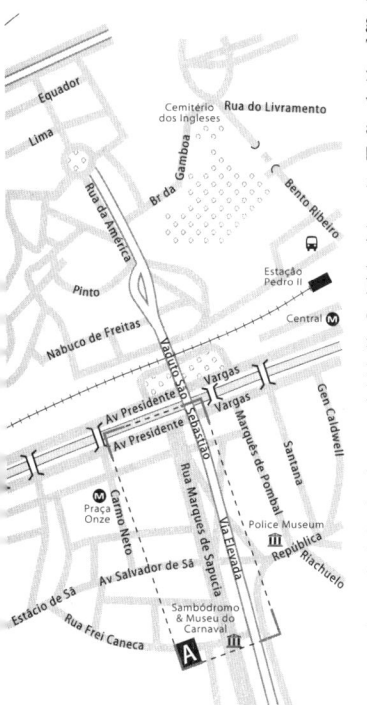

Museu Militar Conde de Linhares, São Cristóvão, Avenida Pedro II 383, São Cristóvão, has a collection of canons, armoured cars and weapons detailing the Brazilian army's involvement abroad from World War II to UN peacekeeping in Angola. ■ *Sat-Sun 1000-1600, T5899034.*

East of the Quinta de Boa Vista is the stadium of **São Cristóvão Clube de Futebol e Regatas**, one of the smaller football clubs in the city and the first team of international footballer Ronaldo.

The **Museu de Astronomia/ National Observatory**, founded 1827, is on São Januário hill, Rua General Bruce 586, São Cristóvão. The building housing the National Observatory was inspired by castles on the river Loire in France. The museum contains scientific instruments, a model of the solar system and an exhibition called The Four Corners of the Universe (*Quatro Cantos de Origem*). ■ *T5807010, www.info.incc.br/mast Tue, Thu, Fri 1000-1700, Thu 1000-2000, Sat-Sun 1600-2000, guided tours 1000-1200; 1400-1600. Viewing of the night sky on Wed, Sat-Sun 1900-2130.*

North of the Morro de São Januário is the stadium of **Clube de Regatas Vasco de Gama**, Rua General Almério de Moura 131, inaugurated in1927 with a 40,000 capacity and popularly known as São Januário. Founded as a rowing club in 1898, a football team was formed in 1915 and today it practices around forty different sports. ■ *T5807373, www.crvasco.com.br*

Other sights **Museu da Vida**, Avenida Brasil 4365, Manguinhos, is an interactive science museum housed in the house and gardens of Oswaldo Cruz, the 19th century scientist. The Palácio Mourisco is also home to the *FIOCRUZ* public health institute which has a permanent collection on scientific history. ■ *T5906747. Tue-Fri 0900-1700. Entry free. Guided visits by appointment.*

Casa de Banho de Dom João VI, Rua Praia do Caju 385, Caju, was declared a national monument in 1938 and restored in 1996. The 19th-century building was used by Dom João VI in 1811 whilst curing an infected tick bite through bathing on the nearby beach. It now houses the **Museu da Limpeza Urbana** which details the urban development of the city as well as holding seminars and cultural events. ■ *T5806033. Tue-Fri 1000-1700, Sat-Sun 1300-1700. Free.*

Museu do Trem, Rua Arquias Cordeiro 1046, Engenho do Dentro, has Brazil's first locomotive Baronesa as well as the imperial carriage used by Dom Pedro II and a presidential car used by Getúlio Vargas. ■ *T2695545. Tue-Fri 1000-1200, 1330-1600, Sat-Sun 1300-1700.*

Museu de Imagens do Inconsciente, Rua Ramiro Magalhães 521, Engenho do Dentro, since 1952 has built up a huge collection of paintings and models produced by patients at the Pedro II Pychiatric Centre. ■ *T5974242. Mon-Fri 0900-1600. Free.*

Capão do Bispo Estate, Avenida Suburbana 4616, Del Castilho, is an 18th-century estate house with an archaeological exhibition. ■ *Mon-Fri 1400-1700.*

Museu Universitário Gama Filho, Rua Manuel Vitorino 625, Piedade, has a collection dealing with the history of education, social development and culture in particularly Northern Rio. ■ *T5997117, iac@ugf.br Mon-Fri 0900-1800.*

Museu Aeroespacial, Avenida Marechal Fontenele 2000, Campo dos Afonsos, has displays of early Brazilian civil and military aircraft such as 14 Bis and Demoiselle by the Brazilian aviation pioneer Santos Dumont, as well as historic weapons and documents. ■ *T33575212, www.musal.maer.mil.br Tue-Fri 0900-1500, Sat, Sun and holidays 0930-1600. Free. Guided visits must be arranged 3 days in advance.*

The church of **Nossa Senhora da Penha**, in the northern suburb of Penha, is on a bare rock in which 365 steps are cut. This staircase is ascended by pilgrims on their knees during the festival month of October; there is a funicular for those unable to do this. The church in its present form dates from the early 20th century, based on an early 18th century chapel. The first religious building, a hermitage, was built in 1632. Its prominent position makes Nossa Senhora da Penha a major landmark and its balustrade provides fine views. ■ *Buses 497 from Copacabana, 340 and 346 from centre go there.*

Essentials

Business travellers merely passing through for meetings might wish to freshen up or break their journey at one of the airport hotels otherwise there are very few good hotels in this area. **L** *Luxor Aeroporto*, 3rd floor of Terminal 1, International airport, T33985460, F33983983, aeroporto@luxor-hotels.com Day and 3 hr use available between 0800-2000. **AL** *Pousada Galeão*, 1st floor of Terminal 1, International airport, T/F33983852. Day and 3 hr use available, bar, restaurant, breakfast not included.

Sleeping

Mid-range *Adegão Português*, Campo de São Cristóvão 212A, São Cristóvão, T5807288. Good *bacalhau*, dishes for two people, open 1130-2300 Mon-Sat, 1130-2030 Sun. *Cheiro do Pará*, Praia da Freguesia 605, Ilha do Governador. Freshwater fish from the Amazon priced by weight, open 1100-Midnight Thu and Sun, 1100-0200 Fri-Sat.

Cheap *Fiorino*, Av Heitor Beltrão 126, Tijuca, T5673368. Good Italian restaurant, open 1800-midnight Mon-Thu, 1800-0100 Fri-Sat, 1200-midnight Sun. Recommended. *Franco & Mayr*, Av Maracanã 782, Tijuca. Good for *moqueca capixaba* and shrimp pasties, open for lunch and dinner Tue-Sat, lunch only Sun. *Siri*, R dos Artistas 2, Vila Isabel. Lively, popular bar/restaurant with good seafood including shredded crab in the shell and very tasty shrimp pasties. Recommended.

Eating
Although not an area particularly known for its restaurants there are a few options worth visiting in this area especially for Brazilian food

Bars *Adega do Peixoto*, R Barão de Mesquita 616, Tijuca. Simple bar with good *chopp*, *cachaça* and *nordestino* food, 0700-0100 Mon-Sat, 0700-1700 Sun. *Chopp Gol*, R Felipe Camarão 8, in front of the state university close to Maracanã stadium. Football theme bar with cable TV showing the games. *Penafiel da Gamboa*, Trav Cunha Matos 3 corner of R do Livramento, Gamboa. Good chilled draught beer in simple bar near the port, 0600-2100 Mon-Sat. *Salete*, R Afonso Pena 189, Tijuca. Good beer and shrimp pasties, 1100-2200 daily. *Só Kana*, R Conde de Bonfim 875, Tijuca, close to Carrefour supermarket. Bar famous for its fruit *batidas* which can be bought by the bottle, 1500-Midnight Mon-Thu, 1500-0200 Fri, 1000-0200 Sat, 1000-Midnight Sun.

Bars & nightclubs

Nightclubs The Sat night before the *Feira de Nordeste* (see below), Campo de São Cristóvão is a maze of improvised bars with people dancing forró to live bands until Sun morning. *Helênico*, R Itapiru 1305, Rio Comprido, T5026448. Club with pagode and forró, 2000-0100 Fri, 1430-0400 Sat. *Malagueta*, R Carneiro de Campos 31, São Cristóvão. A big shed but one of the most popular places for forró in the city, entry US$6.

Zona Norte and the Baixada Fluminense are where most of the samba schools have their quadras which are very lively (and crowded) during the months preceeding carnival. Check the press or ring the schools in advance for full details of rehearsals as days, locations and times often change. This is generally not a very safe area so it's best to take a taxi at night.

Entertainment

Carnival blocos *Banda da Amendoeira*, Traditional working class bloco which parades on Mon and Tue mornings during carnival from the corner of R Quaraim and R Paranapiacaba in Piedade. *Nem Muda Nem Sai de Cima*, Rehearsals at Bar da Dona Maria (see below), on Sat 1400-2200, parades on the Sat afternoon before carnival.

Music *Bar da Dona Maria (Café e Bar Brotinho)*, R Garibaldi 13 almost on the corner with R Conde de Bonfim, Muda (Tijuca). Home to spontaneous *rodas de samba* performed by famous musicians. *Burtiquim do Martinho*, In Shopping Iguatemi, T5777160. Live samba most nights from 1900. *Casa da Mãe Joana*, R São Cristóvão 73, São Cristóvão, T5805613. Very popular traditional club for samba and choro (see short

Mother Joana's House

It was from the ashes of a burnt-out 19th-century former brothel in São Cristóvão, bought by retired policeman Marcos Esteves (o Marquinho) in 1994, that the Casa de Mãe Joana was born. Created as a space for sambistas of all generations to meet and play authentic roots samba, it soon attracted stars like Nélson Sargento, Zé Ketti and the Velha Guarda of the traditional samba schools, Mangueira and Portela to its busy weekend sessions. By 1998 the club had recorded a CD to preserve the music and formed a carnival bloco to take their traditional sambas to the streets once again.

above), open 2200-0300 Fri-Sat. *Olimpo*, Av Vicente de Carvalho 1450, Vila da Penha, T4854747, www.olimpoartbeer.com.br Shows by samba schools and musicians.

Samba schools *Acadêmicos do Grande Rio*, R Almte Barroso 5/6, Duque de Caxias, T7758422, www.granderio.org.br Rehearsals from 2300 Sat, US$1.75. *Acadêmicos do Salgueiro*, R Silva Teles 104, Andaraí, T2385564, www.salgueiro.com.br Rehearsals from 2200 Sat, US$5, mostly white middle-class school where gays are welcome, popular and close to the centre. *Beija Flor de Nilópolis*, Pracinha Wallace Paes Leme 1025, Nilópolis, T7912866, www.beija-flor.com.br Rehearsals from 2100 Thu, US$3. *Caprichosos de Pilares*, R dos Faleiros 1, Pilares, T5945755, www.rioarte.com/caprichosos Rehearsals from 2300 Sat. *Em Cima da Hora*, R Zeferino da Costa 556, Cavalcanti. *Estácio de Sá*, R Miguel de Frias 35, Cidade Nova, T2938944. *Imperatriz Leopoldinense*, R Professor Lacê 235, Ramos, T5608037, www.imperatrizleopoldinense.com.br Rehearsals from 2300 Sat, US$1.75. *Império Serrano*, Av Min Edgar Romero 114, T33594944, Madureira. *Império da Tijuca*, R Conde de Bonfim 1286, Usina. *Inocentes de Belford Roxo*, Av Boulevard 1741, Parque São Vicente, Belford Roxo. *Paraíso de Tuiuti*, Campo de São Cristóvão, São Cristóvão. *Portela*, R Clara Nunes 81, Madureira, T33592921, www.gresportela.com.br Rehearsals from 2200 Wed and Fri, from 1800 Sun, US$2.25. *Primeira Estação de Mangueira*, R Visconde de Niterói 1072, Mangueira, T5674637, www.mangueira.com.br Rehersals from 2300 Sat, US$5, traditional school and good atmosphere with many children and elderly people dancing. Mangueira also have a cultural centre at R Frederico Silva 85, Praça XI. *Tradição*, Estr Intendente Magalhães 160, Campinho, T33906917. Rehearsals from 2300 Fri. *União da Ilha do Governador*, Estr do Galeão 322, Ilha do Governador, T33964951. Rehearsals from 2200 Sat, US$3. *Unidos do Jacarezinho*, Av Suburbana 2233, Jacarezinho. *Unidos da Ponte*, R Olaria 78, São João de Meriti. *Unidos da Tijuca*, R São Miguel 430, Tijuca, T2338976, www.unidosdatijuca.com.br Rehearsals are held at Clube dos Portuários, R Francisco Bicalho 47, Santo Cristo, near Rodoviária Novo Rio from 2200 Sat. *Unidos de Vila Isabel*, R Visconde de Santa Isabel 34, Vila Isabel, T5767052, www.vilaisabel.com Rehearsals are held at Associação Atlética Vila Isabel, Blvd 28 de Setembro 160 from 2200 Sat, US$3. *Unidos do Cabuçu*, R Araújo Leitão 925, Lins do Vasconcelos, T/F5917210.

Shopping

Bookshops *Saraiva* and *Sodiler*, in Shopping Tijuca, Shopping Iguatemi and at the International airport.

Markets *Feira do Nordeste* Northeastern market at Campo de São Cristóvão, with music (forró), *comida nordestina* and magic, on Sun 0800-2200 (bus 472 or 474 from Copacabana or centre).

Shopping centres *Norte Shopping*, Av D Helder Camara 5474, Del Castilho. Supermarkets, cinemas, restaurants open Mon-Sat 1000-2200, Sun 1500-2100. *Shopping Iguatemi*, R Barão de São Francisco 236, Vila Isabel. Cinemas and restaurants, open 1000-2300 Mon-Sat, 1000-2200 Sun. *Shopping Tijuca*, Av Maracanã 987. Cinemas, food hall, open 1000-2200 Mon-Sat, 1500-2100 Sun.

Bus companies

Auto Viação 1001, (Mil e Um), kiosks 53-54 and 68-75, T0800-251001. Buses to Costa do Sol (Búzios, Cabo Frio, Saquarema etc), Campos, Nova Friburgo, Santo Antônio de Pádua.
Cidade do Aço, kiosks 76-78, T2538471. Buses to Itatiaia, Penedo, Visconde de Mauá, Volta Redonda.
Costa Verde, kiosks 86-87, T5162437. Buses to Costa Verde (Angra dos Reis, Mangaratiba, Parati).
Fácil, kiosk 83, T2638792. Buses to Petrópolis.
Macaense, kiosk 51-52, T0800-246555. Buses to Costa do Sol (Araruama, São Pedro da Aldeia, Macaé, Rio das Ostras).
Normandy, kiosks 79-81, T2639424. Buses to Barra do Piraí, Conservatória, Valença, Vassouras.
Salutaris, kiosk 55, T2336786. Buses to Itaipava, Paraíba do Sul, Três Rios.
Sampaio, kiosk 67, T2338325. Buses to Resende, Itatiaia, Engenheiro Passos.
Teresópolis, kiosk 84-85, T2334625. Buses to Teresópolis.
Única Petrópolis, kiosk 83, T2368792. Buses to Petrópolis.

Long distance buses Rodoviária Novo Rio, Av Rodrigues Alves, corner with Av Francisco Bicalho, just past the docks, T2915151. Some travel agents sell interstate tickets, or will direct you to a bus ticket office in the centre. Agencies include **Dantur Passagense Turismo**, Av Rio Branco 156, subsolo loja 134, T2623424/3624. **Itapemirim Turismo**, R Uruguaiana 10, loja 24, T5098543, both in the centre. **Guanatur**, R Dias da Rocha 16A, Copacabana; and an agency at R Visconde de Pirajá 303, loja 114, Ipanema. They charge about US$1 for bookings. Buses run from Rio to all parts of the country; it is advisable to book tickets in advance. For latest bus prices from Rio, check *O Globo's* website, www.oglobo.com.br, click 'Boa Viagem', then 'Guia de Viagem'.

The rodoviária has a Riotur information centre, which is very helpful. Left luggage costs US$3. There are *câmbios* for cash only. The local bus terminal is just outside the rodoviária: turn right as you leave and run the gauntlet of taxi drivers – best ignored. The rodoviária attracts thieves; exercise caution. The air conditioned *Real* bus (opposite the exit) goes along the beach to São Conrado and will secure luggage. If you need a taxi collect a ticket, which ensures against overcharging, from the office inside the entrance (to Flamengo US$7.50). On no account give the ticket to the taxi driver until after your journey.

The main bus station is reached by buses M94 and M95, Bancários/Castelo, from the centre and the airport; 136, 172, Rodoviária/Glória/Flamengo/Botafogo; 127, 128, 136, Rodoviária/Copacabana; 170, Rodoviária/Gávea/São Conrado; 128, 172, Rodoviária/Ipanema/Leblon.

Transport
Details of journey times & fares are given under destinations throughout the chapter

Banks *Banco do Brasil*, 3rd floor of Terminal 1, International Airport. 0800-2200 daily. Good place for changing cash and TCs at weekends. **American Express**, at International airport, VIP room 1st floor, T33984251. Good rates.

Directory

Communications Post Office: Branches at R Almte Cochrane 255B, Tijuca; R Dias da Cruz 182B, Méier; Praça Armando Cruz 120B, Madureira, in Rodoviária Novo Rio (see above) and at International airport (handles international post). **Telephones:** *Telemar* at Novo Rio bus station (see above), open 24 hrs daily, and R Dias da Cruz 182, shop A, Méier. International calls can also be made at the International airport. **Internet:** *@Point*, 3rd floor of Shopping Iguatemi. US$1.25 per quarter hour, open 1000-2300 Sun-Mon, 1000-midnight Fri-Sat.

Places of worship Umbanda: *Cabana Espírita Pai Antonio*, R das Verbenas 371, Vila Valqueire, T5563537. Meeting of Preto Velhos on Mon 1800-2000, meeting of Caboclos on Fri 1800-2000. *Centro Espírita Caminheiros de Verdade*, R Comendador João Carneiro 133, Engenho do Dentro. Ceremonies at 2000 Fri. Candomblé: *Ile Axé D'Oxalá*, R Seridó, Lot 20, Quadra 16, Nova Iguaçú, T5580724. Ceremonies on Sat from 1600. *Palácio de Iansã*, Estr Santa Efigênia 152, Taquara, T33422176. Fortnightly ceremonies on Sat at 2000.

Southern Rio

Beach culture The famous **Zona Sul** begins in **Glória** and follows the coastline until **Barra da Tijuca**. It is in this area that Rio de Janeiro's true *praia* culture comes to the fore. As Priscilla Ann Goslin puts it in *How to be a Carioca* (see under Tourist information, page 39), a Carioca is someone who goes to the beach before, after or instead of work. The beach is divided into numbered *postos*, where the lifeguards are based. Different sections attract different types of people, for example young people, artists and gays. "Where do you go on the beach?" is the defining question for Cariocas (see box 'Where to go on the Beach?'). The safest places are in front of the major hotels which have their own security, for instance the **Meridien** on Copacabana beach or the **Caesar Park** on Ipanema. The *Caesar Park* also has 24-hour video surveillance during the summer season, which makes it probably the safest patch of sand in Rio. Also Brazil's Olympic beach volleyball players practise outside this hotel. Sports of all types, however, can be seen or played all along the beaches: volley ball, football, aerobics, jogging and so on. On all Rio's beaches you should take a towel or mat to protect you against sandflies. In the water stay near groups of other swimmers. There is a strong undertow.

Glória, Catete and Flamengo

The commercial district ends where the Avenida Rio Branco meets the Avenida Beira Mar. This avenue, with its royal palms, bougainvilleas and handsome buildings, coasting the Botafogo and Flamengo beaches (too polluted for bathing), makes a splendid drive; its scenery is shared by the urban motorway, Avenida Infante Dom Henrique, along the beach over reclaimed land (the Aterro), which leads to Botafogo and through two tunnels to Copacabana. To your left as you head south is the bay, ahead of you the Pão de Açúcar (Sugar Loaf) and inland the districts of Lapa, Glória, Catete and Flamengo. Nearby is Santa Teresa, the district west of Glória reached by tram from beside the Catedral Metropolitana (see above).

Another main route runs behind Glória Hill from the centre to Botafogo. Avenida Augusto Severo starts at the Passeio Público, passes Praça Paris, then becomes Rua do Catete as it runs through Catete to the Largo do Machado.

Sights

Marina da Glória Next to the Santos Dumont domestic airport with its airbridge to São Paulo is the Marina da Glória, the only one in the city. The main dock can take vessels up to 30 m whilst there are two piers, one for 10 m boats and the other for 21 m, as well as many anchor buoys. There are many repair facilities, boat sales and marine equipment shops and a sailing school whilst fuel is available just north of the marina. ■ *22° 55.200' S, 043° 10.300' W; VHF 16, 68, 69; HF4431.8, 8291.1; callsign E37*

Parque do Flamengo On the Glória and Flamengo waterfront, with a view of the Pão de Açúcar and Corcovado, is the Parque do Flamengo, designed by Burle Marx (see page 163), opened in 1965 during the 400th anniversary of the city's founding and landscaped on 100 ha reclaimed from the Bay. The park (officially called Parque Brigadeiro Eduardo Gomes) runs from the *aterro* on which Santos Dumont airport stands to the Morro da Viúva and Botafogo beach. The area was reclaimed from the sea using 1.2 million metric tonnes of earth. Behind the War Memorial (see below) is the public yacht marina. In the park are many sports fields; there is a sailboat basin (see above) and model plane flying field; and for children, a marionette theatre, a miniature village and a staffed nursery. There are also night amusements, such as bandstands and areas for dancing. Security in the park is in the hands of vigilante policemen and it is a popular recreation area. On Sunday and holidays between 0700 and 1800 the avenues through the park are closed to traffic.

At the city end of the Parque Flamengo is the **Museu de Arte Moderna**, a spectacular building at Avenida Infante Dom Henrique 85, near the National War Memorial. It suffered a disastrous fire in 1978 but the collection is now being rebuilt and several countries have donated works of art. There is also a non-commercial cinema. The collection of contemporary Brazilian art includes very expressive drawings by Cândido Portinari from the 1940s and 1950s and drawings and etchings of everyday work scenes by Gregório Gruber, made in the 1970s. ■ *T2102188, www.mamrio.com.br Tue, Wed, Fri 1200-1800, Thu 1200-2000, Sat-Sun 1300-2000. US$2.*

The **Monumento aos Mortos da Segunda Guerra Mundial**, Avenida Infante Dom Henrique 75, opposite Praça Paris is the national memorial to Brazil's dead in the Second World War. The Memorial takes the form of two slender columns supporting a slightly curved slab, representing two palms uplifted to heaven. In the crypt are the remains of the Brazilian soldiers killed in Italy in 1944-45. ■ *Crypt and museum are open Tue-Sun 1000-1600, but beach clothes and rubber-thonged sandals are not permitted.*

Praça Paris, built on reclaimed ground near the Largo da Glória, is much admired for the beauty of its formal gardens and illuminated fountains.

The beautiful little church on the Glória Hill, overlooking the Parque do Flamengo, is **Nossa Senhora da Glória do Outeiro**. It was the favourite church of the imperial family; Dom Pedro II was baptized here. The building is polygonal, with a single tower. Construction began in 1735 and was completed in 1791. It contains some excellent examples of blue-faced Brazilian tiling. Its main altar, of wood, was possibly carved by Mestre Valentim. There is also an adjacent museum of religious art. ■ *T5574600, www.outeirodaglória.org.br Tue-Fri 0900-1200, 1300-1700, Sat-Sun 0900-1200. Guided visits by appointment on the 1st Sun of each month. You get to the church by taking bus 119 from the centre or 571 from Copacabana.*

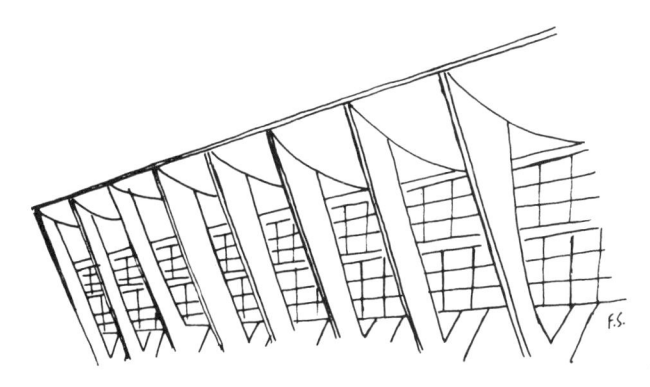

Museum of Modern Art

120 GLÓRIA, CATETE AND FLAMENGO

Local museums **Museu da República**, on Rua do Catete 153, is the former palace of a coffee baron, the Barão de Nova Friburgo. The palace was built in 1858-66. In 1887 it was converted into the presidential seat, until the move to Brasília. The ground floor of this museum consists of the sumptuous rooms of the coffee baron's mansion. The first floor is devoted to the history of the Brazilian republic. You can also see the room where Getúlio Vargas shot himself. The museum is highly recommended. Behind the museum is the **Parque do Catete** with many birds and monkeys. ■ *Tue-Fri, 1200-1700, Sat-Sun 1400-1800, US$2.50, free*

Glória, Santa Teresa, Catete, Flamengo

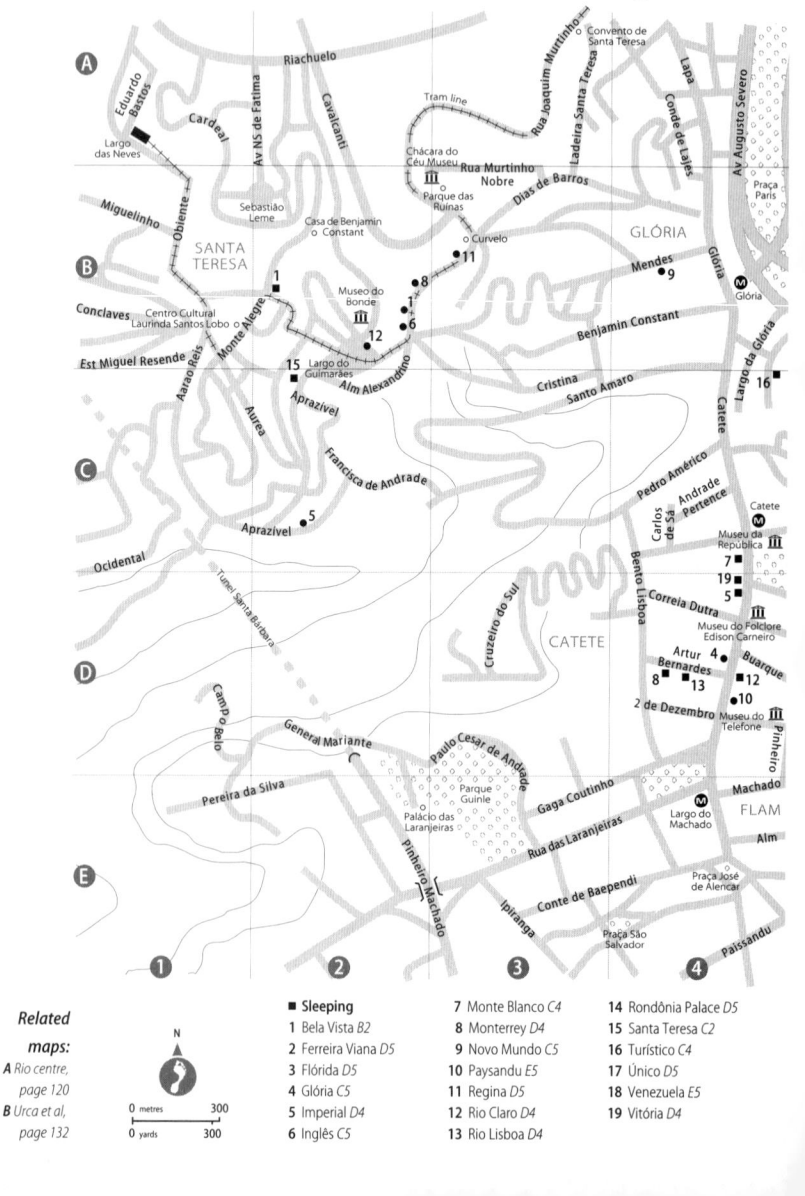

Related maps:
A Rio centre, page 120
B Urca et al, page 132

■ **Sleeping**
1 Bela Vista *B2*
2 Ferreira Viana *D5*
3 Flórida *D5*
4 Glória *C5*
5 Imperial *D4*
6 Inglês *C5*
7 Monte Blanco *C4*
8 Monterrey *D4*
9 Novo Mundo *C5*
10 Paysandu *E5*
11 Regina *D5*
12 Rio Claro *D4*
13 Rio Lisboa *D4*
14 Rondônia Palace *D5*
15 Santa Teresa *C2*
16 Turístico *C4*
17 Único *D5*
18 Venezuela *E5*
19 Vitória *D4*

on Wed, T2856350, F2850795, www.museudarepublica.org.br *Take bus 571 from Copacabana, or the Metrô to Catete station.*

Museu do Folclore Edison Carneiro, on Rua do Catete 181, houses a collection which should not be missed. The very interesting objects have been well selected and arranged, but there are no explanations other than in a book in Portuguese which costs US$2.50. There is a collection of small ceramic figures representing everyday life in Brazil, some very funny, some scenes animated by electric motors. Many artists are represented and displays show the way of life in different parts of the country. There are fine Candomblé and Umbanda costumes, religious objects, ex-votos and sections on many of Brazil's festivals. It has a small, but excellent library, with helpful, friendly staff for finding books on Brazilian culture, history and anthropology. ■ *Tue-Fri 1100-1800, Sat-Sun 1500-1800, free, T2850441, F2050090. Photography is allowed, but without flash. Take bus 571 from Copacabana, or the Metrô to Catete station.*

Museu do Telefone, on Rua 2 de Dezembro 63, exhibits old telephones. On the top floor there is a semi- mechanical telephone exchange from the 1940s plus Getúlio Vargas' golden telephone and a replica of the telephone of Dom Pedro II. The museum is also a busy cultural centre with many exhibitions, plays and shows. Recommended. **NB** The museum will be closed until probably March or April 2001 when it will reopen as **Espaço Telemar**, after an extensive refurbishment, with new interactive exhibits and a cyber café. ■ *Tue-Sun 0900-1900, T5563189, F2054872, www.telemar-rj.com.br/museu*

Museu Carmen Miranda, in Parque do Flamengo in front of Rui Barbosa 560 (beneath the Morro da Viúva), displays over 3,000 items, including the famous singer's gowns, jewellery, reviews, recordings etc. A video compilation is shown, a treat for cinema buffs. ■ *Mon-Fri 1100-1700, US$0.30, T/F5512597 ring in advance for guided tour.*

See map, page 132

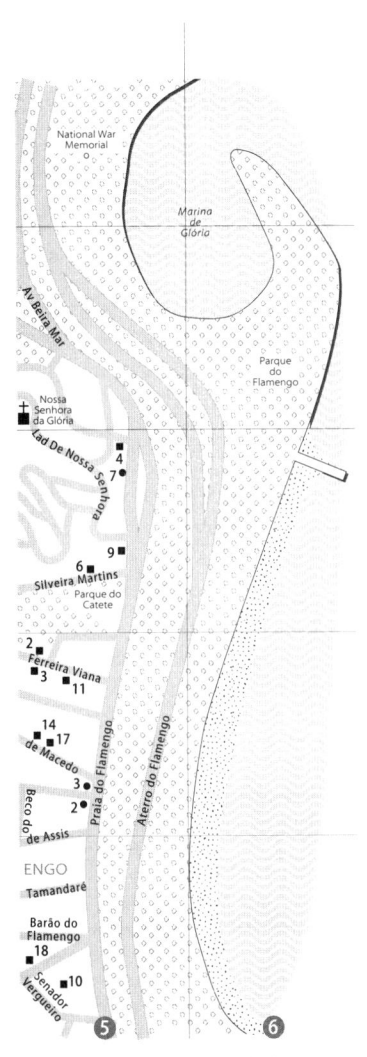

- **Eating**
1 Adega do Pimenta *B2*
2 Alcaparra *D5*
3 Alho e Oleo *D5*
4 Amazônia *D4*
5 Aprazível *C2*
6 Bar do Arnaudo *B2*
7 Café Glória *C5*
8 Cantina Guzzo *B2*
9 Casa da Suiça *B4*
10 Galicia Grill *D4*
11 Sobrado das Massas *B3*
12 Sobrenatural *B2*

Parque Guinle Parque Guinle, Rua Gago Coutinho, near Largo do Machado, is a pleasant wooded area with gardens and playgrounds. Within the park is the **Palácio das Laranjeiras**, the state governor's residence as well as apartment buildings designed by Lucio Costa.

Rua Pinheiro Machado **Palácio Guanabara**, Rua Pinheiro Machado, Laranjeiras, was the official residence of Princess Isabel and today is used by the State government. ■ *Mon-Fri 0900-1200, 1400-1700, Sat-Sun 0800-1600, T2054242.*

Next door is the home ground of **Fluminense Football Club**, Rua Alvaro Chaves 41, with a capacity of 10,000. The club was founded in 1902 and the first stands were built in 1905. In 1915 an expansion began including a new clubhouse and the stadium was inaugurated again in 1919. Although struggling in the lower divisions today, the club has a distinguished history and remains extremely popular with its supporters. ■ *T5537240, www.flu.com.br*

Essentials

Sleeping
■ *on map, page 120*

Glória **L** *Glória*, R do Russel 632, T5557272, F5557282, www.hotelgloriario.com.br Stylish and elegant old building, business and convention centre, fitness centre with two swimming pools. Recommended. **B** *Turístico*, Ladeira da Glória 30, T5577698. With breakfast, a/c, tourist information provided, mixed reports, some highly favourable. **D** *Opera*, R Santo Amaro 75, near Glória Metrô, T2423585. **Camping** If travelling by trailer, you can park at the Marina Glória car park, where there are showers and toilets, a small shop and snack bar. Pay the guards to look after your vehicle.

Catete and Flamengo **L** *Novo Mundo*, Praia Flamengo 20, T5574355, F2652369. Noisy. Recommended. **AL** *Flórida*, R Ferreira Viana 71/81, near Praia de Flamengo, T5565242, F2855777. Sauna, pool, safe, quiet. Good views, great breakfast. Recommended. **AL** *Rondônia Palace*, R Buarque de Macedo 60, T5560616, F5584133, www.ism.com.br/~comsut/hotelrondonia A/c, sauna, TV, safe, bar and restaurant. **A** *Regina*, R Ferreira Viana 29, T5561647, F2852999, hotelregina@hotelregina.com.br Very safe, good breakfast. **B** *Argentina*, Cruz Lima 30, T5587233, F5574447. Best rooms on 5th floor, cheapest on first. Recommended. **B** *Imperial*, R do Catete 186, T5565212, F5585815. A/c, TV, phone, pool, garage, smart. **B** *Paysandu*, R Paissandu 23, T2257270. Very clean, comfortable and good value, helpful staff, good location, organized tours available. **C** *Caxambu*, R Correia Dutra 22, T2659496. With bath, TV, popular cheap hotel. **C** *Inglês*, R Silveira Martins 20, T5583052, F5583447. A/c, TV, phone, reasonable breakfast. **C** *Único*, Buarque de Macedo 54, near Largo do Machado Metrô, T2059932, F2058149. TV, a/c, fridge, safe parking, large breakfast. Recommended. **D** *Ferreira Viana*, R Ferreira Viana 58, T2057396. With breakfast. **D** *Monte Blanco*, R do Catete 160, near Catete Metrô, T2250121. Good breakfast, a/c, radio, clean and friendly, refurbished in 1999. Recommended. **D** *Monterrey*, R Artur Bernardes 39-B, T2659899. Fan, TV, phone, some rooms small and poorly lit. **D** *Rio Claro*, R do Catete 233, T5585180. Small rooms, breakfast, a/c, safe. Recommended. **D** *Rio Lisboa*, R Artur Bernardes 29, T2659599. A/c (but staff will not always turn it on), a few cheaper single rooms **E**, safe, breakfast is just coffee, a roll and some crackers; both hotels in this quiet street are family hotels (luck and patience are needed to get a room, no reservations either by phone or in person). **D** *Serrano*, R Gago Coutinho 22, near Largo de Machado Metrô, T2853233. Pleasant, helpful. **D** *Venezuela*, R Paissandu 34, T5577098, A/c, TV, very clean but small rooms with short/round beds and poor breakfast. **D** *Vitória*, R do Catete 172, T2055397. With breakfast, hot water, a/c, friendly, mixed reports.

Where to go on the beach?

Although everyone is equal on the beach it has over the years become naturally divided into distinct areas frequented by different ages, social classes and interests. Below is a brief guide to help in finding the spot that is right for you:

At Leme the beach is mainly home to families from this residential neighbourhood as well as people from the favela in this area. In Copacabana near Travessa Fernando Mendes at Posto 3 there is a concentration of gays and transvestites. Between Rua Santa Clara and Rua Constante Ramos are younger people and foot volley players. Near Rua Xavier da Silveira is a meeting place for tourists and prostitutes. At Posto 5 are many people from the nearby favela whilst the beach at Posto 6 generally has older and retired people.

At Arpoador you will find many surfers whilst in Ipanema near Posto 8 are mainly people from the nearby favela. Near Rua Farme de Amoedo is a gay meeting point. At Posto 9 there is a mixed group of intellectuals, young people, bohemians and people playing foot volley. The young beautiful people gather near Rua Garcia d'Ávila.

Young people tend to meet at the Barraca do Pepê in Barra da Tijuca whilst Barramares is popular with famous football players.

Beatrix Boscardin

Mid-range *Alcaparra*, Praia do Flamengo 150, T5577236. Elegant traditional restaurant with varied menu, open daily 1200-0200. *Alho e Óleo*, R Buarque de Macedo 13, Flamengo, T5578541. Fashionable but pleasant with international menu, open daily from 1200. Recommended. *Café Glória*, R do Russel 734, Glória. Beautiful Art Nouveau building, helpful staff, excellent food and varied wine list, open daily for lunch and dinner. *Casa da Suíça*, R Cândido Mendes 157, Glória, T2525182. Bar and restaurant with good atmosphere. *Majórica*, R Senador Vergueiro 15, Flamengo, T2056820. Long-established steak house, open daily for lunch and dinner. *Restaurante do MAM*, Av Infante Dom Henrique 85, Aterro do Flamengo, T5337378. Good varied menu, open daily from 1200.

Eating
on map, page 120
There are a lot of eating places on R do Catete & R Cândido Mendes

Cheap *Gaúcha Rio*, R das Laranjeiras 114. Good *churrascaria*. *Luigi's*, R Senador Corrêa 10, Laranjeiras. Good Italian food. *Museum*, in Museu da República, R do Catete 153. Good varied menu in nice surroundings, open daily for lunch and for dinner Fri-Sat.

Very cheap *Amazônia*, R do Catete 234B, downstairs. One price counter service, upstairs for good, reasonably priced evening meals. Recommended. *Catete Grill*, R do Catete 239. Good. *Catelandia*, R do Catete 204. Excellent and cheap, pay by weight. *Restaurante e Pizzaria Guanabara*, R do Catete 150. Excellent value and selection. *Galícia Grill*, R do Catete 265. Very good pizza, good service. *O Bom Galeto*, R do Catete 282, Largo do Machado. Chicken and meats. Next door is *Trattoria Gambino*, recommended for pasta, pleasant on summer evenings. *Rotisseria Sirio Libaneza*, in gallery at Largo de Machado 29. Very good value Arabic food.

This is not a particularly good area for bars and nightlife. Young people do gather in the Largo do Machado but most people are dining in the many restaurants. *Casa Brasil*, R Senador Correia 33, Praça São Salvador. Neighbourhood bar with outside tables, 0600-Midnight Mon-Sat. *Lamas*, R Marquês de Abrantes 18, Flamengo. Excellent value bar and restaurant with good food with great atmosphere, 0730-0300 daily, popular with Brazilian arts/media people. Recommended. *Picote*, R Marquês do Paraná 128 corner of R Marquês de Abrantes, Flamengo. Simple bar with good snacks especially *bolinhos de bacalhau*, 0600-0100 Mon-Sat, 0800-1800 Sun.

Bars & nightclubs

GLÓRIA, CATETE AND FLAMENGO

Entertainment **Art galleries** *Espaço do Catete*, In Museu da República (see above), T2856350.

Carnival blocos *Bloco do Cachorro Cansado*, parades on Mon evening during carnival from Bar Miki, R Barão de Flamengo 35. *Banda da Glória*, parades on Sun afternoon during carnival from the Largo da Glória.

Cinema *Estação Museu da República*, In Museu da República (see above). *Largo do Machado*, Largo do Machado 29. Two screens. *Estação Paissandu*, R Senador Vergueiro 35. *São Luiz*, R do Catete 307. Two screens.

Music *Bistrô Lavazza*, garden of Museu da República (see above). Choro from 1830-2200 Fri-Sat.

Theatre *Teatro Cacilda Becker*, R do Catete 338, T2659933. *Teatro Glória*, R do Russel 632, T5557262. *Teatro do Museu da República*, In Museu da República (see above), T2856350.

Shopping **Bookshops** *Unilivros*, Largo do Machado 29C. French and English bestsellers.

Handicrafts *Brumado*, R das Laranjeiras 486. Baskets, carvings, ceramics and many other items. *Pé do Boi*, R Ipiranga 55, Laranjeiras. Crafts from all over Brazil particularly Pernambuco and Minas Gerais.

Markets Sun market on R da Glória, colourful, cheap fruit, vegetables and flowers. *Feira do Livro*, Largo do Machado, selling books at 20% discount.

Tour operators *Dantur*, in Galeria Condor, Largo do Machado 29, T2051144, F2059918. Helena speaks English and is friendly and helpful. *Marlin Yacht Charters*, Marina da Glória, shop A1, T2257434, Cell99869678. Sailing and motor launch excursions to Angra dos Reis and Búzios. *Sangetur São Geraldo*, in Galeria Condor, Largo do Machado 29, T2050993, F2208268. Credit cards only accepted for airplane tickets. *Saveiros Tour*, R Conde de Lages 44, office 1001, near Glória Metrô, T2246990, F2522227. Boat trips to Angra dos Reis and islands, also rent yachts and speedboats.

Directory **Banks** Money changers: In Galeria Condor, Largo do Machado 29 are *Câmbio Nick* and *Casa Franca*. **Communications** Internet: In Museu da República (see above), US$3.50 per hr. **Laundry** *Fénix*, R do Catete 214, shop 20. *Lavelev*, R Buarque de Macedo 43B, Catete. *Lavlev Flamengo*, RC de Baependi 78, or R das Laranjeiras 43. **Medical services** 24 hr pharmacy: *Drogaria Pachecho*, R do Catete 248. **Places of worship** *Igreja De Santíssima Trinidade*, R Senador Euzébio 366, Flamengo. Roman catholic services in French at 1600 Sat. *Swedish Church (Igreja Escandinava)*, Av Rui Barbosa 170, Flamengo, T5516696. Services in Swedish at 0700 Sun.

Santa Teresa

This hilly inner suburb southwest of the centre is well known as the coolest part of Rio. It boasts many colonial and 19th century buildings, set in narrow, curving, tree-lined streets. Santa Teresa attracted well-to-do and foreign inhabitants not only because of its cooler climate, but also because it was free of the yellow fever which infested the lower parts of the city. Today, Santa Teresa's old houses are lived in by artists, intellectuals and makers of handicrafts. Many buildings between Largo do Guimarães and Largo das Neves are being restored.

Most visitors in the daytime will arrive on the tram (see 'Transport', page 128). If you stay to the end of the line, Largo das Neves, you will be able to appreciate the small-town feel of the place. There are several bars here. Either on the way back, or on the way up from the centre, the essential stop is the Largo do Guimarães, which has some excellent eating places and a great atmosphere.

History

In 1624, Antônio Gomes do Desterro erected a hermitage dedicated to Nossa Senhora do Desterro on the hill which was to become Santa Teresa. The name was changed from Morro do Desterro to Santa Teresa after the construction in 1750 of a convent in honour of two Carmelite sisters, Jacinta and Francisca. The Convento da Santa Teresa, at Rua Joaquim Murtinho and Ladeira de Santa Teresa, can only be seen from the outside; the Carmelite nuns do not admit visitors. From the 17th to the mid-18th century, work was done in various stages to bring water from the Rio Carioca to the city. The final project was the Aqueduto dos Arcos (Arcos da Lapa), which carried water from Santa Teresa to the Chafariz da Carioca, with its 16 fountains, in the centre of the city. The aqueduct's use was changed at the end of the 19th century with the introduction of electric trams in Rio. The inaugural run along the tracks laid on top of the arches was on 1 September 1896. It has been a major task to preserve the Santa Teresa tram, called the *bondinho*, the last such service in Rio.

Sights

Some of the fine historical residences that can be seen include a castle-like house in Vista Alegre (the Casa de Valentim), the tiled Chácara dos Viegas in Rua Monte Alegre, and the Chalé Murtinho, Rua Murtinho Nobre 41. Also in the district is the old hotel known as the *Hotel das Paineiras*. See also the Rua Aprazível and Largo do Guimarães.

The Chácara do Céu, or Fundação Raymundo Ottoni de Castro Maia, Rua Murtinho Nobre 93, has a wide range of art objects and modern painters, including Brazilian; exhibitions change through the year. Castro Maia's former residence is also a museum (see page 159). ■ T5071932, www.visualnet.com.br/cmaya Daily except Tue 1200-1700. US$1. Take the Santa Teresa tram to Curvelo station, walk along Rua Dias de Barros, following the signposts to Parque das Ruínas. **Chácara do Céu**

Parque das Ruínas, Rua Martinho Nobre 169, was the old three storey mansion in which Dona Laurinda Santos Lobo, a rich Brazilian heiress brought up in France, held her famous artistic, political and intellectual salons at the turn of the 20th century. Abandoned for decades after her death, the house was in ruins until it was donated to the city, partially restored and turned into a **Parque das Ruínas** cultural centre in 1998. The outside walls have been kept and the inside rebuilt in a bold architectural style, with modern materials such as iron, rubber and glass. The visitors walk up the steps seeing art exhibits on the walls and superb views of the city through the huge windows. There is a nice garden, an exhibition space, an open-air stage and a snack bar. ■ *T2520112. 1000-1700 Mon-Wed, 1000-2300 Thu, 1000-2000 Fri-Sun. A bridge connects it to the Chácara do Céu (see above).*

Casa de Benjamin Constant Casa de Benjamin Constant, Rua Monte Alegre 255, has a museum in the home of Benjamin Constant de Magalhães, the leader of Brazil's republican movement and the founder of an institute for blind children. The tree lined gardens surrounding the house are also open to the public. ■ *T5091248. Thu-Sun 1300-1700, gardens open daily 0800-1800. Guided visits by appointment.*

Museu do Bonde Until 1998, located in the tram station in Centro, Museu do Bonde, Rua Carlos Brant 14, has very good photographs of old Rio which show the history of trams in the city from the first horse drawn trams to the end of the service in 1960. The collection includes equipment, conductor's uniforms, scale models and a full size tram (made for a TV series). The caretaker Lia is very friendly and will show videos about the district and the trams. ■ *T2422354. Daily 0900-1600, free entry but souvenirs can be bought to support the museum.*

Centro Cultural Laurinda Santos Lobo Centro Cultural Laurinda Santos Lobo, Rua Monte Alegre 306, situated in a huge old mansion built in 1907, it holds cultural activities for local people and has a library, musical performances, videos, conferences, courses as well as a large exhibition space. ■ *T2429741.*

Essentials

Sleeping
Santa Teresa has few places to stay & transport to other parts of the city can be difficult

C *Santa Teresa*, R Almte Alexandrino 660, near Largo do Guimarães, T5089088. 19th century house with good views, breakfast included, pool, parking, rooms can also be rented by the month, US$250, cheaper without private bathroom. **C** *Bela Vista*, R Pascoal Carlos Magno 5, between Largo do Guimarães and Largo das Neves, T2429346. Cheaper without private bathroom, with breakfast, parking.

Eating
● *on map, page 120*

Mid-range *Aprazível*, R Aprazível 62, T/F5089174. Excellent food and service in beautiful surroundings both inside the house or outside on the terrace and garden. Wonderful view over the city, live choro on Thu, open 2000-2400 Thu-Fri, lunch and dinner until 2400 on Sat, 1200-1800 Sun, reservations advised. Recommended.

Cheap *Adega do Pimenta*, R Almte Alexandrino 296, near Largo do Guimarães, T2247554. Very small German restaurant with excellent sausages, sauerkraut and cold beer, open 1130-2200 Mon, Wed-Fri, 1100-1800 Sun. Recommended. *Bar do Arnaudo*, R Almte Alexandrino 316, near Largo do Guimarães, T2527246. One of the best restaurants in Rio it is simple inside, decorated with handicrafts, the cuisine is northeastern, prices are reasonable and portions huge, try the *caipirinhas*, the *carne do sol* (sun-dried beef, or jerky) with *feijão de corda* (brown beans and herbs), or the *queijo coalho* (a country cheese, grilled), open 1200-2200 Tue-Sat, 1200-1600 Sun. Recommended. *Cantina Guzzo*, R Almte Alexandrino 256. Italian restaurant and pizzeria, open 1730-2330 Mon-Thu, 1200-2330 Fri-Sat, 1200-2200 Sun. *Sansuchi*, R Almte Alexandrino 382, T2520581. Japanese food and *tempura* ice-cream, open 1900-2400, Tue-Fri, 1200-1600, 1900-Midnight Sat, 1200-2000 Sun. *Sobrado das Massas*, R Almte Alexandrino 6, at the Curvelo tram stop after Largo do Guimarães on the way to Centro, T2420280. Italian restaurant specializing in pasta

Rio's youth

Many young people in Rio hang out in the streets in areas where the bars are too small for the number of people who come on Friday and Saturday nights. These are often known as Baixos such as the Baixo Gávea around Praça Santos Dumont. The name comes from Baixo Leblon, the famous hang out corner where intellectuals, artists and later young people gathered in the 1970s. Today there are many different youth tribes in Rio. Mauricinhos and Patricinhas are the slang names for the rich young kids who consume every new fashionable product or behaviour from abroad and deny Brazilian cultural roots. Mauricio and Patricia are common names given to children of upper middle class families that have somehow come to represent this new consumerist lifestyle. The young people who visit what's jokingly becoming known as Baixo Santa in Santa Teresa are however generally the sons and daughters of the youth who moved to the district in the early seventies, starting adult life in hippie style communities. They don't go to fashionable dance music discos like Mauricinhos do, but instead dance forró or at least reggae, dress very casually and wear their hair long.

There are also many other youth groups in the city such as the Vanguard clubbers who only go to techno discos as well as the ever popular and very expressive surfer groups who are always to be seen with their boards on Rio's beaches. Pitbulls are shaved head and strong jujitsu fighters that sensible people should stay away from in or when leaving night clubs. Their girlfriends are often referred to as Maria Tatame after the exercise mats in their practice dojos. Another worry for anxious parents is their daughters becoming nicknamed Maria Fuzil (Rifle Mary) and visiting funk parties in the favelas with boyfriends who are sometimes armed drug dealers. These shanty town balls have become the latest fad on the dark dangerous side of town which so often fascinates youth.

Denise Werneck

---

and pizzas but at weekends serves an excellent feijoada, open 1800-2330 Tue-Fri, 1130-2330 Sat-Sun.

Bars *Estação do Chopp*, R Almte Alexandrino 6, at Curvelo tram stop. Open daily 1200-2300 except Tue. *Goiabeira*, Largo das Neves 13. Simple and charming with a nice view of the praça, variety of good *cachaça*. ***Bar do Mineiro***, R Pascoal Carlos Magno 99, near Largo do Guimarães. Bar with good comida mineira, walls are decorated with painted tiles and photographs. ***Salamalekun***, R Progresso 5, near Largo das Neves. ***Sobrenatural***, near Largo do Guimarães. Very good fish, closed Sun. Small bars in Largo do Guimarães such as ***Bar do Marco***, and ***Simplesmente***, good fried aipim, and are popular with young people who quickly fill the square on Fri and Sat nights (see box 'Rio's youth').

Bars & nightclubs

Nightclubs *Lagoinha*, Estr Dom Joaquim Mamede 125. Forró, pagode and reggae, entry US$6.

Art galleries Many artists in Santa Teresa welcome visitors to their workshops but make appointments in advance. *HB 195*, R Hermenegildo Barros 195. Exhibitions of contemporary artists with good views from balcony, 1400-1900 Wed-Sun.

Entertainment

Carnival blocos *Carmelitas de Santa Teresa*, R Dias de Barros corner of Ladeira de Santa Teresa, close to the Carmelites Convent. Rehearsals every Sat from New Year's until Carnival and a parade in the district on the Fri and Tue nights during the festivities.

Music *Parque das Ruinas*, see above. Live Jazz from 1900-2200 on Thu. *Sobrenatural*, see above. Musicians play samba from about 2300, informal but of a high standard, it's hard to find a table after 2230, but you can sit outside, which is still fun. Best nights are Wed, Thu and Fri.

Festivals *Arte de Portas Abertas* (Open Doors Art) is an art festival that happens twice a year during the last weekend of both May and Nov. Created by the neighbourhood movement *Viva Santa*, artists who live in the district open up their beautiful restored old houses, where they usually live and work, to the public who can visit and buy sculptures, paintings, photography and other works of art.

Security In recent years, visitors have been put off going to Santa Teresa because of a reputation for crime which has spilled over from neighbouring *favelas*. It would, however, be a great shame to miss this unique town-within-a-city. The crime rate has been reduced and normally a policeman rides each *bondinho*, but you are advised not to take valuables or look 'wealthy'. A T-shirt, shorts and enough money for a meal should be sufficient. Avoid long walks on streets that are far from the main centres of Largo das Neves and Largo do Guimarães. The area around the Hotel das Paineiras is well patrolled.

Shopping **Handicrafts** *La Vereda*, R Almte Alexandrino 428, near Largo dos Guimarães. Very interesting little store, also open at weekends, selling a great variety of craft pieces from different states of Brazil in particular Minas Gerais and indigenous crafts from Acre. You can also buy the work of Santa Teresa's artists as well as a wooden miniature of the yellow tram.

Tour operators Many tour operators offer Santa Teresa as an option on their city tours. On Sat guided tours of the district are run on the tram (see below). In the morning at 1000 the ecological tram runs from Largo do Carioca through Santa Teresa and the forest to the Silvestre Corcovado train station (there is a project to connect these two rides in the future). In the afternoon at 1400, the historical tram runs to Largo das Neves. Reservations with Fatima at the Tram Museum, T2221003, US$2.50. *Rio Hiking*, R Almte Alexandrino 3226, apartment 404, RJ 20241-262, T/F97210594, Cell97210594, www.riohiking.com.br Offer walking tours of Tijuca Forest and Santa Teresa, Corvocado, Sugar Loaf (climbing if preferred), Pedra da Gávea and other locations in the state such as Ilha Grande and Itaitaia National Park. Small groups only and hotel pick up, friendly guides speak English, French and Spanish.

Transport Santa Teresa is best visited on the traditional open-sided **tram**, the *bondinho* (see 'Arcos da Lapa' above). To get to the *bondinho* station, take the Metrô to Cinelândia, go to R Senador Dantas then walk along to R Professor Lélio Gama (look for *Banco do Brasil* on the corner). The station is up this street. Take the line called Paula Mattos (a second line is Dois Irmãos) and enjoy the trip as it passes over the aqueduct, winding its way up to the district's historic streets. The journey ends at the round praça called Largo das

HIKING IN RIO

HIKING TOURS THROUGH FOREST TRAILS TO THE TOP OF RIO'S MOST FAMOUS MOUNTAINS

Information and Reservation
phone/fax: 55 21 2453630
mobile 55 21 97210594
tours@riohiking.com.br
www.riohiking.com.br

The 'bond'

The tram which runs to and from Santa Teresa is the last example of a form of public transport which used to run in many Brazilian cities. Before electrification, street cars were pulled by mules. The first street car lines were financed by securities, or share bonds, but when one of the first tramway companies failed, its shares became worthless. The term 'bonds', though, stuck, first as a form of rebuke, then as the name for all trolleys and trams. Hence bonde and, in Rio, the even more familiar bondinho.

Neves; here the tram turns round for the journey back to R Professor Lélio Gama. The trams are open-sided; do not carry valuables. Fare US$0.35 one way. **Bus** Nos 206 and 214 run from Avenida Rio Branco in the centre to Santa Teresa. There are also VW Kombis marked Cooper JD which serve the same routes as the buses for the same price, US$0.50. At night, it's best to take a **taxi** (see page 54).

Corcovado and Cosme Velho

To reach the statue of the Cristo Redentor at the summit of Corcovado, you follow the road west out of Catete through Laranjeiras and Cosme Velho past the Museu Internacional de Arte Naif do Brasil, with its colourful collection of folk art, and Largo do Boticário, a pleasant square reminiscent of colonial Rio. From here on the road is steep and curves steadily up the mountain through the Tijuca forest. Another option is the cog railway which climbs to the statue from the station at Cosme Velho. There are magnificent views of Rio and Niterói from the top and this is definitely one of the most famous picture postcard scenes of the city. Other nearby viewpoints such as Mirante da Dona Marta are lower and less crowded with tourists.

Sights

The **Museu Internacional de Arte Naif do Brasil** (MIAN), Rua Cosme Velho 561, is one of the most comprehensive museums of Naive and folk paintings in the world. It is only 30 m uphill, on the same street as the station for Corcovado. There is a permanent collection of some 8,000 works by Naive artists from about 130 countries. The museum also hosts several thematic and temporary exhibitions through the year. Parts of its collection travel to other museums and exhibitions around the world. There is a café and a souvenir shop, where you can buy small paintings by some of the artists on display, books, postcards and T-shirts. Courses and workshops on painting and related subjects are offered. ■ *T2058612, F2058884. Tue-Fri 1000-1800, Sat, Sun and holidays 1200-1800; closed on Mon. The entry ticket costs US$2.50, but there are are special prices for groups, students and senior citizens.*

Cosme Velho
See also box on next page

If you want to see what Rio was like early in the 19th century, go to the **Largo do Boticário**, Rua Cosme Velho 822, a charming small square in neo-colonial style. Much of the material used in creating the effect of the square came from old buildings demolished in the city centre. The four houses that front the square are painted different colours (white, pale blue, caramel, pink), each with different features picked out in decorative tiles, woodwork and stone. The square is close to the terminus for the Corcovado cog railway.

Brazil's International Museum of Naive Art

MIAN, the Museu Internacional de Arte Naif do Brasil, grew out of the private collection of Lucien Finkelstein, a French jewellery designer who lives in Brazil and who, about 40 years ago, started to buy Naive paintings all over Brazil and abroad, on his frequent international trips. As the collection grew so large, he decided to create a foundation and in October 1995 the museum opened its doors to the public. The current director is Jaqueline Finkelstein. The museum is located in a huge, spacious old house surrounded by gardens and trees.

Naive painters have no formal academic training. For this reason, each develops his or her own personal style, using pure, bright colours, as well as peculiar uses of perspective, composition and materials. The subject matter varies from scenes of daily life, to folk festivals, religion and lively landscapes. The international section gathers together works from several countries, from the 17th century to today, including the world-famous paintings on glass from former Yugoslavia (The Hlebine school) and impressive campesino paintings on leather from Ecuador.

The Brazilian section is remarkable for the vibrant tropical colours and the diversity of subjects. Among the most representative Brazilian Naive painters, the museum has several works by Antônio Poteiro, José Antônio da Silva, Rosina Becker do Vale, Lia Mittarakis and others (including our own Fábio Sombra). One of the most interesting works is an enormous painting (four metres by seven metres) by Lia Mittarakis, in the main hall, showing the city of Rio de Janeiro. This colourful work, full of funny details, is considered the biggest Naive painting in the world and took five years to complete.

Corcovado Corcovado is a hunch-backed peak, 710 m high, surmounted by a 30 m high statue of Christ the Redeemer, O Cristo Redentor on an 8m pedestal, which was completed on 12 October 1931. There is a superb view from the top (sometimes obscured by mist), to which there are a cog railway and a road; both cars and train put down their passengers behind the statue. The 3.8 km railway itself offers fine views. The railway was opened on 9 October 1884 by Emperor Dom Pedro II. Steam trains were used to begin with, but electric trains replaced them in 1910. The current rolling stock is Swiss and dates from 1979. Average speed is 15 kph on the way up and 12 kph on the way down. From the upper terminus there is a climb of 220 steps to the top (although an escalator is being installed and should be operational by the end of 2000), near which there is a café. To see the city by day and night ascend at 1500 or 1600 and descend on the last train, approximately 1815. Mass is held on Sunday in a small chapel in the statue pedestal. The floodlighting, which has changed back to its original greenish tinge, was designed in 1931 by Marconi and came into operation in the following year. ■ *T/F5581329, www.corvocado.com.br Daily 0830-1900. Take a Cosme Velho bus to the cog railway station at Rua Cosme Velho 513: from the centre or Glória/Flamengo No 180, 184; from Copacabana take No 583, from Botafogo or Ipanema/Leblon No 583 or 584; from Santa Teresa Microônibus Santa Teresa. The train runs every 20-30 mins according to demand between 0800 and 1830, journey time 10 mins (cost: US$9 return; single tickets available). Also, a 206 bus does the very attractive run from Praça Tiradentes (or a 407 from Largo do Machado) to Silvestre (the railway has no stop here now). An active walk of 9 km will bring one to the top and the road is shady. Take the narrow street to the right of the station, go through the gate used by people who live beside the tracks and continue to the national park entrance. Walkers are not usually charged entrance fees. Allow a minimum of 2 hrs (up to 4 depending on fitness) for the climb. For safety reasons go in company, or at weekends when more people are about. If going by car to Corcovado, the entrance fee is US$4 for the vehicle,* plus US$4 for each passenger. Coach trips tend to be rather brief and taxis which wait in front of the station offering tours of Corcovado and Mirante Dona Marta are expensive and offer no information.

A nearby Viewpoint is the **Mirante da Dona Marta** (340 m) off the Corcovado road, with the same direction of view as the Corcovado, but as it is lower, the details can be seen more clearly. There is no public transport.

Botafogo, Urca and Pão de Açúcar

As the crow flies, the district of Botafogo sits roughly mid-way between the Pão de Açúcar and Corcovado. On the ground, access to either peak from this part of the city is quite straightforward, but it involves many more twists and turns than a bird would take. There are also plenty of other attractions at ground level.

For a long time, Botafogo was the terminus of Linha 1 of the Metrô, but an extension to Arcoverde in Copacabana has now been constructed. It is a major road junction for routes from the centre to Urca, Copacabana and Jardim Botânico. In the district is the Morro do Pasmado, which has fine views of the bay. Also in Botafogo is one of the city's main shopping malls, Rio Sul, a good place to go for entertainment, services, eating and, of course, shopping.

Sights

The **Casa de Rui Barbosa**, Rua São Clemente 134, former home of the Brazilian jurist and statesman, contains his library and other possessions and a public library specializing in law and literature. ■ *T5370036, www.casaruibarbosa.gov.br Tue-Fri 0900-1600, Sat, Sun and holidays 1400-1700, free entry on Sun. The large garden is also open to the public. Buses 106, 176, 178 from the centre; 571 from Flamengo; 591 from Copacabana.*

Botafogo

Centro de Arquitetura e Urbanismo, Rua São Clemente 117, has exhibitions of architecture and city planning in a 19th-century mansion restored in 1995. ■ *Tue-Sun 1200-1900.*

The **Museu do Índio**, Rua das Palmeiras 55, is being partly renovated so there is only a small exhibition. It houses 12,000 objects from many Brazilian Indian groups, including basketry, ceramics, masks and weapons. There is also a small, well-displayed handicraft shop (shop closes for lunch 1200-1400). It belongs to the *Fundação Nacional do Índio* (Funai) and was set up by Marechal Rondon. There is also a library of ethnology open during the week, which has friendly and helpful staff. ■ *T2868799, www.museodoindio.org.br Tue-Fri 1000-1730, Sat-Sun 1300-1700. From Botafogo Metrô it's a 10 min walk; from Catete, bus 571 (Glória-Leblon) passes Ruas Bento Lisboa and São Clemente.*

Museu Villa-Lobos, Rua Sorocaba 200, houses a collection of personal objects belonging to the great composer, with instruments, scores, books and recordings. ■ *T/F2663845. Mon-Fri 1000-1730.*

Museu dos Teatros, Rua São João Batista 103/105, has documents and exhibits from the history of theatre in Rio de Janeiro including photographs and costumes. There is also a library with books dating back to the 17th century. ■ *T2863234. Mon-Fri 1100-1630.*

On Praia de Botafogo is the **Guanabara Regatta Club** see page 76 whilst close to the Universidade Federal do Rio de Janeiro is the clubhouse of **Clube Botafogo de Futebol e Regatas**, Avenida Venceslau Braz 71. The football club dates back to 1904 (the rowing club to 1892) and they began to play at General Severiano in 1912. Famous players have included both Garrincha and Bebeto. ■ *T/F5437272, www.botafogo.com.br*

Immediately opposite the university is the **Iate Clube do Rio de Janeiro** (see page 76), founded in 1920 by Carioca high society for regattas, cruises and fishing, on the piece of land where the Morro da Viúva Fort once stood.

Casa da Ciência, Rua Lauro Müller 3, part of the Federal university has concerts, plays as well as interactive scientific exhibitions. ■ *T5427494, www.cciência.ufrj.br Tue-Fri 0900-2000, Sat-Sun 1000-2000.*

Urca The suburb of Urca was built in 1922 when an *aterro* was made at the base ot the Pão de Açúcar on its north side. It is mostly residential. Note the small **statue of São Pedro** holding the keys to heaven on a rock in the sea in front of the church. From the esplanade there are lovely views of the sunset behind Corcovado.

The **Fortaleza de São João**, Avenida João Luis Alves, was built by Estácio de Sá in 1565 and has been expanded many times since. Garrisoned by the coastal artillery until 1991 it now houses a physical training center and staff college. ■ *T5433323, extension 2056. Mon-Thu 0900-1200, 1400-1600, Fri 0900-1100.*

Museu de Ciências da Terra, Avenida Pasteur 404, 2nd floor, Praia Vermelha, has a collection of minerals, rocks, ore, mateorites and fossils. ■ *T2950032, www.dnpm.gov.br/museu Mon-Fri 1000-1600, free entry. Guided tours by appointment via F2953895.*

Pão de Açúcar At 396 m, the Pão de Açúcar, or Sugar Loaf, is a massive granite cone at the entrance to Guanabara Bay. The bird's eye view of the city and beaches that it affords is very beautiful. There is a restaurant (great location, shame about the food, closes 1900) and a playground for children on the Morro da Urca, half

Urca, Botafogo, Cosme Velho

way up, where there are also shows at night (consult the cultural sections in the newspapers). You can also get refreshments at the top.

The sea level cable car station is in a military area, so it is safe to visit. At Praia Vermelha, the beach to the south of the rock, is the *Círculo Militar da Praia Vermelha* restaurant, which is open to the public (no sign). It has wonderful views, but is not so good for food or service; stop there for a drink anyway. From Praia Vermelha, the Pista Cláudio Coutinho runs around the foot of the rock. It is a paved path for walking and jogging and gives access to various climbing places. It is open until 1800, but you can stay on the path after that. Here you have mountain, forest and sea side-by-side, right in the heart of the city. You can also use the Pista Coutinho as a way of getting up the Pão de Açúcar more cheaply than the US$12.50 cable-car ride. About 350 m from the path entrance is a track to the left which leads though the forest to Morro de Urca, from where the cable car can be taken for US$10 (you can come down this way, too, but if you take the cable car from sea level you must pay full fare). You can save even more money, but use more energy, by climbing the Caminho da Costa, a path to the summit of the Pão de Açúcar. Only one stretch, of 10 m, requires climbing gear (even then, some say it is not necessary), but if you wait at the bottom of the path for a group going up, they will let you tag along. This way you can descend to Morro de Urca by cable car for free and walk down from there.

There are 35 rock routes up the mountain, with various degrees of difficulty. The best months for climbing are April to August. See 'Sports' in Essentials chapter, page 68, for climbing clubs; there is also a book on climbing routes.

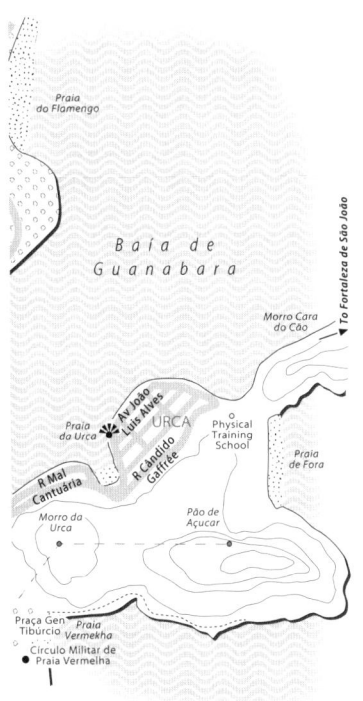

■ *Bus: 107 (from the centre, Catete or Flamengo) and 511 from Copacabana (512 to return) take you to the cable-car station, Avenida Pasteur 520, at the foot. Cable car: Praia Vermelha to Morro de Urca: first car goes up at 0800, then every 30 mins (or when full), until the last comes down at 2200. From Urca to Sugar Loaf, the first connecting cable car goes up at 0815 then every 30 mins (or when full), until the last leaves the summit at 2200; the return trip costs US$8 (US$6 to Morro da Urca, half-way up). The old cableway has been completely rebuilt. Termini are ample and efficient and the present Italian cable cars carry 75 passengers. Even on the most crowded days there is little queuing.*

Essentials

Sleeping
These are mainly residential areas with few hotels

C *Real*, R Real Grandeza 122, Botafogo, T2863093, F2863331. Comfortable and good value, close to restaurants.

Youth hostel E pp *Chave do Rio de Janeiro*, R Gen Dionísio 63, Botafogo, T2860303, F2865652. IYHA, slightly more expensive for non-members, clean, laundry and cooking facilities, good breakfast, can be noisy. Recommended. This excellent youth hostel is one of the best places to stay in Rio for budget travellers.

Eating
There are many good places to eat to suit all budgets. R Visconde de Caravelas in Botafogo has several interesting bars & restaurants whilst Rio Sul Shopping Center between Botafogo & Urca has a lot of choice for food

Expensive *Carême*, R Visconde de Caravelas 113, Botafogo, T5375431. Excellent food but reservations necessary, open from 1900 Tue-Sat.

Mid-range *Adega do Valentim*, R da Passagem 178, T5411166. Portuguese with good *bacalhau* cod, open daily 1200-0100. Portuguese music from 2200 Fri-Sat. *Clube Gourmet*, R Gen Polidoro 186, T2951097. Excellent French cuisine, open 1200-1530, 2000-0030 Thu-Fri, 2000-0100 Sat, 1200-1700 Sun. *Kotobuki*, in *Botafogo Praia* shopping center, T5599595. Japanese with traditional tables and sushi bar, good view, open daily 1100-Midnight. *Zen*, basement of *Centro Empresarial*, Praia de Botafogo 228, T5535060. Popular Japanese, open 1200-1430, 1900-2330 Mon-Fri, 1900-2330 Sat. Recommended.

Cheap *Aurora*, R Capitão Salomão 43. Bar and restaurant with dishes that serve two, walls display old photographs of Rio, 1100-Midnight Mon-Thu, 1100-0200 Fri-Sat. *Botequim*, R Visconde de Caravelas 184. Varied menu of good value Brazilian food, steak, fries and *chopp* is the house's speciality, open 1130-0100 Mon-Thu and Sun, 1130-0200 Fri-Sat. *Pizza Park*, in *Cobal de Humaitá*, Rua Voluntários da Pátria 446. 25 flavours of pizza but check your bill, open daily 0800-Late. *Raajmahal*, R Gen Polidoro 29. Indian food. *Yorubá*, R Arnaldo Quintela 94, T5419387. Excellent Bahian food, open 1200-1500. 1900-Midnight Wed-Sat, 1200-2000 Sun, best to reserve in advance.

Very cheap Many different places to eat in Shopping Rio Sul, eg. *Chez Michou*, 4th floor. For crêpes and chopp; *Habib's* 1st floor. Fast Arabic food. *Cobal de Humaitá* is a fruit market with many popular restaurants such as Mexican *tacos*, pizzería, etc. *Manolo*, R Bambina and Marquês de Olinda. Very good value. *Violeta Café*, R Dona Mariana 277, Botafogo. Pay by weight buffet, lunch only Mon-Fri.

Bars & nightclubs

Botafogo has many bars and clubs popular with the city's gay and lesbian community especially near the corner of Rua Visconde de Silva and Rua Real Grandeza. Shopping Rio Sul also has many clubs and bars.

Bars *Adega da Velha*, R Paulo Barreto 25, Botafogo. Good chopp and cachaça as well as food from the Northeast of Brazil, 1100-0100 daily. *Big Ben Pub*, R Muniz Barreto 374, Botafogo. Bar games and live music, open 1500-0130 Mon-Thu, 1800-0200 Fri, 2100-0300 Sat. *Circulo Militar*, Praia Vermelha, Urca. Bar and restaurant with good views of Pão de Açúcar. *Loch Ness*, R Visconde de Silva 22. Popular gay meeting point. *Porão*, under the Anglican church hall, R Real Grandeza 99, Botafogo. Meeting place for British ex-pats on Fri only.

Nightclubs *The Ballroom*, R Humaitá 110. Buffet restaurant by day, disco and live music by night from 2200, pagode on Tue, forró on Thu, US$15 entry and minimum consumption. *Fun Club*, in *Shopping Rio Sul*, 4th floor. Popular disco bar. Open all night, very young crowd. *Le Maxim's Club*, at the top of the *Shopping Rio Sul* tower. Club with superb night view of Rio, entry for single women and couples only, open from 2230 Mon-Sat. *Terraço Rio Sul*, G3 *Shopping Rio Sul*. 80s night on Fri.

Art galleries *Fábio Sombra's Art Studio*, 5 mins walk from Sugar Loaf, please ring in advance to arrange visit (see 'Tour operators' below), www.fasombra.cjb.net (many of his paintings are on this website). Fábio is a well known Brazilian contemporary folk painter with works on display in the International Museum of Naive Art Anatole Jakovsky in Nice as well as in the Brazilian International Museum of Naive Art (see page 129). Self taught, he specializes in painting Rio's famous landscapes and street life in bright colours and joyful compositions. By visiting his studio you will have the opportunity to learn some of the secrets of his work, as well as to listen to interesting facts about Rio's history and culture. He also sells his original paintings, colour reproductions, posters and colourful T-shirts at very reasonable prices. If you are interested, please ask him to present his 10 min slide show, *The Rio Folk Experience*, a virtual city tour in Rio through 40 paintings.

Carnival blocos *Barbas*, meets on Sat afternoon during carnival at the "Bermuda Triangle" of R Assis Bueno, R Arnaldo Quintela and Gen Polidoro in Botafogo, so called due to the tendency for people to disappear in the crowd only to reappear after carnival with a smile on their face. *Dois Pra Lá, Dois Pra Cá*, meets on Sat afternoon during carnival in front of R da Passagem 145 and heads towards Copacabana accompanied by percussionists from the Grande Rio samba school. Known as the ballroom dancer's bloco, T-shirts, US$5, are compulsory and the group is cordoned off. Other blocos in Botafogo are *Bloco de Segunda* and *Boka de Espuma*.

Cinema Hollywood films mainly showing in Botafogo Praia, Rio Off-Price and Rio Sul shopping centres. *Espaço Unibanco*, R Voluntários da Pátria 35. Three screens showing mainly art house films, also has a good café. *Estação Botafogo*, R Voluntários da Pátria 88. Three screens of usually art films.

Music Many young Cariocas congregate in Botafogo for live music. *Canecão*, R Venceslau Brás 215, Botafogo, T5431241. Live shows of top Brazilian musicians and groups. Musical shows on Sun from 1900 at the *Mercado Forte* (see below).

Samba schools *São Clemente*, Sede Náutica do Botafogo F.R., Av Repórter Nestor Moreira, Praia de Botafogo, T5802121.

Theatre *Teatro Bibi Ferreira*, R Visconde de Ouro Preto 78, Botafogo.

Bookshops *Saraiva Megastore*, 3rd floor of Shopping Rio Sul. Very wide stock of books, CDs and multimedia. *Siciliano Megastore*, 4th floor of Botafogo Praia shopping centre. *Sodiler*, A03 Shopping Rio Sul. Second-hand English books at the Anglican church, R Real Grandeza 99.

Handicrafts *Artíndia*, In Museu do Índio (see above). Indian crafts including masks, musical instruments and weapons. *Jeito Brasileiro*, R Ererê 11A, Cosme Velho, next to the train to Corvocado. Crafts from all parts of Brazil.

Photography For processing, *One Hour Foto*, in Shopping Rio Sul. Recommended.

Shopping centres *Botafogo Praia*, Praia de Botafogo 400. Shops, cinemas and food hall with a view of the bay. *Rio Off Price*, Av Venceslau Brás 72, Botafogo. Fashion shops, snackbars and cinemas, open 1000-2200 Mon-Sat, 1500-2100 Sun. *Shopping Rio Sul*, at the Botafogo end of Túnel Novo, has almost everything the visitor may need. It is convenient and very safe. Some of the services in Rio Sul are the *Ibeas Top Club* gym; and a cinema. Eating places include fast food restaurants, 2 branches of *Kotobuki* sushi bar (another branch on the road to Praia Vermelha, recommended) and *Chaika* for milkshakes, ice creams and sandwiches (fourth floor, original branch on Praça Nossa Senhora da Paz, Ipanema). A US$5 bus service runs as far as the *Sheraton* passing the main hotels, every 2 hrs between 1000 and 1800, then 2130.

Tour operators *Deep Blue*, R Marquês de Olinda 18, Botafogo, T5532615. Offers boat trips. *Fábio Sombra*, T2959220 (answer phone 2758605), Cell97295455 (please don't leave messages on this number), fasombra@altavista.net Entertaining and educational tailor-made guided tours focusing on the cultural and historical aspects of Rio and Brazil. Recommended.

Directory **Banks** *Banco do Brasil*, Praia de Botafogo, 384A, 3rd floor. Changes US$ TCs minimium US$200. **Money changers** *Câmbio Belle Tours*, in Rio Sul Shopping Center, ground floor, shop 101, part A-10, Mon-Fri 1000-1800, Sat 1000-1700, changes cash. **Communications** Post Office: Branches at Praia de Botafogo 324 and G2, Shopping Rio Sul. **Telecommunications:** International calls can be made at Urca, near the Pão de Açúcar cable car. Also *Telemar*, A10-A Shopping Rio Sul, Mon-Sat 1000-2200. **Internet:** *Bell Sul*, Posto Telefônico, loja 101, Rio Sul Shopping Center, US$2.50 for 30 mins. *El Turf Cyber Place* G3, Shoping Rio Sul. US$3 per ½ hr, open daily 1200-2000. *Saraiva Megastore*, 3rd floor of Shopping Rio Sul. **Cultural centres** *Australian Trade Commission*, R Voluntários da Pátria 45, 2nd floor, Botafogo, T2867922 (for visas etc you must go to Brasília). *British Council*, R Elmano Cardim 10, Urca, T2957782, F5413693. *British School of Rio de Janeiro*, R Real Grandeza 99. **Laundry** *Lavelev*, in Shopping Rio Sul. Self-service laundrettes about US$7 for a machine, including detergent and drying, 1 hr. *Lavelev*, R Voluntários da Patria 248, Botafogo. **Medical services** *Policlínica de Botafogo*, Av Pasteur 72, Botafogo, T5431804. A good public hospital for minor injuries and ailments is *Hospital Municipal Rocha Maia*, R Gen Severiano 91, Botafogo, T2952295/2121, near Rio Sul Shopping Centre. Free, but there may be queues. 24 hr pharmacy: *City Farma*, R Humaitá 95, Humaitá. **Places of worship** *Associação Religiosa Israelita*, R Gen Severiano 170, Botafogo, T2956444. Services in Hebrew at 1830 Fri and 0930 Sat. *Chapel of Our Lady of Mercy (Capela de NS das Mercês)*, R Visconde de Caravelas 48, Botafogo. T2465664. Roman Catholic services in English at 1800 Sat and 0930 Sun. Also has primary school. *Christ Church (Igreja de Cristo)* R Real Grandeza 99, Botafogo, T5382978 (Church of England/American Episcopalian). Services in English at 0800 and 1800 Sun. The proceeds of books sold here go to help the Boys' Town Charity for street kids. The British School, for children of 5-16, is nearby. *Masonic Temple*, in the British School at R da Matriz 76, Botafogo.

Copacabana and Leme

Built on a narrow strip of land (only a little over 4 sq km) between mountain and sea, Copacabana began to develop when the Túnel Velho (Old Tunnel) was built in 1891 and an electric tram service finally reached the neighbourhood. Weekend villas and bungalows sprang up but all have now gone, replaced by modern skyscrapers and apartment blocks. In the 1930s the Copacabana Palace Hotel was the only tall building on the beach, now it is one of the lowest. The opening of the Túnel Novo (New Tunnel) in the 1940s led to a population explosion (Copacabana has one of the highest population densities in the world: 62,000 per square kilometre, or 250,000 in total) which shows no sign of having spent its force. However, there are some still unspoilt pockets such as the Art Deco blocks towards the Leme (city) end of Copacabana, which are now under a preservation order.

There is almost everything in this 'city within a city'. This is the ultimate area of Rio in which to watch, or participate in, the city's glamorous and world famous nightlife; and the shops, mostly in Avenida Nossa Senhora de Copacabana and the Rua Barata Ribeiro, are excellent, although even more stylish shops can be found nearby in Ipanema and Leblon.

Streetwise in Copacabana

Although Rio is no more dangerous for tourists than any large modern city in the world many people are still apprehensive about visiting and unfortunately a small minority still get into trouble usually after displaying a lack of common sense. Being streetwise and observing a few simple rules won't spoil your holiday and will help to avoid you having to bother the very helpful tourist police.

Be aware that Copacabana is one of the most densely populated places on earth and with some very poor neighbourhoods nearby. When on the beach it can be a good idea to choose a spot near one of the barracas serving food and drink. If you are a customer they will generally keep an eye on your things while you take a swim - however don't expect them to take responsibility for your expensive camera, passport, credit cards and travellers cheques which you should have left in your hotel! As a general rule of thumb you are safe wherever there are people around but it's not a good idea to take a midnight swim on the beach when it is deserted. (Tourist police patrol Copacabana beach until 1700.) If you are walking at night in areas which are empty you should definitely think about taking a bus or taxi to your destination instead.

Copacabana is one of the world's most famous red light districts although most of the industry is hidden from view in termas and the sex clubs around Av Prado Júnior and Praça do Lido. However, if you are on your own you may well be approached in the sidewalk bars on the city side of Avenida Atlântica and in the Help disco. Cariocas don't usually converse much with foreigners here due to the large number of professionals working the area. Your new friend however pleasant will be mainly interested in the contents of your wallet and may turn nasty if you are wasting their time or arguing the price. Most hotels either charge extra for guests or ban them all together due to thefts of belongings from the rooms sometimes after the victim has had their drink drugged.

Cariocas are very friendly and spontaneous but they also know from experience not to believe everything they are told by others. On meeting new friends and acquaintances in the city don't take for granted that appointments will be met, telephone calls returned and be a little suspicious of anyone who seems too persistent or over friendly. A true Carioca will understand a polite refusal or a broken appointment and the few who don't may have other interests beside the pleasure of your company. Remember if you rent an apartment from someone you met in the street you may not be the only one with a key.

Sights

The **Forte Duque de Caxias**, Rua Almirante Júlio de Noronha, at the Leme end of the beach was built between 1776 and 1779. Tiradentes, leader of the *Inconfidência Mineira*, served here in 1789 as a member of the Minas dragoons. It became an army staff college in 1965. ■ *Sat-Sun 0900-1700.*

The **Forte do Vigia**, built in 1779 at 210 m above sea level on the **Pedra da Leme** can be visited when accompanied by a guide. There are good views from the top and many plants and animals can be seen during the walk. ■ *T2757696. Sat-Sun 0900-1200, 1400-1700. Visits only by appointment.*

The **Forte de Copacabana**, at the far end of the beach was an important part of Rio's defences and prevents a seashore connection with the Ipanema and Leblon beaches. It was innaugurated in 1914 on the promontory where the Nossa Senhora de Copacabana chapel stood and on 5th July 1922 distinguished itself in the "18 of the Fort" rebellion against the government. Inside the fort is a military museum. ■ *T5211032. Tue-Sun 1000-1600.*

The **Parque da Chacrinha**, Rua Guimares Natal, is a rare green space in between the modern blocks, with *micos* (monkeys) and many birds in the trees. ■ *Daily 0800-1700.*

Essentials

Sleeping

■ *on map, page 138*
Many hotels on Av Atlântica charge about 30% more for a room with a sea view, but some town-side upper rooms have equally fine views of the mountains

Leme A much quieter area than Copacabana and with less traffic noise. **LL** *Le Méridien*, Av Atlântica 1020, T5460866, F5416477, sales@meridien-br.com World renowned hotel chain but rooms quite small and best on upper floors, pool, huge breakfast, good restaurants (see below), business centre, events rooms, nightclub. **L** *Leme Othon Palace*, Av Atlântica 656, T/F2758080. Good hotel popular with tour groups. **AL** *Luxor Continental*, Gustavo Sampaio 320, T5411946, F5411946. **A** *Acapulco Copacabana*, R Gustavo Sampaio 854, T2750022, F2753396. Parking, bar, quiet location, simple but comfortable. Recommended. **A** *Parthenon Real Residence*, Av Princesa Isabel 500, T5466565, F5466581. Rooms and long-stay lets, well-equipped and well-run, studios and rooms with sitting room and kitchen. **A** *Rio Copa*, Av Princesa Isabel 370, T2756644, F2755545, www.riocopa.com.br Restaurant, meeting room, roof top pool, sauna and bar, English spoken, good value. Recommended.

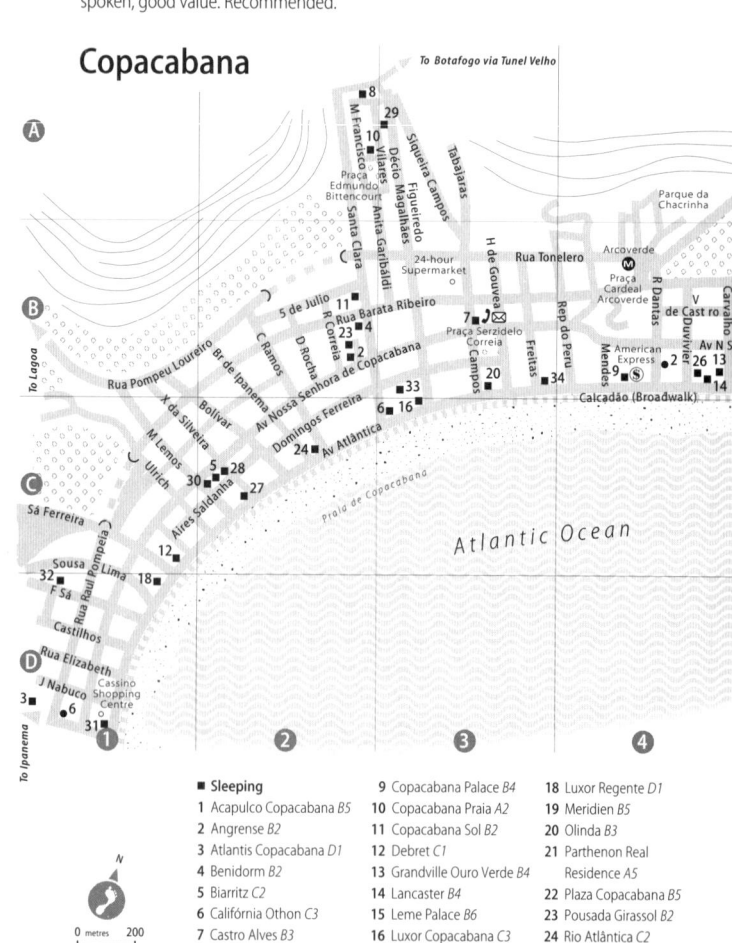

Copacabana

■ Sleeping
1 Acapulco Copacabana *B5*
2 Angrense *B2*
3 Atlantis Copacabana *D1*
4 Benidorm *B2*
5 Biarritz *C2*
6 Califórnia Othon *C3*
7 Castro Alves *B3*
8 Copacabana Chalet *A2*
9 Copacabana Palace *B4*
10 Copacabana Praia *A2*
11 Copacabana Sol *B2*
12 Debret *C1*
13 Grandville Ouro Verde *B4*
14 Lancaster *B4*
15 Leme Palace *B6*
16 Luxor Copacabana *C3*
17 Luxor Continental *B6*
18 Luxor Regente *D1*
19 Meridien *B5*
20 Olinda *B3*
21 Parthenon Real Residence *A5*
22 Plaza Copacabana *B5*
23 Pousada Girassol *B2*
24 Rio Atlântica *C2*
25 Rio Copa *B5*

Copacabana LL *Copacabana Palace*, Av Atlântica 1702, T5487070, F2357330, www.copacabanapalace.com.br World famous hotel built in 1923 with a distinguished guest list of royalty, heads of state and film stars (see box 'Scandal at the Palace'), comfortable rooms some with a beach view, childminders, art gallery, theatre, medical facilities, beach service, bar, good restaurants (see below), business centre, tennis courts, gym, pool popular with local high society. **LL** *Rio Othon Palace*, Av Atlântica 3264, T5221522, F5221697, www.hoteis-othon.com.br Childminders, business centre, auditorium, beach service, rooftop bar with good view, restaurant, heated pool, sauna, gym, parking. **LL** *Sofitel Rio Palace*, Av Atlântica 4240, T5251232, F5251200, sofitelrio@accor.com.br Childminders, nightclub, two pools to cover morning and afternoon sun, good tearoom, restaurant and piano bar.

Hotels on Av N S de Copacabana can be quite noisy because of the traffic

L *Califórnia Othon*, Av Atlântica 2616, T/F2571900, gevenrio@othon.com.br Art deco style, bar and restaurant with Brazilian cuisine, 3 meeting rooms. **L** *Lancaster Othon*, Av Atlântica 1470, T/F5431834. Easy to change TCs, non-smoking rooms, balconies overlook the beach, helpful management, airline discount can cut price. Recommended. **L** *Olinda Othon*, Av Atlântica 2230, T/F2571890. Restaurant with North Italian cuisine, meeting room. **L** *Rio Atlântica*, Av Atlântica 2964, T5486332, F2556410, rioatlan@netgate.com.br Sea view rooms have balconies, pool on roof terrace, two restaurants and business facilities, good views. Recommended. **L** *Rio Internacional*, Av Atlântica 1500, T5431555, F5425443, www.riointernacional.com.br Excellent suite hotel, Japanese spoken, bar, restaurant, gym, sauna, pool, beach service. **L** *Trocadero Othon*, Av Atlântica 2064, T/F2571834.

AL *Atlantis Copacabana*, Av Bulhões de Carvalho 61, T5211142, F2878896. Pool, sauna, good breakfast, close to both Ipanema and Copacabana beaches. **AL** *Benidorm Palace*, R Barata Ribeiro 547, T5488880, F2566396. Suites and double rooms, sauna. Recommended. **AL** *Grandville Ouro Verde*, Av Atlântica 1456, T5421887, F5424597. Rooms set around courtyard, restaurant, terrace overlooks beach. Recommended. **AL** *Luxor Copacabana*, Av Atlântica 2554, T5482245, F2551858. **AL** *Luxor Regente*, Av Atlântica 3716, T2677693, F2677693. Good well placed hotel. **AL** *Plaza Copacabana*, Av Princesa Isabel 263, T5860000, F5738071, www.windsorhoteis.com.br Modern hotel opened in 1999, business centre with internet connection, meeting rooms, gym, rooftop pool, parking, English spoken. **AL** *Savoy Othon*, Av NS de Copacabana 995, T/F5220282. Very central, popular, friendly and helpful staff, front rooms quite noisy from traffic. **AL** *South American Copacabana*, R Francisco de Sá 90,

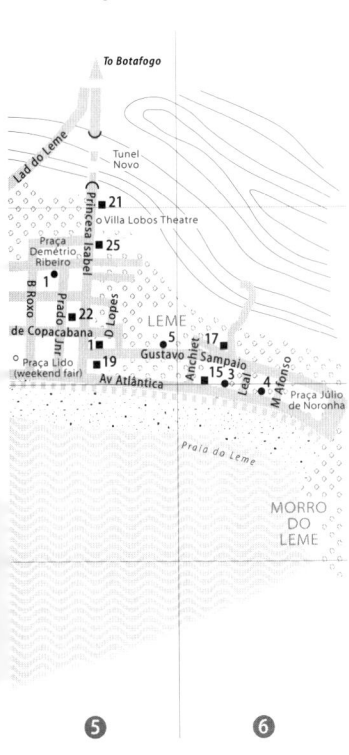

26 Rio Internacional *B4*
27 Rio Othon Palace *C2*
28 Rio Roiss *C2*
29 Santa Clara *A3*
30 Savoy Othon *C2*
31 Sofitel Rio Palace *D1*
32 South American Copacabana *D1*
33 Toledo *B3*
34 Trocadero *B3*

• **Eating**
1 Cervantes *B5*
2 Churrascaria Palace *B4*
3 Da Brambini *B6*
4 Marius *C6*
5 Shirley *B5*
6 Siri Mole & Cia *D1*

Scandal at the Palace

A Rio landmark to this day the Copacabana Palace Hotel opened in 1923 as one of the very few luxury hotels anywhere in South America. In that day and age gambling was legal in Brazil and extremely popular with guests who came from far and wide to lose their wedge at the Copa's tables. Distinguished visitors included presidents, royalty and the stars of stage and screen who were entertained by the best performers money could buy.

It was the guests from Hollywood, however, who were to make the most notorious entries in the Copa's history books. Orson Welles arrived in 1942 to film an unfinished documentary on Rio, but after the break up of his affair with a local starlet tempers began to fly and so did the furniture - right out of the window! Jayne Mansfield fared no better in the late 1950s with her supposedly accidental topless displays by the poolside and during a Carnival ball which outraged the local high society.

Despite being such an integral part of the Copacabana landscape and social scene it was only a preservation order and a refurbishment by a British company that has saved the Palace from becoming yet another faceless modern apartment block facing the beach. There was, however, further controversy in April 2000 after plans to tear down the theatre and art gallery in order to build a new annex were revealed to wide spread disapproval from the local community.

T5216040, F2670748. Good location 2 blocks from the beach, safe area, front rooms noisy, helpful front desk staff, highly rated.

A *Castro Alves Othon*, Av NS de Copacabana 552, T/F5488815, srorio@othon.com.br Central location, very comfortable and elegant. Recommended. **A** *Copacabana Sol*, R Santa Clara 141, T2571840, F2550744, www.hpm.com.br/copacabanasol.html Modern, safe, quiet, good breakfast, helpful. **A** *Debret*, Av Atlântica 3564, T5220132, F5210899, sales@debret.com Good, helpful staff, some inner rooms dark whilst some have beach view. **A** *Rio Roiss*, R Aires Saldanha 48, T5221142, F5227719. Very good, restaurant.

B *Angrense*, Trav Angrense 25, off Av NS de Copacabana, T/F5480509, angrense@antares.com.br Triple and quadruple rooms available, cheaper without private bathroom, luggage store, English spoken. **B** *Biarritz*, R Aires Saldanha 54, T5220443, F2877640. Good, accepts Amex. **B** *Pousada Girassol*, Trav Angrense 25A, T/F2566951, www.hpm.com.br/girassol.html With breakfast, triple and quadruple rooms available. **B** *Santa Clara*, R Décio Vilares 316, T2562650, F5474042. 2-star, best rooms at front, quiet. Recommended. **B** *Toledo*, R Domingos Ferreira 71, 1 block from beach, T2571995, F2877640. Good breakfast, single rooms are gloomy, but excellent value.

Youth hostels E (pp) *Copacabana Chalet*, R Henrique Oswald 103 (near the Old Tunnel), Bairro Peixoto, RJ 22041-020, T2360047, www.geocities.com/thetropics/cabana/7617 Kitchen, individual lockers, roof fans, open 24 hrs, very friendly staff. Recommended. **E** (pp) *Copacabana Praia*, R Tte Marones de Gusmão 85, Bairro Peixoto, RJ 22041-060, T5475422, F2353817, www.wcenter.com.br/cop-apraia Dormitory but apartments also available **B** , quiet location, luggage store.

Self-catering apartments The following agencies and individuals rent apartments in residential blocks and are much safer: *Yvonne Reimann*, Av Atlântica 4066, Apto 605, T5130281/2670054. Rents older apartments, all with phone for local calls, near beach, a/c, maid service, English, French, German spoken, all apartments owned by the agency, prices from US$50 per flat. *Yolanda Thiémard*, Av Prado Junior 165 CO2, T2952088. Multilingual, good value. Recommended. *Dona Lígia*, R Ministro Viveiros de Castro 141 apto 101, T5416367. Speaks English, lower-price apartments. *Fantastic Rio*, Av Atlântica 974, Suite 501, T/F5432667, hpcorr@hotmail.com, all types of furnished accommodation from US$20 per day. Owned by Peter Corr. Recommended. *Copacabana Holiday*, R Barata Ribeiro 90A, T5421525, F5421597, www.copacabanaholiday.com.br Well equipped apartments from US$500 per month, minumum 30 days let. Recommended. *Rio Residences*, Av Prado Júnior 44, room 508, T5414568, F5416462. Swiss run, includes airport transfer. *Holidays in Copacabana*, Av Atlantica, T2270281.

Be very wary about renting apartments from people you meet in the street however good the deal may seem. You may not be the only person with a key

Eating Some of Rio's best restaurants and cafés are in the main Copacabana hotels (see above for locations). There are also many cheap places to eat in the streets either side of Av NS de Copacabana and R Barata Ribeiro. The restaurants on Av Atlântica have outside tables and are excellent for people-watching but beware of overcharging and international food is the norm.

Leme Expensive: *Le Saint Honoré*, in *Hotel Le Méridien*, T5460880. Excellent French cuisine and desserts with wonderful view, open 1900-0100 Mon-Sat. **Mid-range**: *Café de la Paix*, in *Hotel Le Méridien*. Afternoon tea 1600-1830 from Mar-Nov. *Da Brambini*, Av Atlântica 514B, Leme, T2754346. Good Italian, open daily 1200-0100. **Cheap**: *Marius*, Av Atlântica, 290B, Leme. Excellent all you can eat churrasco. Recommended. *Shirley*, R Gustavo Sampaio 610, Leme, T2751398. Spanish seafood, small so best to book in advance.

Copacabana Expensive: *Cipriani*, in *Hotel Copacabana Palace*, T5458747. One of the best Italian restaurants in the city, reservations advisable, open daily 1230-1430, 1900-0100. *Le Pré Catalan*, in *Sofitel Rio Palace Hotel*, T5251160. Excellent French cuisine with some of the best desserts in the city, open 1900-0100 Mon-Sat.

Mid-range: *Don Camillo*, Av Atlântica 3056, T5499958. Good Italian and seafood, open daily from 1200. *Moenda*, in *Trocadero Othon Hotel*. Bahian cuisine with good views. *Monte Carlo*, R Duvivier 21, T5414097. Good varied cuisine with *feijoada* on Sat and *cozido* on Sun, open daily from 1130. *Pergula*, in *Copacabana Palace Hotel*. Café open 1400-1700 Mon-Fri. Recommended. *Siri Mole & Cia*, R Francisco Otaviano 50, T2670894. One of the best Bahian restaurants in the city, don't miss coffee after the meal from an old-fashioned coffee machine, open 1800-2400 Mon and 1200-2400 Tue-Sun.

Cheap: *Alfaia*, R Inhangá 30B. Good Portugese, open daily from 1200. *Arataca*, R Figueiredo de Magalhães 28. Try *carne-de-sol* and *lagosta ao molho*, excellent duck.

HOLIDAYS IN COPACABANA
BEAUTIFUL FURNISHED APARTMENTS
1 block from the beach

Fully equipped: air conditioning, telephone, color TV, wall-safe, refrigerator, linen & towels, maid service.

SWISS MANAGEMENT   ENGLISH, FRENCH AND GERMAN SPOKEN

Call: Yvonne tels.: 227-0281 or 267-0054
RIO DE JANEIRO, AVENIDA ATLANTICA 4.066 APT. 605

Beach snacks

The first thing you'll notice when going to the beach in Rio is a multitude of vendors strolling around who have everything you could need for sale or hire: umbrellas, sun block, sunglasses, deck chairs, refreshments. They will be shouting out many strange words that may be puzzling for the beginner. Don't worry they are not intrusive and the majority of them are really nice and friendly to tourists as well as often being very helpful. Here is a short description of what they normally say and what is on offer:

Natural or **Sandwich Natural** is a Rio beach invention and is made of whole wheat sliced bread, filled with mayonnaise and usually either chicken breast (natural de frango), tuna (natural de atum) or cottage cheese (natural de ricota) as well as many other combinations including raisins (passas), carrot (cenoura) and olives (azeitonas). They are a good, light snack but before buying, check if the sandwiches are kept in a Styrofoam box. Avoid the ones offered on a plate or that have been under direct sunlight as mayonnaise tends to go bad quickly in these conditions.

Mate (pronounced 'Maahtee') is a very refreshing Brazilian iced tea. The best brand is known as Mate Leão and the seller will proudly announce it! You can also try Mate com Limão which has added lime juice. They are sold in sealed plastic cups and my experience with foreigners is that you will either love it forever or hate it immediately. But there's only one way to find out - Try the bloody tea!

Globo or **Biscoito Globo** are a very light kind of baked salt biscuit recommended for those who are very hungry and need to chew something but at the same time don't want to miss a nice meal afterwards. Believe me, you can eat a whole package of these crispy biscuits and still be hungry. Safe and healthy.

Picolé is a kind of ice cream on a stick made from tropical fruits. The best in my opinion are those made from limes (limão), grapes (uva), passion fruit (maracuja) and coconut (coco) but there are many other flavours.

Espetinho de Camarão are fried shrimps on a wooden skewer and are great appetizers if you are drinking beer. They come with a slice of lime which you should squeeze on top of the shrimps before eating to get the full flavour.

Agua de Coco is coconut water which you can find in any of the small snack bars along the beach. The coconuts are kept in ice and the seller will choose one for you then cut a hole with a machete so that you can insert a straw to drink this sweet and refreshing water straight from the coconut. This is totally hygienic and when you finish drinking the water, don't forget to give the coconut back to the seller. He will immediately cut the fruit in two halves and make a small spoon out of the coconut peel so you can eat the delicious white flesh on the inside. It is a ritual and Brazilians say that nothing in the world is a better hangover cure than drinking coconut water on the morning after.

Fábio Sombra

Azumi, Av Ministro Viveiros de Castro 127. Good Japanese, open 1900-0200 Tue-Sun. *Casarão*, Souza Lima 37A. Café. *Cervantes*, Prado Júnior 335B. Stand-up bar or sit-down, a/c restaurant, open all night, queues after 2200, specializes in meats and sandwiches (all with a slice of pineapple). Recommended. *Chá e Simpatia*, in *Sofitel Rio Palace Hotel*. Café open 1600-1830 Mon-Fri. *Churrascaria Palace*, R Rodolfo Dantas 16B. 20 different kinds of meat, very good food and value. *Gallo Nero*, Av Atlântica 1424. Good Italian, open from 1800 Mon-Fri and from 1200 Sat-Sun. *Mab's*, Av Atlântica 1140, corner with Av Prado Júnior. Good Brazilian and Spanish food but many prostitutes at outside tables, open daily 1200-0300. *Mala e Cuia*, R Raimundo Correia 34. *Comida mineira* in traditional setting with music in the evenings. Self service buffet at lunchtimes with a variety of tasty dishes to choose from. Excellent selection of cachaça including the *Salinas Havana* at US$7.50 a shot! Recommended.

A Marisquera, R Barata Ribeiro 232. Good seafood, open daily 1100-Midnight. *Nino*, R Domingos Ferreira 242. Italian cuisine and Argentine beef. *A Polonesa*, R Hilário de Gouveia 116. Polish, open 1800-0100 Tue-Fri, 1200-Midnight Sat-Sun. *Ponto de Encontro* R Barata Ribeiro 750. Portuguese, try baked *bacalhau*. *Rian*, R Santa Clara 8. International cuisine, very popular. *Siquiera Grill*, R Siquiera Campos 16. Good pay by weight buffet with seafood and churrasco available. *Traiteurs de France*, Av NS de Copacabana 386. Delicious tarts and pastries. *La Trattoria*, R Fernando Mendes 7A. Good Italian food and service. Recommended.

Very cheap: There are many cheap pay by weight or set price buffet restaurants in the streets off Av NS de Copacabana. Galetos which specialise in fried chicken can also be good value and there are a wide range of fast food places. *Kicê Sucos*, Av NS de Copacabana 1033 corner of R Miguel Lemos. Good juice bar with sandwiches, hamburgers etc. *Marakesh*, Av NS de Copacabana 599. Good quality and value, pay by weight. *Vindobona*, R Paula Freitas 55. Set price self service buffet, eat as much as you like, lunch only. *Yonza*, R Miguel Lemos 21B. Café serving pancakes with savoury or sweet fillings. Popular with younger people in the evenings.

Bars & nightclubs

The small kiosks on the *calçadão* which runs alongside Copacabana beach are excellent for people watching and home to occasional samba sessions. The big hotels also have good cocktail bars. There are many sex shows in the area around Av Prado Júnior and Praça do Lido. Prostitutes also gather in the bars at the other end of Av Atlântica near the *Help* disco. Be careful in these areas late at night when there are fewer people around.

Bars *Adega Pérola*, R Siquiera Campos 138. Traditional Portuguese bar with good chopp and wide range of bar snacks, 1000-2400 Mon-Sat. *Alla Zingara*, corner of Ministro Viveiros de Castro and Belfort Roxo. Friendly bar with outside tables. *Blue Angel*, R Julio de Castilhos 15. Café bar popular with gay community. *Copacabana Palace*. Poolside bar. Recommended. *Manuel e Juaquim*, Av Atlântica corner of R República de Peru. *Botequim* style bar with good snacks. *Sindicato do Chopp*, Av Atlântica 3806. Popular bar with good beer.

Nightclubs *Club B.A.S.E.*, in *Shopping Cassino Atlântico*, Av Francisco Otaviano 20A. House, techno, and trance, open from 2300 Tue-Sun, best night reported to be Thu, entry and minimum consumption about US$15. *Barman Club*, R Belford Roxo 58. Drum'n'bass Fri-Sat from 2300, US$6. *Bunker 94*, R Raul Pompéia 94. Dance club with good atmosphere for trance, house, techno, open Wed-Sun, entry US$10, cheaper before midnight. Recommended. *Copa Show*, Av NS de Copacabana 435. Live forró downstairs, disco upstairs from Midnight onwards Fri-Sat, entry US$3.50. *Le Boy*, R Raul Pompéia 102. Techno disco, very popular with gays, lesbians and supporters, from 2200 Tue-Sun, US$5 cheaper before midnight. *Help* Av Atlântica. Large disco with good music although many prostitutes, opens around midnight, US$8.50 entry does not include drink, women with female friends and a sense of humour can have a lot of fun (but not recommended for couples). *Sobre as Ondas*, Av Atlântica 3432. Live bands for dancing, good view from terrace, open 1800-0400.

Entertainment

Carnival blocos *Banda da Sá Ferreira*, parades on Sat and Sun afternoons during carnival. *Bloco do Bip-Bip*, meets at the *Bar Bip-Bip* (see below) and parades on Sat and Tue during carnival. Famous musicians playing *marchas* and traditional carnival music, T-shirts US$5 but are not obligatory to join in. There are many others such as *Clube do Samba* and *Banda da Santa Clara*.

Cinema *Art Copacabana*, Av NS de Copacabana 759. *Copacabana*, Av NS de Copacabana 801. *Novo Jóia*, Av NS de Copacabana 680. *Roxy*, Av NS de Copacabana 945. Three screens.

Music *Bar Bip-Bip*, R Almte Gonçalves 50. Small bar home to occasional samba sessions on Fri and Sun featuring many famous musicians. Very friendly regulars, the walls are decorated with photos and cartoons of *sambistas*, Botafogo and Alfredo, the bar's owner. Recommended. *Horse's Neck*, in Sofitel Rio Palace (see above). Piano bar with live jazz from 1900-0100 daily. *Razão Cultural*, inside bookshop (see below). Café with outside tables, nice atmosphere with live choro at weekends from 1900.

Samba schools *Unidos de Vila Rica de Copacabana*, Ladeira dos Tabajaras 681, T2559743.

Theatre *Teatro Sesc Copacabana*, R Domingos Ferreira 160, T5481088. *Teatro Villa Lobos*, Av Princesa Isabel 440, T2756695.

Shopping **Bookshops** *Livraria Kosmos*, Av Atlântica 1702, shop 5. International stock. *Livraria Nova Galeria de Arte*, Av NS de Copacabana 291D. International stock. *Livrarias Siciliano*, Av NS de Copacabana 830. Second-hand books at Av NS de Copacabana 400, small selection, US$1 per book. *Razão Cultural*, inside gallery at Av NS de Copacabana 1133. Good selection of art, esoteric, literature and guide books.

Jewellery There are several good jewellery shops at the Leme end of Av NS de Copacabana: *Lido*, R Rodolfo Dantas 26B, T5418098. Recommended. For mineral specimens as against cut stones, try *Mineraux*, Av NS de Copacabana 195. Belgian owner.

Markets Markets on Wed 0700-1300 on R Domingos Ferreira and on Thu, same hours, on Praça do Lido, both Copacabana (Praça do Lido also has a *Feirarte* on Sat-Sun 0800-1800). There is an *artesania* market nightly near the *Rio Othon Palace* hotel, near R Miguel Lemos: one part for paintings, one part for everything else.

Music *Modern Sound Música Equipamentos*, R Barata Ribeiro 502D. Large selection of Brazilian music, jazz and classical. *Top Sound*, Av NS de Copacabana 1103. New and secondhand Brazilian and international records, tapes and CDs.

Photography *Camera Service Miyazaki*, R Djalma Ulrich 110, upstairs shop 214, T/F5224894. Camera and equipment repairs.

Shopping centres *Shopping Cassino Atlântico*, next to Hotel Rio Palace Sofitel with entrances in Av NS de Copacabana and R Francisco Otaviano. Art galleries, antique stores and jewellers, open 0900-2100. *Shopping Center de Copacabana*, R Siqueira Campos 143. Shops and theatres, open 0900-1800 Mon-Fri, 0900-1400 Sat.

Tour operators *América Exchange Tur*, Av NS de Copacabana 346A, T5487909, www.highway.com.br/america Carnival tickets for stands and boxes. *BIT*, R Barão de Ipanema 56, 5th floor, T2565657, F2565868, www.bitourism.com Swiss run agency specializing in congresses and events. *Cultural Rio*, R Santa Clara 110, apartment 904, RJ 22041-010, T33224872, Cell99113829 (24 hrs), F5474774. Tours by day or night with Professor Carlos Roquette, English and French spoken, hundreds of options available on almost anything you could want to know about Rio (or didn't want to know for the more adventurous spirits). *Ékoda*, Av NS de Copacabana 583, office 406, T5495332, F2562406. Guided tour to Maracanã stadium. *Instituto de Estudos Turísticos do Rio de Janeiro*, Av NS de Copacabana 195, office 309, T5422163, F5422596. Cultural and historical city tours, 0900-1800 Mon-Fri. *Fantasia Turismo*, Av NS de Copacabana 583, office 504, T5490399. Boat trips to Angra dos Reis and Búzios. *Fenician Tours*, Av NS de Copacabana 335, T2353843, F2573782. Offer a cheaper Samba show tour than some at US$30 including transport from/to hotel. *Guanatur Turismo*, R Dias da Rocha 16A, Copacabana, T2353275, F2353664. Sells long distance bus tickets. *Marlin Tours*, Av NS de Copacabana 605, office 1204, RJ 22050-000, T5484433, F2352081, bbm.robin@openlink.com.br Hotel bookings, flights and tours, Robin and Audrey speak English. Recommended. *Turismo Clássico*, Av NS de Copacabana 1059/805, RJ 22060-000, T5233390, F5214636. Recommended. *Turismo Diferente*, R Barão de Ipanema 32, office 1103, T2363846, F5378983. Cultural guided city tours, 1800-2000 Mon, Wed, Fri. *Quality Travel*, Av NS de Copacabana 387, T2356888, F2366985. Helpful with hotel bookings.

Buses Buses to and from the city centre are plentiful and cost US$0.50. The buses to take are Nos 119, 154, 413, 415, 455, 474 from Avenida Nossa Senhora de Copacabana. If you are going to the centre from Copacabana, look for 'Castelo', 'Praça 15', 'E Ferro' or 'Praça Mauá' on the sign by the front door. 'Aterro' means the expressway between Botafogo and downtown Rio (not open on Sun). From the centre to Copacabana is easier as all buses in that direction are clearly marked. The 'Aterro' bus does the journey in 15 mins.

Transport

Banks *Banco do Brasil*, Av NS de Copacabana 594. Changes cash and TCs Mon-Fri 1000-1630. Also Visa ATMs at many branches in Av NS de Copacabana. *Bradesco*, corner of Av NS de Copacabana and R Santa Clara. Visa ATMs. Many other branches. *Itaú*, on Av Atlântica, next to *Copacabana Palace*. Mastercard and Cirrus cash machines. **Money changers** Copacabana (where rates are generally worse than in the centre) abounds with *câmbios*. *American Express*, Av Atlântica 1702, loja 1, T2552148 Mon-Fri 0900-1800. Good rates. **Communications** Post office: Av NS de Copacabana 540A. Handles international post and can send faxes, fax number for receiving messages F5474774. Three other branches in Av NS de Copacabana at 1059A, 1113 and 1298, shop A-B, as well as R Dias da Rocha 45B and Av Princesa Isabel 323A, Leme. **Poste Restante**: *American Express*, Av Atlântica 1702 loja 1, Copacabana (for customers only). *Correios*, Av NS de Copacabana 540A and all large post offices (letters held for a month, recommended, US$0.10 per letter). **Telephone**: International calls can be made at Av NS de Copacabana 540, 2nd floor which is open 24 hrs (although it has been known to be closed at times). **Internet**: *Clube Israelita Brasileira* (CIB), Av Barata Ribeiro 489, US$3 per hr. *Copa Cyber Café*, Centro Comercial de Copacabana, R Siqueira Campos 43, room 901. US$1.75 per 20 mins. 0930-2200 Mon-Fri, 1100-2200 Sat-Sun, also has tourist information and tour guides speaking several languages. *Estação Internet*, R Xavier da Silveira 19B. *Internet House*, Av NS de Copacabana 195, shop 106, US$2.25 per ¼ hour, open 0930-2200 Mon-Sat. **Cultural centres** *Sociedade Brasileira de Cultura Inglesa*, in Copacabana, T2674048 (central information). **Laundry** Laundromat at Av NS de Copacabana 1225 corner of R Souza Lima. Also at R Barata Ribeiro 662. Self-service. *Lavelev*, Av Prado Junior 63B. **Medical services** 24 hr medical clinics: *Galdino Campos Cárdio Copa*, Av NS de Copacabana 492, T5489966. *Medtur*, Av NS de Copacabana 647, room 815, T2353339. 24 hr dentist: *Polîclinica Barata Ribeiro*, R Barata Ribeiro 51, T2754697. 24 hr pharmacies: *Drogaria Pachecho*, Branches at Av NS de Copacabana 115 and 534. *Farmácia do Leme*, Av Prado Júnior 237. **Places of worship** *Israelita Bethel*, R Barata Ribeiro 469, T2355545. Synagogue and kosher bakery. *Sinagoga Beit Yaacov*, R Capelão Alvares da Silva 15, T2550191. Services in Hebrew.

Directory

Ipanema and Leblon

Beyond Copacabana are the beautiful seaside suburbs of Ipanema (a good place from which to watch the sunset) and Leblon. The two districts are divided by a canal from the Lagoa Rodrigo de Freitas to the sea, beside which is the Jardim de Alá. The name Ipanema comes from the Indian word for 'bad water' and the area was first developed by the Barão of Ipanema in 1896. However, it was not until the arrival of the tram in 1902 that the area began to become popular. In the late 1950s and early 1960s, during the so-called Republic of Ipanema, the area became a meeting place for intellectuals and bohemians and today there are still many places in the neighbourhood which can be visited that are linked to that epoca.

Ipanema and Leblon are a little less built-up than Copacabana and their beaches tend to be cleaner. Praia de Arpoador at the Copacabana end of Ipanema is a peaceful spot to watch surfers, with the beautiful backdrop of Morro Dois Irmãos; excellent for photography, and walks on the rocks. (There is now night-time illumination on these beaches). The seaward lane of the road running beside the beach is closed to traffic until 1800 on Sundays and holidays, making it great for rollerskating and cycling (bicycles can be hired). Parts of the nearby military areas are now being handed over to civilian use, the first being the Parque Garota de Ipanema at Arpoador, the fashionable Copacabana end of the Ipanema beach whose name comes from a colony of whalers who lived in the area during the 19th century.

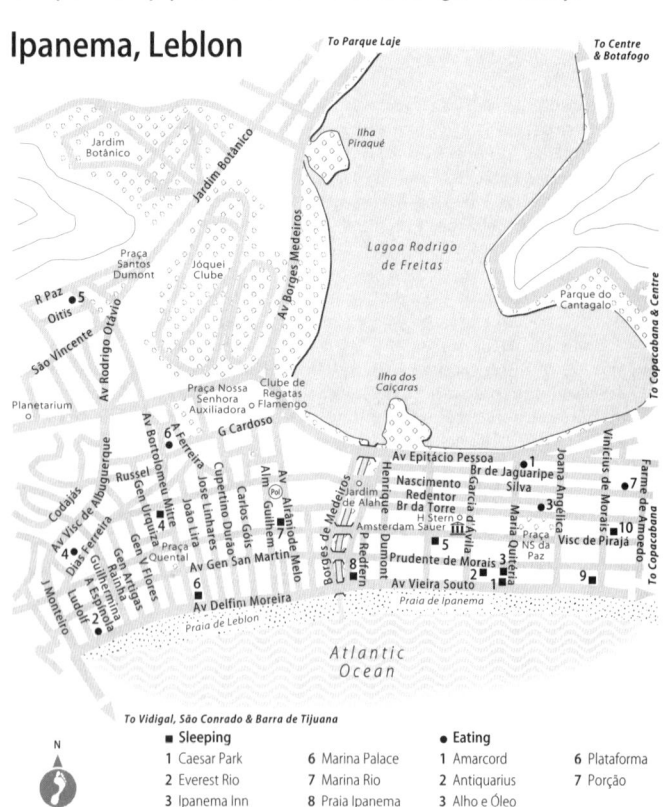

Ipanema, Leblon

■ Sleeping
1 Caesar Park
2 Everest Rio
3 Ipanema Inn
4 Le Blond Monsieur
5 Mar Ipanema
6 Marina Palace
7 Marina Rio
8 Praia Ipanema
9 Sol Ipanema
10 Vermont

● Eating
1 Amarcord
2 Antiquarius
3 Alho e Óleo
4 Celeiro
5 Guimas
6 Plataforma
7 Porção

The Tanga

For many decades Rio de Janeiro was at the forefront of Brazilian fashion. Traders from all over Brazil would invade the Copacabana boutiques, principally those of Rua Santa Clara, searching for new clothes to resell in other cities. Today, however, the best boutiques are probably in Ipanema and the main market for fashion in São Paulo. It was in the seventies that the famous tanga was created and the Cariocas, considered the most beautiful and liberal women in Brazil, soon adopted this new style on the beach. As the ideal garment for showing off their bodies, the tanga and the fio dental (dental floss) bikini had definitely arrived in the right place.

Beatrix Boscardin

Sights

Toca de Vinicíus, Rua Vinicíus de Moraes 129C is a record and bookshop with friendly and helpful staff that has become a shrine to Bossa Nova. Upstairs is a museum dedicated to the famous songwriter and a small auditorium for concerts and films. There are also displays on the lives of Tom Jobim, Nara Leão and other musicians. ■ *T2475227. Mon-Fri 0900-2000, Sat 0900-1800, Sun 1000-1700.*

In Ipanema are the headquarters of two stores which have successfully adapted the Brazilian gemstone industry to the modern world: Amsterdam Sauer and H Stern. Both have exhibitions which you can visit without any pressurized selling attached.

Amsterdam Sauer Museum, R Garcia d'Ávila 105 and Visconde de Pirajá, has reproductions of two Brazilian mines and a large exhibition of gemstones In both their rough state and cut into precious stones. ■ *T5121132, www.amsterdamsauer.com Mon-Fri 0930-1730, Sat 0930-1300. Free.*

H Stern, R Garcia D'Ávila 113, has a self-guided exhibition which shows the complete process of turning an uncut stone into a piece of jewellery. As you walk around the display, you can see the experts at work in front of you. There is also a permanent exhibition of jewellery, including items which have won international prizes. ■ *T2597442, www.hstern.com.br Mon-Fri 0830-1800, Sat 0830-1300.*

Essentials

Sleeping
■ *on map, page 146*

Ipanema LL *Caesar Park*, Av Vieira Souto 460, T5252525, F5216000, www.caesarpark-rio.com 5-star hotel regarded as possibly the city's best with a very high standard of service, childminders, restaurant is good for seafood and sushi, business centre with large meeting rooms, pool with bar, beach patrol. **L** *Everest Rio*, R Prudente de Morais 1117, T5232282, F5213581, reservas@everest.com.br Quiet, modern and functional, rooftop pool with good view. **L** *Mar Ipanema*, R Visconde de Pirajá 539, Ipanema, 1 block from the beach, T5129898, F5114038, maripa@domain.com.br Helpful, good buffet breakfast. **L** *Praia Ipanema*, Av Vieira Souto 706, T5404949, F2396889, ipanema@ism.com.br All rooms with seaview, pool, helpful, good security. **L** *Sol Ipanema*, Av Vieira Souto 320, T5252020, F2478484, hotel@solipanema.com.br Best Western chain hotel, near Posto 9 on beach. Recommended.

AL *Everest Park*, R Maria Quitéria 19, T5232282, F5213198, reservas@everest.com.br **A** *Arpoador Inn*, Francisco Otaviano 177, Arpoador, T5230060, F5115094. Close to beach, more expensive rooms have sea view, with breakfast, quiet location and good value. Recommended. **A** *Ipanema Inn*, R Maria Quitéria 27, behind Caesar Park, T5233092, F5115094. Good value and location. **A** *Tiffany's*, R Prudente de Morais 302, T5214418. Apartment hotel. **A** *Vermont*, R Visconde de Pirajá 254,

The Liberal City

Over the years Rio de Janeiro has gained a reputation as the most liberal city in South America. This rather open behaviour mainly came about during the era of the military dictatorships which held practically all of the subcontinent in their iron grip during the 1960s and 1970s. In other countries such as Argentina or Chile anyone who had a beard was quickly labelled as a communist or of having left-wing sympathies. Under such harsh regimes many people were arrested for no other reason than the length of their hair. In those repressive times the city of Rio de Janeiro became a haven for refugees from neighbouring countries as here the military rulers were less brutal and long hair, beards and earrings were slightly more acceptable. The city has also become extremely popular with homosexuals as their sexuality is less discriminated against here than in many other Latin American cities. Apart from these important factors, Rio's beaches with their agreeable climate all year round attracted many Argentines and Chileans from their more temperate southern countries.

Beatrix Boscardin

T5220057, F2677046. With breakfast, small meeting room. **B *San Marco***, R Visconde de Pirajá 524, T/F5405032. 2-star, simple breakfast. Recommended.

Leblon L *Marina Palace & All Suites*, Av Delfim Moreira 630 and 696, T2941794, F2941644, hotelmarina@callnet.com.br Facing beach, all rooms have sea view, meeting room, parking, bar, restaurant, sauna, massage, pool.

AL *Leblon Palace*, Av Ataulfo de Paiva 204, T5128000, F2745741, leblonpalace@radnet.com.br Meeting room, restaurant, pool. **AL *Monsieur Le Blond***, Av Bartolomeu Mitre 455, T5393030, F5293220. Good quality apartment hotel. **A *Carlton***, R João Lira 68, T2591932, F2593147, carlton@mandic.com.br **A *The Claridge***, R Rainha Guilhermina 156, T/F5112692, info@promenade.com.br Apartment hotel.

Eating **Ipanema** Quieter than Copacabana, there are many nice places round Praça Gen
• on map, page 146 Osório. **Expensive**: *Esplanada Grill*, R Barão de Torre 348. T5122970. One of the best meat restaurants in the city, open daily 1200-late. *Madame Butterfly*, R Barão de Torre 472, T2674247. One of the best Japanese restaurants in the city, open daily 1200-0200. *Margutta*, Av Henrique Dumont 62, T2593887. Chic Italian popular with celebrities, open 1200-1600, 1900-0100 Tue-Fri, 1200-0130 Sat-Sun.

Mid-range: *Arlecchino*, R Prudente de Morais 1387, T2597745. Good Italian open 1930-0200 Mon-Fri, 1200-0100. *Satyricon*, R Barão de Torre 192, T5210627. Excellent fresh fish and seafood as well as Italian and Japanese dishes, open 1800-0200 Mon, 1200-0200 Tue-Sun. *Grottammare*, R Gomes Carneiro 132, T5231596. One of the best seafood and fish restaurants in the city, open 1800-2400 Mon-Fri, 1200-2400 Sat-Sun. *Marius*, R Francisco Otaviano 96, Arpoador. All you can eat *churrascaria*, open daily 1200-Midnight. *Mostarda*, Av Epitácio Pessoa 980. Excellent food often seasoned with mustard sauce, nightclub upstairs, entry fee can be avoided if you eat in the 1st floor restaurant before 2200-2300. Recommended.

Cheap: *Alho e Óleo*, R Barão de Torre 348. Fashionable, friendly. Recommended. *Amarcord*, R Maria Quitéria 136, T2870335. Italian. Recommended. *Bistro 1800*, Av Vieira Souto 110, T2870085. Good Brazilian menu, fish and meat. *La Bonne Table*, R Visconde de Pirajá 580 sala 407. Café. *Casa da Feijoada*, R Prudente de Morais 10. Serves an excellent *feijoada* daily 1200-2400. *Concorde*, Av Prudente de Morais 129. Café. *Del Mare*, at corner of Prudente de Morais and Vinícius de Morais. Recommended.

La Frasca, R Garcia d'Ávila 129. Good Italian, pleasant atmosphere. **New Garden**, R Visconde de Pirajá 631, T2593455. Good modern cuisine, some tables with own beer taps. *La Maschera de Pulcinela*, R Farme de Amoedo 102, Good Italian, open 1900-0100 Tue-Thu, 1900-0200 Sat, 1200-0100 Sun. **Pax Delícia**, R Maria Quitéria 99. Good light food and salads, lively crowd, open Mon from 2000 and Tue-Sun from 1200. **Porção**, R Barão de Torre 218. Very good *churrascaria*. **Yemanjá**, R Visconde de Pirajá 128. Bahian food, open 1800-2400 Mon-Thu, 1200-2400 Fri-Sat, 1200-2200 Sun.

Very cheap: *Delicats*, Av Henrique Dumont 68. Good Jewish delicatessen. *Delícias da Bahia*, R Vinícius de Morais 71B. Pay by weight buffet with *vatapá* and other Bahian specialities open daily at lunchtimes and afternoons. **Empório Saúde**, Visconde de Pirajá 414. Sandwiches and vegetarian food, open 1100-1900 Mon-Fri, 1100-1600 Sat.

Leblon Expensive: *Antiquarius*, R Aristides Espínola 19, T2941049. One of the best Portuguese restaurants in the city, seafood and international cuisine, open daily 1200-0200. **Garcia & Rodrigues**, Av Ataulfo de Paiva 1251, T5128188. Excellent and varied cuisine, open 2000-2400 Mon, 1200-1530, 2000-2400 Tue-Sat, 1300-1600 Sun.

Mid-range: *Bel Beef*, Av Afrânio Melo Franco 131. Good *churrascaria rodízio*. **Ettore**, Av Ataulfo de Paiva 1321A, T2595899. Excellent Italian. **Sushi Leblon**, R Dias Ferreira 256, T2741342. Popular Japanese, open 1900-0330 Mon-Thu, 1230-1600 Sat-Sun, 1300-midnight Sun. **Tanaka San**, R Bartolomeu Mitre 112, T2390198. Good Japanese, open daily for lunch and dinner. **Un, Deux, Trois**, R Bartolomeu Mitre 123. Very fashionable, restaurant, nightclub.

Cheap: *Celeiro*, R Dias Ferreira 199. Some of the best salads in the city, also light food and desserts, pay by weight, open 1000-2220 Mon-Tue, 1000-1800 Wed-Sat. **Mediterráneo**, R Prudente de Morais 1810. Excellent fish. **Pizza Park**, R Gilberto

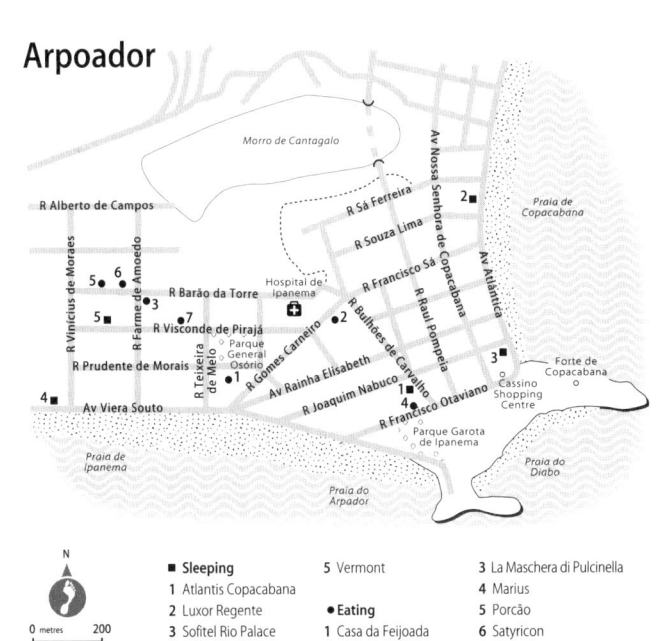

Arpoador

- **Sleeping**
  1 Atlantis Copacabana
  2 Luxor Regente
  3 Sofitel Rio Palace
  4 Sol Ipanema
  5 Vermont

- **Eating**
  1 Casa da Feijoada
  2 Grottamare
  3 La Maschera di Pulcinella
  4 Marius
  5 Porção
  6 Satyricon
  7 Yemanjá

The Girl from Ipanema

Despite Brazil's varied musical tradition the only Brazilian composer ever to really achieve fame outside their home shores is of course Antônio Carlos Jobim or Tom as he is rather better known abroad. The song that carried him to fame on the new wave of Bossa Nova was A Garota de Ipanema sung by Astrud Gilberto and accompanied by Stan Getz's tenor sax. Co-written in 1962 by his fellow intellectual and poet Vinicius de Moraes the song was inspired by young schoolgirl Heloisa Pinheiro whose daily journey past their favourite sidewalk bar entranced the two bohemians. The rest, as they say, is history and today the bar is named after the song, the street after Vinicius and the International airport, that brings so many tourists to visit the spot where it was written, after Tom.

Cardoso. Good pizzas, open evenings only and it's best to arrive early (about 2000) to get a table on Sun when it is very popular with younger Cariocas. *Ragi*, R Conde Bernadotte 26A. Arabic food, open daily.

Bars & nightclubs **Bars** *Academia da Cachaça*, R Conde de Bernadotte 26-G, Leblon. Bar serving various cocktails made from sugar cane spirit. *Barril 1800*, Av Vieira Souto 110, Ipanema. Seafront bar and a nice place to watch the sunset. *Bofetada*, R Farme de amoedo 87, Ipanema. Popular botequim generally considered the most bohemian of the neighbourhood. *Bracarense*, R José Linhares 85B, Leblon. Chilled beer with prawn pasties and other snacks. Was recently voted best bar in Rio. *Caneco 70*, Av Delfim Moreira 1026. Bar and restaurant on Leblon beach. *Clipper*, R Carlos Góes 263, in front of Cinema Leblon. Popular street bar. *Empório*, R Maria Quitéria 37, Ipanema. Popular *chopperia* with young crowd. Recommended. *A Garota de Ipanema*, R Vinícius de Morais 49, Ipanema. Very lively bar where the song 'Girl from Ipanema' was written (see box). *Jobi*, Av Ataulfo de Paiva 1166, Leblon. Popular with a wide variety of locals and foreigners, 0900-0430. *The Lord Jim Pub*, R Paul Redfern 63, Ipanema. For those missing darts and British food.

Nightclubs *Hippopotamus*, R Barão de Torre 354, Ipanema. Buddha restaurant open from 2030, nightclub from 2300 daily. The socialites choice with a strict door policy, US$15 entry and minimum consumption. *People*, Av Bartolomeu Mitre 370, Leblon, T5128824. Popular and select night spot for many years, techno, trance, hip hop, open from 2300, entry and minimum consumption US$15, Sun is reported to be the best night. *Plataforma I*, R Adalberto Ferreira 32, Leblon, T2744022. Lavish samba show, arrive by 2100, show starts at 2200 and ends at 2350, expensive drinks. *Scala*, Av Afrânio de Melo Franco 296, T2394448. Home to many carnival balls in particular the extremely popular *Baile Gay*. *W*, R Visconde de Pirajá 22, Ipanema. New club with dance floor, theatre, Japanese and Italian restaurants, popular with local celebrities, entry and minimum consumption US$15, open from 2100 daily, best night reported to be Thu.

Entertainment **Carnival blocos** *Banda da Carmen Miranda*, parades on the Sun afternoon before carnival. Famous gay banda dressed in the style of the famous actress. *Banda da Ipanema*, parades on Sat and Tue afternoons during carnival in Praça General Osorio (also parades on the Sat two weeks before carnival). Formed in 1965 as a political protest against the dictatorship today the banda is popular with gays and transvestites whose costumes are always colourful and inventive. *Simpatia é Quase Amor*, parades on the Sat afternoon before carnival and the Sun afternoon during carnival in Praça General Osorio. Popular bloco with politically incorrect banners and good percussion section. There are many others such as *Bloco Rôla Preguiçosa* and *Cordão Carnavelesco Folia do Pingüim*.

Cinema *Candido Mendes*, R Joana Angélica 63. *Cineclube Laura Alvim*, Av Viera Souto 176. Art cinema. *Leblon*, Av Ataulfo de Paiva 391. *Star Ipanema*, R Visconde de Pirajá.

Music *Bar do Tom*, in Plataforma nightclub (see above). Live Bossa Nova, Jazz and MPB from 2230 Thu-Sat, 2000-midnight Sun. *Vinícius*, R Vinícius de Morais 39, 2nd floor. Live music (Jazz, Bossa Nova, MPB) and international cuisine from 2030 Tue-Sat.

Theatre *Casa da Cultura Laura Alvim*, Av Viera Souto 176, T2671647. Small theatre. *Teatro do Leblon*, R Conde de Bernadotte 26. Divided into Sala Marília Pera, T2940347 and Sala Fernanda Montenegro, T2743536.

Bookshops *Livraria Argumento*, R Dias Ferreira 417, Leblon. Sells imported English books, also has a café, 0900-2430 Mon-Sat, 1400-2400 Sun. *Dazibao*, R Visconde de Pirajá 571, Ipanema, www.dazibao.com.br Good stock on many subjects. *Letras e Expressões*, R Visconde de Pirajá 276, Ipanema, www.letras.com Good bookshop with English and German magazines. *Livraria da Travessa*, R Visconde de Pirajá 462, Ipanema. Good selection of guidebooks.

Shopping

Jewellery *H Stern*, R Visconde de Pirajá 490 with R Garcia D'vila 113. 10 outlets plus branches in major hotels throughout the city; see page 147. *Amsterdam Sauer*, R Garcia D'Ávila 105, have 10 shops in Rio; they offer free taxi rides to their main shop; see page 147. The headquarters of these 2 establishments are next door to each other. *H Stern* is much the bigger of the 2 in terms of premises, shop space, tours etc.

Markets *Feirarte I* is a Sun open-air handicrafts market (everyone calls it the *Feira Hippy*) at Praça Gen Osório, Ipanema, 0800-1800, mainly popular now with tourists but still fun: items from all over Brazil. Early-morning food market, 0600-1100, R Min Viveiros de Castro, Ipanema. Excellent food and household-goods markets at various places in the city and suburbs (see newspapers for times and places). *Feira do Livro*, Nossa Senhora da Paz, selling books at 20% discount.

Photography For processing, *Flash Studio*, R Visconde de Pirajá 156. Expensive. *Honório*, R Vinícius de Moraes 146E. Stocks lithium batteries. Nikon camera repairs.

Shopping centres *Rio Design Center*, Av Ataulfo de Paiva 270. Antiques, boutiques and art galleries, open 1000-2200 Mon-Sat.

Blumar Turismo, R Visconde de Pirjajá 550, basement 108/109, RJ 22410, T5113636, F5113739, www.blumar.com.br Run extensive tours throughout Brazil as well as reservations for Rio. *Helisight*, R Visconde de Pirajá 580, ground floor 107, T5112141, F2945292, www.helisight.com.br Helicopter sightseeing tours from US$45 pp for 6-7 mins from Morro de Urca over Sugar Loaf and Corcovado, to US$150 pp for 30 mins over the city. *Jeep Tour Ecologia e Cultura*, Av Rainha Elizabeth 664, 1st floor, T/F5221620, Cell99779610, www.antares.com.br/~jeeptour Tours to Candomblé ceremony, Rocinha favela, Tijuca Forest and Western Rio. *Rio Life*, R Visconde de Pirajá 550, office 215, Ipanema, T2595532, Cell96372522, www.travelrio.com Personalized tours on all aspects of Rio with groups of 2 to 4 maximum. Luiz Felipe Amaral speaks excellent English. *Novos Rumos*, R Visconde de Pirajá 550, T/F5127799, nrumos@openlink.com.br Cultural tours and visits to operas, ballets and concerts. *Stella Barros*, R Visconde de Pirajá 647, Sl 701/726, T2946740, F2947392. *Tour Brazil*, R Farme de Amoedo 75/605, near Ipanema, T5214461, F5211056. Very good English spoken.

Tour operators

Transport Buses Buses run from Botafogo Metrô terminal to Ipanema: some take integrated Metrô-Bus tickets; look for the blue signs on the windscreen. Many buses from Copacabana run to Ipanema and Leblon.

Directory Banks *Itaú*, R Visconde de Pirajá, close to Praça Gen Osório. Mastercard and Cirrus cash machines. **Communications Post Office:** Branches at R Visconde de Pirajá 452, basement, and R Ataulfo de Paiva 822. **Telephone:** International calls can be made at *Telemar*, R Visconde de Pirajá 111. **Internet:***Café.com.arte*, Av Ataulfo de Paiva 566/100B. US$1.25 per hour, open daily 0700-midnight. *Café Ubaldo*, R Visconde de Pirajá 276, 2nd floor of *Letras e Expressões* bookshop. US$2.75 per ½ hr, open 0800-0200 Mon-Thu and 24 hrs Fri-Sun. *Estação*, R Visconde de Pirajá 572. Macs and PCs, US$1.75 per ¼ hr, good food, live music on Thur, open daily 0800-2300. *Image Link*, R Visconde de Pirajá 207, room 216. Slow PC, US$3 per ½ hr, 0900-1800 Mon-Fri. *Internexus*, Av Ataulfo de Paiva 1079, 3rd floor. **Laundry** *Fénix*, Praça Gen Osório. **Medical services** Dentist: Dr Mauro Suartz, R Visconde de Pirajá 414, room 509, T2876745. Speaks English and Hebrew, helpful. **Places of worship** *International Baptist Church*, R Desembargador Alfredo Russel 146, Leblon, T2460900. Services in English at 1100 and Portuguese at 1900.

Lagoa, Jardim Botânico and Gávea

Backing Ipanema and Leblon is the middle-class residential area of Lagoa Rodrigo de Freitas, next to a saltwater lagoon frequented by Rio's rowing and small-boat sailing clubs. The lake is too polluted for bathing, but the road which runs around its shores has pleasant views. The avenue on the eastern shore, Avenida Epitácio Pessoa, leads to the Túnel Rebouças which runs beneath Corcovado and Cosme Velho. Once out of the tunnel, the urban motorway meets up with the Linha Vermelha for the north, or continues to Avenida Presidente Vargas and the Rodoviária.

On the western side of the lake is the Hipódromo de Gávea, the city's horseracing track. By the track and the lake is the residential area known as Jardim Botânico, so called because of its proximity to the Botanical Gardens.

Sights

Lagoa The Lagoa was originally called Sacopenapã by the Tamoios Indians after a local bird. After the arrival of the Portuguese it became known as Engenho del Rei and later Engenho de Nossa Senhora da Conceição as well as receiving the name of its many owners before finally sticking with that of Rodrigo de Freitas Mello e Castro. The area passed to the posession of the monarchy in the early nineteenth century. At this time the lake was much larger but has shrunk over the years as has its canal to the sea. Many foreign visitors such as the German botanist Von Martius in 1817 and the English naturalist Charles Darwin in 1832, have commented on its beauty.

Running for 7.5 km around the Lagoa Rodrigo de Freitas, the **Parque Tom Jobim** has a cycle way and jogging track. It joins three other parks Parque Brigadeiro Faria Lima, Parque do Cantagalo and Parque das Taboas to form an extensive leisure area with playgrounds and facilities for many different sports such as volleyball and rollerskating. In the area known as Parque dos Patins there are kiosks serving a variety of food from Arabic to Japanese. Recently this has become a very popular spot with Cariocas who come on warm evenings for live shows and forró. ■ *Daily.*

Parque Carlos Lacerda in Parque da Catacumba, Avenida Epitácio Pessoa, is an open air art gallery with sculptures by local artists in a landscaped park shaded by ornamental trees. ■ *Daily 0800-1900.*

£4000 worth of holiday vouchers to be won!

... that can be claimed against any **exodus**, **Peregrine** or **Gecko's** holiday, a choice of around 570 holidays that set industry standards for responsible tourism in 90 countries across seven continents.

exodus

The UK's leading adventurous travel company, with over 25 years' experience in running the most exciting holidays in 80 different countries. We have an unrivalled choice of trips, from a week exploring the hidden corners of Tuscany to a high altitude trek to Everest Base Camp or 3 months travelling across South America. If you want to do something a little different, chances are you'll find it in one of our brochures.

Peregrine

Australia's leading quality adventure travel company, Peregrine aims to explore some of the world's most interesting and inaccessible places. Providing exciting and enjoyable holidays that focus in some depth on the lifestyle, culture, history, wildlife, wilderness and landscapes of areas that are usually quite different to our own. There is an emphasis on the outdoors, using a variety of transport and staying in a range of accommodation, from comfortable hotels to tribal huts.

Gecko's

Gecko's holidays will get you to the best places with the minimum of hassle. They are designed for younger people who like independent travel but don't have the time to organise everything themselves. Be prepared to take the rough with the smooth, these holidays are for active people with a flexible approach to travel.

To enter the competition, simply tear out the postcard and return it to Exodus Travels, 9 Weir Road, London SW12 OLT. Or go to the competition page on www.exodus.co.uk and register online. Two draws will be made, Easter 2001 and Easter 2002, and the winner of each draw will receive £2000 in travel vouchers. If you do not wish to receive further information about these holidays, please tick here. ☐

To receive a brochure, please tick the relevant boxes below (maximum number of brochures 2)

exodus	Peregrine	Gecko's
☐ Walking & Trekking	☐ Himalaya	☐ Egypt, Jordan & Israel
☐ Discovery & Adventure	☐ China	☐ South America
☐ European Destinations	☐ South East Asia	☐ Africa
☐ Overland Journeys	☐ Antarctica	☐ Thailand & Laos
☐ Biking Adventures	☐ Africa	☐ India

Please give us your details:

Name: ....
Address: ....
....

Postcode: ....
e-mail: ....
Which footprint guide did you take this from?
....

exodus *The Different Holiday*

getaway tonight on www.exodus.co.uk

getaway tonight on
www.exodus.co.uk

exodus
The Different Holiday

---

exodus

**9 Weir Road
LONDON
SW12 0BR**

BUSINESS REPLY SERVICE
Licence No SW4909

Fundação Eva Klabin Rapaport, Avenida Epitácio Pessoa 2480, is a private art collection including paintings, sculptures, furniture and ceramics from all parts of the world. ■ *Mon-Fri 0900-1800, T2479016, arrange visits in advance.*

The Jardim Botânico (Botanic Gardens) at Rua Jardim Botânico 1008, are well worth a visit. Covering 137 ha, they were founded in 1808 by the king, Dom João VI, as a garden for acclimatizing plants on land in the Real Fazenda. When the electric tram line arrived in this part of the city, housing and industries soon followed, but the gardens, then as now, remained a haven of peace. The most striking features are the transverse avenues of 30 m high royal palms. Among the more than 7,000 varieties of plants from around the world are examples of the *pau-brasil* tree (see page 229), now endangered, and many other threatened species. (Look for monkeys in the trees.) There is a herbarium, an aquarium and a library as well as the **Museu Botânico**, housing exhibitions on the conservation of Brazilian flora, and the **Casa dos Pilões**, the first gunpowder factory in Brazil. A new pavilion contains sculptures by Mestre Valentim transferred from the centre. Many improvements were carried out before the 1992 Earth Summit, including a new Orquidário, an enlarged bookshop, an expensive *lanchonete*, replanting and cleaning up. Visitors needing information in English should ask for Beatriz Heloisa Guimarães, of the *Society of Friends of the Garden*.

Jardim Botânico

Birdwatchers should visit the Botanical Gardens, preferably early in the morning; 140 species of birds have been recorded here: flycatchers are very prominent (the social flycatcher, great and boat-billed kiskadees, cattle tyrant); also tanagers (the sayaca and palm tanagers and the colourful green-headed tanager) and over 20 different kinds of hummingbird. Birds of prey include the roadside hawk, the laughing falcon and the American kestrel, and there are doves, cuckoos, parakeets, thrushes and woodpeckers and occasional flocks of toucans. ■ *T2947494, www.jbrj.gov.br Daily 0800-1700. US$2. They are 8 km from the centre; take bus No 170 from the centre, or any bus to Leblon, Gávea or São Conrado marked 'via Jóquei'; from Glória, Flamengo or Botafogo take No 571, or 172 from Flamengo; from Copacabana, Ipanema or Leblon take No 572 (584 back to Copacabana).*

Parque Laje, near the Jardim Botânico at Rua Jardim Botânico 414, almost jungle-like, has small grottoes, an old tower and lakes, as well as the Escola de Artes Visuais (Visual Arts School) housed in the mansion. ■ *Daily, 0900-1700, free.*

South of the Jóquei Club, as the racetrack is also known, is the **Clube de Regatas do Flamengo**, Praça Nossa Senhora Auxiliadora. Originally formed as a rowing club in 1895, today the club practices many sports such as Athletics and Judo whilst its football team is one of the most popular throughout Brazil. ■ *www.flamengo.com.br*

Gávea

The **Planetário** (Planetarium), on Rua Padre Leonel Franco 240, Gávea, was inaugurated in 1979, with a sculpture of the Earth and Moon by Mario Agostinelli. On Wednesday evenings at dusk, in clear weather, astronomers give guided observations of the stars that are visible (entry free); on Saturday and Sunday there are shows for children at 1630 and for adults and children over 12 at 1800 and 1930; also on Sunday at 1800 there are observations. There are occasional *chorinho* concerts on Thursday or Friday; check the press for details. ■ *T2740096, www.rio.rj.gov.br/planetario Visits by appointment. Buses 176 and 178 from the centre and Flamengo; 591 and 592 from Copacabana.*

Parque da Cidade, Estrada de Santa Marinha 505, a pleasant park a short walk beyond the Gávea bus terminus, has a great many trees and lawns, with views over the ocean. The proximity of the Rocinha favela (see below) means that the park is not very safe. It is advisable to carry a copy of your passport here because of the frequent police checks. ■ *Daily 0700-1700. Free. Buses, Nos 593, 592, 174, 170, 546, leave you just short of the entrance, but it should be OK to walk the last part if in a group. Similarly, do not walk the trails in the park alone.* In the park is the **Museu Histórico da Cidade**, a former coffee *fazenda* with historical exhibits. Every third Sunday in the month it holds a gastronomic event with music from 1400. See the Capela de São João Bautista whose murals by Carlos Bastos so scandalized the patrons for their inclusion of famous people into the life of Christ that they were never finished (only open weekends). ■ *T5122353, www.rio.rj.gov.br/cultura Tue-Sun 1100-1700. US$1.*

Instituto Moreira Salles, Rua Marquês de São Vicente 476, is a cultural centre in a 19th-century mansion with gardens landscaped by Burle Marx. There are a number of exhibition halls, library and a small auditorium for concerts and films. ■ *T5126448. Tue-Fri 1300-2000, Sat-Sun 1300-1800.*

Essentials

Sleeping These are rich residential areas with few hotels and most visitors stay in nearby Ipanema or Leblon.

Eating **Jardim Botânico Expensive**: *Claude Troisgros*, R Custódio Serrão 62, T5378582. One of the best French restaurants in the city, elegant, open 1200-1530 and 1900-0030 Mon-Fri, 1900-0030 Sat. Recommended. ***Quadrifoglio***, R JJ Seabra 19, T2941433. Excellent Italian, open 1200-1530, 1900-0100 Mon-Fri, 1930-0100 Sat and 1230-2400 Sun.

Mid-range: *Allons Enfants*, R Visconde de Carandaí 5, T2393397. Excellent French cuisine. *Le Sommelier*, R Frei Leandro, T5279003. Good French cuisine, open from 2000 Mon-Sat and from 1200 Sun.

Cheap: *Boteco 66*, Av Alexandre Ferreira 66. Cosy bistro, open from 1130 Tue-Sun.

Gávea Mid-range: *Guimas*, R Macedo Soares 5, T2597996. Good international cuisine.

Cheap: *Garota da Gávea*, Praça Santos Dumont 142. Good food especially *picanha* (beef) which you cook to your taste on a hot plate. Some tables have their own beer taps so you can fill your glass at your leisure for which you are charged per litre (indicated by a counter). Recommended.

Bars & nightclubs **Bars** On some weekday evenings, younger Cariocas congregate at *Hipódromo*, and other bars around Praça Santos Dumont, often spilling out into the streets (the area has become known as the *Baixo Gávea*). The most popular day is *Segunda sem lei* (Monday without laws) and the appropriate night to go out without one's boyfriend or girlfriend. Thursday is also a popular night but the bars now have to close at 0100 due to complaints by local residents. *Bar Lagoa*, Av Epitácio Pessoa 1674, Lagoa. Art deco bar founded in 1934, good draught beer and German food, arty crowd, 1800-0200 Mon, 1200-0200 Tue-Sun. *Queen's Legs*, Av Epitácio Pessoa 5030, Lagoa. British pub with bar games and live music.

Nightclubs *El Turf* (aka *Jockey Club*) , opposite the Jardim Botânico, Praça Santos Dumont 31, T2741444. Opens at 2200, gets going at 2300, you may have to wait to get in at the weekend if you arrive after midnight, no T-shirts allowed, very much a singles and birthday party place. *Hipódromo Up*, Praça Santos Dumont 108, upstairs.

Live forró, and MPB, open from 2100 Tue-Sun. **Méli Mélo**, Av Borges de Medeiros 1426, Lagoa. Spacious club with two dance floors, Japanese restaurant and free cybercafé, from 2000 Tue-Sun, entry and minimum consumption about US$15 (after 2200), best night reported to be Wed. **Prelude**, Av Epitácio Pessoa 1484. Small club with Japanese restaurant, open daily from 2200 (best to arrive early). **Skipper**, Praça Santos Dumont 80. Club which is more popular during the week especially Thu, entry on Fri-Sat is US$5 (free during week) with US$8.50 minimum consumption.

Entertainment

Carnival blocos *Suvaco de Cristo*, is popular with young people, has a large percussion section and is considered the ideal bloco for flirting. It parades on the Sun before carnival from Bar Jóia, R Jardim Botânico 594. T-shirts, US$5, are compulsory and can be bought on the day of the parade or before from Bar Jóia.

Cinema *Sala Instituto Moreira Salles*, R Marquês de São Vicente 476 (see above).

Music *Chiko's Bar*, Av Epitácio Pessoa 1560. MPB and Jazz from 2130 daily. *Mistura Fina*, Av Borges de Medeiros 3207, T5372844. Classy restaurant with popular and friendly nightclub upstairs with live Jazz and Latin music. *Rhapsody*, Av Epitácio Pessoa 1104, T2472104. Restaurant with piano bar, dance floor with Brazilian and Italian music.

Theatre In Shopping da Gávea: *Teatro das Artes*, 2nd floor, T5406004. *Teatro Clara Nunes*, 3rd floor, T2749696. *Teatro dos Quatro*, 2nd floor, T2749895. *Teatro Vannuci*, 3rd floor, T2747246.

Shopping

Handicrafts *O Sol*, R Corvocado 213, Jardim Botânico. Wide variety of Brazilian arts and crafts.

Markets Every other weekend the very lively and popular **Babilônia Feira Hype** is held at the Jockey Club racetrack from 1400-2300 with fashion clothes, arts, shiatsu massage as well as live music and dance performances. An antiques fair is also held on Sun from 0900-1700 in Praça Santos Dumont opposite the racetrack.

Shopping centres *Shopping da Gávea*, R Marquês de São Vicente 52. Fashions, art galleries, restaurants, cinemas and theatres, open 1000-2200 Mon-Sat.

Vidigal and São Conrado

The Pedra Dois Irmãos mountain overlooks Leblon. On the slopes is Vidigal favela. From Leblon, two inland roads take traffic west to the outer seaside suburb of Barra da Tijuca: the Auto Estrada Lagoa-Barra, which tunnels under Dois Irmãos, and the Estrada da Gávea, which goes through Gávea passing the American School of Rio de Janeiro.

Beyond Leblon the coast is rocky. A third route to Barra da Tijuca is the Avenida Niemeyer, which skirts the cliffs on the journey past Vidigal, a small beach where the Sheraton is situated. Avenida Niemeyer carries on round the coast to São Conrado, with its Fashion Mall and the Gávea golf club; a very exclusive neighbourhood and few tourists stop here. On the slopes of the Pedra da Gávea, through which the Avenida Niemeyer has two tunnels, is the Rocinha favela.

Sights

Favela Tour It is possible to visit Vila Canoas and Rocinha *favelas* close to São Conrado. This is very interesting and leads to a greater appreciation of Rio and its people. Rocinha has a tourist information post with guides from the community who will take visitors on an hour long tour, minimum of four people, US$6 per person. It is best to visit on an organized tour. ■ *See Tour operators below, for guides who can offer a safe, different and interesting experience.*

The flat-topped **Pedra da Gávea** can be climbed or scrambled up for magnificent views, but beware of snakes. Some say that the rock is sphinx-like and from the Tijuca Forest side there is clearly a conformation similar to a face with a beard. Claims have been made that Phoenician inscriptions have been found and many other legends surround the rock. The trek to the top and back takes about five hours for the reasonably fit. People sometimes camp on top especially during full moons.

Behind the Pedra da Gávea is the **Pedra Bonita** which can be reached in about 30 minutes at an easy pace from the parking place for the hang-gliders. There are good views of Barra da Tijuca, Rio and the Ilhas Cagarras from the top. A road, the Estrada das Canoas, climbs up past these two rocks on its way to the Tijuca National Park. There is a spot on this road which gives access to the *rampa de asa delta*, which is one of the chief **hang-glider** launch sites in the area (see 'Sports', page 68).

Close to Praia de São Conrado **Vila Riso**, Estrada da Gávea 728, is a well preserved colonial 18th-century *fazenda* with a small chapel. Inside are furniture, antiques and art objects. ■ *T33221444.*

Essentials

Sleeping **LL** *Sheraton Rio Hotel & Towers*, Av Niemeyer 121, Vidigal, T2741122, F2395643, www.sheraton-rio.com 5-star located directly on beach front, several restaurants and pools, childminders, medical facilities, tennis courts, travel agency and business services. **LL** *Intercontinental Rio*, Av Prefeito Mendes de Moraes 222, São Conrado, T33222200, F33225500, rioha@intercont.com 5-star on the beach with mountain views, childminders, restaurants, tennis courts, gym, disco.

Eating **Mid-range**: *Alfredo*, in Hotel Inter-Continental. Italian restaurant with piano music, open 1930-2330 Mon-Fri. *Enotria*, 2nd floor of *Fashion Mall* shopping centre, T33226064. Excellent Italian food, service, atmosphere and prices. Recommended. *Guimas*, in *Fashion Mall* shopping centre, T33225791. Good international cuisine. *Oásis*, Estr do Joá 136, São Conrado, T33223144. Good churrascaria open daily from 1100 to midnight. *Sushi Garden*, in *Fashion Mall* shopping centre, T33224932. Excellent Japanese, open daily 1200-0200.

Bars & nightclubs **Bars** *Bar 121*, in *Sheraton Hotel*. Happy hour from 1800-2000 daily, Jazz from 2100 Mon-Sat. *Zeppelin*, Estr do Vidigal 471. Cosy bar with beautiful views and live music (MPB), open from 2000 Fri-Sat. *Alvaro's* and *California Dream*, In Fashion Mall (see below).

Nightclubs *Papillon Club*, in *Hotel Inter-Continental*. Disco open from 2200 Fri-Sat.

Entertainment **Cinema** *Art Fashion Mall*, in São Conrado Fashion Mall. Four screens.

Samba schools *Acadêmicos da Rocinha*, R Bertha Lutz 80, São Conrado, T33225948, www.artes.com/rocinha Rehearsals from 2300 Sat and 1300 Sun.

Handicrafts *Borogodó*, Ground floor of Fashion Mall. Handmade laces from North- **Shopping**
east Brazil, clothes, tablecloths etc.

Shopping centres *São Conrado Fashion Mall*, Estr da Gávea 899. Small and stylish but expensive mall with art galleries, cinemas and restaurants, open 1000-2200 Mon-Thu, 1000-2300 Fri-Sat, 1500-2100 Sun.

Favela Tour, Estr das Canoas 722, Bl 2, apt 125, RJ 22610-210, T33222727, Cell99890074 **Tour operators** and 97721133, F33225958, www.favelatour.com.br Marcelo Armstrong was the pioneer of favela tourism and offers guided tours of Vila Canoas and Rocinha favelas, safe, different and interesting, US$25 (part of which helps fund a community school), 3 hrs. Also ask about eco tours, river rafting and other excursions. He speaks English, French, Spanish, Italian and can provide guides in German and Swedish. For the best attention and price call Marcelo direct rather than through a hotel desk. See box on page 98. *The Gray Line*, in *Hotel Intercontinental*, T5129919, F2595847. Regular sightseeing tours and bay trips.

Barra da Tijuca

This rapidly developing residential area is also one of the principal recreation areas of Rio, with its 20-km sandy beach and good surfing waves. At the westernmost end is the small beach of Recreio dos Bandeirantes, where the ocean can be very rough. The channels behind the Barra are popular with jetskiers and it gets very busy on Sundays. There are innumerable bars and restaurants, clustered at both ends, campsites (see page 160), motels and hotels: budget accommodation tends to be self-catering. The facilities include the huge Barra Shopping and Carrefour shopping centres.

Although buses do run as far as Barra, getting to & around here is best done by car. A cycle way links Barra da Tijuca with the centre of the city

Nature is an important and undeniable part of Rio and nowhere is this more evident than in the Maciço da Tijuca that divides the city in two with its ridges and dramatic peaks. As the largest urban park of tropical forest in the world, Parque Nacional da Floresta da Tijuca is the preferred option for Cariocas and tourists wishing to swap the noisy traffic and crowded beaches of the city for its shaded trails, cool streams and waterfalls. Plants and animals to be seen include eucalyptus, humming birds and monkeys but be sure not to stray off the marked paths without a guide.

Sights

The **Autódromo** (motor racing track) is behind Barra and the Lagoa de Jacarepaguá, in the district of the same name. The Brazilian Grand Prix was held here during the 1980s before returning to Interlagos, São Paulo.

See also Sleeping section on page 159

Riocentro, Avenida Salvador Allende 6555, Jacarepaguá, is a 600,000-sq m convention complex which is becoming an increasingly popular site for international congresses and trade fairs. ■ *T4421300, F4421155, riocentro@rio.rj.gov.br*

A bit further out is the **Museu Casa do Pontal**, Estrada do Pontal 3295, Recreio dos Bandeirantes. Set in a pleasant site near the Grumari mountains this museum houses a collection of Brazilian folk art, put together by the French designer Jacques van de Beuque. The exhibits consist of expressive figurines made from painted wood or clay that show many different aspects of the country's culture and history such as bandits, carnival and rural life. Some of the displays are animated with sound and there is a discrete erotic section in a separate closed room. Recommended. ■ *T4903278. Tue-Sun, 0900-1730. US$2.75 entry. Best visited on a tour of Barra or Western Rio as the museum is difficult to reach by public transport.*

Parks **Terra Encantada**, Avenida Ayrton Senna 2800, is a 300,000 sq m theme park in Barra whose attractions are based on the different cultural heritages of Brazil: the indigenous, African and European. Among the attractions are roller coasters, river rapids, a cinema and shows. Rides close at 2200 and on the main street restaurants, bars and nightspots open. ■ *T4219444, www.terra-encantada.com.br Thu-Sun 1000-2300.*

There are two aquatic theme parks in Recreio dos Bandeirantes. **Rio Water Planet**, Estrada dos Bandeirantes 24000, with artificial beaches, water slides and a go-kart track. ■ *T0800-242220, www.riowaterplanet.com.br Tue-Sun 1000-1900.* **Wet'nWild Rio**, Avenida das Américas 22000. ■ *T4289300, www.wetnwildrio.com Daily 1000-1900.*

The **Bosque da Barra/Parque Arruda Câmara**, at the junction of Avenida das Américas and Avenida Ayrton Senna, preserves the vegetation of the sandbanks which existed on this part of the coast before the city took over. Many birds and small animals can be seen around the natural lagoons and there are cycle and jogging paths. ■ *Daily 0700-1800, T33256519.*

Parque Ecológico Municipal Chico Mendes, Av Jarbas de Carvalho 679, Recreio dos Bandeirantes, is a 400,000 sq m park with ecological trails and includes the Lagoinha das Tachas. The park preserves the *restinga* marsh ecosystem and provides a home for broad nose caymans, beach butterflies and many birds. ■ *T4376400. Daily 0900-1730. Free entry.*

Other parks in this area include **Parque Trevo das Palmeiras**, junction of Avenida Arrton Senna and Avenida das Américas. ■ *Daily 0700-1900.* **Parque Marapendi**, Avenida Alfredo Baltazar da Silveira, Recreo dos Bandeirantes. ■ *Daily 0800-1700.*

Tijuca National Park

History The vegetation in the Parque Nacional da Tijuca, for all its abundance, is not primeval. Most of what is now the largest urban, forested national park in the world, is reforested. The first Europeans in the area cut down trees for use in construction and as firewood. The lower areas were cleared to make way for sugar plantations. When coffee was introduced to Rio de Janeiro in 1760, the logical place to start cultivating it was on the hillsides surrounding the city. Huge tracts of the forest were cut down and coffee estates created. Conditions for the bushes were ideal, but for the city itself, it did not prove ideal. Although many people made lots of money, deforesting the hills disrupted the rainfall pattern and the water supply for the expanding city became insufficient. In 1861, therefore, the Imperial government decided that the whole area should be reforested. The job was given to Major Manuel Gomes Archer who, with just six slaves, completed the task in 13 years. They used saplings taken from neighbouring areas, but added to the native species many exotic varieties. The work was continued by Tomás de Gama. A national park of 3,300 ha, which united various different forests, was set up in 1961.

Exploring the The **Pico da Tijuca** (1,022 m) gives a good idea of the tropical vegetation of the **park** interior and a fine view of the bay and its shipping. A two to three hour walk leads to the summit. On entering the park at Alto da Boa Vista (open 0600-2100), follow the signposts (maps are displayed) to Bom Retiro, a good picnic place (1½ hours' walk). At Bom Retiro the road ends and there is another hour's walk up a fair footpath to the summit (take the path from the right of the Bom Retiro drinking fountain; not the more obvious steps from the left). The last part consists of steps carved out of the solid rock; look after children at the summit as there are several sheer drops, invisible because of bushes. The route is shady for almost its entire length. The main path to Bom Retiro passes the **Cascatinha Taunay** (a 30 m waterfall) and the **Mayrink Chapel** (built 1860). Panels painted in the Chapel by Cândido Portinari have been replaced by copies and the originals will probably be installed in the Museu de Arte Moderna. Beyond the Chapel is the restaurant *A Floresta* and Major Archer's house, now in ruins.

Other places of interest not passed on the walk to the peak are the **Paulo e Virginia Grotto**, the **Vista do Almirante** and the **Mesa do Imperador** (viewpoints). Allow at least five to six hours for the excursion. Maps of the park are available. If hiking in the national park other than on the main paths, a guide may be useful if you do not want to get lost: *Sindicato de Guías*, T2674582.

Viewpoints include the Vista Chinesa (420 m), where from a Chinese-style pavilion one can see the Lagoa Rodrigo de Freitas, Ipanema and Leblon. There is no public transport.

Museu Açude, Estrada do Açude 764, Alto da Boa Vista, Floresta da Tijuca, Castro Maia's former residence is a museum and every Sunday it has a 'brunch' with music, 1230-1700. ■ *T4922119, www.visualnet.com.br/cmaya Thu-Sun 1100-1700.*

Jeep tours are run by *Atlantic Forest Jeep Tour*, T4959827, Cell99740218. Also to Angra dos Reis and offshore islands, Vargem Grande in Western Rio, coffee *fazendas* in the Paraíba Valley, Itaipava, Teresópolis and the Serra dos Órgãos. *Jeep Tour Ecologia e Cultura*, T/F5221620, Cell99779610, www.jeeptour.com.br Also offer many other tours in the city (see page 151). *Qualitours Jeep Tour in Rio*, T/F2329710, Cell91751225. English, French, German and Hungarian spoken. Also offer tours to Fortaleza de Santa Cruz near Niterói, Grumari in Western Rio and many other tours in the city.

Walking tours are run by *Aventuras Rio*, T38130312, Cell96999633, www.aventurasrio.com.br Also offer abseiling and rafting at weekends. *Cume Calmo*, T5725063 (André), Cell91160652 (Gustavo), www.alpinismo.com Also offer mountaineering courses as well as trekking and climbing in Serra dos Órgãos. *Rio Hiking*, T/F2454036, Cell97210594, www.riohiking.com.br Also offer tours in the city as well as to Ilha Grande and Itatiaia (see page 128). *Trilharte Ecoturismo*, Caixa Postal 50070, RJ 20062-970 T/F2731798, trilharte.com.br. Also offer trekking in Pedra Branca state park and nature photography courses.

Park tour operators

Buses Take bus No 221 from Praça 15 de Novembro, No 233 (which continues to Barra da Tijuca) or 234 from the rodoviária or from Praça Sáens Pena, Tijuca (the city suburb, not Barra – reached by Metrô), or No 454 from Copacabana to Alto da Boa Vista, for the park entrance.

Transport

Essentials

Barra da Tijuca **AL** *Barraleme*, Av Sernambetiba 600, T33893100, F33893396. Restaurant, pool, sauna, beauty saloon. **AL** *Barra Palace*, Av Sernambetiba 2916, T33891212, F33891244. Restaurant, pool, sauna, gym, tennis court, beauty saloon, parking. **AL** *Barra Sol*, Av Sernambetiba 690, T/F4942658. **AL** *Entremares*, Av Érico Verissimo 846, T4943887, F4931868. Small meeting room, bar, restaurant, parking. **AL** *Praia Linda*, Av Sernambetiba 1430, T4942186, F4942198. Meeting room, restaurant, parking. **AL** *La Reserve*, Av Sernambetiba 5730, T33851200, F33851390. Bar, restaurant, pool, sauna, beauty saloon, parking. **A** *Barra Beach*, Av Sernambetiba 1120, T33896358, F33896222. **A** *Signus*, Estr da Barra 25, T4939515, F4930487. Restaurant, parking.

Sleeping
Most of the accommodation in this area is apartment hotels & flats

Recreio dos Bandeirantes A *Atlântico Sul*, R Professor Armando Ribeiro 25, T4902050, F4901818. Meeting room, restaurant, pool, sauna, parking. **A** (half board) *Pousada Fetiche*, Av AW 700, Praia da Macumba, T4903307, Cell99893944, www.hps.com.br/pousadafetiche On the beach, TV, roof fans, snack bar, barbecue, games room, parking.

Camping *Camping Clube do Brasil* has 2 beach sites at Av Sernambetiba 3200, T4930628 (bus 233 from centre, 702 or 703 from the airport via Zona Sul, US$5 – a long way from the centre), sauna, pool, bar, café, US$12 (half price for members) and a simpler site at Estrada do Pontal 5900, T4378400, lighting, café, good surfing, US$6. Both have trailer plots. *Ostal*, Av Sernambetiba 18790, T4378350.

Eating **Mid-range** *La Botticella*, R Prof Ferreira da Rosa 88, T4944776. Good Italian, open 2000-0100 Tue-Sat, 1300-1800 Sun. *La Louisiane*, in Itanhangá Center, T4942360. New Orleans creole cuisine, open Mon-Fri 1900-0100, Sat-Sun 1200-0200. *Outback*, Av das Américas 6101 and in New York City Center, www.outbackintl.com Very popular American steak house, open 1800-0100 Mon-Fri, 1200-0130 Sat, 1200-2300 Sun. *Porcão*, Av Armando Lombardi 591, T4922001. Good churrasco rodízio, open 1100-0100.

Cheap *Azzurra*, Av Lúcio Costa 5706, T33851171. Italian restaurant popular with football players, open daily for lunch and dinner. *Koskenkorva*, Av Germário Dantas 439, Jacarepaguá, T33928320. Finnish restaurant specializing in fish. *El Patio Porteño*, Av Rodolfo de Amoedo 360. Argentine barbeques, tango on Mon, open daily 1200-2400. *Royal Grill*, in Casa Shopping, T33256166. Good churrasco, open 1200-2400.

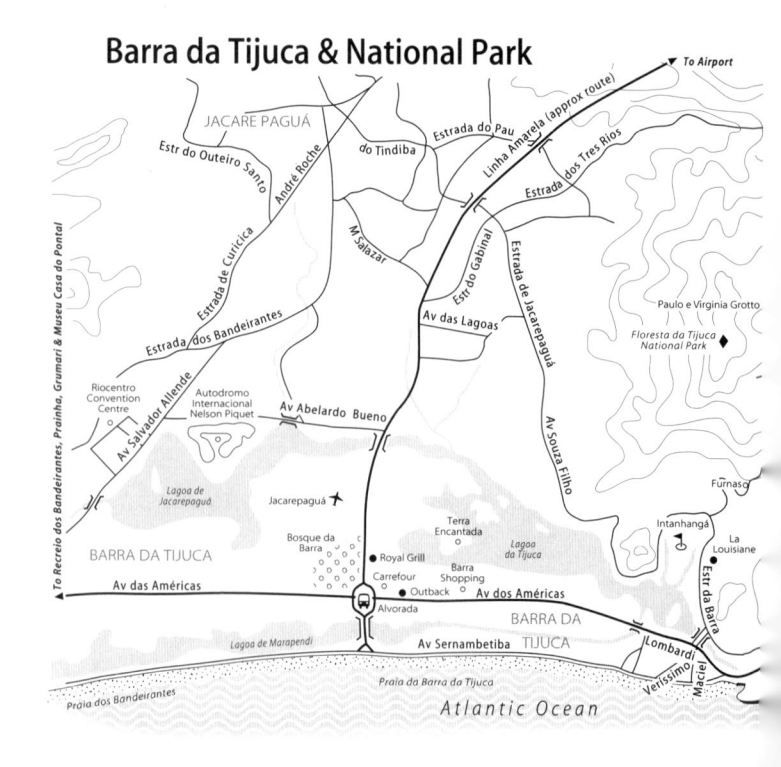

Barra da Tijuca & National Park

Very cheap *Amarelinho*, Av Ayrton Senna 3000. Excellent lanchonete. Recommended.

Bars & nightclubs

Bars *Academia da Cachaça*, Av Armando Lombardi 800. Bar and restaurant serving various cocktails made from sugar cane spirit. ***Bar do Oswaldo***, Estr da Joá 3896. Simple yet historic bar with excellent batidas mixed from tropical fruits, *coco* (coconut) is a good choice, open from 1200-0100. ***Barraca do Pepê*** at Posto 2, Barra da Tijuca beach. Very popular with young people.

Nightclubs *Dado Bier*, in Downtown shopping centre. Disco bar with its own beer, open Tue-Sun from 1830 until late. *Greenwich Village*, Av Sernambetiba 4462, at Posto 6 on the beach front. Disco with good reputation, open Wed-Sat from 2100 and Sun 1700-2200. *Ilha dos Pescadores*, Estra da Barra da Tijuca 793, on an island in the lagoon. Often has live samba and Bahian music. *Rock in Rio Café*, in Barra Shopping, T4319500. Bar, restaurant and disco, good food, young crowd, a long way from the centre (taxis hard to find in the early morning), open Mon from 1800 and Tue-Sun from 1200 until late. *Slavia*, 1st floor of New York City Centre, T4324700. Lager and dark beers brewed on site, restaurant open daily for dinner and Fri-Sat for lunch as well, club is open from Midnight, Wed-Sat.

Entertainment

Carnival blocos *Banda da Barra*, parades along Av Sernambetiba on Sat morning one week before carnival. T-shirts are sold or given away but are not obligatory, a water truck sprays the crowd to relieve the heat and there is a float with the band's monarchs and their court.

Cinema Mainly Hollywood films on show at multiscreen cinemas in Barra Shopping, Downtown (12 screen), Barra Point, New York City Center (18 screen), Via Parque and other shopping centres.

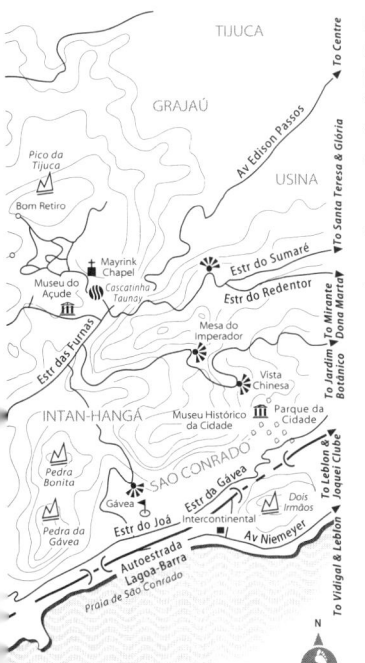

Music *Garden Hall*, in Shopping Barra Garden, T4315527. Features mainly Brazilian artists. *ATL Hall (ex Metropolitan)*, in Via Parque shopping centre, T5321919, www.metropolitan.com.br Large concert hall featuring famous Brazilian and international artists.

Theatre *Teatro dos Grandes Atores*, Barra Square, Av das Américas 3555, T33251645. Two large theatres. Also in Barra Shopping, T4319721.

Shopping

Bookshops *Eldorado*, in Barra Shopping, shop 207. *Saraiva Megastore*, in New York City Center. *Sodiler* in Barra Shopping and Via Parque shopping centres.

Photography For processing, *One Hour Foto*, in Barra Shopping. Recommended.

Shopping centres *Barra Garden*, Av das Américas 3255. Mall lined with trees, cinemas, ice skating, concert hall, open 1500-2100 Sun-Mon, 1000-2200 Tue-Sat. *Barra Point*, Av Armando Lombardi 350, on banks of Tijuca Lagoon. Many fashion boutiques, cinemas and food hall, open 1000-2200 Mon-Sat. *Barra Shopping*, Av das Américas 4666. Huge mall with shops, cinemas, theatre, bowling, children's play area and restaurants, open 1000-2200 Mon-Sat, Sun 1500-2100. *Casa Shopping*, Av Aryton Senna 2150. Mall specializing in everything for the home, open 1000-2200 Mon-Sat, 1500-2000 Sun. *Downtown*, Av das Américas 500. Shops, cinema, leisure areas, open daily 1000-2200. *Itanhangá Center*, Estr da Barra da Tijuca 1636. Shops and restaurants, open 1000-1630 Mon-Fri. *New York City Center*, Av das Américas 5000. Restaurants, night club, 18 screen cinema, open daily 0800-2400. *Via Parque*, Av Ayrton Senna 3000. Cheaper prices at this mall, cinema and *ATL Hall* for concerts (see above), open daily 1000-2200.

Tour operators *Lagunar*, T4470079, www.pantanalcarioca.com.br, has a 1½ hr catamaran tour of the mangroves of Marapendi lagoon during which many birds such as the *Maguari* can be seen. Daily departures every 2 hrs between 0900-1700 from the Fazenda Clube Marapendi, Av das Américas 3979. *Leizer Air*, Av Luiz Carlos Prestes 431, T4319494, F4319343. Helicopter sightseeing tours from US$20. *Stella Barros Rio*, Av das Américas 297/306, T4930186, F4959927.

Transport **Buses** Buses from the city centre to Barra are Nos 175, 176; from Botafogo, Glória or Flamengo take No 179; Nos 591 or 592 from Leme; and from Copacabana via Leblon No 523. A taxi to Zona Sul costs US$15 (US$22.50 after midnight). A comfortable bus, *Pegasus*, goes along the coast from the Castelo bus terminal to Barra da Tijuca and continues to Campo Grande or Santa Cruz, or take the free 'Barra Shopping' bus. Bus 700 from Praça São Conrado (terminal of bus 553 from Copacabana) goes the full length of the beach to Recreio dos Bandeirantes.

Directory **Communications** Post Office: Branch at Av Olegário Maciel 30. **Internet:** *@Point*, 2nd floor of Barra Shopping, shop 215 and kiosk in the food hall on 1st floor. US$1.50 per ¼hr, open daily 1000-2300. *Cyber Cofee & Book*, Saraiva Megastore in New York City Centre. US$1.75 per ¼hr, open 1200-midnight Mon-Fri, 1000-midnight Sat, 1400-2200 Sun. *Web Station*, in Barra Point shopping centre. **Places of worship** *Union Church* (Protestant nondenominational), services held at R Parque da Lagoa de Marapendi, CP 37154, Barra da Tijuca.

Western Rio

Almost half of the municipal area of Rio de Janeiro is in what is referred to as the Zona Oeste (the West Zone) and supports around 1½ million inhabitants. Once a mainly agricultural region, today it is home to light industry and is being developed for tourism. The coastline stretches from Barra de Tijuca past the beaches at Prainha (a little cove, good for surfing) and Grumari (very attractive, rustic beach bars), neither accessible by public transport, but attracting heavy traffic at weekends. Further west still are the Barra de Guaratiba and Pedra de Guaratiba beaches and, finally, those at Sepetiba (on the bay, with calm sea and medicinal mud). This stunning coastal road (the start of the Costa Verde highway) is becoming obliterated by executive housing developments – visit soon, if you can. Near Guaratiba is the Restinga de Marambaia, a reserve that divides the Baía de Sepetiba from the Atlantic ocean.

Inland are the suburbs of Realengo, Padre Miguel, Bangu, Campo Grande and Santa Cruz, whilst in the centre of the zone is the Parque Estadual da Pedra Branca. Historical sites, such as the Capela Magdalena, abound throughout the zone as well as a few curiosities such as a well preserved Zeppelin hanger. There are a number of parks providing a variety of different activities, often orientated towards families and children. Rodeos are also very popular in this part of Rio and competitions are held regularly.

Sights

Sítio Roberto Burle Marx, Estrada da Barra de Guaratiba 2019. This was the home of the great landscape designer from 1949 to 1994. Roberto Burle Marx (1909-94) was world-famous as a landscape designer and artist. His projects achieved a rare harmony between nature, architecture and man-made landscapes. He created many schemes in Brazil and abroad; in Rio alone his work includes the Parque do Flamengo, the pavements of the Avenida Atlântica in Copacabana, Praça Júlio de Noronha in Leme, the remodelling of the Largo da Carioca, the gardens of the Museu Nacional de Belas Artes and of the Biblioteca Nacional and the complex at the Santa Teresa tram station near the Catedral Metropolitana. — **Barra de Guaratiba**

Covering 350,000 sq m, the estate contains an estimated 3,500 species of plants, mostly Brazilian. It is run now by the *Instituto do Patrimônio Histórico e Artístico Nacional* and one of its main aims is to produce seedlings of the plants in its collection. Also on view are Burle Marx's collection of paintings, ceramics, sculptures and other objets d'art, plus examples of his own designs and paintings. The library houses 2,500 volumes on botany, architecture and landscape design. ■ *T4101171. Daily 0900-1300 by prior appointment only.*

The **Igreja Matriz Salvador do Mundo**, Estrada de Guaratiba 6496, was built around 1755 by the Ordem de Nossa Senhora de Carmo. Founded by the Marquês de Valença in a strategic position to warn against attacks by the French, with thick walls and iron windows, the church has good views of the whole coast. ■ *T4107033. Tue-Sat 0900-1700. Mass on Sun at 0900.* — **Ilha de Guaratiba**

The 19th-century **Capela Magdalena**, Estrada do Mato Alto 6024, with its castle-like exterior is decorated inside with byzantine and baroque syle frescos. ■ *T4107183, arrange visits in advance.* The **Igreja Nossa Senhora do Desterro**, Rua Barros de Alarcão, was built in 1629 after a slave claimed to have seen a vision of Our Lady and is one of the oldest churches in Rio. ■ *Open for mass Thu 1930, Fri 1830, Sat 1500.* — **Pedra de Guaratiba**

Campo Grande This large town is the main transport hub for the region. The name Campo Grande came from the Jesuits due to the large amount of land served by the parish. The **Igreja Matriz de Campo Grande**, Rua Amaral Costa 141, was rebuilt in 1882 after a fire which destroyed the Capela de Nossa Senhora do Desterro dating from 1673. ■ *T4134837. Tue-Fri 0800-1100, 1400-1700.*

Santa Cruz The most western town in Zona Oeste is Santa Cruz close to the start of the Rio-Santos highway. The area has many sites of historical interest such as the **Ponte dos Jesuítas**, Avenida do Cortume, finished in 1752 as a dam to regulate the water level of the Rio Guandú. The museum of the Batalhão Vilagran Cabrita, the first Brazilian military engineering unit, is situated in the **Convento dos Jesuítas**, Praça Ruão 35. ■ *T33950573. Mon-Fri 0800-1130, 1330-1600.* Nearby are stone posts dating from 1826 used to mark the boundary between the Fazenda Imperial and the land belonging to the Padres Carmelitas. The **Mirante Imperial** on Morro do Mirante, Rua Pindaré, was originally used to watch over the slaves at work. An octagonal observatory popular with the royal family and foreign visitors was later built on the spot.

The *Núcleo de Orientação e Pesquisa Histórica de Santa Cruz* (NOPH) in the Igreja Matriz, Praça Dom Romualdo 11, has a small library which can be consulted for information on local history, T33950260. Also in Praça Dom Romualdo is the **Fonte Wallace**, donated to the Brazilian government in 1876.

Nearby is the **Base Aérea de Santa Cruz**, Rua do Império, home of the last surviving Zeppelin hanger (those in Germany were destroyed during World War Two), which was completed in 1936. The airships Graff Zeppelin and Hindenburg plied the route between Europe and Brazil until 1938 when the Hindenburg exploded in the United States. ■ *T33950080, arrange visits in advance.*

Parque Estadual da Pedra Branca The State Park of Pedra Branca, created in 1974 is the largest natural reserve in the city with 12,500 ha. Centred on **Pico da Pedra Branca**, at 1,025m the highest point in Rio, the park encompasses mountain ranges and dense forests especially around Vargem Grande. It also includes agricultural communities in Rio da Prata and many reservoirs such as that formed by the Represa de Camorim which provide a ready source of water for the city. The park headquarters is at Rua Professor Francisca Piragibe 80, Taquara. ■ *T4453387. Mon-Fri 0700-1700. Authorized visits only.*

Parks **Criadouro Zoobotânico da Pedra Branca**, Rua Agapanto 550, Vargem Grande, at the bottom of the Pedra Branca mountain. Ecological tours of the site's many rare animal and plant species are conducted by the owner and landcape architect Luiz Carlos Gurken. ■ *T4281909. Daily 0900-1700 by prior appointment only. www.ptdonline.com/pedrabranca*

There are many activity parks in this area which are popular with families: **Fazenda Alegria**, Estrada da Boca do Mato, Vargem Pequena is a large forest park with natural swimming pools, restaurants, sports facilities and childrens play areas as well as hiking trails in the nearby Mata Atlântica. ■ *T/F4421991. Wed-Fri 0900-1700, Sat-Sun 1000-1800.* **Bwana Park**, Estrada da Pedra 2728, Santa Cruz, has a zoo and swimming pool. ■ *T4172564. Wed-Fri 0900-1700, Sat-Sun 0900-1700.* **Parque Rio Rural**, Estr Santa Eugênia 3200, Paciência, is a large park with a boating lake, small zoo, restaurants and rodeos. Activities include horseriding, fishing and helicopter flights over the surrounding countryside. ■ *T33954902. Sat-Sun 0900-1800.*

Essentials

Sleeping

B *Pousada do Mar*, Estr da Barra de Guaratiba 9510, Barra de Guaratiba, T4108104, F4477250. With breakfast, a/c, phone, fridge, bar, restaurant, pool, sauna, parking.
B *Recanto das Águias*, Estrada de Morro Cavado 1920, Ilha de Guaratiba, T/F4107131. With breakfast, bar, pool, sauna, bar, TV.

Camping *Novo Rio*, at Km 17 on the Rio-Santos road, T4376518.

Eating

Many good fish & seafood restaurants in often beautiful surroundings can be found around Vargem Grande & Guaratiba both, however, are a long drive from the city

Expensive *Quinta*, R Luciano Gallet 150, Vargem Grande, T4281396. Excellent food in a beautiful garden with tables on the varanda, open 1900-2200 Fri, 1300-1800 Sat-Sun.

Mid-range *Barreado*, Estr dos Bandeirantes 21295, Vargem Grande, T4422023. Good seafood and fish in rustic house, open 1200-2400 Tue-Sun. *Restaurante do Bira*, Estr da Vendinha 68, Barra de Guaratiba, Cell99620161. Excellent seafood and fish, open 1200-1800 Thu-Fri, 1200-2000 Sat-Sun. *Cândido's*, R Barros de Alarcão 352, Pedra de Guaratiba, T4172674. Good Portuguese seafood, open for lunch only. *Tia Palmira*, Caminho do Souza 18, Barra de Guaratiba, T4108169. Seafood banquet, open 1100-1800 Tue-Sun.

Cheap *476*, R Barros de Alarco 476, Pedra de Guaratiba. Set in an old fisherman's house with sea view and nice breezes from the varanda, good for fish and seafood *moqueca*, open 1200-1900 Wed-Sun.

Bars & nightclubs

Bars *Bar Budo*, R Barros de Alarcão 283, Praça São Pedro, Pedra da Guaratiba. Good seafood, shrimp pasties and view of Sepetiba Bay, 1000 until last client Thu-Mon.

Entertainment

Samba schools *Acadêmicos de Santa Cruz*, R do Império 573, Santa Cruz. *Mocidade Independente de Padre Miguel*, R Coronel Tamarindo 38, Padre Miguel, T3325823, www.mocidade.com Rehearsals from 2200 Sat, US$4.50.

Transport

Buses A/c buses and minibuses travel the route between Centro to Campo Grande or Santa Cruz passing through Copacabana and Barra da Tijuca, US$3. Local buses can be caught in Santa Cruz for Sepetiba. From the *Terminal Rodoviário* in Campo Grande to Barra de Guaratiba, take bus 867; to Ilha de Guaratiba, 869; to Pedra de Guaratiba, 852 or 866; to Rio da Prata, 846; to Sepetiba, 871; to Barra de Tijuca, 854.

Train There are suburban train services from Dom Pedro II station in Centro to Santa Cruz with stops at Realengo, Padre Miguel, Bangu and Campo Grande.

Guanabara Bay

Today around 10 million people live around the 381 sq km bay which is fed by over 35 rivers and streams. Pollution has been a serious problem and despite recent efforts to clean up, most of the wildlife, including the dolphins, have moved elsewhere. The bay is dotted with many islands of which the largest are Ilha do Governador and Ilha de Paquetá. Nearby is Ilha do Brocoio. Close to the city centre are Ilha das Cobras and Ilha Fiscal (see page 100). Near the domestic airport in central Rio is Ilha de Villegaignon, site of the 16th-century French colony. Many islands in the bay such as Ilha das Enxadas and Ilha da Boa Viagem are used by the navy and marines as schools or forts.

Boat trips

Sambaiba Bay Tours, R Santa Luzia 776, office 904, T2200009, Cell99795851, sambaiba@radnet.com.br 2½ hr tours around the bay leaving from the harbour in front of *Restaurante Albamar*, Praça Marechal Âncora at 1030 Sat. ***Saveiros Tour***, R Conde de Lages 44, near Glória Metrô, T2246990, F2522227, saveiros@skydome.com.br 3 hr tours around the bay in a 75 person sailing schooner leaving from Marina da Glória at 0930 Tue-Sun, can buy ticket at departure, US$8.50 per person. Also 'Baía da Guanabara Histórica' historical tours. Also offering boat trips are ***Passamar***, R Siqueira Campos 7 (T2364136), ***Soletur*** (Bay trips Saturday and Sunday only) and ***American Sightseeing***, Avenida Nossa Senhora de Copacabana 605, Sala 1204, T2363551. All offer a day cruise, including lunch, to Jaguanum Island (see page 206, under Itacuruçá) and a sundown cruise around Guanabara Bay, also deep-sea fishing expeditions and private charters.

Ilha de Paquetá

The island, the second largest in Guanabara Bay, is noted for its gigantic pebble shaped rocks, butterflies and orchids. Its name means 'many shells' in Tupi, but it has also been called the Ilha dos Amores. There are a few places of interest, suach as the **house of José Bonifácio**, the opponent of slavery and the **Solar del Rei**, which today houses the Biblioteca Popular de Paquetá. At the southwest tip of the island is the interesting **Parque Darke de Mattos**, with beautiful trees, lots of birds and a lookout on the Morro da Cruz. The island has several beaches, but ask about the state of the water before bathing. The island is very crowded at weekends and on public holidays, but is usually quiet during the week. The prices of food and drink are reasonable.

Sleeping & eating **A** *Flamboyant*, Praia Grossa 58, T/F33970028. Restaurant. **B** *Lido*, Praia José Bonifácio 59, T/F33970377. A/c, bar and restaurant. **C** *Paquetá*, Praça Bom Jesus 15, T/F33970052.

Sports *Paquetá Yacht Club*, Praia das Gaivotas (22° 45.800' S, 043° 06.300'), T33970113 (VHF 69, callsign E44). Very welcoming to visiting sailors with a naval festival on 15 August, landing quay has a depth of 3m whilst boats can anchor in 5m on the eastern side of the island.

Transport **Local** The only means of transport on the island are bicycles (which can be hired) and **horse-drawn carriages** (many have harnesses which cut into the horse's flesh). Neither is allowed into the Parque Darke de Mattos. A tour by **trenzinho**, a tractor pulling trailers, costs US$1.50, or just wander around on foot, quieter and free.

Ferry Paquetá Island can be visited by ferry services that leave more or less every 2 hrs from Praça 15 de Novembro, where there is a general boat terminal; there are boats from 0515 (0710 on Sun and holidays) to 2300, T5336661, or hydrofoils between 1000 and 1600, Sat and Sun 0800-1630 hourly, T33970656 (fare US$1 by boat, 1 hr, US$4 by hydrofoil, 20 mins' journey, which more than doubles its price Sat, Sun and holidays). Buses to Praça 15 de Novembro: No 119 from Glória, Flamengo or Botafogo; Nos 154, 413, 455, 474 from Copacabana, or No 415 passing from Leblon via Ipanema.

Niterói

Just across Guanabara Bay is Niterói, capital of Rio de Janeiro state until 1975 when it was unified with Guanabara state and the capital moved to Rio. To the north is São Gonçalo and to the east is the Região dos Lagos. It is a pleasant excursion providing a good view of Rio and some interesting fortresses and beaches nearby.

Population: 450,000
Phone code: 0xx21

History

When the French under Villegagnon, with their Tamoio allies, established their colony on the western side of the mouth of the Baía de Guanabara, the Portuguese and the Temiminós set up camp on the eastern shore. The formal founding of the settlement of São Lourenço here was in 1573 by Araribóia the Tamininós chief's son who had received land for services to the Portuguese. However after his death and the elimination of the tribe by bubonic plague in 1587, these lands were subdivided into smaller settlements. Once the Portuguese had established sovereignty, the area became a centre for sugar growing in the 17th century. It only really became important after Dom João VI's visit in 1816, when it was given the name of Vila Real da Praia Grande. In 1834 it was renamed Niterói ('hidden waters' in Tupi-Guarani) and was made capital of the province and in 1902 of the state of Rio de Janeiro. Industrialization began early here due to the visionary Barão de Mauá who bought a shipyard at Ponta da Areia in 1846 and introduced modern techniques from Europe.

Sights

Many buildings associated with the city's period as state capital are grouped around the Praça da República (none open to the public). The main avenue is Av Ernâni do Amaral Peixoto, with buildings similar to Av Presidente Vargas in Rio. At the end of the avenue is the dock for Rio, a statue of the Indian chief Araribóia and *Bay Market* shopping centre. The main green area in the centre is Campo de São Bento, which has many trees and handicraft stalls at weekends.

The centre of Niterói is easily explored on foot

There are various **tourist information** points. *Neltur*, Estr Leopoldo Fróes 773, São Francisco, T7102727, is open daily. *Centro de informações*, 2nd floor of Plaza Shopping (see below), T7149949, Mon-Sat 1000-2200. A monthly newspaper, *Niterói, Esporte, Lazer, Turismo e Cultura*, is free.

Churches Colonial churches include **São Lourenço dos Índios**, Praça General Rondon, which dates from at least 1627 and the **Capela da Boa Viagem** (1663), which stands on a fortified island, attached by a causeway to the mainland (open one day a month for mass). By Gragoatá beach in the city is the **Capela São Domingos** (1662) and the **Forte de Gragoatá**, from the same period (closed to the public).

The **Basílica de Nossa Senhora Auxiliadora**, Rua Santa Rosa 207, is an early 20th-century church. Its famous organ, made in Italy, was bought by the Salesian order during the Second World War and is one of the largest pipe organs in the world, certainly the largest in Latin America. ■ *Daily 0600-1100, 1500-2000.*

Forts The town's most important historical monument, however, is the 16th century **Fortaleza de Santa Cruz**, which is still a military establishment. It is situated on a promontory which commands a fine view of the entrance to the bay. Tours show the Capela de Santa Bárbara, whose statue was destined for Santa Cruz dos Militares in Rio. All attempts to move the saint were accompanied by great storms, which was taken as a sign to leave her at the fortress. Also shown are the dungeons, fortifications, execution sites and gun batteries. It is about 13 km from the centre of Niterói, on the Estrada General Eurico Gaspar Dutra, by Adão e Eva beach. ■ *T7149297. Daily 0900-1600. US$1.50, tours have a compulsory guide, Portuguese only.*

Forte Imbuí, Alameda Marechal Pessoa Leal 265, Jurujuba, was started in 1863 and designed to link its arcs of fire with nearby Forte Barão do Rio Branco and Fortaleza de Santa Cruz. It has a strenghened dome and German cannons added in 1894. ■ *T7107840. Sat-Sun 0900-1600.*

Forte Barão do Rio Branco (Forte de São Luiz), also in Jurujuba was first used as a watchpoint in 1567 and construction of the fort started in 1770. Modernized in 1918 with the addition of four cannons it received its current name in 1938. Like Forte Imbuí it has wonderful views of Rio and Guanabara Bay.

Museums **Museu Antônio Parreira**, Rua Tiradentes 47, Ingá, is in the house of the eponymous artist (1860-1937). It houses a collection of 19th- and 20th-century art. ■ *T7198728. Sat-Sun and holidays 1400-1700.*

The **Museu de Arqueologia de Itaipu** is in the ruins of the 18th-century Santa Teresa Convent and also covers the archaeological site of Duna Grande on Itaipu beach. It is 20 km from the city. ■ *T7094079. Wed-Sun 1300-1800.*

Museu de Arte Contemporânea, Mirante da Praia da Boa Viagem, regarded by Condé Nast Traveller magazine as one of the architectural marvels of the world, is an Oscar Niemeyer project and worth visiting for the views from its surrounding balcony as well as its contemporary modern art collection. It is best seen at night, expecially when the pond beneath the flying saucer like design is full of water. The exhibition inside changes. ■ *T6202400, www.macnit.com.br Tue-Sun 1100-1900. US$1. Sat 1300-2100. Free.*

Beaches The beaches closest to the city centre are unsuitable for bathing (Gragoatá, *To get to the ocean* Vermelha, Boa Viagem, das Flechas). The next ones, also in the city with pol-
beaches, take a 38 or luted water (Icaraí – the smartest district, good nightlife, São Francisco – even
52 bus from Praça better nightlife, eg Rua das Pedras, and Charitas), have more in the way of
Gen Gomes Carneiro

restaurants, bars and nightlife. The road continues round the bay, past Preventório and Samanguaiá to Jurujuba, a fishing village at the end of the bus line, beautiful ride (take Bus No 33 from the boat dock; sit on the right-hand side). About 2 km from Jurujuba along a narrow road are the attractive twin beaches of Adão and Eva beneath the Fortaleza da Santa Cruz, with lovely views of Rio across the bay.

Piratininga, Camboinhas, Itaipu (note the archaeology museum, above) and Itacoatiara are fabulous stretches of sand and the best in the area, about 40 minutes' ride through picturesque countryside (buses leave from the street directly ahead of the ferry entrance, at right angles to the coast street). The undertow at Itacoatiara is dangerous, but the waves are popular with surfers and the beach itself is safe. Itaipu is also used by surfers.

Essentials

Sleeping **AL** *Niterói Palace*, R Gen Andrade Neves 134, T7192155, F7192800. Restaurant, pool, parking. **A** *Clube Piratininga*, Estr Frei Orlando 161, Piratininga, T6094581. **A** *Residencial Icaraí* , R Mariz e Barros 109, Icaraí, T7145242, F7195554. Parking. **A** *Icaraí Praia*, R Belisário Augusto 21, T7141414, F7106142. Bar, restaurant, parking. **A** *Plaza*, R São Sebastião 118, T6208008, F6205618. Parking. **A** *Pousada Trovador*, Av Almte Tamandaré 4698, Piratininga, T6099330, pool, sauna, parking. **B** *Flat Icaraí* , R Col Moreira César 19, Icaraí, T7167176, F7167178. Bar, restaurant, pool, sauna, gym, parking.

Camping *Piratininga*, Estr Frei Orlando Km 2, T6094581.

Eating **Mid-range** *Cantina Buonasera*, Estr Leopoldo Fróes 34, Icaraí, T6102762. Italian food with good view of the bay. *Bicho Papão*, Jurujuba. Good seafood. *Coelho à Caçarola*, Km 4 on the road to Várzea das Moças, T6097228. Many dishes based on rabbit, open 1200-2300 Tue-Wed, Fri-Sat, 1200-2000 Sun. There are three good value restaurants opposite the Ruínas de Estação da Cantareira (which has occasional shows and handicraft market): *Tio Cotó*, *Vila Real* and *Zia Amélia*.

Bars & nightlife **Bars** *Acrópole*, Av Quintino Bocaiúva 185, Praia de São Francisco. Cocktails, 1800-0200 Tue-Sun, disco on Fri-Sat from 2230, US$15 entry and minimum consumption.

Entertainment **Cinema** Hollywood films: *Art Plaza*, R 15 de Novembro 8. *Center*, R Col Moreira César 265. *Icaraí*, Praia da Icaraí 161. Art films: *Estação Icaraí*, R Col Moreira César 211. *Cine Arte UFF*, R Miguel de Frias.

Samba schools *Acadêmicos de Cubango*, R Noronha Torrezão 560, Cubango. *Porto da Pedra*, R João Silva 84, Porto da Pedra, São Gonçalo, T6052984, www.portodapedra.com.br Rehearsals from 2200 Fri, US$3. *Unidos da Viradouro*, Av do Contorno 16, Barreto, T6287840, www.viradouro.com Rehearsals from 2200 Sat, US$3.

Festivals **March/April** and **May**, *Festa do Divino*, a festival which traditionally begins on Easter Sunday and continues for the next 40 days, in which the Bandeira (standard) do Divino is taken around the local municipalities. The festival ends at Pentecost with sacred and secular celebrations. **24 June**: *São João*. **22 November**: founding of the city.

Shopping **Shopping centres** *Plaza Shopping*, R XV de Novembro 8.

Sports **Clubs** *Rio Cricket Associação Atlética* (RCA), R Fagundes Varela 637, T7175333. Bus 57 from ferry.

Yachting There are many clubs and facilities in Jurujuba Bay, with a depth of 4-5m, as well as nearby Saco de São Francisco and Charitas beach. *Clube Naval de Charitas*, Av Carlos Ermelindo Marins 68, Charitas (22° 56' 8" S, 043° 6' 27" W), T7105612, F7106295 (VHF 16, 68, HF 4431.6, callsign E30). Pier with water, electricity, crane and repair area. *Iate Clube Icaraí*, Estr Leopoldo Froes 450, São Francisco (22° 54.900' S, 043° 06.300' W), T/F7114022 (VHF 68, 69, HF 4431.8, callsign E38). Pier with water, electricity, crane for 41' vessels, visits only. *Jurujuba Iate Clube*, R Lauro Sodré Jurujuba (22° 56.200' S, 043° 06.500 W), T/F7112370 (VHF 68, 69, callsign E45). Pier and anchor buoys, visits only. *Rio Sailing Club* (Iate Clube de Niterói), Estr Leopoldo Fróes 418, lote 338, T6105810. Bus 33 marked 'via Fróes'.

Tour operators *Stella Barros*, Av Roberto Silveira 196, shop 1, Icaraí, T/F6116669.

Transport **Boats** Niterói, across Guanabara bay, is reached by ferries and launches crossing every 10 mins (15-20 mins, US$0.50) from the 'Barcas' at Praça 15 de Novembro (ferry museum at the terminal). There are also catamarans ('aerobarcas') every 10 mins (about 3 mins, US$2.50; the fare is US$1.25 between 0700 and 1000 Rio-Niterói and after 1700 Niterói-Rio). The slow, cheaper ferry gives the best views. Ferries and catamarans to Rio de Janeiro leave from the terminal at Praça Araribóia.
  Road Buses: Buses 996 Gávea-Jurujuba, 998 Galeão-Charitas, 740-D and 741 Copacabana-Charitas, 730-D Castelo-Jurujuba, US$0.60-0.75. **Car**: The toll on the 14 km Rio-Niterói bridge for cars is US$0.65 (paid only when entering Niterói). If you are crossing the bridge frequently, there is a phone number and website available for checking traffic conditions. High winds can close the bridge. (The approach to the bridge is on the elevated motorway Av Rio de Janeiro in the Caju district, take Av Rodrigues Alves past the docks.) Bus 999 from the corner of R Sen Dantas and Av Beira Mar, crosses the bridge to Niterói and Icaraí (US$0.85); also 996 and 998 from the Jardim Botânico and the Rodoviária.

Directory **Banks** *Banco 24 Horas*, Niterói Shopping, R da Conceição 188. *Bradesco*, R Gavião Peixoto 108. **Communications** Internet: *O Lido Cyber C@fé*, Av Rui Barbosa 29, shop 124, São Francisco, T6119641, Mon-Wed 1000-2000, Thu-Sat 1100-2200. **Medical services** *Universitário Antônio Pedro*, Av Marques do Paraná, T6202828. **Laundry** *Lavlev*, R Pres Backer 138. **Voltage** 110 volts, AC, 60 cycles.

Excursions

4

Excursions

174	**The Costa do Sol**	194	Nova Friburgo
174	Maricá	195	Três Rios
175	Saquarema	196	**Towns in the Coffee Zone**
176	Araruama	197	Vassouras
177	São Pedro da Aldeia	200	Barra do Piraí
177	Arraial do Cabo	200	Valença
178	Cabo Frio	201	**West of Rio de Janeiro**
180	Búzios	201	Volta Redonda
183	Macaé	202	Penedo
183	**Northeast of Rio de Janeiro**	203	Visconde de Mauá
184	Campos	206	**The Costa Verde**
186	**Inland resorts**	207	Angra dos Reis
186	Petrópolis	209	Ilha Grande
191	Teresópolis	211	Paraty
193	Serra dos Órgãos		

Should you wish to venture out from the city there are many beach and mountain resorts within easy reach. East of Rio is the Costa do Sol with windswept beaches that are ideal for surfing, saltwater lagoons and the fashionable resorts of **Cabo Frio** *and* **Búzios**. *West of Rio and reached by the spectacular coastal road of the Costa Verde is* **Angra dos Reis** *and the historic colonial town of* **Paraty**. *Offshore there are many islands such as the once pirate lair of* **Ilha Grande** *which can be visited by schooner. Just north of Rio you will find the imperial palace at* **Petrópolis** *and the* **Serra dos Órgãos** *national park near Teresópolis, which is ideal for trekking, as is the area around* **Nova Friburgo**, *founded by Swiss settlers. Near the northern border with Minas Gerais is* **Três Rios**, *the main rafting destination in the state. The mansions and grounds of the many* **coffee plantations** *around Vassouras and Valença can be visited as a day trip from the city. In the northwest corner of the state is the spectacular mountain scenery of the* **Itatiaia national park** *and around Visconde de Mauá, an ideal escape from the city heat.*

The Costa do Sol

To the east of Niterói lie a series of saltwater lagoons, the Lagos Fluminenses. Two small lakes lie behind the beaches of Piratininga, Itaipu and Itacoatiara, but they are polluted and ringed by mud. The next lakes, Maricá and Saquarema (with other lagoons between), are much larger. Although they are still muddy, the waters are relatively unpolluted and wildlife abounds in the scrub and bush around the lagoons. This is a prime example of the restinga environment. The RJ-106 road runs behind the lakes en route to Cabo Frio and Búzios, but an unmade road goes along the coast between Itacoatiara and Cabo Frio, giving access to the many long, open beaches of Brazil's Costa do Sol (also known as Região dos Lagos). The whole area is perfect for camping.

Maricá

Phone code: 0xx21
Population: 60,000

The first main town just off the RJ-106 road (Rodovia Amaral Peixoto) is Maricá, a small fishing village on its own lagoon. The best season for fish is August to September, many varieties such as *bagres*, *tainhas* and shellfish can be caught from the beaches or in the lagoas. The Restinga de Maricá is a narrow sand spit, 35 km long, that follows the coastline east from Praia de Itaipu-Açu. There is good walking in the Serra do Silvado, 14 km away on the road to Itaboraí. Between Maricá and Saquarema are Ponta Negra and Jaconé, both good surfing beaches. **Tourist information** from *Casa do Turismo*, Av Ver Francisco Sabino da Costa 477, T6371999.

Sleeping & eating
A *Fazenda Ubatá*, Estr do Caxito 540, T/F6372493, hfubata@uol.com.br Restaurant, pool, sports facilities, hotel transport. **B** *Pousada Colonial*, Ponta Negra, T/F6481707. Suites and bungalows with breakfast. Recommended. **B** *Solar Tabaúna*, R Caxambú, Ponta Negra, T6481626. Pool. Recommended. **D** *Malocas Van*, Av Central, T6481313. Pool. **Camping F** *Fazenda de Maricá*, Estr do Retiro, T6371003. Snackbar, fishing. *Caranguejo e Cia*, Estr do Boqueirão. Cheap seafood restaurant.

Costa do Sol

Arts and crafts market in the Praça de Câmara at weekends 1800-2300. **Shopping**

Luctua, R Domício da Gama 89, Centro, T6372002. **Tour operators**

Buses From **Rio Rodoviária** every hour (every 30 mins in summer) with *Mil e Um* **Transport** *(1001)* (buses don't enter town but pass by on Rodovia Amaral Peixoto). Bus terminal at Av Roberto Silveira, T6372955. *Viação NS do Amparo*, operate local buses every 40 mins to **Ponta Negra, Guaratiba, Bambui**, and to **Jaconé** about every 2 hrs between 0430-2230 and every 30 mins between 0720-2050 to **Rio** (Castelo and Praça Mauá).

Banks *Bradesco*, R Sen Macedo Soares 44. **Medical services** *Clínica São Vicente*, R Domicio da **Directory** Gama 355, Centro, T6372593. Private clinic but also deals with emergencies.

Saquarema

At the outlet to the sea of the Lagoa de Saquarema (turn right off the RJ-106 at *Phone code: 0xx24* Bacaxá) is the holiday village of Saquarema. Today Saquarema is still a fishing *Population: 44,000* town, but is much better known as one of the main centres for surfing in Brazil. Its cold, open seas provide consistent, crashing waves of up to 3 m (there is a **surfing school** at Avenida Oceânica in Itaúna) but beware of strong currents. Frequent national and international championships take place here. There are many beaches in the area particularly popular with young people: Barra Nova and Praia da Vila are closest to the town.

The small white church of **Nossa Senhora de Nazaré** (1675) is on a green **Sights** promontory jutting into the ocean with good views. The local legend has it that on 8 September 1630, fishermen, saved from a terrible storm, found an image of the Virgem de Nazaré in the rocks. A chapel was founded on the spot and subsequent attempts to relocate the Virgin (as when the chapel was falling into disrepair) resulted in her miraculously returning to the original site. The **Reserva Florestal de Jacarepiá** at the end of Praia de Itaúna is a good place to see birds and animals that inhabit the region. The **Cemitério Arqueológico de Sambaqui** at Barra Nova is an open air site displaying artefacts from the prehistoric inhabitants of the region.

AL *Pousada Pedra d'Água Maasai*, Trav de Itaúna 17, Praia de Itaúna, T/F6511092. **Sleeping** Near the beach, seafood restaurant and pool. **A** *Laje de Itaúna*, Av Oceânica 1900, *Most accommodation is* close to Itaúna beach, T6512389. Good breakfast, pool, barbecue, safe parking. *at Itaúna beach, 3 km* **B** *Pousada Airumã*, R das Garoupas, Itaúna, T/F6514295, www.aktuell.com.br/ *from Saquarema. Prices* airuma Fan, restaurant, pool. **C** *Pousada Solar de Itaúna*, R das Pitangas 700, *are around 30% cheaper* T6515158. Pool, gym, games room, bar. **D** *Pousada dos Socós*, R dos Socós 592, *in low season* Itaúna, T6511205. With breakfast, bar, pool, parking. **Youth hostel D** *Pousada das Ilhas Gregas*, R Prado 671, close to Itaúna beach, T6511008. Rooms and dormitory, pool, sauna, bar, restaurant, surfboard, bicycle and buggy hire. **Camping** *Itaúna's*, R dos Tatuís 999, access from Av Oceânica, T6511711.

Cheap *Le Bistrô*, Av São Rafael 1134, Itaúna. Portuguese food. *Passadiço*, in *Lake's* **Eating** *Shopping* (see below). Seafood restaurant. **Very cheap** *Do'n Jacinto*, Av Oceânica 1662, next to Point do Itaúna. Selection of pasta dishes made by friendly Argentine owner.

Festa do Divino, see page 169; **town's founding day**, 8 May; **festival of São Pedro**, **Festivals** 29 Jun at the end of the Festas Juninas; **Nossa Senhora de Nazaré**, 7 Sep, the town's patron saint's day.

Shopping *Lake's Shopping*, Av Saquarema 567, open 1000-2200 daily. There is a *Feira de Artesanato* with arts and crafts in the central praça at weekends.

Transport **Buses** From **Rio de Janeiro** frequent departures from 0630-2030 with *Mil e Um (1001)*, 1¾ hrs, US$3.75. Local bus terminal is in Praça Oscar Macedo Soares, T6512054.

Directory **Banks** *Banco do Brasil*, Av Saquaremea 5395. **Medical services** *Hospital Municipal*, R Adolfo Bravo 10, T6513123. *Pró Lagos Serviços Médicos*, R Prof Souza, Bacaxá, T6533436. Private clinic open 24 hrs daily.

Araruama

Phone code: 0xx24
Population: 66,000

The largest lake is Araruama (220 sq km), famous for its medicinal mud. The salinity is high, the waters calm and almost the entire lake is surrounded by sandy beaches, making it popular with families looking for unpolluted bathing. Praia dos Amores behind Clube Náutico is popular with young people for parties. The constant breeze makes the lake perfect for windsurfing and sailing. The major industry of the area is salt, and all around one can see the salt-pans and the wind pumps used to carry the water into the pans. Churches in the area include **Matriz de São Sebastião** in the centre of Araruama, situated at the western end of the lake on the inland shore, 116 km from Rio, 101 from Niterói. The **Igreja de Nossa Senhora de Conceição** at Praia Seca has a festival on 8 December. There are good views over the lake to Cabo Frio from the **Mirante de Paz** on Morro de Itatiquara, 5 minutes from the bus terminal on the RJ-124 to Rio Bonito. The town and area are host to a varied calendar of festivals throughout the year.

Sleeping & eating **A** *Ver a Vista*, R São Sebastião 400, near Praia da Pontinha, T/F6654721. Restaurant, pool, some apartments adapted for disabled people. **C** *Pousada do Péu*, Estr da Praia Seca, Km 12, T6653614. With breakfast, restaurant, pool, TV room. **D** pp *Pousada Bela Vista*, Rod São Pedro 864. With breakfast, restaurant, pool. **Camping** *Camping Clube do Brasil*, 5 km from town on the RJ-124 to Saquarema, T6650352. *Veneza*, Estr de Praia Seca at Km 13, T6652667. *Gigi*, about 2 km from town on RJ-106 to São Pedro da Aldeia is a cheap seafood restaurant with a shop selling hand-painted ceramics.

Bars & nightclubs *Danceteria Magique*, Rod Amaral Peixoto Km 90, Coqueiral.

Shopping Arts and crafts market in the Casa da Cultura, Praça São Sebastião, every weekend 0800-2200.

Tour operators *Terra do Sol Turismo*, Av John Kennedy 150, shop 110, Centro, T6658200. Various packages.

Transport **Buses** From **Rio de Janeiro** there are frequent bus departures from 0600-2200 with *Mil e Um (1001)*, 2 hrs, US$4.75. To **Niterói** from 0700-1900. To **Rio Bonito** every 30 mins (every hour on Sun) between 0545-2200 with *Rio Ita*.

Directory **Banks** *Banco do Brasil*, Av Nilo Peçanha 151. **Medical services** *Casa da Caridade de Araruama*, R Major Félix Moreira 267, T6651509. Hospital with emergency ward.

São Pedro da Aldeia

At the eastern end of the lake, also inland, is São Pedro da Aldeia which, despite intensive development, still retains much of its colonial charm and has a lovely Jesuit church built in 1723. Like Saquarema, São Pedro celebrates the feast of São Pedro (the town's patron saint) on 29 June, but also its founding on 16 May. **Tourist information** is on Avenida São Pedro, T6211559.

Phone code: 0xx24
Population: 55,000

AL *Enseada das Garças*, R José Costa 1088, Ponta da Areia, about 5 km from town, T/F6211924, www.alohanet.com.br/garcas Boat trip included and other tours, fishing, horse riding available. A member of the Roteiros de Charme group. **A** *Pousada Pontal da Praia*, Praia do Sudoeste, T6212441, F6216596. **B** in low season, watersports, tours available. **D** *Pousada Elefantinho*, Rod RJ-140 Km 5. No breakfast, TV room. **Youth hostel** **E** pp *Albergue da Juventude Praia do Sudoeste*, R Pedro Américo, Lot 27, take bus to Praia do Sudoeste from beside the *rodoviária* and get off at the first stop before the end of the beach, T6212763. IYHA, open high season only. **Camping** **F** pp *da Colina*, RJ-106, Km 108, Praia da Teresa, T6211919. *Don Roberto*, Av Getúlio Vargas 272. Cheap pizzas.

Sleeping & eating

There is an arts and crafts fair in Praça Dr Plínio de Assis Tavares on weekend afternoons (open until midnight) during the summer.

Shopping

From **Rio de Janeiro** there are frequent bus departures from 0500-1415 with *Mil e Um (1001)*, 2½ hrs, US$5.50. *Viação Salineira* run buses to the beaches and neighbouring towns every 15-25 mins.

Transport

Banks *Bradesco*, Av São Pedro 120. **Medical services** *Missão de São Pedro*, Av Getúlio Vargas 290, Centro, T6211063. Hospital with emergency ward.

Directory

Arraial do Cabo

The lake and the ocean are divided by the Restinga de Massambaba, mostly deserted except for the beaches of Massambaba and Praia Seca at the western end and Praia Grande in the east. Arraial do Cabo is at the end of the Restinga de Massambaba, on the southern side of Cabo Frio. The majority of the population live from fishing but tourism is increasing in the area. Sights include the Museu Oceanográfico, **Museu Regional**, the **Igreja de Nossa Senhora dos Remédios** and the **ruins of Farol Velho**.

Phone code: 0xx24
Population: 21,000

The town's main beach, **Praia Grande**, is ideal for surfing, but the water is cold most of the time. Arraial has lots of other small beaches on the bays and islands which form the cape. Those on the east side of the town vary with moderate to flat, calm waves but all have clear, warm water. **Praia do Forno**, reached by boat from the port or by a track over a deserted hill (beware robberies if walking alone), and Prainhas at **Pontal do Atalaia** have been recommended. Excursions can be made by boat around the islets and by jeep or buggy over the sand dunes.

Beaches

Praia do Farol, on the Ilha do Cabo Frio, is considered one of Brazil's best beaches. It has dunes and crystal clear water. To get there you must obtain a free permit from the Navy (Marinha) office in Arraial do Cabo, then go to Praia dos Anjos from where fishermen will take you to Farol, about US$60 for nine people. You must arrange a pick up time, take your own food and water and leave no rubbish behind. A stop at the Gruta Azul, a cave carved in the rocks by the ocean can be included in the price. **Tourist information** is on Praça da Bandeira, T6205039.

Sleeping **A** *Caminho do Sol*, R do Sol 50, Praia Grande, T6221347, F6222029, www.caminhodosol.cuc.de Overlooks the beach, pool, sauna, secure parking. **A** *Pousada Nautilus*, R Marcílio Dias 100, T6221611. Bar, games room, pool. Recommended. **A** *Pousada da Prainha*, Rua D 90, Prainha, T/F6222512, www.alohanet.com.br/users/pprainha Close to beach, sitting room, restaurant, pool, laundry, boat trips. **B** *Pousada Orlamar*, Av Beiramar 111, Recanto da Prainha, T/F6222410. Comfortable with good restaurant (see below). **B** *Pousada dos Atobás*, R José Pinto Macedo 270, Prainha, T6222461. TV, fridge. **Camping** *Camping Clube do Brasil*, Praia dos Anjos, T6221023. Crowded beach.

Eating **Mid-range** *Oriental*, R José Pinto Macedo 356 (not a nice area of town), T6221576. Well prepared and presented Japanese food with excellent service. *Todos os Prazeres*, R José Pinto Macedo, south end of Prainha beach, T6222365. Large menu of interesting dishes and ice cream, book table in advance, English spoken. Recommended. **Cheap** *Orlamar*, in Pousada Orlamar (see above). Good seafood, mainly caught locally. Recommended. *Picanha na Brasa*, R Oswaldo Cruz, edge of Praça Tiradentes. Barbecue and salads, good quality and quantity. **Very cheap** *Agua na Boca*, near the town centre bus station. Pay by weight buffet kept both fresh and hot.

Festivals **Founding of the town**, 13 May, and **Corpus Christi** in May/Jun.

Sports As the self-styled "Capital of Diving", the town has many diving schools, good facilities and interesting sites for more experienced divers. Bring your qualifications as the better dive companies will not risk their reputations on a word of mouth assurance.

Tour operators *Trilhas do Mar*, R Washington Luis 69, Praia Grande, T/F6222118, trilhasdomar@mar.com.br Walking tours, boat trips, helpful with airfares, accommodation, carnival tickets, owner Marco speaks some English.

Transport **Buses** From **Rio de Janeiro** there are frequent bus departures from 0330-2400 with *Mil e Um (1001)*, 3½ hrs, US$6.50. Good services to **Rio de Janeiro**, **Niterói** and other parts of the state. Very frequent local bus to **Cabo Frio** and hourly departures to **Búzios** and **São Pedro da Aldeia**.

Cabo Frio

Phone code: 0xx24
Population: 100,000

Situated 168 km from Rio, the town is a popular holiday and weekend haunt of Cariocas because of its cool weather, white sand beaches and dunes, scenery, sailing and good underwater swimming (mosquitoes, however, are a problem). During some of the summer months there is loud music from a *trio electrico* on the main beach. You can take pleasant schooner trips from the quayside, and dive into the crystal clear waters. Refreshments and fresh fruit are also served as part of the package. **Tourist information** is on Avenida Américo Vespúcci 200, Praia do Forte, T6471689, www.cabofrio.tur.br There is another information centre run by the local hotel association at Avenida América Central 950, Praia do Siquiera, T0800-260004, www.cabofriotur.com.br ■ *0900-1800 Mon-Sat and holidays.*

History The navigator Americo Vespucci landed at nearby Arraial do Cabo in 1503 and after making contact with the local Indians returned to Portugal with a boatload of *pau-brasil*. Since the wood in these parts was of better quality than that further north, the area became the target for loggers from France, the Netherlands and England. The Portuguese failed to capitalize on their colony here and it was the French who established the first defended settlement. Their presence was strengthened after the Portuguese had driven the French from Guanabara Bay. By 1575, the Portuguese had had enough of the corsairs operating from Cabo Frio and they took it by force. It was not until the second decade of the 17th century that they planned their own fortification, Forte São Mateus, which was started in 1616 on the foundations of the French fort. It is now a ruin at the mouth of the Canal de Itajuru.

Beaches

The canal, which connects the Lagoa Araruama and the ocean, has a small headland at its mouth, which protects the nearest beach to the town, **Praia do Forte**. Backed by hotels, restaurants and bars, the water is calm and clear, the sand fine. The beach stretches south for about 7½ km to Arraial do Cabo, its name changing to **Praia das Dunas** and **Praia do Foguete**. These waters are much more suited to surfing. North of the canal entrance are the small, surfing **Praia Brava** (not too easy to get to, naturist beach) and the small, calm **Praia das Conchas**, which is ideal for watersports. Next is **Praia do Peró**, 7 km of sand on the open sea; it is used by surfers, fishermen and by sandboarders, who slide down the dunes on wooden boards.

Sleeping

Reservations are necessary from Dec-Feb

L *La Plage*, R dos Badejos 40, Praia do Peró, T/F6435690. Close to the beach, restaurant, pool. **AL** *Pousada Porto Veleiro*, Av dos Espadartes 129, T/F6473081, www.portoveleiro.com.br Private beach and boat dock, restaurant, pool, sports facilities. **A** *Pousada do Albatroz*, at Praia do Foguete, T/F6431577, www.pousadadoalbatroz.com.br Very close to beach, rooms with sea view, hammocks, sitting room, safe parking. **A** *Âncora*, Av dos Pescadores 1, Praia do Peró, T6431153, F6431841, www.hotelancora.com.br Restaurant, pool, gym, parking, arranges boat trips. **B** *Pousada Porto Peró*, Av dos Pescadores 2002, Praia do Peró, T0800-268866, www.pousadaportopero.com.br Restaurant, pool, meeting room, internal parking. **B** *Pousada Suzy*, Av Júlia Kubitschek 48, 100 m from the rodoviária, T6431742. **C** *Jangada*, Granaola 220, near the canal. Good breakfast. Recommended. **D** *Praia das Palmeiras*, Praia das Palmeiras 1, T/F6432866. **D** pp *Remmar Residence*, Av Teixeira e Souza 1203 (main route into town), close to the main beach and bus station, T6432313, F6455976. Short stay apartments with kitchen, bathroom and laundry. **Youth hostel E** pp *Albergue da Juventude São Lucas*, R Goiás 266, Jardim Excelsior, RJ 28915-170, 3 mins from the rodoviária near Supermercado ABC, T6453037. IYHA. **Camping** *Camping Clube do Brasil*, Estr dos Passageiros 700, 2 km from town, T6433124. On the same road, at No 600, is *Bosque Clube*, T6450008, and No 370 *Camping da Estação*, T6431786. *Dunas do Peró*, Estr do Guriri 1001, Praia do Peró, T6292323, F6292411, www.dunasdoperu.com.br Chalets, space for trailers and tents, pool, bar.

Eating

There are now many restaurants in the town. **Mid-range** *Picolino*, R Mcal Floriano 319, T6432436. Good seafood. **Cheap** *Restaurante do Zé*, on the canal quayside. Ample quantities of well cooked food at reasonable prices.

Festivals

Corpus Christi, May or Jun. Colourful designs are made from coloured salt in the streets of Cabo Frio and other towns in the region. **São Pedro**, 29 Jun (as above). **Founding of the town**: 13 Nov. **Patron saint's day, Nossa Senhora da Assunção**, 25 Dec.

Shopping

Peró Shopping, Rua do Moinho corner with Av dos Pescadores, Praia do Peró. Beach wear, arts and crafts, food hall with occasional live music at night.

Sports

Yachting The local branch of the *Iate Clube do Rio de Janeiro* has supplies but permission to use facilities must be obtained first from Rio (see page 76).

Tour operators *Boulevard Brazil Tour*, in Shopping Boulevard Canal R Major Belegard 584, T/F6474752, boulevardbraziltour@mar.com.br Flights, boat trips, tours available for older people. *Ver Tour*, T6216642, Cell0xx24-99015901, guiacabofrio@hotmail.com Hotel reservations, ecological, historical and city tours by day or night.

Transport **Air** A new airport has opened linking the area with **Santos Dumont** airport in Rio de Janeiro. So far only small operators and private aircraft however are using it. Flights from **Buenos Aires** via Rio de Janeiro may be introduced in the future. **Buses** The rodoviária is 2 km from the centre. From **Rio de Janeiro** there are frequent departures from 0500-2400 with *Mil e Um (1001)*, 2¾ hrs, US$7 (US$8.50 with a/c). To Rio every 30 mins and after midnight every hour. Frequent buses to **Niterói**, **Campos**, **Macaé**, **Itaperuna** and **Bom Jesus** in the north of the state. Daily service to **Petrópolis**. To Búzios, from the local bus terminus in the town centre, every hour, US$1. **Car rental** *Localiza*, R Teixeira e Souza 1703, T6436822.

Directory **Banks** *Banco 24 Horas*, Av Assunção 925. *Bradesco*, Av Assunção 904. *HSBC*, Praça Porto Rocha 74. **Medical services** There is an emergency post at R Governador Valaderes 22, T6454391. Dentist: *Luiz Henrique Lanna Drumond*, R Teixeira e Souza 30, upstairs, T/F6432132.

Búzios

Phone code: 0xx24
Population: 10,000

From Cabo Frio the RJ-102 heads 25 km northeast to the next resort up the coast, the sophisticated yet informal Búzios. This charming seaside town (full name Armação de Búzios) is well-spread out with low-rise, but attractive development. It is situated on a peninsula and is the perfect choice for those who want to enjoy the sun and the sea by day and, after dark, its internationally famous nightlife and gastronomy. Its climate is sunny and windy all year round.

Unless it is absolutely necessary, avoid visiting Búzios at Carnival, New Year's Eve and other main holidays. The city gets crowded, the price of food, accommodation and other services rises substantially and the long, stressful traffic jams on the roads will be an experience to be remembered forever.

History Originally a small fishing community, founded in 1740 when a trader called Braz de Pina started a whale fishery, Búzios remained virtually unknown until the 1950s when its natural beauty started to attract the Brazilian jet-set who turned the village into a fashionable summer resort. In 1964, Brigite Bardot visited Búzios and the photos of her, walking barefoot along the beach, brought the focus of the world's press to this 'lost paradise in the tropics'. Soon many wealthy families, foreign tourists and the travel and leisure industry started to move to Búzios, building over 150 *pousadas*, around 50 restaurants as well as open-air cafés, bars, clubs, art galleries and fashion shops. As many of these businesses are foreign-owned, English, French, German and Spanish are widely spoken. A local joke says that, in population, Buenos Aires is the second city in the world in summer; Búzios is the first.

Beaches During the daytime, the best option is to head for the beaches, of which there are 25. The most visited are Geribá (many bars and restaurants; popular with surfers), Ferradura (deep blue sea and calm waters), Ossos (the most famous and close to the centre), Tartaruga and João Fernandes. To help you to decide which beach suits you best, a good idea is to join one of the local two to three hour schooner trips which pass many of the beaches. These trips cost around US$10-15 and can be arranged with through: *Escuna Buziana*, T6236760/6232157, and *Escuna Queen Lory*, T6231179/6232286.

L *Colonna Park*, Praia de João Fernandes, T6232245, colonna@colonna.com.br Fantastic view of the sea, restaurant, pool. **L** *Galápagos Inn*, Praia de João Fernandinho, T6236161, F6232297, www.buziosonline.com.br/galapagos Right on the beach with good views, restaurant, pool. **AL** *Brigitta's Guest House*, Rua das Pedras 131, T/F6236157, www.buziosonline.com.br/brigitta Beautifully decorated little pousada on the beach with a good restaurant, bar, tea house and excellent breakfast. **AL** *Cabanas de Búzios*, Av José Bento Ribeiro Dantas 1313, Bosque de Geribá, T6236650, F6236721, www.buziosonline.com.br/cabanas Very comfortable hotel with ample grounds, tennis court, pool. Owner Alexandre Bomeni makes guests feel at home. Recommended. **AL** *La Mandrágora*, Av José Bento Ribeiro Dantas 1010, Portal da Ferradura, T6231348, F6232190, www.buziosonline.com.br/mandragora One of the most famous pousadas in Búzios, rooms or chalets (**L**), restaurant, pool. **AL** *Pousada Vila D'Este*, Morro do Humaita, T0800-210799. Othon chain pousada with rooms or bungalows, pool. **AL** *Fazendinha Blancpain*, Estr Velha da Raza, T/F6236490, fazendinha@mar.com.br Close to golf course, good seafood restaurant and wine list, pool, horse riding, a member of Roteiro de Charme group, see page 47. **A** *Pousada Casa de Pedra*, Trav Lúcio Antônio Quintanilha 57, T6231499, F6232410. Parking. **A** *Pousada do Corsário*, Praia dos Ossos, T0800-210799. Othon chain pousada with pool, gardens and hammocks. **A** *Pousada Hibiscus Beach*, R 1, No 22, Quadra C, Praia de João Fernandes, T6236221. Run by its British owners, 15 pleasant bungalows, garden, pool, light meals available, help with car/buggy rentals and local excursions. **B** *Pousada dos Tangarás*, R dos Namorados 6, lote 4, Geribá, T6231275. Pool. **B** *Pousada La Coloniale*, R das Pedras 52, T/F6231434, lacoloniale@uol.com.br Ideally located for nightlife, but you will hear all the noise of Rua das Pedras until the early hours. **D** *Casa da Ruth*, R dos Gravatás, Geribá, T6232242. **Youth hostel E** pp *Albergue da Juventude Praia dos Amores* (IYHA), Av José Bento Ribeiro Dantas 92, get off before the bus station at the stop in front of the youth hostel in Tartaruga, T6232422, Cell0xx21-99982464. Recommended. Several **private houses** rent rooms, especially in summer and holidays. Look for the signs: 'Alugo Quartos'. **Camping** *Country Camping Club*, near Praça da Rasa, Praia Rasa, T6291122, 12 km from Búzios.

Mid-range *Satryicon*, Av J B Ribeiro Dantas 412, T6231595. Excellent Italian restaurant. **Cheap** *El Lorenzo*, Travessa dos Arcos, Loja 6, Rua das Pedras 100. Good for Italian food. *La Tropezienne*, Av José Bento Ribeiro Dantas 712, Armação. French, with a nice view of the sea. *Muqueca Capixaba*, R Manoel de Carvalho 116, Centro. Brazilian seafood. *Estância Don Juan*, R das Pedras, 178, Centro. Grill and restaurant. *Kassai*, R das Pedras 275. Japanese. **Very cheap** *Chez Michou*, R das Pedras, 90, Centro. An open-air bar with videos and music, dozens of choices of pancakes accompanied by ice cold beer. Always crowded. *Pastello*, in front of the *Shopping One*, at the entrance to R das Pedras. A stand serving pastéis, thin, fried pastries filled with cheese, meat, chicken or preserve. *Skipper*, Av J B Ribeiro Dantas 392, Praia do Canto. Pizza House.

Sleeping
Even though there are more than 150 pousadas, prior reservations are needed in summer, at holidays such as Carnival, the New Year's Eve, & weekends

Eating
Búzios has plenty of restaurants for all tastes and budgets. International cuisine can be found mostly in the R das Pedras and the streets surrounding it, in the centre

---

POUSADA HIBISCUS BEACH – BÚZIOS

Alice and Kevan Prior, and David Smith, are the British owners of this delightful, small hotel overlooking one of Búzios most attractive beaches, the Praia de João Fernandes. The spacious, individual bungalows, with a sea-view from their balconies, are all equipped with air-conditioning, colour T.V. and mini-bar. They are set in beautiful tropical gardens adjacent to the guest lounge, breakfast room and swimming pool.

For reservations and information, phone or fax:
(55) 246-23-6221 (Brazil), or write to
POUSADA HIBISCUS BEACH, RUA 1, No. 22, QUADRA C, PRAIA DE JOÃO FERNANDES, BÚZIOS, R.J., BRAZIL.
E-mail: hibiscus@buziosonline.com.br

Bars & nightclubs Nightlife is a must in Búzios. All you have to do is walk along the R das Pedras (Stone Street, as it is paved with irregular, huge blocks of stone). Here is where you will find the best choice of restaurants, cafés, art galleries and bars. It gets very crowded at weekends and during the holidays, especially after 2300. Good options are: *Zapata Mexican Bar*, R das Pedras. One of the hottest spots at night. *Number One*, R das Pedras 1. A 2-storey shopping centre just at the entrance to the street. There are some good bars here with live pop music at night. *Ta-ka-ta ka-ta*, R das Pedras 256. One of the craziest bars in Búzios: weird decoration, owned by a foreigner who obstinately refuses to tell where he came from, but who can speak fluent Portuguese, Spanish, English, German, Dutch, worth a visit.

Sport **Diving** *Casamar*, T6232441 (located in Rio de Janeiro). A highly professional dive operation offers 1 day diving trips costing US$25 pp if you bring your own equipment, US$50 pp if you rent equipment, both prices include 2 bottles of air. Casamar is closed in May and on Tue during low season. Recommended.

Yachting *late Clube Armação dos Búzios*, 22° 44.800' S, 041° 53.000' W, VHF 16, 68, callsign E43. A fee is required to use the club's facilities, there is a refuelling dock next door at the *Shell* service station.

Tour operators *Malizia*, see 'Banks' below. *Mister Tours*, R das Pedras 168, Centro, T6232100. *Webtur*, Av J B Ribeiro Dantas 1144, Armação, T6236661. Guided tours in English: Adriana Rainho, T6232146, arainho@mar.com.br

Transport
192 km to Rio
37 km to Arraial do Cabo

Road By car via BR-106 takes about 2½ hrs from Rio. **Buses** From **Rio de Janeiro** ther are frequent departures from 0630-2015 with *Mil e Um (1001)*, 2¾ hrs, US$7, (be at the bus terminal 20 mins before departure). 1300 from **Búzios** a/c. You can also take any bus to **Cabo Frio** (many more during the day), from where it's 30 mins to Búzios and vice versa. Buying the ticket in advance is only recommended on major holidays. The Búzios rodoviária is a few blocks' walk from the centre. Some pousadas are within 10 mins on foot, eg La Coloniale, Brigitta's, while others need a local bus (US$0.50) or taxi. The buses from Cabo Frio run the length of the peninsula and pass several pousadas.

Directory **Banks** *Banco do Brasil*, R Manuel de Carvalho 70, Centro. *Malizia*, R das Pedras, T6232022. **Medical services** Public hospital: *Posto Municipal de Saúde de Manguinhos*, Av J B Ribeiro Dantas, Manguinhos, T192. **Private hospital**: *Clínica Búzios*, Av J B Ribeiro Dantas 3000, Manguinhos, T6232465.

Rio das Ostras
Phone code: 0xx24
Population: 28,000

Continuing to the north, one comes to Barra de São João and Rio das Ostras. The beaches in this area are at the northern end of the Costa do Sol, all containing sheltered coves with good swimming and scuba diving. In Rio das Ostras is an archaeological museum with finds from the **Sambaqui da Tarióba**, in the Casa da Cultura, Rua Dr. Bento Costa Júnior 70, T7641749. The municipal park at Rodovia Amaral Peixoto Km 155 preserves some of the Mata Atlântica with information on the plants.

Sleeping and eating There are many hotels and pousadas along Rodovia Amaral Peixoto. **A** *Pousada do Wagner*, R Nova Iguaçu 1199, Costa Azul, T/F7641973. Restaurant, pool, tours and boat trips available. **C** *Hotel Mirante do Poeta*, Rod Amaral Peixoto, Centro, T7641910. **C** *Pousada Praia Virgem*, R Túlio de Alencar, Costa Azul, T7641139. Bar, restaurant, pool. **Cheap** *Bar da Boca*, R Teresópolis 69, Praia Boca da Barra. Seafood.

Transport From **Rio de Janeiro** there are bus departures at 0330, 1000, 1415 with *Rápido Macaense*, 3½ hrs, US$6.75. All buses to Macaé with *Rápido Macaense* (see below) also go to **Rio das Ostras**. *Auto Viação 1002* run buses to the beaches (also *Leão Dourado*) and to **Barra de São João** every 15 mins during the day.

Macaé

Macaé is the supply centre for the offshore oil industry but is attempting to develop tourism as well. There are good views from the **Igreja de Santana** on Morro de Santana, 2 km away. Cavaleiros beach is good for surfing and has many bars and restaurants whilst at Praia das Conchas is the **Forte de Marechal Hermes**. Nearby is the Archipélago de Santana with Ilha de Santana and Ilha do Francês, good for beaches, fishing and a lighthouse. **Tourist information** is *Macaé Tur* on Av Rui Barbosa 780, 2nd floor, T7628456, www.macaetur.com

Phone code: 0xx24
Population: 118,000

Sleeping **AL** *Lagos Copa*, Av Elias Agostinho 500, Praia de Imbetiba, T7721405, F7722050, www.copasul.com.br Restaurant, meeting rooms, pool. **A** *Colonial*, Av Elias Agostinho 140, Praia de Imbetiba, T/F7225155. Helpful, comfortable, restaurant. **A** *Ouro Negro*, Av Pres Sodré 466, Praia do Forte, T7723305, F7723205. Restaurant, pool. **A** *Panorama*, Av Elias Agostinho 290, T7724455, F7625536. Restaurant. **B** *Rosa Mar*, R Jesus Soares Pereira, T7727007, F7625613. Restaurant, pool. **C** *Central*, R Rui Barbosa. Nice place, good breakfast, secure parking. **Camping** *Costazul*, Av Heleno Nunes, Costa Azul, T7641389.

Eating **Cheap** *Albatroz*, Av Atlântica 2374, Praia dos Cavaleiros. Seafood. **Very cheap** *Xandoca's Bar*, R Col José de Lima 365. Seafood.

Transport **Air** Airtaxis with *Líder*, T7723202, and *Aeróleo*, T7725995. **Buses** Bus station, Av Vereador Abreu Lima, T7724500. From **Rio de Janeiro** there are frequent departures 0420-2230 with *Mil e Um* 2½ hrs, US$7.50 (US$9 with a/c); frequent departures 0530-2300 with *Rápido Macaense*, 3 hrs, US$7.50. To **Rio de Janeiro**, every 30 mins. To Campos, 1¾ hrs, US$4.

Directory **Banks** *Bradesco*, Av Rui Barbosa 614. **Medical services** *Casa de Caridade*, Praça Veríssimo de Melo 391, T7721005.

Parque Nacional Restinga de Jurubatiba

Close to Macaé and 228 km from Rio de Janeiro is the Restinga de Jurubatiba national park extending for 40 km along the Atlantic coast. With a width never greater than 5 km, this strip of coastal plains and lagoons is a breeding ground for many species of flora and fauna. The area was declared a Biosphere Reserve in 1992 by UNESCO due to its great importance for the global network of wildlife and in 1998 the national park was created by Ibama from a project developed by researchers from Brazil, Sweden and the United States. Park information: Rua Francisco Portela 489, Macaé, RJ 27910-200, T7725035.

Northeast of Rio de Janeiro

From Rio and Niterói, the BR-101 runs north east to Campos and the border with Espírito Santo. Rio Bonito is 64 km from Niterói, where the RJ-124 toll road branches off south to Araruama and the Cost do Sol. There are many *fazenda* hotels in the area around the town.

Rio Bonito

Sleeping **AL** *Fazenda Pedras Negra*, turn off at Km 257 of BR-101, T/F7340425. Pool, horse riding, fishing. **A** *Fazenda Serra dos Cambê*, BR101 Km 265, T7340027. Pool.

Transport From Rio de Janeiro bus to São Pedro da Aldeia stops at Rio Bonito frequent departures 0500-1415 with *Mil e Um* 1½ hrs, US$4.50

Biological Reserve of Poço das Antas
See also box next page

At Km 222 is the Biological Reserve of Poço das Antas, the only natural habitat of the *mico-leão*, Golden Lion Tamarin (two hours' drive from Rio); it is not open to the general public). ■ *Contact Ibama, Av Pres Antônio Carlos 607, 12th floor, Rio de Janeiro.*

Campos

Phone code: 0xx24
Population: 385,000

Campos (dos Goitacazes – after the Indian tribe which used to inhabit the area) is a busy industrial city, some 276 km from Rio de Janeiro and 70 km from Macaé. It stands 56 km from the mouth of the Rio Paraíba, up which coffee planting originally spread into São Paulo state. Coffee is still grown near Campos, but the region has always been one of the largest sugar-producing zones in Brazil.

In the 1970s, Brazil's answer to rocketing oil prices was the conversion of sugar into alcohol fuel for cars, where Campos became one of the major centres for this industry. Subsequently, important offshore oil and gas discoveries have been made nearby. On a historical note, this was the first Brazilian city to install electric lighting, inaugurated in 1883. The **Basílica de São Salvador** in Praça São Salvador dates from 1652.

Beaches The sea can be reached by the road to **São João da Barra** (41 km). It is then a further 4 km to **Atafona**, at the mouth of the Rio Paraíba do Sul. The outflow of the river here pollutes the beach, but if you go further south to **Grussaí** or **Açu**, the sea is generally cleaner. Further south still are beaches around **Farol de São Tomé**, **Barra do Furrado** and **Quissamã**. North of the Rio Paraíba are several beaches in the vicinity of **São Francisco** and **Itabapoana**.

Sleeping & eating **A** *Antares*, R Vig João Carlos 19, T7334055, F7220011. Restaurant, parking. **B** *Palace*, Av 15 de Novembro 143, T7332277, F7223661. Restaurant, parking. **B** *Terrazo Tourist*, R Joaquim Távora 22, T7331405, F7221605, terazzo@censa.com.br Two-star. **C** *Planície*, R 13 de Maio 56, T7234455, F7223377. **C** *Tuyuyú Praia*, Praia da Barra do Furado, Quissamã, T/F7471498. A/c, pool. For eating, try the very cheap *Kantão do Líbano*, Av Pelinca 101, which serves Arabic food. *Picanha Grill*, in Shopping Estrada, Av Nilo Peçanha 614 for Churrasco.

Festivals **Founding of the city**, 28 Mar; **Corpus Christi**, May or Jun; **São Pedro**, 29 Jun (as above); **patron saint's day**, Santíssimo Salvador, 6 Aug.

Transport **Air** Airport, BR-101, Km 5, T7330144. Flights to **Rio de Janeiro**. **Buses** Bus station, BR 101, T7331001. From **Rio de Janeiro** there are frequent departures from 0030-2130 with *Mil e Um (1001)*, 3¾ hrs, US$10.

Directory **Banks** *Banco 24 Horas*, Parque Centro Shopping, Av Pelinca 116. *Bradesco*, Blvd Francisco P. Carneiro 28. **Medical services** *Beneficência Portuguesa*, R Barão de Miracema 142, T7330055.

Santo Antônio de Pádua
Phone code: 0xx24
Population: 34,000

Santo Antônio de Pádua is a pleasant town on the Rio Pomba near the border with Minas Gerais, 106 km from Campos via São Fidélis, Cambiasca and Itoacara. The large number of rapids in the area make **canoeing** very popular around here. The **hydromineral spring** at Avenida Dr Themístocles de Almeida is unique for the chemical composition of its waters. ■ *Mon-Fri 0700-1100, 1300-1600, Sat 0700-1100.* The RJ-393 road leads out of town to **Itaperuna** and **Bom Jesus do Itabapoana** on the border with Espírito Santo.

The golden lion tamarin

The tamarin, or mico-leão in Portuguese, is a primate of the genus Leontopithecus. It is a small mammal, about the size of a squirrel, which lives off fruit, flowers, tender vegetation and insects. In Brazil there are three species of tamarin, all under threat of extinction: L rosalia, the mico-leão-dourado or golden lion tamarin; L chrysopygus, the mico-leão-preto or black lion tamarin; and L chrysomela, the mico-leão-de-cara-dourada or golden-headed lion tamarin. The main problem for the tamarins is that their habitat, the mata atlântica of São Paulo, Rio de Janeiro, Espírito Santo and Bahia, has all but been destroyed and there has been further threat from predation by man.

These engaging creatures are quite beautiful, so much so that they were popular pets with European royalty in the 17th and 18th centuries. The golden lion tamarin, with its face surrounded by a bright, silky mane, was considered the most beautiful. It has been described as having a coat that "shines like gold dust in the light." And thereby hangs another of the animal's problems; its attractiveness made it a prize pet for non-royal collectors and demand in the trade soon contributed to the golden lion tamarin's dwindling numbers. By the 1970s it seemed a foregone conclusion that the golden lion tamarin and its Brazilian relatives were doomed to extinction.

Fortunately, the Golden Lion Tamarin Conservation Project, set up in 1983 at the Poço das Antas Biological Reserve (which was created in 1974), has been successful in breeding tamarins in captivity and returning them to the wild. Around the world, zoos have been helping with the breeding programme. In 1997, a WWF estimate for the number of golden lion tamarins living in the wild in Poço das Antas was put at 800, but other figures suggest 550 (some even as low as 150). Whatever the number, the severest test for the survival of the species is the creation of more forest in which the tamarins can live. Corridors of suitable vegetation have to be set up so that the tamarins can move about safely and breed freely in their natural surroundings. This goal was undermined during the drought of 1997 which led to an increase in forest fires in Brazil (the majority started by man), posing a renewed threat to the tamarin's habitat. So the mico-leão-dourado's future is by no means secured; despite this, the animal has become a symbol of hope for forest conservation throughout Brazil. Many Brazilian and international agencies and specialist centres have contributed to its survival, but as with all such projects, the work never stops.

Besides the mico-leão-dourado population at Poço das Antas, there is a conservation project for the mico-leão-da cara-dourada at Una in Bahia, and the mico-leão-preto can be seen near Praia do Forte, north of Salvador.

Sources WWF Update (World Wide Fund for Nature), Summer 1997, website http://www.wwf-uk.org; in the UK T01483-426444, F01483-426-409, or contact your local office. Marya Rowan, 'Breeds Apart', South American Explorer (25 May 1990), pages 32-3. Wildlife Fact File, International Masters Publishers Ltd (London), #120.

Sleeping C *Hotel das Águas*, R Luís da Silva Magacho 170, T38510805. A short walk from the centre it is set in a park and associated with the health centre and bottling plant for the local mineral water.

Transport The bus station is at Rua José de Alencar Leite, T38510823. From **Rio de Janreiro** there are frequent departures from 0700-2400 with *Mil e Um (1001)*, 4½ hrs, US$8.50.

Inland resorts

There are three main resorts in the Serra do Mar (the area from Rio Grande do Sul to Espírito Santo) close to Rio de Janeiro: Petrópolis, Teresópolis and Nova Friburgo. Among the principal reasons for their existence are their altitude, which gives cooler temperatures than Rio; the lack of yellow fever and other diseases which festered in the unhealthy port on the bay in the 19th century; and the access provided by the routes which brought first gold, then coffee, to the coast. The mountains at first sight appear to be a rugged barrier between the coast and the interior, but once mule trains had established permanent roads through to the Rio Paraíba and Minas Gerais, it became obvious to early travellers that the highlands had many benefits. Nowadays weekenders from Rio and other tourists tend to agree. One such visitor was Dom Pedro I, the emperor, who in 1822 stopped at a fazenda belonging to Padre Correia on his way to Minas Gerais. He was so taken with the place that he subsequently made frequent visits. At the prompting of his wife, Dona Amélia, he purchased a nearby estate, Córrego Seco, in 1830, setting in motion the process which led to the building of Petrópolis.

Petrópolis

Phone code: 0xx24
Population: 270,000

Standing at 809 m in the Serra da Estrela range of mountains in the Serra do Mar, Petrópolis was once known as the 'summer capital' of Brazil. It was also referred to as *A Cidade Imperial* (see history below), a name given to it in 1881 or *Cidade das Hortênsias* (hydrangeas) because of the abundance of these flowers there. Now it combines a manufacturing industry (particularly textiles) and tourism with floral beauty and hill scenery. This is a great place for hiking, climbing, riding and cycling.

The pleasant **climate** which attracted the imperial family has an average high temperature of 23°C and a low of 14°C. The warmest months are from September to December. The wettest months are from January to March, although it can start getting wet in November and rain can be expected at any time. It can get chilly at night all year round, but especially in winter. A unique climatic feature of the area is a dense fog, called *o ruço*, which usually forms in the late afternoon. While this can be atmospheric, it can also be dangerous for drivers as the fog can descend very quickly.

Tourist information is at *Petrotur*, in the Prefeitura de Petrópolis, at the rear of the Casa do Barão de Mauá, Praça da Confluência 03, T2433561, F2420639. It has a list of tourist sites and of hotels and a good, free coloured map of the city. ■ *Petrotur is open Mon-Thu 0830-2000, Fri 0830-2100, Sat 0900-2100, Sun 0900-1500. The tourist kiosk on Praça Dom Pedro II is open Tue-Sat 0900-1700, Sun 0900-1500, closed for lunch 1300-1400.* News stands sell a *Guia de Petrópolis* (Guia Castor) for US$9, which has a full description of the city's attractions, hotels, restaurants and services. The map, though artistic, is not too helpful.

History Because the emperor Pedro I abdicated in 1831, he never realized his dream of building a summer palace in the Serra. Córrego Seco was rented out, lastly to Júlio Frederico Koeler, a German engineer who worked on the construction of a road to Minas Gerais. Koeler proposed the colonization of Córrego Seco by Germans. When the new emperor, Dom Pedro II, approved this plan in 1843, he stipulated that a summer palace should be built in addition to a town and the settlement scheme. Petrópolis dates its founding from 1843 and in little over a decade became an important place. Once the imperial palace was built, the emperor and his family began to spend six months of each year there (November to April). His court had to accompany him, so other fine residences sprang up in the city that Koeler had designed. In April 1854, Brazil's first railway line was opened, from Porto Mauá on Guanabara Bay to Raiz da Serra, which greatly shortened the journey time between Rio and Petrópolis. By the 1880s the railway had crossed the mountains to Petrópolis itself. So by the time the Republic was proclaimed in 1889, Petrópolis was administrative capital of the country for half the year, an intellectual centre for the same months, had its own commercial importance and was directly connected to Brazil's rapidly growing transport links.

In the early 20th century, it became the official summer seat of the president of the republic (the residence being the Palácio Rio Negro). In the 1940s it had a brief flirtation with gambling, when the *Hotel e Cassino Quitandinha* attracted Hollywood stars and other members of the international jet set until the banning of gaming in 1946. Since then, the city has thrived industrially and, most recently, in tourism.

Sights

Three **rivers** are dominant features in the design of Petrópolis: the Piabanha, Quitandinha and Palatino. In the historic centre (Centro Histórico), where most of the sites of tourist interest are to be found, the rivers have been channelled to run down the middle of the main avenues. Their banks, especially the Quitandinha, are planted with fine trees and flowers and the overall aspect is completely different from elsewhere in Brazil. You quickly get a sense that this was a city built with a specific purpose and at a specific time in Brazil's history.

Petrópolis

- **Sleeping**
  1. Bragança Palace
  2. Casablanca
  3. Casablanca Center
  4. Casablanca Palace
  5. Comércio
  6. Margaridas
  7. Pousada dos Pássaros
  8. York

- **Eating**
  1. Bauernstube
  2. Cantina Italiana
  3. Casa d'Ângelo
  4. Casa Itarare
  5. Falconi
  6. Majórica

The main commercial streets are **Rua do Imperador**, which runs southwest from the Praça da Inconfidência by the Rodoviária and **Rua 16 de Março**. At right angles to Rua do Imperador is the stately **Rua da Imperatriz**, which passes the Imperial Museum, bends round to the cathedral as Avenida Tiradentes, then turns again, as Avenida Koeler, towards **Praça Rui Barbosa**. The view from Praça Rui Barbosa, up the canal and Avenida Koeler to the cathedral, gives a fine impression of Petrópolis' design. These three avenues straddle the Rio Quitandinha, which now turns northwest, then northeast, until it meets the Rio Piabanha by the Palácio de Cristal.

The **Museu Imperial** (Imperial Palace), which seems to express faithfully what we know of Dom Pedro II's character, is a modest but elegant building, neoclassical in style, fully furnished and equipped. It contains the Crown Jewels of both Pedro I and Pedro II and other imperial possessions. It is extremely well-kept and you might think the imperial family had left the day before your visit, rather than in 1889. Many of the rooms and salons are open to visitors. In a separate building is the Salão das Viaturas (vehicles), which houses coaches, litters, the *Leopoldina* locomotive which worked the Rio-Petrópolis line from 1883-1964 and a Merryweather of London fire engine (entry free). There are pleasant gardens in front of the palace. Horse-drawn carriages wait to be hired outside the gate (not all the horses are in good shape). ■ *Rua da Imperatriz 220, T2427012. Tue-Sun, 1200-1700. US$3, you pay at a small kiosk outside the entrance, then queue to deposit any bags and be admitted. On Sun, expect long queues.*

The Gothic-style **Catedral de São Pedro de Alcântara**, completed in 1925, contains the tombs of the Emperor and Empress. The Imperial Chapel is to the right of the entrance. ■ *Tue-Sat 0800-1200, 1400-1800.*

The summer home of air pioneer **Alberto Santos Dumont**, known as 'A Encantada', is at Rua do Encanto 22, west of Praça Rui Barbosa. The small house was built in 1918 as a mock Alpine chalet. Downstairs is an exhibition devoted to his flying career. His first flight was on 23 October 1906: the plane *14 Bis* flew 60 m in seven seconds; on 12 November 1906 it flew 220 m in 21.5 seconds. Upstairs is Santos Dumont's office/bedroom, with information on other aspects of his life. ■ *Tue-Sun 0900-1700. US$1.*

'A Encantada' stands on a bluff, below which is the Universidade Católica de Petrópolis. Outside the university is the **Relógio das Flores** (Flower Clock), built in 1972. Above the university, on the hill of Quinta do Sol, is the **Trono de Fátima**, a shrine to Nossa Senhora de Fátima, with good views. ■ *Daily 0700-1830.*

The **Palácio de Cristal** in Praça da Confluência (where the Rios Quitandinha and Piabanha meet), was designed in the same style as several similar crystal palaces in Europe. This one was built in France in 1879, with the original intention of being an exhibition hall for local products. However, it became the imperial ballroom, but has now reverted to being an exhibition centre.

Opposite the Palácio de Cristal, across Rua A Pachá, is the Bohemia brewery. The **Bohemia Beer Festival** is held in June.

Fine mansions built by the aristocracy of both the imperial and republican eras can be seen on Avenida Koeler and Avenida Ipiranga. Among them are the neoclassical Palácio Rio Negro and the Palácio da Princesa Isabel at Avenida Koeler 255 and 42 respectively and the Casa de Rui Barbosa, in the eclectic style, at Avenida Ipiranga 405. Another palace is the mid-19th century Casa do Barão do Rio Branco, Avenida Barão do Rio Branco 279. It was here that the Treaty of Petrópolis was signed, settling with Bolivia the issue of the annexation of Acre (1903). The house is not open to the public.

Parks & praças

The twin praças of dos Expedicionários and Dom Pedro II (in which there is a tourist kiosk) are at the junction of Rua do Imperador and Rua da Imperatriz. A short distance up Rua da Imperatriz, on the same side as Praça Dom Pedro II, is the **Praça Visconde de Mauá**, in which there is a statue of an eagle and a snake. On one side of the praça is the Palácio Amarelo (1850), now the Câmara Municipal, and on another the modern Palácio da Cultura. On Sundays in the square is a small antiques market. **Praça Rui Barbosa** is very busy on Sunday, with goat-drawn carriages for children and occasional open-air concerts.

Excursions

Southwest of the centre is the **Museu Casa do Colono**, Rua Cristóvão Colombo 1034, Castelânea, with exhibits on the way of life of the early German colonists. ■ *Tue-Sun 0900-1700.* Also southwest is the **Parque Cremerie**; and the **Palácio Quitandinha**, Avenida Estados Unidos 2, T421012. This vast, grandiose palace, built in 1944 as a casino and hotel, is now a tourist centre that holds events. The lake in front of the building is in the shape of South America. ■ *Tue-Sun 0900-1700.*

Museu das Armas Ferreira da Cunha, Km 40 on the BR-040 (on the old road to Rio), shows a large collection of arms. ■ *By appointment only, T420373.*

The Avenida Barão do Rio Branco, which heads north out of the city, passes the turning to the **Orquidário Binot**, Rua Fernandes Vieira 390. This has a huge collection of orchids from all over Brazil (plants may be purchased). ■ *T420833. Mon-Fri 0800-1100, 1315-1630, Sat 0700-1100. Take bus to Vila Isabel.*

Sleeping
■ *on map, page 187*
Price codes: see inside front cover

In the Roteiros de Charme group (see page 47) are **L** *Locanda della Mimosa*, Al das Mimosas 30, Vale Florido, T/F2425405 and **L** *Pousada da Alcobaça*, R Agostinho Goulão 298 (Estr do Bonfim), Corrêas, T2211240, F2213390. Both are set in quiet gardens with the highest levels of multilingual service, local food in the excellent restaurants (see below), pool, sauna and sports facilities. **A** *Margaridas*, R Bispo Dom José Pereira Alves 235, Trono de Fátima, T2424686, F2435422. A chalet-type hotel set in lovely gardens with a swimming pool, charming owners. There are 3 *Casablanca* hotels: **A** *Casablanca*, R da Imperatriz 286, T2426662, F2425946, good atmosphere in the older part, pool, very clean; **A** *Casablanca Center*, Gen Osório 28, T2422612, F2426298, restaurant, games room; and **A** *Casablanca Palace*, R 16 de Março 123, T2420162, F2425946. **A** *Riverside*

Façade of the Imperial Palace

Parque, R Hermogéneo Silva 522, Retiro, 5 mins from the centre, T2310730, F2432312. Restaurant, pool and sports facilities. **B** *York*, R do Imperador 78, a short walk from the Rodoviária, T2432662, F2428220. Convenient, helpful, the fruit and milk at breakfast come from the owners' own farm. Recommended. **B** *Comércio*, R Dr Porciúncula 55, opposite Rodoviária, T2423500. Shared bath, basic.

On R Raul de Leoni (the continuation of R da Imperatriz) are: **A** *Pousada dos Pássaros*, whose prices are in the **C** range Mon-Fri; and almost opposite, at No 109, *Bragança Palace*, T2420434, F2435276.

Eating
• on map, page 187

Mid-range *Locanda della Mimosa*, Al das Mimosas 30, T2425405. Excellent Italian, open 2000-2400 Thu, 1230-1600, 2000-2400 Fri-Sat, 1230-1600, 1900-2300 Sun, best to reserve at weekends. *Pousada da Alcobaça*, (see above). Brazilian cuisine typical of the mountain region such as trout with herbs, open daily 1300-2400.

Cheap *Bauernstube*, Dr Nelson de Sá Earp 297. German, closed Mon. *Falconi*, R do Imperador 757. Italian. Recommended. *Cantina Italiana*, R Paulo Barbosa, just by Praça Sodré. Upstairs, popular, cheap, Italian, pizzas, Brazilian daily specialities. *Majórica*, R do Imperador 754. Churrasco.

There are several **bars and cafés** in the centre, eg *Casa d'Ángelo*, R do Imperador 700, by Praça Dom Pedro II and *Casa Itarare*, at the corner of R do Imperador and R Dr Porciúnculo.

Festivals Foundation of the town, 16 Mar. Its **patron saint's day**, São Pedro de Alcântara, is 29 Jun. There is also the **Bohemia beer festival**, see page 188.

Shopping R Teresa, southeast of the centre, is where the textile industry exhibits its wares. In common with Itaipava (see below), it draws buyers from all over the country and is a good place to find good quality knitwear and other goods.

Transport
68 km north of Rio

Buses Frequent departures from **Rio de Janeiro** along a steep, scenic mountain road (sit on the left hand side for best views) from 0540-2400 (every 15 mins 0800-2200, every hour on Sun) with *Única Fácil*, 1½ hrs, US$3.25. Return tickets are not available, so buy tickets for the return on arrival in Petrópolis. The ordinary buses leave from the rodoviária in Rio; a/c buses, hourly from 1100, from Av Nilo Peçanha, US$4. Bus to **Niterói**, US$4.50; to **Cabo Frio**, US$10. To **Teresópolis**, *Viação Teresópolis*, 8 a day, US$3.

Directory **Banks** *Banco do Brasil*, R Paulo Barbosa 81. There are several banks on R do Imperador and R Marechal Deodoro. A *Banco 24 Horas* ATM is located by the Varig office at R Mcal Deodoro 98. The following travel agencies change money: *BKR*, R Gen Osório 12, *Goldman*, R Barão de Amazonas 46 (between Praça Rui Barbosa and the Universidade) and *Vert Tur*, R 16 de Março 244, from 1000-1630. **Communications** **Post Office**: R do Imperador 350 in the Palácio dos Correios (built 1922) at the corner of Av Epitácio Pessoa. **Telephone**: R Mcal Deodoro, just above Praça Dr Nelson de Sá Earp, no fax.

Itaipava
Phone code: 0xx24

Continuing north from Petrópolis, the road becomes the Estrada União-Indústria, going through Corrêas, where you will find the **Casa do Padre Correia** (see Petrópolis' history, above), although it is not open to the public. Further out is Itaipava, about 20 km from Petrópolis, near where this road joins the BR-040 highway to Belo Horizonte and at the junction of the road to Teresópolis. This district is rapidly becoming a popular centre for eating, shopping and weekend breaks for Cariocas. There are outlets and boutiques for the local textile industry, a *feira* every Wednesday and Friday night and at weekends, a wide variety of good restaurants and several good *pousadas*.

Sleeping **L** *Pousada das Araras*, Estr Bernardo Coutinho 4570, Araras (access at Km 65 of BR-040), T2251143, www.pousadadasararas.com.br Chalets in a garden with mountain views, good restaurant, two pools, dry and wet saunas. Two Roteiro do Charme hotels are **L** *Pousada Capim Santo*, 2 km on the road to Teresópolis (RJ-130), T2221395, www.capimsanto.com.br Set in a pine forest, suites or chalets, good restaurant, walking trails, heated pool, gym, and **L** *Pousada Tankamana*, Estr Aldo Gelli, Vale do Cuiabá, T2222706, www.tankamana.com.br Chalets set in wooded area with mountain biking trails and horse riding. **AL** *Pousada Tambo Los Incas*, Estr Ministro Salgado Filho 2761, Vale do Cuiabá, T2221313, www.compuland.com.br/tambo Restaurant, dry sauna and heated pool, no children under 12. **A** *Pousada das Águas*, Estr da Rocinha Km 6, Secretário, T0xx21-2330288, www.pousadadasaguas.com.br Simple yet well maintained pousada with a lake, waterfalls and natural pools, restaurant serving trout.
Camping *Associação Brasileira de Camping and YMCA*, Araras district. Space can be reserved through Rio YMCA, T021-2319860.

Eating Cheap: *Araras*, in Pousada das Araras (see above). Good mix of international cuisine, open daily from 1300 until late. *Faraona*, Estrada União Indústria 13984, T2221503. Restaurant specialising in *faraona* (chicken), open Thu for dinner and Fri-Sun for lunch and dinner. *Tankamana*, in Pousada Tankamana (see above). Specializes in trout, open Mon-Sat for lunch and dinner, Sun for lunch only.

Tour operators *Cavalgada Ecológica*, Haras Analu, Estrada do Vale do Cuiabá 5230, T2221261, www.cavalgadaecologia.com.br Guided horse riding tours.

Transport Buses from **Rio de Janeiro** depart from 0700-2030 with *Salutaris*, US$3.75, 2 hrs.

Teresópolis

Near the Serra dos Órgãos, 91 km northeast of Rio, at an altitude of 910 m, this is the highest city in the state of Rio de Janeiro. The town was the favourite summer residence of Empress Teresa Cristina, and was accordingly named after her.

Phone code: 0xx21
Population: 125,000

Tourist information is in the bus station, T7420999; *Secretaria de Turismo*, Praça Olímpica, T7423352 extension 284; *Terminal Turístico Tancredo Neves*, Av Rotariana at the entrance to town from Rio, T7423352, extension 2106.

Because of its height above sea level and the relatively low temperatures, the area was not exploited by the early colonists since they could not grow the tropical crops which were in demand in Europe. The Michelin guide points out that the existence of *fazendas* in the region was first documented in the early 19th century, the best known being that belonging to an Englishman, George March. To accommodate a constant stream of visitors, March added lodgings to his farm and, not long after, other landowners followed suit. Before taking the name of the Empress, the parish was called Santo Antônio de Paquequer. Building in recent years has destroyed some of the city's character, but most visitors do not go only to see the town. Its location, at the foot of the Serra dos Órgãos, with the associated outdoor activities, is an essential part of the charm.

History

See the **Colina dos Mirantes** hill, a 30-minute steep climb from Rua Jaguaribe (2 km from the centre), which has sweeping views of the city and surroundings (a taxi up is not expensive). Around the town are various attractions, such as the Sloper and Iaci lakes, the Imbui and Amores waterfalls and the **Fonte**

Sights

Judith, which has mineral-rich water, access from Avenida Oliveira Botelho, 4 km southwest. Just off the road to Petrópolis is the **Orquidário Aranda**, Alameda Francisco Smolka, T7420628, 5 km from the centre.

The road to Nova Friburgo (see below) is known as the Vale das Hortaliças because it passes through a zone where vegetables and some flowers are cultivated. There is a rock formation called A Mulher de Pedra (The Stone Woman), 12 km out of Teresópolis on this road.

Sleeping
L *Fazenda Rosa dos Ventos*, Km 22 on the road to Nova Friburgo, T6428833, F6428174. In the Roteiros de Charme group (see page 47). Set in a park with lake, walking trails, horse riding, tennis courts, pool, meeting rooms. **AL** *São Moritz*, outside on the Nova Friburgo Rd, Km 36, T/F6411115. Swiss-style with meals. **AL** *Pousada Toca Terê*, Praça dos Namorados, Ingá, T6425020. Set in a wood with waterfalls, natural and thermal pools. **A** *Alpina*, Av Pres Roosevelt 2500, Parque Imbui, on Petrópolis Rd, T/F7425252. **A** *Fazenda Montebello*, at Km 17 on the same road, T/F6446313. A modern hotel with pool, price includes 3 meals. Recommended. **C** *Várzea Palace*, R Sebastião Teixeira 41, T7420878. Recommended. There are many cheap hotels in R Delfim Moreira, near the Praça.

Youth hostel *Retiro da Inglesa*, 20 km on road to Nova Friburgo, Fazenda Boa Esperança, in the beautiful Vale dos Frades, T7423109, F5312234. Book in advance in Jan-Feb, dormitory accommodation and family rooms, camping beside the hostel. **Camping** *Quinta de Barra*, R Antônio Maria 100, Km 3 on Petrópolis Rd, T6431050.

Eating
Cheap *Da Irene*, R Tte Luís Meireles 1800, T7422901. Russian. Reservations necessary. *Taberna Alpina*, Duque de Caxias 131, German cuisine. *Bar Gota d'Água*, Praça Baltasar da Silveira 16, for trout or *feijoada* (small but recommended) and for *batidas*. There is also a cafetería in the ABC supermarket. Clean and very cheap. Recommended.

Festivals
Patron saint's day, 13 Jun, Santo Antônio; **São Pedro**, 29 Jun, is celebrated with fireworks. **Foundation of the city**, 7 Jul. Another saint's day is **Santa Terezinha**, 15 Oct. **Festa das Colônias**, is in May.

Transport
Buses There are frequent departures from **Rio de Janeiro** from 0600-2200 every hour from the Novo Rio rodoviária with *Viação Teresópolis*, 1½ hrs, US$4. Book the return journey as soon as you arrive at Teresópolis. Rodoviária at R 1 de Maio 100. From Teresópolis to **Petrópolis**, 8 departures daily, US$3. **A suggested day trip from Rio de Janeiro**: leave Rio at 0800 or before for the 1¾ hour ride into the mountains to Teresópolis (sit on the right side). Upon arrival, buy a ticket right away for Petrópolis (Viação Teresópolis) for the 1200 bus. This gives you 2¾ hrs to wander around. The 90-min drive from Teresópolis to Petrópolis is beautiful. The views on either side are spectacular. Again, upon arrival in Petrópolis, buy your ticket to Rio with *Única Fácil*. Take the 1715 bus 'via Quitandinha' and you might catch the sunset over the mountains (in May, Jun, Jul, take the 1615 bus). This gives you time to visit most of the attractions listed above.

Directory
Banks Cash or TCs at *Teretur*, Trav Portugal 46. English spoken. **Communications Internet**: *Cott@ge Cybercafe*, R Alfredo Rebello Filho 996, 2nd floor. US$5 per hr, 1800-2400 Tue-Thu, 1800-0400 Fri-Sat, 1800-2300 Sun.

Serra dos Órgãos

Eleven thousand hectares of the Serra dos Órgãos, (so called because their strange shapes are said to recall organ-pipes), are a national park (created in 1939, it is the second oldest in the country). The main attraction is the precipitous **Dedo de Deus** ('God's Finger') Peak (1,692 m). The highest point is the 2,263 m Pedra do Sino ('Bell Rock'), up which winds a 14-km path, a climb of three to four hours. The west face of this mountain is one of the hardest climbing pitches in Brazil. Another well known peak is the **Pedra do Açu** (2,245 m – the name is a Tupi word meaning 'large'). Many others have names evocative of their shape: for example, O Escalavrado ('The Scarred One'), O Dedo de Nossa Senhora ('Our Lady's Finger'), A Cabeça de Peixe ('Fish Head'), A Agulha do Diabo ('The Devil's Needle') and A Verruga do Frade ('The Friar's Wart'). Near the Sub-Sede (see below) is the **Von Martius** natural history museum, named after a German naturalist, Karl Friedrich Philipp Von Martius (1794-1868), who visited Brazil in 1817-20. ■ *0800-1700.*

Flora & fauna The park belongs to the Mata Atlântica ecosystem which, as frequently mentioned, is seriously threatened. There are 20-30 m high trees, such as paineiras (floss-silk tree), ipês and cedros, rising above palms, bamboos and other smaller trees. Flowers include begonias, bromeliads, orchids and quaresmeiras (glorybushes). The park is the home of the very rare and endemic grey-winged cotinga, as well as a number of other cotingas, berryeaters and other rare endemic birds. Less rare birds include hummingbirds, guans, araçaris and tinamous. Mammals include some species of monkey, wild cat, deer, armadillo, agouti and peccary. There are also a number of frogs and toads, including the *sapo-pulga* (the flea-toad, at 10 mm claimed by local literature to be the smallest amphibian in the world; although other sources say that the Cuban pygmy frog is the smallest).

Serra dos Órgãos

Park essentials The park has two dependencies, both accessible from the BR-116: the Sede (headquarters, T/F6421070) is closer to Teresópolis (from town take Avenida Rotariana), while the Sub-Sede is just outside the Park proper, off the BR-116. By the Sede entrance is the Mirante do Soberbo, with views to the Baía de Guanabara. Anyone can enter the Park and hike the trails from the Teresópolis gate, but if you intend to climb the Pedra do Sino, you must sign a register (those under 18 must be accompanied by an adult and have authorization from the park authorities). Entrance to the park is US$1, with an extra charge for the path to the top of the Pedra do Sino. For information from **Ibama** for the state of Rio de Janeiro, T0xx21-2311772.

A good way to see the park is to do the Rio-Teresópolis-Petrópolis-Rio circuit; a scenic day trip by car. It can also be hiked in 2-3 days (take a tent)

Sleeping & eating Ibama has some hostels, US$5 full board, or US$3 1st night, US$2 thereafter, although they are a bit rough. At the Petrópolis side of the Park, **A** *Campo de Aventuras Paraíso Açu*, Estr do Bonfim 3511, T0xx24-1426275, or T0xx21-9733618. Has various types of accommodation, from rooms to chalet, and specializes in adventure sports (credit cards not accepted); on the same road, at Km 3.5 and in the same price bracket, is *Cabanas Açu*, T0xx21-9835041, inside the Park, cabins, restaurant, sports include riding, canoeing and fishing (credit cards accepted). **Camping** Two sites in the Sub-Sede part, 1 close to the Museum, the other not far from the natural swimming pool at Poço da Ponte Velha; 1 site in the Sede part. The Sede has a restaurant and the Sub-Sede a *lanchonete*.

Sports At both the Sede and Sub-Sede there are natural swimming pools, although between May and Oct the temperature may be a little too chilly for bathing. In the Sub-Sede they are called Poços Verde, da Preguiça and Ponte Velha. It is possible to trek right through the park, from Teresópolis to Petrópolis, a distance of 42 km, but it is essential to take a guide; contact *Campo de Aventuras Paraíso Açu* (see 'Sleeping' above).

The Serra dos Órgãos is considered Brazil's climbing capital & the park is also good for trekking

Tour operators Tours of the park are offered by Francisco of *LazerTours*, recommended; T7427616, or find him at the grocery shop on R Sloper 1. *Focus Tours* (see page 22) offers birdwatching tours to this area.

Nova Friburgo

Phone code: 0xx24
Population: 169,000

At 846 m, in a beautiful valley with excellent walking and riding, the town is a popular resort during the summer months. It was founded by Swiss settlers from Fribourg, the first families arriving in 1820. Apart from the holiday business, Nova Friburgo has an important textile industry, specializing in lingerie, and also produces cheeses, preserves, sweets and liqueurs. **Tourist information** from the *Centro de Turismo*, on Praça Demerval Barbosa Moreira, T5238000, extension 236.

Sights A cable car from Praça dos Suspiros goes 650 m up the **Morro da Cruz**, from where you get a magnificent view of the rugged country for US$5. Most of the interesting sites are in the surrounding countryside, so a car may be necessary to see everything. The **Furnas do Catete**, 10 km northeast, is an area of forest, caves, waterfalls and rock formations – one of which is called the Pedra do Cão Sentado ('The Seated Dog'). ■ *There is a small entry fee.* Other natural attractions are the Pico da Caledônia (2,310 m) 15 km southwest, and the Véu de Noiva waterfall, 9 km north. The district of **Lumiar**, 34 km southeast, has beautiful scenery, waterfalls, natural swimming pools and good canoeing in the Rios Macaé and Bonito. These two rivers meet at a point called Poço do Alemão, or Poço Verde, 4½ km south of Lumiar.

AL *Bucsky*, 5 km out on the road to Niterói (Km 76.5), T5225052, F5229769, **Sleeping** www.hotelbucsky.com.br With meals, large meeting rooms, tennis courts, city tour and ecological walks available. **AL** *Pousada do Riacho*, Estr Teresópolis to Nova Friburgo (RJ-130), turn off at Km 8 near Cardinot, T5222823, riacho@openlink.com.br A Roteiro de Charme hotel (see page 47) set in gardens with pool, sauna, games room, tennis court and walking trails. **A** *Garlipp*, at Muri, 8 km south, Km 70.5 from Rio, T/F5421330. German-run, in chalets, with meals. **A** *Fazenda São João*, 11 km from *Garlipp* (under the same ownership) up a side road, T5421304. Riding, swimming, sauna, tennis, hummingbirds and orchids. The owner will meet guests in Nova Friburgo or even in Rio. **B** *Everest*, R Manuel Ventura 75, T5227350. Comfortable, good breakfast. **B** *Fabris*, Av Alberto Browne 148, T5222852. Central, TV, hot showers, plentiful breakfast buffet. **C** *Maringá*, R Monsenhor Miranda 110, T5222309. **D** without bath. Good breakfast. Recommended. **Camping** *Camping Clube do Brasil* has sites on the Niterói Rd, at Caledônia (7 km out, T5220169) and Muri (10 km out, T5422275). There is a private site at Fazenda Sanandu, 20 km out on the same road.

There are many options to choose from, several in European styles which reflect the **Eating** background of the people who settled in the area. You can also find Brazilian food, pizzas and *confeitarias*. **Cheap** *Auberge Suisse*, R 10 de Outubro, T5411270. Swiss; *Chez Gigi*, Av Euterpe Friburguense 21, T5230107. French.

Founding of the city, 16 May. Throughout the month the town holds a festival: **Festivals** *Maifest*. **Patron saint's day**, 24 Jun, São João Batista.

Buses Bus station, Ponte da Suadade, T5220400. From **Rio de Janeiro** there are frequent departures from 0500-2130 with *Mil e Um (1001)*, 2½ hrs, US$5.50. **Transport**

Banks *Bradesco*, Praça Demerval Barbosa Moreira. **Directory**

Near the state's northern border, this town is just off the BR-040 which connects Rio and Belo Horizonte. The region was previously known as Paraíba Nova and was part of the gold route between Paraty and the mines in Minas Gerais. An imperial customs post had to be maintained in the area to prevent smuggling. **Três Rios**
Phone code: 0xx24

Sleeping & eating C *Comendador*, R Nélson Viana 210, Praça Salim Chimelli, T2520533. Central location, a/c, TV.

Sports The town is the main centre for whitewater rafting in Rio de Janeiro. *Klemperer Turismo*, T2434052, in Rio, T0xx21-2528170, arranges descents on the junction of rivers Paraibuna, Piabanha and Paraíba do Sul. Recommended. *World River*, R Dr Bezerra 4, Centro, RJ 25806-100, T2553622, Cell0xx21-96755497, www.worldriver.com Rafting packages which can include accommodation, meals and a river descent at night. See also 'Rafting' page 71.

Transport Buses depart from **Rio de Janeiro** from 0700-2030 with *Salutaris*, US$6, 2¾ hrs. The bus terminal is in Rua Condessa do Rio Novo.

Towns in the Coffee Zone

Although coffee no longer dominates this part of Brazil, as it did in the 19th century, there are still many reminders of the wealth of this trade. It can be seen in the towns of Vassouras, Valença and especially in the fazendas which were the homes and production headquarters of the coffee barons. Today many of these plantations have been well and truly incorporated into a rural, cultural and historic tourist circuit, with some small towns in the Vale do Rio Paraíba do Sul such as Conservatória maintaining the serenading street musician tradition. Nearer to Rio, the train journey from Miguel Pereira has spectacular views of this mountainous terrain whilst the Museu da Cachaça at Pati dos Alferes is a shrine to this strong sugar cane spirit.

History The coffee zone was the valley of the Rio Paraíba do Sul and neighbouring hills and valleys. Before the coming of the railways in the second half of the 19th century, mule trains carried the coffee from the interior to the coast on roads such as the Estrada do Comércio, which ran from Minas Gerais, through Valença and Vassouras, to the town of Iguaçu on the river of the same name. At the end of the 19th century, the abolition of slavery, the exhaustion of the land and lower international prices for coffee caused the collapse of the coffee trade. The towns had to adapt to new economic activities or die, but many of the fazendas remain. Although not easy to get to, a visit is well worth the effort. *Fazendas: As Casas Grandes Rurais do Brasil*, by Fernando Tasso Frajoso Pires (Abbeville Press), is a beautiful book showing these magnificent houses.

Fazendas A number of these fazendas have become hotels whose prices start in most cases in our **AL** range. Besides lodging and food, most offer riding and other outdoor activities. Others offer day visits, usually guided tours and lunch at around US$15. Details should be obtained locally from the fazendas or municipal tourist offices (see below) or phone the Instituto de Preservação de Desenvolvimento do Vale do Paraíba (Preservale) T0xx21-2407539, who are coordinating the inclusion of 36 fazendas near Barra do Piraí, Valença, Rio das Flores and Vassouras into a cultural corridor for tourism.

Vale do Rio Paraíba do Sul

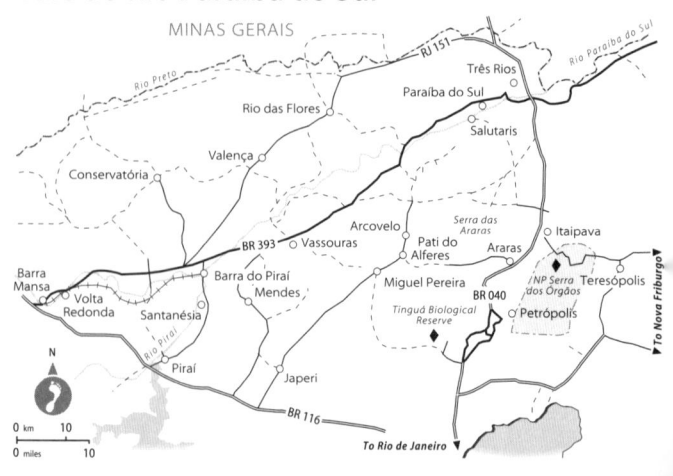

This town, 113 km north of Rio de Janeiro, has an excellent mountain climate. In the mid-19th century the area was entirely given over to coffee. Other industries were introduced when a railway branch line reached here in the late 19th century. The town was named after a doctor who, in the 1930s, promoted the region for holidays away from the coast. Three kilometres from town on the road to Rio is the **Javari lake**, a popular recreational spot. Mountain roads through the Serra do Mar head east to Petrópolis (see above) and west to Vassouras (see below), but ask about their condition before using either of them. *Setur*, Avenida Manuel Guilherme Barbosa 375, T4841616, has **tourist information**.

Miguel Pereira
Phone code: 0xx24
Population: 20,000
Altitude: 613 m

A tourist train, also known as the *Trem Azul*, on the **Miguel Pereira-Conrado** railway: a started operations in 1993 and affords beautiful views of mountains, rivers and waterfalls. The diesel train follows a meter gauge line constructed to take coffee to the port of Rio. Among the attractions of the journey is the Paulo de Frontin iron bridge, built in 1889 and said to be the only railway bridge built in a curve. The line is operated by *Montmar Turismo* of Angra dos Reis (see page 208). There is a museum at the railway station. ■ *The round trip of 56 km takes 4½ hrs, costs US$25 and leaves Miguel Pereira at 0930 on Sat, Sun and public holidays. The museum is open Thu-Sun 0900-1200, 1300-1700. T4844342.*

Sleeping AL *Fazenda Javary*, Praça Frutuoso Fernandes 35, Baro de Javary, T/F4843611 (or Rio T0xx21-2409335). Restaurant, pool, sports courts. B *Pousada Caçarola*, R Luís Marques 1204, 5 km from town, T4841499.

Transport From Rio de Janeiro bus to Arcozelo passes Miguel Pereira, every 2 hrs 0700-2000 with *Normandy*, 2 hrs, US$5.50 (with a/c US$6.75).

About 5 km north east of Miguel Pereira on the RJ-125 road is the town of Pati do Alferes which holds a **Festa do Tomate** in June. It also is home to the **Museu da Cachaça** in Rua Nova Mantiquira 227, www.muca.com.br, which also has its own distillery producing aguardiente for sale.

Pati do Alferes
Phone code: 0xx24
Population: 22,000
Altitude: 610 m

Sleeping A *Fazenda Quindins*, 3 km east on the road to Araras, T4851020.

Transport Buses: from **Rio de Janeiro** the bus to **Arcozelo** passes Pati dos Alferes, every 2 hrs 0700-2000 with *Normandy*, 2¼ hrs, US$5.50 (with a/c US$6.75).

Vassouras

It is hard to believe that the small town of Vassouras, northwest of Miguel Periera, was once considered one of the most important cities of the Brazilian Empire. During the coffee boom in the 19th century, Vassouras was surrounded by coffee farms whose owners became immensely rich. These coffee barons acquired noble titles and, as their power increased, they built enormous, opulent town houses in Vassouras. The majority of these buildings are still there, surrounding the beautiful main Praça Barão de Campo Belo. The emperor Pedro II visited the city several times.

Phone code: 0xx24
Population: 29,000
Altitude: 434 m

The climate is up here in the hills much cooler than Rio & it rains a lot in Jan & Feb

In 1875 the railway station was opened in Vassouras, allowing the local farmers to send their produce directly to Rio de Janeiro. But the town went into decline when the coffee boom ended and for many years it had almost no economic activity, except for some cattle ranching and small-scale agriculture. Nowadays, it has a university and is being rediscovered by the tourist industry. It still retains its small-town calm, but the reminders of its golden past mix with the student nightlife in the bars along a street called, unofficially, 'The Broadway'.

Sights The best way to explore Vassouras is on foot. Starting at the rodoviária, walk as far as the **Estação Ferroviária**, the former railway station. Recently restored, it is now the headquarters of the Universidade de Vassouras. Carry straight on to the **Praça Barão de Campo Belo**, where you will find the most important old houses and public buildings, all dating from the 19th century. Note the neoclassical influence. One of these old 'baronial' houses, at Rua Custódio Guimarães 65, on the lefthand side of the square as you enter, houses the **Casa da Cultura**, a municipal cultural centre which also provides **tourist information** and temporary exhibitions of local art and folklore. Ask if you can go upstairs and, on the second floor, at the top of some of the internal walls, look for where the paint has peeled. You can see the 19th century method of house construction, using clay over a frame of interwoven wood and bamboo.

At the top end of the praça is the church of **Nossa Senhora da Conceição**, the most important in the city, finished in 1853 in neoclassical style. Behind the church is the small **Praça Sebastião Lacerda**, surrounded by huge fig trees. Locals believe there is one fig tree for each of the rich coffee barons who lived in Vassouras in the last century. Keep on walking until you come to the **cemetery**. A visit is recommended. Most of the wealthiest men of Brazil's second empire are buried there. Rich mausoleums decorated with Italian and Portuguese marble sculptures show the competition among the families. Two of the most important clans are represented: the Teixeira Leite family and the Correa e Castro family. In the cemetery is one of the most curious legends of Vassouras: the 'flesh flower'. Growing on the grave of a catholic priest who died in 1866, Monsenhor Rios, a strange purple flower blooms every year in November on the 'Day of the Dead'. Its intense smell is reminiscent of rotting flesh. Scientists have studied it, but no definitive conclusions have been reached as to its origins or nature. The flower vanishes in a few days and the small bush lives on until January or February. It is now protected by a small iron fence and miracles are reported to have occurred there.

Back at Praça Barão de Campo Belo, on Rua Barão de Vassouras, is the **Palacete do Barão do Ribeirão**, the former residence of a coffee baron, later converted into the town's court. Nowadays it is closed for restoration as it has been badly attacked by termites. Turn right, and at the end of Rua Dr Fernandes Junior (No 89) you will find the fascinating **Casa da Hera** museum, an old country house covered with ivy, which belonged in the 19th century to one of the richest men in the town, Joaquim Teixeira Leite. After his death the house was inherited by his daughter, Eufrásia Teixeira Leite, who lost interest in the coffee business. She went to Paris, living a life of parties and luxury for many years. After her death in 1930, the house was made into a museum, according to her will. All the furniture, decoration and architecture is original, from the golden years of coffee. The wide variety of imported tapestries, pianos and porcelain contrasts with very rough building materials: a fantastic portrait of how life was in the 1850s. On some Sundays, depending on the number of visitors, they serve tea in a style that recreates the atmosphere of the old coffee *fazendas*. ■ *T4712342. Wed to Sun 1100-1700.*

The nightlife of Vassouras has more variety than in other towns of a similar size. Being a university centre, many students go out at night for a drink, especially on Friday and Saturday. The action is concentrated in Rua Expedicionário Oswaldo de Almeida Ramos, but you won't need to pronounce that: simply ask for the 'Broadway' and everybody will direct you to the right place. There are many bars and open-air restaurants to suit all tastes and budgets.

Another possibility is a guided visit to the food technology centre at the **Senai**, close to the main praça. Here students learn how to process fruit, vegetables, meat and also how to work in a brewery. Most of the hotels can arrange a guided visit at weekends.

Excursions

As yet, Vassouras lacks a well-developed tourist infrastructure. There is a lot to see around the city, especially the old *fazendas*, but they are only just starting to open to the public. The majority of them are privately owned and can only be visited with a prior appointment. The bigger hotels can arrange guided tours with transport at weekends. During the week, the only option is to go by car, as some of the *fazendas* are a long way away, down dirt roads. The best *fazendas* in the vicinity are: Fazenda Santa Mônica, Fazenda São Fernando, Fazenda Paraíso and Fazenda Oriente. More information can be obtained from the Casa da Cultura, R Custódio Guimarães 65, or from the Tourism Secretary, in the Municipalidade, Praça Barão de Campo Belo, T4711367. English is not normally spoken, but the staff will try to help you.

Sleeping

AL *Santa Amália*, Av Sebastião Manoel Furtado 526, close to the rodoviária, T4711038, F4711897. Located in a very pleasant and quiet park, swimming pool, sauna, volleyball and soccer pitches, one of the best in town, try to negotiate in the low season (Mar to Jun and Aug to Nov) and during the week. **B** *Gramado da Serra*, R Aldo Cavalcanti 7, T/F4712314. Bar, restaurant, pool, sauna. **B** *Mara Palace*, R Chanceler Dr. Raul Fernandes 121, T4711993, F4712524, www.marapalace.com.br House built in 1870, fully and tastefully preserved, swimming pool, bar, sauna, sports, nice atmosphere and good service, owner (Gerson) can arrange visits to *fazendas*. Also **Pousada Bougainville**, T4712451, and **Pousada Veredas**, T4712728.

Eating

The best restaurants are located in the centre, on R Expedicionário Oswaldo de Almeida Ramos/'The Broadway'. There are many to choose from, but the two best-known are **Sputnik** and **Mafioso** (both in the cheap category). They are close neighbours and have similar layouts and prices, with dishes varying from pasta (around US$8 for 1), steak (around US$13 for 1) and pizzas in different sizes and toppings (pizzas at *Sputnik* are good value). During the week they both offer meals 'by weight' at lunchtime, with a buffet of salads, cold and hot dishes. On warm nights you can sit outside, but be sure to arrive before 2000 to avoid the crowds, especially at weekends. Try the *chopp* (beer) and ask for one of the interesting appetizers, such as *mandioca frita* (fried manioc), similar to French fries.

Bars & nightclubs

Nightlife is found mostly in the bars and restaurants. University students often organize parties at weekends; look for the advertisements posted on the walls or in other public places. For people watching, stroll along 'The Broadway' on a Friday night.

Festivals

Carnival, Feb or Mar, is one of the best in the region, with its own Samba schools and balls. In Jun, the days of **Santo Antônio**, **São Pedro** and **São João** are celebrated with traditional parties. The **feast of Nossa Senhora da Conceição**, the city's patron saint, in on 8 Dec, with a mass and procession.

Shopping

Vassouras doesn't have any speciality handicrafts or souvenirs, other than the country cheese and the preserves made with local fruits.

Transport

Buses There are frequent departures from **Rio de Janeiro** from 0600-2030 with *Viação Normandy*, 2¼ hrs, US$5.50. (with a/c US$6.50) Try to buy your ticket at least 30 mins before departure. The average time between departures is 1½ hrs. Returning to Rio, the 1st bus is at 0430, then 0645, 0815 and others with an average time of 1½ hrs between them; the last 1 departs at 1900. These schedules may alter on holidays and during the summer, when more buses are added.

Directory

Banks The city is definitely not prepared for international tourism and foreign currencies are unlikely to be accepted. Change all the money you will need in Rio before departing. As a last resort, try the local *Banco do Brasil* at R Caetano Furquim, in the centre. **Communications** Post Office: R Irmã Maria Agostinha. **Telephone**: long distance and international calls at the office between R Caetano Furquim and R Expedicionário Oswaldo de Almeida Ramos(there are entrances in each street). **Medical services** *Hospital Eufrásia Teixeira Leite*, Praça Provedor Félix Machado 110, T4711796.

Barra do Piraí

Phone code: 0xx24
Population: 85,000
Altitude: 363 m

An asphalted road from Vassouras follows the Rio Paraíba for 20 km to Barra do Piraí, a major distribution centre for coffee and other goods in the mid-19th century. It was a main rail junction and has retained its importance as a commercial centre. There are many coffee fazendas in the area which can be visited. **Tourist information** is at the *Secretaria de Turismo*, T4420102.

Sleeping **AL** (full board) *Fazenda do Arvoredo*, 10km south on the RJ-145 to Piraí, T4422904, F4420278. Once the property of the Conde Modesto Leal, the plantation's slaves quarters have been reformed for guests but are still very simple. Pool, sauna, horse riding, ox cart rides, fishing and many other activities. **AL** (full board) *Pousada Fazenda Ponta Alta*, near Santanésia, 11km south on the RJ-145 to Piraí, T/F4423399. Built in 1830 by the Barão de Mambucaba, it was a favoured retreat of President Getúlio Vargas. Pool, horse riding. **Youth hostel E** pp *Albergue da Juventude Na Toca* (IYHA), Estr Mun. Rui Pio Davi Gomes 1876, Fazenda Santa Rita, Dorândia, RJ 27160, T4425323. To get there from Praça Oliveira Figueiredo in Barra do Piraí take *Viação Gran Eufrása* bus to Vargem Alegre via Dorândia, get off in Dorândia near the post office and walk 1½ km to the hostel.

Transport There are frequent daily departures from **Rio de Janeiro** every hour from 0600-2000 with *Viação Normandy*, 2 hrs, US$5.50 (with a/c US$6.50).

Valença

Phone code: 0xx24
Population: 62,000
Altitude: 560 m

Like Vassouras, Valença is a historical monument and its history follows much the same pattern, with wealth from the coffee trade followed by some small-scale industry and agriculture. There are a number of *fazendas* nearby and in the town a Faculty of Medicine. Secretaria de Turismo, T4522696.

Sleeping **AL** *Fazenda Repouso dos Guerreiros*, Estr da Figueira, 17km from town. T4522705. Pool, horse riding. **B** *dos Engenheiros*, R Teodorico Fonseca 525, T4520522.

Transport **Road** Although there is a dirt road which heads directly north from Vassouras, the best road follows the Rio Paraíba west to Barra do Piraí for 20 km, then doubles back for 30 km to Valença. **Buses**: there are frequent daily departures from **Rio de Janeiro** every 2 hrs from 0600-2000 with *Viação Normandy*, 2¾ hrs, US$7 (with a/c US$8.50).

Rio das Flores
Phone code: 0xx24

Some 20 km from Valença, near the border with Minas Gerais is the small town of Rio das Flores. There is a museum and the Igreja Santa Teresa d' Ávila which dates from 1858. Secretaria de Turismo, T4581115.

Sleeping **AL** *São Polycarpo*, Estr da Divisa, T0xx21-4395161, Cell9690060. Built in 1854 and once belonging to the Visconde de Rio Preto, the house has period furniture and gardens with palm trees.

Transport Buses: There are frequent daily departures from **Rio de Janeiro** to **Valença** (see above), from where you can change for Rio das Flores.

About 35 km from Valença and 30 km from Barra do Piraí, is Conservatória, another town in the coffee zone. Until the end of the 17th century the area was still inhabited by the Araris Indians before they were exterminated by the colonists. The town was founded on 19th March 1839 with the name Vila Santo Antônio de Rio Bonito. The railway arrived in the 1880s to transport the coffee grown in the nearby plantations and although the station closed in 1961, old locomotives can still be seen. Although it did not become as wealthy as Vassouras or Valença, it still has some fine 19th century houses and today, it is quieter than the other two towns. In Conservatória, local farm produce can be bought, as well as blankets, macrame and crochet work. A local custom is the serenade through the streets; serenaders meet at the Museu da Seresta on Rua Osvaldo Fonseca on Friday and Saturday. The three day Festa de Santo Antônio takes place in June and includes a cross country race. This region can also be reached via the Japeri turn-off on the BR-116 (a beautiful mountain drive). Secretaria de Turismo, T4381188.

Conservatória
Phone code: 0xx24
Population: 3,500
Altitude: 535 m

Sleeping There are many *fazenda* hotels in the area with lakes for fishing. **AL** *Fazenda Vilarejo*, 1 km on road to Barra da Piraí, T4381274. Horse riding available. **A** *Fazenda São Sebastião*, Estr São Sebastião 2301, T0xx21-2620262. **B** *Pousada do Lago*, Estr São Sebastião 487. T0xx21-2887610, Cell9670558.

Transport Buses: departures from **Rio de Janeiro** on Fri at 2015 with *Viação Normandy*, 3 hrs, US$6.

West of Rio de Janeiro

This western corner of Rio de Janeiro state, bordering the states of Minas Gerais and São Paulo, has beautiful mountain scenery with many rivers and waterfalls especially around Visconde de Mauá. It is also home to the Itatiaia national park and the imposing peak of Agulhas Negras as well as the only Finnish colony in Brazil at Penedo.

Volta Redonda

On a broad bend of the Rio Paraíba, 113 km west of Rio along the railway to São Paulo, Volta Redonda has one of the largest steel works in Latin America. The mills are on the river bank and the town spreads up the surrounding wooded and gardened slopes. To visit, apply for a permit from the *Companhia Siderúrgica Nacional*, Avenida Treze de Maio 13, Rio de Janeiro (10 days in advance), or locally from the *Bela Vista* hotel. Visits of 2½ to 3 hours start at 0900.

Phone code: 0xx24
Population: 226,000

A *Bela Vista*, Alto de Boa Vista, on a hill overlooking town, T33482022, F33482066. **A** *Sider Palace*, Av Alberto Pasqualini, T/F33481032.

Sleeping

Buses From **Rio de Janeiro** at 1700 daily, with *Viação Cidade de Aço*, 2 hrs, US$5.25. The hourly daily departures between 2030-2230 to **Barra Mansa** (see below) go via Volta Redonda. Also minibuses.

Transport

An industrial town at the crossroads of the BR-116 (Via Dutra between Rio de Janeiro and São Paulo) and the BR-393 which follows the Rio Paraíba do Sul north east to Três Rios close to the border with Minas Gerais. A railway for freight runs south to Angra dos Reis on the coast.

Barra Mansa
Population: 166,000

Resende Some 30 km west of Volta Redonda, in the town of Resende, is the Military Academy of Agulhas Negras at Km 306 Rodovia Presidente Dutra. The grounds, with captured German guns from the Second World War, are open to the public. There is a military museum. ■ *0800-1700*.

Population: 94,000
Phone code: 0xx24

Sleeping & eating A *Castel Plaza*, Av Mcal Castelo Branco 301, T33551091, F33544025. Bar, restaurant, sauna. **A** *River Park*, Av Nova Resende 262, T33353344, F33547314. Bar, restaurant, pool, sauna. *Peixe Boi*, R Nicolau Taranto 151, a cheap fish restaurant.

Transport From **Rio de Janeiro** there are frequent bus departures 0700-2100 with *Viação Cidade de Aço*, 2¾ hrs, US$4.75 (executive US$6.50) and *Sampaio* between 0615-1800. Buses also from **Volta Redonda**. There are buses to **Barra Mansa** with *Resendense*, 40 mins, US$2.50.

Penedo

Phone code: 0xx24
Population: 5,000
Altitude: 600 m

In the same region, 175 km from Rio, is the small town of Penedo and the only Finnish colony in Brazil, formed in 1929 by settlers who brought the first saunas to the country. Here they created a pacifist and vegetarian community closely linked to nature. Due to the difficulty of farming the land after the years of coffee cultivation, they turned to the production of crafts, chocolate, jams and chutneys as well as health tourism. Today there is a **Finnish museum**, open Wednesday-Sunday, and a **cultural centre** with Finnish dancing on Saturdays. This popular weekend resort is also ideal for horse riding and swimming in the **Portinho River**. There are many waterfalls in the area such as the Cachoeira de Deus on the Rio das Pedras. **Tourist information** is at Avenida Casa das Pedras, next to Hotel Girassol, T33511876. There is a Scandinavian festival in June, a Trout festival in August and a traditional Christmas with Papa Noel.

Sleeping There are many pousadas and hotels. **A** *da Cachoeira*, Estr das Três Cachoeiras, T33511262, F33511180. With its own waterfall, guide will take guests to the more distant *cachoeiras*, bar, restaurant, pool, sauna, gym, parking. **A** *Girassol*, Av Casa das Pedras 766, T33511237. President Cardoso has stayed here, chalets or rooms (some with own sauna and jacuzzi), pool, playground. **B** *Bertell*, R Harry Bertell 47, T/F33511288. Chalets or rooms, a/c, fridge, TV, phone, bar, pool, sauna, parking. **B** *Hotel do Campanário*, R do Lago 62, centre of town, T33511166. With bathroom and breakfast, TV, fridge, phone, bar, pool, sauna, playground, volleyball court, parking. **B** *La Cave*, R Projetada, close to Museu Finlandês, T33511232, lacave@resenet.com.br Chalets or rooms with bathroom and breakfast, a/c, TV, phone, pool, sauna, gym, games room, small meeting room. **B** *Pousada Serra da Índia*, Estr Vale do Ermitão, T33511185. Chalets or rooms with bathroom and breakfast, a/c, TV, fridge, bar, pool, sauna, games room, gym. **B** *Pousada Penedo*, Av Finlândia, T33511309, F33511255. Safe, TV, fridge, phone, pool, sauna, parking. Recommended. **Camping** *Bandeirante*, Av Brasil 440, T3511358. *Hans*, T33511184.

Eating In the town centre there are many restaurants with a wide variety of different cuisines such as fondues, salmon and herring. **Cheap** *Biergarten*, Av Casa das Pedras 1017. German, closed Mon. *Pequena Suécia*, R Toivo Suni, T33511275. Swedish, closed Tue. *Rei das Trutas*, Av das Mangueiras. Trout and other fish.

Tour operators *Cachoeira Tur*, in Penedo Shopping, T33521947. Tours throughout this mountain region. Horse riding tours with *Haras Katmandu*, Av Penedo 1580, Jardim Martinelli, T33511129, and *Centro Hípico Vale das Montanhas*, on the road to Resende, T33511040.

Buses Departures from **Rio de Janeiro** at 1100 and 1700 with *Viação Cidade de Aço*, 3 hrs, US$6.75. Five buses a day from **Resende** with *Viação Tupi*, T33551706, 40 mins.

Visconde de Mauá

Some 33 km beyond Penedo (part of the road unpaved) is the small village of Visconde de Mauá in the **Serra da Mantiqueira**. Swiss and German immigrants came to this area in the early 20th century. The surrounding scenery is fine, with valleys, cold rivers and lots of flowers. Temperatures range from under 10°C to highs of around 30°C. There are opportunities for good walks and other outdoor activities. Lots of holidaymakers visit the town and the atmosphere is very pleasant. Many places offer acupuncture, shiatsu massage, macrobiotic food etc, and there is a hippy feel to the crafts on sale. Horses can be rented in Visconde de Mauá from Berto (almost opposite *Vendinha da Serra*), or Pedro (Lote 10) and 9 km away at *Fazenda Aguas Claras*, excellent countryside rides with well trained horses, 3 hours, US$30. Many places in Maringá arrange riding. The Rio Preto is good for canoeing and there is an annual national event (dates change; check in advance). **Tourist information**, *Mauátur*, is at the entrance to town, T33871283. Open 0900-1800, Mon-Sun.

Phone code: 0xx24
Altitude: 1,200 m

There are roads to three other small hill towns: to **Mirantão**, at about 1,700 m, with semitropical vegetation; to **Maringá**, which is just across the state border in Minas Gerais and is a delightful two hours' walk; and to **Maromba**. On the way to Maromba is the Mirante do Posto da Montanha, a lookout with a view of the Rio Preto, which runs through the region and is the border between Rio de Janeiro and Minas Gerais states. Also in Minas Gerais, 6 km up river from Maringá but on a different road, are the Santa Clara falls (turn off before Maromba). Between Visconde de Mauá and Maringá is a natural pool in the river (turn left before crossing the bridge). After Maromba follow the signs to Cachoeira e Escorrega, a small fall and waterslide with a cold natural swimming pool, a 2 km walk. A turning off this road leads to another waterfall, the Cachoeira Véu da Noiva.

Excursions

Visconde de Mauá **LL** *Fronteira*, Estr Visconde de Mauá to Campo Lindo, Km 4, T33871219, F33871388. Restaurant, pool, sauna, sitting room with paintings and gardens with sculptures by Brazilian artists. A Roteiro de Charme hotel (see page 47). **A** *Fazenda do Mel*, 5 km from Visconde de Mauá on the road to Campo Alegre, T33871308. Chalets, restaurant, heated pool, sauna. **B** *Pousada da Lua*, Praça da Maringá, T33871230. Chalets on a hill overlooking the Rio Preto. **B** *Pousada Recanto de Mauá*, on the road to Maringá, T33871182. Chalets. *Hotel Turístico*, ½ km on road to Maringá. With handicrafts and homemade food. Italian owner, Nino, and his Brazilian wife run excursions. Cheap lodgings are limited: enquire at *Vendinha da Serra*, an excellent natural food restaurant and store (also has information on horse riding); next door is *Dona Mariana*, a recommended budget place to stay.

Sleeping
There are many fazendas, pousadas & chalés in the vicinity but very few are cheap places to stay

 Maringá **A** (half board) *Beira Rio*, T33541801. Chalets or rooms. Recommended. **A** (full board) *Pousada Vale das Hortênsias*, T33543030. Chalets, pool. Recommended. **A** *Pousada no Caminho do Marimbondo*, Estr do Vale do Pavão, T0xx21-7111292. Chalets, pool, sauna. **A** *Cabanas do Visconde*, on the banks of the Rio Preto, 5 km from Visconde de Mauá on the road to Maringá, T33871115. Chalets, restaurant, heated pool, sauna. **B** *Pousada Sitio Portal da Travessia*, on the left bank of Rio das Cruzes, T33871154, pousitio@unisys.com.br Chalets. **Camping** There are several sites, including *Barragen's*, in Maringá, T33871354 and *Ipê Amarelo*, T33540945.

Eating *Cheap Fazenda do Mel*, see above. Very small restaurant. *Gosto com Gosto*, R Wenceslau Brás 148, T33871382. Excellent mineiro cuisine and trout, open 1200-1700 Sun-Thu, 1200-2200 Fri-Sat and holidays. **Very cheap** *Bar do Jorge*, café.

Everywhere in town shuts at about 2200

Bars & nightclubs *Adega Bar*, open till midnight, live music and dancing (Sat only). *Forró da Marieta* for forró dancing.

Transport **Buses** Direct bus from **Rio de Janeiro** at 1930 Fri and 0745 Sat with *Viação Cidade de Aço*, 3½ hrs, US$8. To Visconde de Mauá from **Resende**, 1500 and 1630, 2 hrs, return 0900-0830, US$5.

Itatiaia

Phone code: 0xx24
Population: 21,000
Altitude: 390 m

Itatiaia is surrounded by picturesque mountain peaks and lovely waterfalls and is the entrance point for the national park. The town was formed around 1820 but was part of Resende until 1988. Today it depends on fishing and some small industrial activity. The Festa de São José is on 19th March and the anniversary of the town's formation is celebrated on 1st June. **Tourist information**, T33521660, F33521338.

Most accommodation is on the road to the national park (see below)

Sleeping **Youth hostel** E pp *Albergue da Juventude Ipê Amarelo*, R João Maurício Macedo Costa 352, Campo Alegre, ask at the bakery (only one in the neighbourhood), 800 m from the bus station, T/F3521232. IYHA. **Camping** *Camping Clube do Brasil* site is entered at Km 148 on the Via Dutra.

Transport There are departures from Rio de Janeiro from 0615-1800 with *Viação Cidade de Aço*, US$8.25 and *Sampaio*, US$5.25, 3 hrs. See below for buses to the national park.

Itatiaia National Park

The park is one of the most popular excursions in the state of Rio de Janeiro & is a good area for climbing, trekking & birdwatching

Founded 1937 on the Serra de Itatiaia in the Mantiqueira chain of mountains, the park was the first to be created in Brazil. Its entrance is a few kilometres north of the Via Dutra (Rio-São Paulo highway). The road to it is paved. The curious rock formations of Pedra de Taruga and Pedra de Maçã and the waterfalls Poranga and Véu de Noiva (many birds) are definitely worth seeing. Climbing is good: for instance on the Pico das Agulhas Negras (2,787 m) and the peaks in the Serra das Prateleiras (up to 2,540 m). The average temperature is 11°C.

Flora & fauna The vegetation is determined by altitude, so that the plateau at 800-1,100 m is covered by forest, ferns and flowering plants (such as orchids, bromeliads, begonias), giving way on the higher escarpments to pines and bushes. Higher still, over 1,900 m, the distinctive rocky landscape has low bushes and grasses, isolated trees and many unique plants adapted to the high winds and strong sun. There is also a great variety of lichens.

The southern masked titi monkey is common, recognizable by its loud hee-haw-like call. There are also

Around Itatiaia

agoutis, sloths, peccaries and other rarer mammals. Sources vary on the number of bird species in the park, from 270 to 300 to 400, but there are many endemics making it a top birding destination. Specialities include swallow-tailed, shrike-like and black-and-gold cotingas, white-bearded ant shrike, black-capped manakin, gilt-edged, brassy-breasted, brown and olive-green tanagers, and a number of hummingbirds. Needless to say, insects are plentiful, including some of the largest flies in the world, and there is a wide range of amphibians. There is a **Museu de História Natural** near the headquarters. ■ *1000-1600, closed Mon*. Also nearby is a wildlife trail, **Três Picos**, which starts near the *Hotel Simon* (see below).

Park essentials

Information and maps can be obtained at the park office. The Administração do Parque Nacional de Itatiaia operates a refuge in the park which acts as a starting point for climbs and treks. Information can be obtained from **Ibama**, T33521461, for the local headquarters, or T0xx21-2246463 for the Rio de Janeiro state department. Information on treks can be obtained from Clube Excursionista Brasileira or Tour operators in Rio de Janeiro (see page 69). It is very difficult to visit the park without a car and some parts are only possible in a four-wheel drive vehicle (it is 70 km from the *Hotel Simon* to the other side).

Sleeping

Basic accommodation in cabins and dormitories is available in the park; you will need to book in season, say 30 days in advance, by writing to Administração do Parque Nacional de Itatiaia, Caixa Postal 83657, Itatiaia 27580-000, RJ, telephone as above. **A** *Simon*, Km 13 on the road in the park, T33521122, F33521230. With meals, sauna, lovely views, beautifully set, helpful with advice on getting around the park. Recommended. **A** *Hotel do Ypê*, on the road in the park, Km 14, T/F33521453, www.hoteldoype.com.br Rooms or cabins with meals, pool, sauna, offers guided walks in the park. Recommended. **A** *Repouso Itatiaia*, Km 11 on the park road, T33521110, F33521509. With meals. **A** *Fazenda da Serra*, Via Dutra Km 151, T33521611. With meals. **B** *Pousada do Elefante*, 15 mins walk back down hill from *Hotel Simon*. Good food, swimming pool, lovely views, may allow camping; cheap lodging at R Maricá 255, T33521699. Possibility of pitching a tent on the premises, located close to the National Park. **D** *Hotel Alsene*, at 2,100 m, 2 km from the side entrance to the Park, take a bus to São Lourenço and Caxambu, get off at Registro, walk or hitchhike from there (12 km). Very popular with climbing and trekking clubs, dormitory or camping, chalets available, hot showers, fireplace, evening meal after everyone returns, drinks but no snacks.

Transport

Buses A bus from **Itatiaia**, marked *Hotel Simon*, goes to the park at 1200 and returns at 1700; coming from **Resende** this may be caught at the crossroads before Itatiaia.

Engenheiro Passos
Population: 3,000
Phone code: 0xx24

Further along the Dutra Highway (186 km from Rio) is the small town of Engenheiro Passos, from which a road (BR-354) leads to São Lourenço and Caxambu in Minas Gerais. By turning off this road at the Registro pass (1,670 m) on the Rio-Minas border, you can reach the **Pico das Agulhas Negras**. The mountain can be climbed from this side from the Abrigo Rebouças refuge at 2,350 m which is manned all year round. Take your own food, US$2.50 to stay.

Sleeping & eating Around Engenheiro Passos there are many *fazenda* hotels. **L** *Fazenda Villa Forte*, 1 km from town, T/F33571122. With meals, bar, sauna, massage, gym and other sports. **AL** *Fazenda Palmital*, Km 11 BR-354 towards Caxambu, T/F3571108. The local cuisine is strongly influenced by the *mineira* food of Minas Gerais. *Cachaça* is made in the area and there is a festival.

Transport From **Rio de Janeiro** there are bus departures from 0615-1900 with *Viação Cidade de Aço*, US$7.25 and *Sampaio*, US$5.50, 3 hrs.

The Costa Verde

The Rio de Janeiro to Santos section of the BR101 is one of the world's most beautiful highways, hugging the forested and hilly Costa Verde southwest of Rio. All along the coast are islands, beaches, colonial settlements and mountain fazendas. Angra dos Reis, Paraty and Ilha Grande are the most popular excursions but there are many other beaches, islands and waterfalls that can be visited by those with time and their own transport.

Road west from Rio to Paraty The BR101 is now complete through to Bertioga in São Paulo state and buses run from Rio to Angra dos Reis and Paraty. Hotels and pousadas have sprung up all along the road, as have expensive housing developments, though these have not spoiled the views. The drive from Rio to Paraty should take four hours, but it would be better to break the journey and enjoy some of the attractions. The coast road has lots of twists and turns so, if prone to motion sickness, get a seat at the front of the bus to make the most of the views.

Itacuruçá
Phone code: 0xx21
Population: 3,500

The BR-101 does not take the coastal route through Barra da Tijuca out of the city, but goes around the north side, eventually hitting the coast at Coroa Grande. This fishing village with summer houses and beach (the sea is polluted), together with Itacuruçá and Mangaratiba, are all on the shore of the Baía de Sepetiba, which is protected from the open sea by a long sand spit, the Restinga da Marambaia. At the spit's western end is the Ilha da Marambaia. The mouth of the bay is protected by Ilha Grande.

Itacuruçá, 91 km from Rio, is a delightful place to visit: there is fine scenery, peace and quiet, with islands off the coast. The sea in the town is too polluted for bathing, but you can walk along the railway to Castelo where the beach is cleaner. Separated from the town by a channel is the Ilha de Itacuruçá, the largest of a string of islands stretching into the bay. Further offshore is Ilha de Jaguanum, around which there are lovely walks. Both islands have beaches from which bathing is possible. *Saveiros* (schooners) sail around the bay and to the islands from Itacuruçá; T7801776 for details. Ilha de Itacuruçá can also be reached from **Muriqui**, a popular beach resort 9 km from Itacuruçá; bathing is also possible in the Véu de Noiva waterfall. The next beach along the coast is Praia Grande, then **Praia do Saí** which has the ruins of an old port. There is a Marina with three piers

Costa Verde

of 4m depth which can handle up to 55m boats, a service station and the usual facilities. ■ *22° 55' S, 043° 54' W; VHF 16, 68; HF 4431.8; callsign E28.*

Sleeping On Ilha de Itacuruçá are **AL** *Elias C*, Praia Cabeça do Boi, T2537444. Chalets, pool, restaurant, sports courts. **AL** *Hotel Pierre*, Praia da Bica, reached by boat from Coroa Grande on the mainland, 5 mins (boats also go from Itacuruçá), T/F6881560. Restaurant, bar, sports courts. For bookings in Rio, T0xx21-2534102. **A** *Pousada Praia Grande*, Praia Grande, T99794882 (cellular).

Twenty two kilometres down the coast, this fishing village halfway from Rio to Angra dos Reis. It stands on a little bay within the Baia de Sepetiba and in the 18th century was a port for the export first of gold, later coffee and for the import of slaves. During the coffee era, it was the terminus for the Estrada São João Marcos from the Rio Paraíba do Sul. Mangaratiba's beaches are muddy, but the surroundings are pleasant and better beaches can be found outside town, for example Ibicuí (2 km) and Brava (between Ibicuí and Saí – see above) to the east, at the head of the bay Saco, Guiti and Cação, and further west São Brás.

Mangaratiba
Phone code: 0xx21
Population: 20,000

Sleeping D *Sítio Santo Antônio 12*, T7892192. Family-run, owner Carlito is proud of his shell collection. Recommended. At Rio das Pedras is **LL** *Club Mediterranée*, BR-101 Km 445, T6885050, F6883333, with all the facilities associated with this French chain; in Jul and Dec-Mar, stays of 7 days minimum are required.

Transport Buses from **Rio de Janeiro** Rodoviária departures every 2-3 hrs from 0520-1845 with *Costa Verde*, 2¼ hrs, US$4.50. **Ferries**: daily boats to **Ilha Grande** (see below) charge US$30 return. This is a highly recommended trip. You can enquire in advance what *Conerj* sailings are operating. Ferry departures and destinations can be checked at the ferry station at Praça 15 de Novembro, Rio de Janeiro (see page 166).

Angra dos Reis

Said to have been founded on 6 January 1502 (O Dia dos Reis – The Day of Kings), Angra dos Reis is 151 km southwest of Rio by road. A small port with an important fishing and shipbuilding industry, it has several small coves with good bathing within easy reach and is situated on an enormous bay full of islands. It is one of the most sophisticated resorts on the Rio de Janeiro coast. **Tourist information** is at Largo da Lapa, opposite the bus station, T33651175, extension 2186. Very helpful.

Phone code: 0xx24
Population: 90,000

Angra's past and present are bound to the sea, in earlier times through its importance as a port, nowadays through tourism. Once a harbour had been established here, Angra became a stop on the sea route to São Vicente (Santos). In the 18th century it was used by the gold traders making their way to and from Minas Gerais. When coffee replaced gold as the boom product, it became the harbour for the exports carried down the Estrada do Caramujo. It was one of the most important ports in the country until the railway shifted the transport emphasis away from the old roads onto the direct route into Rio.

History

Several buildings remain from Angra's heyday. Of particular note are the church and convent of **Nossa Senhora do Carmo**, built in 1593 (Praça General Osório), the Igreja Matriz de **Nossa Senhora da Conceição** (1626) in the centre of town and the church and convent of **São Bernardino de Sena** (1758-63) on the Morro do Santo Antônio. On the Largo da Lapa is the church of **Nossa Senhora da Lapa da Boa Morte** (1752) and a museum of sacred art.
■ *Thu-Sun 1000-1200, 1400-1800.*

Sights

208 ANGRA DOS REIS

Excursions On the Península de Angra, just west of the town, is the **Praia do Bonfim**, a popular beach and a little way offshore the island of the same name, on which is the hermitage of Senhor do Bonfim (1780). 15 km east are the ruins of the **Jacuecanga** seminary (1797).

Boat trips around the bay are available, some with a stop for lunch on the island of Gipóia (five hours). Several boats run tours from the Cais de Santa Luzia and there are agencies for *saveiros* in town.

Train The historic *Trem da Mata Atlântica* or *Trem Verde* has been reopened, making the coastal trip to Lidice. A steam locomotive and six carriages were renovated for the line, but the train may be pulled by a diesel engine. The six-hour round trip runs through beautiful countryside (hence the name 'Green Train'). It leaves Angra railway station at 1030 on Saturday, Sunday and public holidays and has a restaurant car; the fare is US$44. The operator is *Montmar Turismo*, Rua do Comércio 11.

Sleeping **L** *do Frade*, on the road to Ubatuba, Km 123 BR-101, 33 km from Angra, T33692244, F33692254. Luxury hotel on the Praia do Frade with restaurants, bar, sauna, sports facilities on land and sea. **AL** *Porto Aquarius*, Saco de Itapirapuã, out of town access from Km 101 BR-101, 13 km, T33651642, F33651766. Lots of facilities, pleasant, helpful staff. **A** *Pousada Porto Marina Bracuhy*, Km 115 BR-101, 23 km from Angra dos Reis, T33651153, F33631122. Lots of facilities for watersports, nightly shows and dancing, restaurant.

There are many hotels around Angra

In town are **A** *Londres*, Av Raul Pompéia 75, T33650044, F33650511. **A** *Angra Palace*, same avenue No 90, T33653207, F33652656. **A** *Caribe*, R de Conceição 255, T33650033, F33653450. Central. Recommended.

Youth hostel E pp *Rio Bracuí* (IYHA), Estr Santa Rita 4, Bracuí, on the road to Santos at Km 115, take any bus going beyond Angra to the bridge over the Rio Bracuí, one stop after the Bracuhy Marina, T33631234, www2.quick.com.br/albergue Open all year.

Eating **Cheap** *Taberna 33*, R Raul Pompéia 110. Italian, good, popular, moderate prices. *Tropicalitá*, Largo do Convento do Carmo.

Festivals In Jan there are several festivals: at New Year there is a **Festa do Mar**, with boat processions; on the 5th is the **Folia dos Reis**, the culmination of a religious festival that begins at Christmas; the 6th is the anniversary of the founding of the city. In May is the **Festa do Divino** and, on the 2nd Sun, the **Senhor do Bonfim** maritime procession. As elsewhere in the state, the **Festas Juninas** are celebrated in Jun. On 8 Dec is the festival of **Nossa Senhora da Conceição**.

Sports **Diving** *Aquamaster*, Praia da Enseada, take bus marked 'Retiro' from the port in Angra, T33652416. US$60 for 2 dives with drinks and food.

Transport **Road** A road runs inland (about 18 km beyond Angra), through Getulândia, to join the BR-116 either just south of Piraí or near Volta Redonda, through nice mountain scenery. **Buses**: from **Rio de Janeiro's** rodoviária 0415-2100 with *Costa Verde*, 3 hrs, US$6.50, several direct, accepts credit cards, new comfortable buses, several go through Copacabana, Ipanema and Barra then take the 'via litoral', sit on the left, (you can flag the bus down in Flamengo, Copacabana, Ipanema, Barra de Tijuca, but it may well be full at weekends).

Ferries 1½ hrs by boat with *Conerj* to **Ilha Grande**, US$2 during the week, US$8 at weekends, one-way (Mon to Fri at 1500 and 1700, return 1000, so you have to stay overnight; Sat, Sun and holidays leaving Angra at 1000, returning from Abraão at

1600; for day trips, go from Mangaratiba). Fishing boats also take passengers from Angra for about US$5, or there is the *Santa Isabel* schooner, T9828287, which costs about US$10 1-way.

Banks *Banco 24 Horas*, R do Comércio 250, *Bradesco*, R do Comércio 196. **Medical services** *Santa Casa*, R Dr Coutinho 84, T33650131.

Ilha Grande

A two-hour ferry makes a most attractive trip through the bay to **Vila do Abraão**, the main village on Ilha Grande. If you have a couple of days to spare, the island is definitely worth a visit because it encapsulates most of what the name 'Emerald Coast' suggests. It is mountainous, covered in Atlantic forest, surrounded by transparent green waters and largely unspoiled. The weather is best from March to June; it is best to avoid the peak summer months. In fact, visit the island soon, before it becomes overdeveloped. You will see the very helpful **tourist office** as you get off the boat. It is run by Angela, who speaks some English and will act as a trekking guide.

Phone code: 0xx21

Ilha Grande remained relatively untouched by the pressures of development because of what has been called "a strange protection afforded by the forces of evil". It was once an infamous lair for European pirates, then a landing stage for slaves. In the 19th century, it was the site of a leper colony (which we should call unfortunate, rather than evil now). In the 20th century one of Brazil's larger high security prisons deterred visitors. A famous inmate was the writer Graciliano Ramos (see 'Literature', page 238), whose *Memórias do cárcere* relate his experiences. The prison was closed in 1994 and is now overgrown rubble.

History

In the past, sugar cane and coffee were cultivated on parts of the island, but now most of it is a state park, including the **Reserva Biológica da Praia do Sul**. The main industry is fishing. Cars are not allowed on the island, so transport is either by boat, or on foot.

Ilha Grande

Beaches & There are about 100 beaches around the island, about three dozen of which are
excursions regular tourist spots. Those on the landward side are good for watersports, diving is good around most of the coast, there is fishing and some surfing. From Vila do Abraão there are trails to most of the beaches, but it is much less effort to go by boat. Even so, some parts of the island are a long journey.

Popular excursions include: the 20-minute walk from Abraão to the peaceful and clean beach at **Abraãozinho**. Another two hours in the same direction will take you to **Palmas beach**, which is also calm, and another 20 minutes to **Lopes Mendes**, good for surfing. This beach can be reached by boat, too, as can other lovely beaches: **Lagoa Azul**, with crystal clear water and excellent snorkelling, **Freguesia de Santana** and **Saco do Céu**.

To Provetá, at the eastern end, for instance, takes 6½ hours by boat. You can ask in the port at Angra dos Reis for a fishing boat going to Provetá, where you can stay in boat sheds or, if lucky, with a fisherman. It is a beautiful village, from which you can walk through tropical forest over the mountain to Praia do Aventureiro (a day's leisurely walk each way), or go by boat. Take mosquito precautions when walking in the forest.

A couple of good treks are over the mountains to **Dois Rios**, where the old jail was situated. There is still a settlement of former prison guards here who have nowhere to go. The walk is about 13 km one way and takes about three hours; beautiful scenery and superb views. You can also hike to **Pico do Papagaio** (980 m) through forest; a stiff, three hours climb for which a guide is essential. The view from the top is breathtaking. **Pico da Pedra d'Água** (1,031 m) can also be climbed.

Sleeping **A** *Fazenda Paraíso do Sol*, Praia Saco das Palmas (full board), 2 hrs' walk from Abraão, or 40 mins by boat, for reservations in Rio T2621226. Hotel reservations are necessary. Many new *pousadas* have been opened, most in Abraão: eg, in our **A** range on R da Praia: *Água Viva*, No 26, T/F9862519, *Solar da Praia*, No 32, T9863396 and *Tropicana*, No 28, T99896609, T024-33522073 for reservations. French run. Recommended, good but expensive open-air restaurant. **B** *Pousada da Vanda*, R Antônio Moreira 95, T2852429. In green surroundings. **B** *Pousada do Canto*, 2 blocks from centre, T5950940/97747871. Quiet location, good value. **B** *Beto's*, T7801202, central. Recommended. **B** *Hotel Ori*, R Prof Lima. Recommended. **B**Recanto dos Tiés, R do Bicão 38 (outskirts of Abraão), T33615253, Cell0xx21-96443797. Set in forest with monkeys and many birds, 3 rooms with bathroom (hot water), fridge, fan and excellent breakfast (fresh fruit and home baked cakes), owner Hilda speaks English. Recommended. **B** *Sonia/Tuti*, R Antônio Moreira 80, 5 mins from the beach, T654512. A small house with 2 rooms to let. Recommended. **B** *Albatroz*, R das Flores 108, T6271730. Recommended. **C** *Pousada Canto Verde*, near cemetery, T5940225. English spoken, 5 rooms with fan and bath, welcoming, good breakfast. **C** *Pousada Cachoeira*, at the end of the village. Friendly, run by German-Brazilian couple, English spoken, bungalows in green surroundings, pleasant. **C** *Estalagem Costa Verde*, T0XX11-31047940. Pleasant surroundings near beach, ask for Márcia or Marly. Also *Pousada Beija Flor*, R da Assembléia 70, Vila do Abraão, T0xx21-5481037, Cell0xx21-96488177. Swedish owned, English, French and Spanish also spoken, with good breakfast, a/c, fridge, book exchange, games room and bar. Recommended. **Youth hostel F** pp *Albergue da Juventude Ilha Grande*, R Pres Vargas, Praia do Abraão, RJ 20271-021,T0xx21-2646147, Cell0xx21-99446444. IYHA. Alternatively, you can rent a room in Abraão.

Eating **Cheap** *Casa da Sogra*, Trav do Beto. Recommended. *Minha Deusa*, R Prof Alice Coury 7, next to church. Brazilian, excellent food, reasonable prices.

Ferries For boats to Ilha Grande, see above under Angra dos Reis and Mangaratiba. **Transport**
There are 5 ferries called *Isabel*, check which is going to the mainland destination you
want. **Boats** Boat trips cost US$10 without food or drinks, but includes fruit. Recommended boats are *Anna Paula*, *Jeremias* (owned by Mario, an Argentine) or *Nina* (owned by 'Baiano'). There is some good scuba diving around the coast but the bottom is becoming littered in places with picnic rubbish.

Banks It is very difficult to exchange cash or TCs on the island. **Directory**

Paraty

Beyond Angra dos Reis the road continues 98 km along the coast. Inland is the *Phone code: 0xx24*
Parque Nacional da Serra da Bocaína (see below). The BR-101 goes past the *Population: 27,000*
nuclear-power plant at Itaorna and an array of beaches on the shore of the Baía
da Ilha Grande to Paraty, a charming colonial town. The centre has been
declared a national historic monument in its entirety. The streets, which are
paved with large, irregular stone slabs, have curves to provide ambush points
should the town (in colonial times) be attacked by pirates. In the colonial
buildings are a great many art galleries, tourist shops and eating places, but
none is allowed to impose its presence or disrupt the tranquility of the streets.
The hills that surround the town are covered in tropical forest and the coastline
has hundreds of beaches within easy reach. Paraty is normally cooler than Rio
de Janeiro. The wettest times of year are January-February and June-July.
Tourist information is at *Centro de Informações Turísticas*, Av Roberto
Silveira, near the entrance to the historical centre, T3371266 ext 218. The
website www.paraty.com.br has lots of information.

The coast road continues from Paraty into the State of São Paulo through
the Serra do Mar. At the state border, the sea becomes visible again and the
route is as attractive as before. Another road, rough but scenic, climbs the
Serra do Mar to Cunha and Guaratinguetá, also in São Paulo.

Paraty was officially founded in the first half of the 17th century. Its name **History**
derives from the indigenous word for a small fish common in these waters,
called *paratii*. Having a good harbour and a well-worn trail into the interior
(used by the Guianas Indians before the Portuguese colonizers), Paraty was a
natural choice for a port. Some parts of the old trail can still be walked; ask tour
operators (see below). It became the chief port for the export of gold in the
17th century and thus grew rich. Most of its colonial churches date from this
period, as do the fortresses which were built to prevent pirates and foreign
ships stealing the valuable cargo (see the Forte do Defensor Perpétuo). Walls
protected the landward side and the ruins of an old gate can be seen close to the
football field at the entrance to town. Commerce prospered and farms around
the city produced sugar and fine brands of *cachaça* (the name Paraty is still
synonymous with *cachaça*). When a road was built to Rio de Janeiro from the
mining regions at the beginning of the 18th century, shortening the journey by
some 15 days, Paraty's importance declined.

It recovered in the 19th century as a coffee-exporting port for the *fazendas*
of the valley of the Paraíba do Sul. At the same time, through its wharf came the
imported European luxuries which furnished the barons' houses. It is now
hard to imagine that slaves had to carry French furniture, pianos and fine porcelain over the hills through dense forest.

In the second half of the 19th century, the opening of the railway from the
Paraíba Valley to Rio led to Paraty being effectively isolated again. The port
being redundant, almost all its inhabitants left. Those that remained grew

bananas, but the old sugar plantations were for the most part abandoned. Because so few people stayed in the town, there was no urge to modernize the buildings. In this way, Paraty has become an open air museum.

Only in the 1950s was the town 'rediscovered' as a tourism and cultural centre. It was declared a national historic monument in 1966. Whereas in colonial times Paraty was dependent for its livelihood on the roads across the mountains, in the late 20th century the Rio-Santos road has brought a new prosperity. And even though Paraty is easily accessible to tourists, they only come in great numbers at weekends and on holidays, so the rest of the time it keeps its small-town atmosphere.

Sights In keeping with all Brazilian colonial towns, Paraty's churches were built according to social status and race. There are four churches in the town, one for the 'freed coloured men', one for the blacks and two for the whites. **Santa Rita** (1722), built by the 'freed coloured men' in elegant Brazilian baroque, faces the bay and the port. It is probably the most famous 'picture postcard' image of Paraty. It houses an interesting **Museum of Sacred Art**. ■ *Wed-Sun 0900-1200, 1300-1800, entry US$1.* **Nossa Senhora do Rosário e São Benedito** (1725, rebuilt 1757), Rua do Comércio, built by black slaves, is small and simple; the slaves were unable to raise the funds to construct an elaborate building. ■ *Tue 0900-1200.* **Nossa Senhora dos Remédios** is the town's parish church, the biggest in Paraty. In fact, the church was never completely finished. Started in 1787, but finished only in 1873, it was built on unstable ground, so the architects decided not to add weight to the structure by putting up the towers. The façade is leaning to the left, which is clear from the three doors: only the one on the right has a step. The church was built with donations from the whites and it is rumoured that a certain Dona Geralda Maria da Silva contributed with gold from a pirate's hoard found buried on the beach. ■ *Mon, Wed, Fri, Sat 0900-1200, Sun 0900-1500.* **Capela de Nossa Senhora das Dores** (1800) is a small chapel facing the sea. It was used mainly by the wealthy whites in the 19th century. ■ *Thu 0900-1200.*

There is a great deal of distinguished Portuguese colonial architecture in delightful settings. **Rua do Comércio** is the main street in the historical centre. It was here that the prominent traders lived, the two-storey houses having the commercial establishments on the ground floor and the residences above. Nowadays the houses are occupied by restaurants, *pousadas* and curio shops.

The **Casa da Cadeia**, close to Santa Rita church, is the former jail. It belongs to the Secretaria da Cultura e Turismo and is being converted into a historical museum. Note the iron grilles in the windows and doors.

Santa Rita Church

On the northern headland is a small fort, **Forte do Defensor Perpétuo**, built in 1822. The cannons and the ruins of the thick walls can be seen. From the fort there are good views of the sea and the roofs of the town. To get there, cross the Rio Perequê Açu by the bridge at the end of the Rua do Comércio; climb the small hill, which has some nice *pousadas* and a cemetery, and follow the signs to 'Forte'. It's about 15 minutes' walk from the centre. Also here is the **Museum of Arts and Popular Traditions** in a colonial-style building. It contains carved wooden canoes, musical instruments, fishing gear and other handmade items from local communities. In 1997 it was closed for repairs to the damage done by termites. Also on the headland is the gunpowder store and, set in the grass, enormous hemispherical iron pans which were used for extracting whale oil to use in lamps and to mix with sand and cement for building.

The town centre is out of bounds for motor vehicles; heavy chains are strung across the entrance to the streets. In spring the roads are flooded, while the houses are above the water level.

Excursions

Beaches **Praia do Pontal**, 10 minutes' walk, is not very clean; **Praia do Forte** and **Praia do Jabaquara** are worth visiting. There are other beaches further from town, many of which make worthwhile excursions. **Paraty Mirim**, a small town 27 km away with old buildings and nice beaches, is reached by four buses a day (three on Sunday).

There are several waterfalls (*cachoeiras*) in the area, such as the **Cachoeira da Penha**, near the church of the same name. It is 10 km from town on the road to Cunha; take a local bus from the rodoviária, US$1. There are good mountain views on the way. The tourist office and travel agencies (see below) can give details on trips to waterfalls and other hikes, plus information on boat trips around the bays and islands (good value, US$10 per day, lunch extra).

Fazenda Murycana, an old sugar estate and 17th century *cachaça* distillery, is a recommended excursion. You can taste and buy the different types of *cachaça*; some are aged in oak barrels for 12 years (try the *cachaça com cravo e canela*, with clove and cinnamon). The original house and water-wheel are still there. There is an excellent restaurant and horse riding is available. English is not spoken by the employees. Mosquitoes can be a problem at the *fazenda*, take repellent and don't wear shorts. Take a Penha/Ponte Branca bus from the rodoviária, four a day; alight where it crosses a small white bridge and then walk 10 minutes along a signed, unpaved road. Returning to Paraty, there is a good chance of hitching a lift.

Sleeping

■ *on map, page 214*
Price codes: see inside front cover
There are a great many pousadas, more than we can mention here. If you have time & you are here mid-week when hotels are not at a premium, look around & find a place that suits you best

AL *Pousada do Sandi*, Largo do Rosário 1, T33712100, F33711236. 18th century building, charming, spacious rooms. **AL** *Pousada do Ouro*, R Dr Pereira (or da Praia) 145, in the historical centre, T/F33712221, ouro@contracthor.com.br **A** *Pousada Pardieiro*, R do Comércio 74, T33711370, F33711139. Attractive colonial building with lovely gardens, delightful rooms facing internal patios, extremely pleasant, swimming pool, calm, sophisticated atmosphere, but always full at weekends, does not take children under 15. **A** *Pousada Porto Parati*, R do Comércio, T33711205, F33712111. Good value. Recommended. **A** *Pousada do Príncipe*, Roberto Silveira 289, T33712266, F33712120. Belongs to descendents of the former imperial family, lovely atmosphere with genuine works of art from the Brazilian Empire, all facilities, pool. Highly recommended. **A** *das Canoas*, R Silveira 279, T33711133, F33712005. Pool. Recommended. **A** *Morro do Forte*, R Orlando Carpinelli, T/F33711211. Lovely garden, good breakfast, pool, German owner Peter Kallert offers trips on his yacht. Recommended. **A** *Pousada do Portal*, Av Beira-Rio 100, T33712221. Charming, but some distance from the centre, relaxing. **A** *Pousada do Forte*, Al Princesa Isabel 33, Pontal, on the way to the fort, T/F33711462. **B** *Pousada Capitão*, R Luiz do Rosário 18, T3711416, www.paraty.com.br/capitao.htm Charming, close to historical centre, swimming pool, English and Japanese spoken. **B** *Pousada Mercado do Pouso*, Largo de Santa Rita 43, close to the port and Santa Rita, T/F33711114. Recommended. **B** *Pousada do Corsário*, Beco do Lapeiro 26, T33711866 (in Rio T5220262), F33711319. A/c, TV, fridge, pool, sauna. Recommended. **B** *Pousada Villaggio*, R José Vieira Ramos 280, between historical centre and rodoviária, T33711870. Pleasant, pool, garden, good. **C** *Pouso Familiar*, R José Vieira Ramos 262, near bus station, T33711475. Run by Belgian (Joseph Yserbyt) and his Brazilian wife (Lucia), laundry facilities, English, French, German and Flemish spoken. Recommended. **C** *Solar dos Gerânios*, Praça da Matriz, T/F33711550. Beautiful colonial building, hard beds, but recommended.

D *Pousada Konquista*, R Jango Pádua 20, between bus station and historic centre, T/F33711308. A/c rooms with fridge, TV and breakfast, sitting room, safe deposit, laundry, parking. **D** *Marendaz*, R Patitiba 9, close to the historical centre, T33711369. Family-run, simple, charming. **D** *Pousada da Matriz*, R da Cadeia, close to corner of R do Comércio, in historic centre. Basic but clean rooms, with bath, without breakfast, friendly if a little noisy. **D** *Pousada Miramar*, Abel de Oliveira 19, T33712132. One room has its own kitchen, good value. Recommended. **D** *Tia Palminas Lua Nova*, R Mcal Deodoro. Cheap, pleasant, central.

Outside Paraty If arriving by car, there are 2 good options for staying outside the town: *Refúgio das Caravelas*, Praia da Boa Vista, T/F33711270, 5 km south, on seafront with its own harbour and scuba diving facilities; **B** *Le Gite d'Indaiatiba*, access from Km 172 BR-101, 20 km away. Country *pousada* with chalets, waterfalls and forest, French owner, superb cuisine. Both places can be reached by taxi from the rodoviária.

Camping *Camping Club do Brasil*, Av Orlando Carpinelli, Praia do Pontal. Small, good, very crowded in Jan and Feb, US$8 pp, T33711877. Also at Praia Jabaquara, T33712180. *Camping Beira-Rio*, just across the bridge, before the road to the fort.

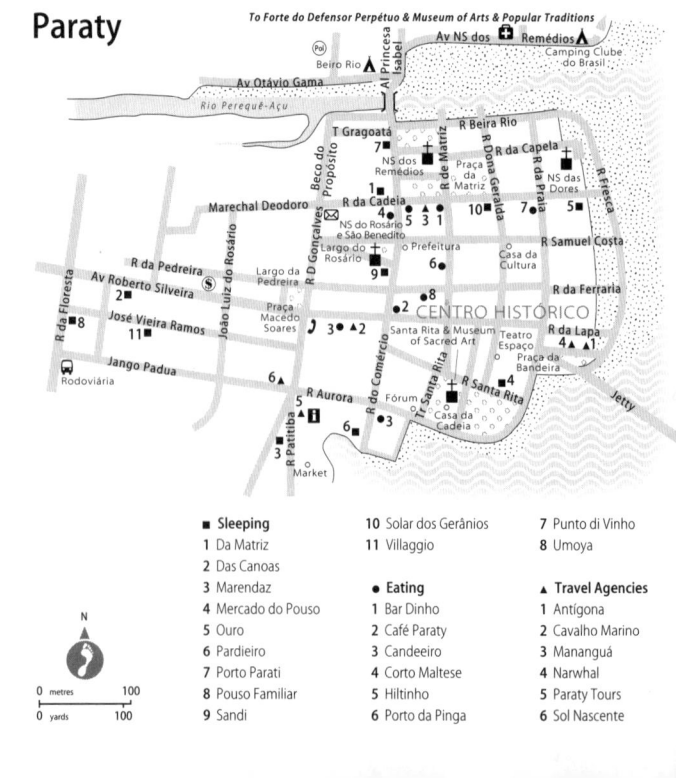

Paraty

- **Sleeping**
- 1 Da Matriz
- 2 Das Canoas
- 3 Marendaz
- 4 Mercado do Pouso
- 5 Ouro
- 6 Pardieiro
- 7 Porto Parati
- 8 Pouso Familiar
- 9 Sandi
- 10 Solar dos Gerânios
- 11 Villaggio

- **Eating**
- 1 Bar Dinho
- 2 Café Paraty
- 3 Candeeiro
- 4 Corto Maltese
- 5 Hiltinho
- 6 Porto da Pinga
- 7 Punto di Vinho
- 8 Umoya

- **Travel Agencies**
- 1 Antígona
- 2 Cavalho Marino
- 3 Mananguá
- 4 Narwhal
- 5 Paraty Tours
- 6 Sol Nascente

Eating
on map, page 214

The best dishes to try in Paraty are those with seafood, eg *peixe à Parati* (local fish cooked with herbs, green bananas and served with *pirão*, a mixture of manioc flour and the sauce that the fish was cooked in); also popular is the *filé de peixe ao molho de camarão* (fried fish filet with a shrimp and tomato sauce). A recommended appetizer is *aipim frito*, fried pieces of manioc, which look like French fries. The *caipirinhas* in Paraty are among the best in Brazil because they include the excellent local *cachaça*.

Mid-range *do Hiltinho*, R Mcal Deodoro 233, historical centre, T/F 33711432. Local dishes. Excellent seafood, good service, expensive but worth it. **Cheap** *Candeeiro*, R da Lapa 335. Good local food. *Corto Maltese*, R do Comércio 130. Italian, pasta. *Punto Divino*, R Mcal Deodoro 129. Excellent Italian. *Dona Ondina*, R do Comércio 2, by the river. Family restaurant, well-prepared simple food, good value (closed on Mon between Mar and Nov). *Kontiki*, Ilha Duas Irmãs, an island 5 mins from the harbour where a stand offers trips for US$2.50 return, T9999599, www.paraty.com.br/kontiki.htm Wonderful view, seafood, main courses US$13.50-25, bar, private beach. Recommended. **Very cheap** *Café Parati*, R da Lapa and Comércio. Sandwiches, appetizers, light meals, also bar at weekends with live music. The less expensive restaurants, those offering *comida a quilo* (pay by weight) and the fast food outlets are outside the historical centre, mainly on Av Roberto Silveira. *Bar do Turquinho*, on the side street off Av Roberto Silveira opposite the petrol station. Tasty and cheap *prato do dia*.

Bars & nightclubs

Bars *Umoya*, R Comendador José Luiz. Video bar and café, live music at weekends. *Bar Dinho*, Praça da Matriz at R da Matriz. Good bar with live music at weekends, sometimes mid-week.
Nightclubs *Clube Bandeirantes*, for dancing (Friday Brazilian, Saturday funk, Sunday dance and disco music), an interesting place to meet local people, popular, entry US$3-5.

Entertainment

Theatre *Teatro Espaço*, The Puppet Show, R Dona Geralda 327, T33711575, F3711161, ecparati@ax.apc.org Wed, Sat 2100, US$8.50. This world-famous puppet show should not be missed. The puppets tell stories, without words, which are funny, sad, even shocking, with incredible realism. It is high quality theatre of an unusual kind.

Festivals

Carnival, Feb/Mar, hundreds of people cover their bodies in black mud and run through the streets yelling like prehistoric creatures (anyone can join in). **Semana Santa**, Mar/Apr, with religious processions and folk songs. **Semana de Santa Rita**, Mid-Jul, traditional foods, shows, exhibitions and dances. **Festival da Pinga**, Aug, the *cachaça* fair at which local distilleries display their products and there are plenty of opportunities to over-indulge. **Semana da Nossa Senhora dos Remédios**, Sep (around the 8th), processions and religious events. **Spring Festival of Music**, Sep/Oct, concerts in front of Santa Rita church. The city is decorated with lights for Christmas. **Reveillon**, 31 Dec, a huge party with open-air concerts and fireworks (reserve accommodation in advance). As well as the *Dança dos Velhos* (The Dance of the Old Men), performed to the accordion, another common dance in these parts is the *ciranda*, in which everyone, young and old, dances in a circle to songs accompanied by guitars.

Shopping

The town has plenty of handicraft and souvenir shops. The most interesting items are the small, wooden canoes and boats, oars carved in wood with peculiar designs and colourful T-shirts. You can find paintings and painted wall tiles. Don't forget to buy a bottle of *cachaça*; there are shops such as **Porto da Pinga**, R da Matriz. All the local brands are good, but if you are visiting the distilleries, don't hesitate to buy there (see *Fazenda Murycana* above).

Tour operators *Antígona*, Praça da Bandeira 2, Centro Histórico, T/F33711165. Daily schooner tours, 5 hrs, bar and lunch on board. Recommended. *Paraty Tours*, Av Roberto Silveira 11, T/F33711327. English and Spanish spoken. *Sol Nascente*, Av Roberto Silveira 58, T/F33711536. *Mananguá*, R Domingos Gonçalves de Abreu 3, T33712188. All can arrange schooner trips, city tours, trekking in the rain forest and on the old gold trail, visits to Trindade beach, mountain biking, sugar estate visits and transfers. *Narwhal*, T33711399, and *Cavalho Marinho*, R da Lapa, T/F33712148, offer diving. *Soberana da Costa*, T33711114, and others offer schooner trips in the bay, US$15-US$20, 6 hrs, meals sometimes included. Recommended. *Fausto Goyos*, T99145506, offers off-road tours in an ex-US military jeep to rainforest, waterfalls, historical sites, also photo safaris, He also has highly professional horse riding tours and offers lodging in youth-hostel style rooms for US$5, or US$7.50 with 2 meals.

Transport **Buses** There are frequent departures from **Rio de Janeiro** from 0415-2200 with *Costa Verde*, 241 km, 4 hrs, US$9, only the 0630 from Rio and the 1730 from Paraty go through **Barra da Tijuca** (Tue, Thu, Sat-Sun). Paraty has a new rodoviária at the corner of R Jango Padua and R da Floresta. To **Angra dos Reis**, every 1 hr 40 mins, 98 km, 1½ hrs, US$4.

On holidays & in high season, the frequency of bus services usually increases

Directory **Banks** *Banco do Brasil*, Av Roberto Silveira, not too far from the bus station. Exchange 1100-1430, ask for the manager. **Communications** Post Office: R da Cadeia and Beco do Propósito, 0800-1700, Sun 0800-1200. Telephone: International calls, Praça Macedo Soares, opposite the tourist office. Local and long distance calls can be made from public phones; buy phone cards from the newspaper stand by the tourist information centre. **Medical services** *Hospital Municipal São Pedro de Alcântara* (Santa Casa), Av Dom Pedro de Alcântara, T33711623. **Voltage** 110 volts.

Parque Nacional Serra da Bocaina

Straddling the border of Rio de Janeiro and São Paulo states is the Parque Nacional Serra da Bocaina, which rises from the coast to its highest point at Pico do Tira (or Chapéu) at 2,200 m, encompassing three strata of vegetation. Up to 1,000 m the forest is mainly made up of large trees such as *maçaranduba* (milk, or cow trees), *jatobá* (courbaril), cedar and *angelim* (angely). Between 1,000 and 2,000 m the predominant varieties are pines and myrtles. Higher than this, the landscape is more grassy and open, with bromeliads, orchids and lichens. The main river flowing through it is the Mambucaba, which cascades down the mountainsides in a series of waterfalls. Trails lead to some of the falls and an old gold trail leads through the park (a three to four day hike).

Park essentials Permission to visit must be obtained in advance from Ibama, T0xx21-2246489 in Rio de Janeiro although some tour operators in the city are now offering tours in the park. The local Ibama office is in São José do Barreiro in São Paulo state, T0xx12-5771225. There are hotels and trekking agencies here, including *Vale dos Veados*, Estr da Bocaina, Km 42, T0xx12-5771194, F0xx12-5771303, part of the Roteiros de Charme hotel group, see page 47.

Background

5

Background

219	**History**
224	**Modern Rio de Janeiro**
224	Government and politics
224	Economy
225	Society
226	Environment
226	**Land and environment**
226	Geography
227	Climate
227	Flora and fauna
228	National parks
230	**Arts and architecture**
230	Fine art and sculpture
232	Architecture
236	Literature
240	**Culture**
240	People
241	Religion
245	Music and dance

History

Although there is some evidence of human occupation of the area surrounding what is now Rio de Janeiro from 5000 years ago, the history of Rio de Janeiro really begins with the advent of European settlers and the written word. Guanabara Bay was discovered by the Portuguese at the beginning of the 16th century, although the French were the first settlers in the area. However, their stay did not last long and they were driven out in 1567 by Estácio de Sá who founded the city of Rio de Janeiro. The city's wealth and prestige grew steadily through the years of the gold rush in Minas Gerais and as a result of the slave trade with Africa, before becoming the colony's capital in 1763. The arrival of the Portuguese royal family in the early 19th century brought further kudos as well as new building projects, which continued after the proclamation of the Republic in 1889. But it was not until the 1920s that the city became the popular tourist destination that we know it as today – something which has given the city a new sense of purpose since the transfer of the administrative capital to Brasília in 1960.

Indigenous peoples

Evidence from *sambaquis* (shell mounds used as dwellings and burial sites) indicates that there were settled coastal communities along the whole length of the Rio de Janeiro seaboard about 5,000 years ago: there are a number of interesting sites along the Costa do Sol east of Rio de Janeiro such as the one near Saquarema. When the Europeans arrived in the region, the indigenous inhabitants belonged to the Tupi or Tupi-Guarani, Puri, Botocudos and Maxacali linguistic groups. Few Indian people in what is now Rio de Janeiro state survived the European incursions – they either fled inland or were destroyed by the colonists.

Discovery & colonization

The Portuguese navigator, Gonçalo Coelho, arrived at what is now Rio de Janeiro on 1 January 1502. Thinking that the Baía de Guanabara (the name the local Indians used) was the mouth of a great river, they called the place the January River. Although the bay was almost as large and as safe a harbour as the Baía de Todos os Santos to the north, the Portuguese did not take of advantage of it. In fact, it was first settled by the French, who, under the Huguenot Admiral **Nicholas Durand de Villegagnon**, occupied Lage Island on 10 November 1555, but later transferred to Seregipe Island (now Villegagnon), where they built the fort of Coligny. The fort has been demolished to make way for the Naval College (Escola Naval) and the island itself has become a part of the mainland, since the narrow channel was filled up. Villegagnon set up a colony as the starting point for what he called Antarctic France. Although it was not a peaceful place, it was reinforced by 300 colonists led by Villegagnon's nephew, Bois-le-Comte. Among them was the chronicler **Jean de Léry**.

In early 1559-60, **Mem de Sá**, third governor of Brazil, mounted an expedition from Salvador to attack the French, who were supported by Tamoio Indians. The Portuguese succeeded in capturing the French fort, and thus putting an end to Antarctic France, but they did not colonize the area. The French were able, therefore, to continue trading with the Tamoio: offending the Portuguese not only territorially, but also on religious grounds, since most of the French were protestants or non-conformists. Battles on land and sea culminated in Mem de Sá sending his son **Estácio de Sá**, with Temiminó allies, to destroy the French in 1565. The Portuguese finally took control in 1567 when they transferred their settlement to the Morro de São Januário. It was also called the Morro do Castelo – and the Esplanada do Castelo covers the site today. 1567 is generally considered the date of the founding of the city of São Sebastião do Rio de Janeiro, so called in honour of the Portuguese prince who would soon assume the throne. Though constantly attacked by Indians, the new city grew rapidly and when King

Sebastião divided Brazil into two provinces, Rio was the chosen capital of the southern captaincies. Salvador became sole capital again in 1576, but Rio again became the southern capital in 1608 and the seat of a bishopric.

Inland roads

In the early years of colonization, the Baía de Guanabara was the focus of a lot of attention. The bay and then Rio de Janeiro itself were initially part of the Capitania de São Vicente (São Paulo) and São Tomé. As in the rest of the Portuguese colony, great efforts were put into enslaving the Indians so they could work on the plantations and also converting them to Christianity. Gradually, routes up and down the coast were made to connect the far-flung outposts. Similarly, trails followed Indian tracks into the interior, as pioneers explored for wealth and mule drivers transported goods over the Serra do Mar. The history of the state was therefore closely associated with the development of and settlement along the roads. In the 16th century, the first established road became that which linked Paraty with the valley of the Rio Paraíba, continuing into southern Minas Gerais. This became a route for exporting gold later in the 18th century and it was followed by the Caminho Novo, also from Minas Gerais, which ended on the shores of the Baía de Guanabara. Other gold routes were later created, including one between Rio and São Paulo. The city itself slowly grew during the 17th century, partly due to Portugal's need to find another port after Recife, in the Northeast of Brazil, had been occupied by the Dutch.

Colonial capital

There were further French incursions in 1710-11 as a result of the tension between France and Portugal during the war of Spanish Succession, and because of the flow of gold out of Minas Gerais through the city's port. Rio de Janeiro was by now becoming the leading city in Brazil – with a population of around 30,000, which was comprised mainly of African slaves. Not only was it now the colony's main port, but it was also the focus of the export and import trade (of crops such as sugar) of the surrounding agricultural lands. On 27 January 1763, it became the seat of the Viceroy and the city continued to prosper with the paving of streets, improved fortifications and new public works such as the canal which brought the water of the Rio Carioca to the public fountain in Largo do Carioca, as well as the rest of downtown Rio. A new commercial centre was built around what is known today as Praça XV, and the Passeio Público was created from a landfill. In 1794, however, the city was the scene for a revolutionary plot against the Portuguese colonial masters which was soon repressed.

The arrival of the court

In November of 1807 the French dictator Napolean Bonaparte invaded and occupied Portugal. The Prince Regent decided to evacuate the court to Brazil and under British escort sailed to Rio de Janeiro, which became the capital of the Portuguese Empire in 1808. The court stayed there even after 1814 and the defeat of Napoleon but King João VI was forced to return to Portugal in 1820, leaving his son Dom Pedro as Prince Regent in Brazil.

Attempts to return Brazil to its former colonial status caused friction with the native Brazilians and on 7 September 1822 Dom Pedro declared independence which was finally recognized by Portugal in 1825. However, due to his favouring Portuguese minsters there was resentment from all the planter oligarchy – especially as a result of the **Anglo-Brazilian Treaty of 1826**. This treaty granted British recognition of the independent Brazil in return for certain trading privileges, but, almost more importantly, stipulated that the Atlantic slave trade should come to an end in three years. Mistrust between the Portuguese and the Brazilians became even more pronounced. Portuguese merchants were blamed for the rising cost of living and in 1831 rioting broke out in Rio de Janeiro. Dom Pedro shuffled and reshuffled his cabinet to appease different factions but nothing worked and on 7 April 1828 he abdicated in favour of his five-year-old son, Dom Pedro II, choosing to leave Brazil a week later on a British warship.

Imperial Capital

After independence, in 1834, Rio de Janeiro was declared capital of the **Brazilian Empire** and remained so for another 125 years. During the 10 years of the young prince's boyhood, there were many separatist movements and uprisings by the oppressed lower classes and by 1840 there was a general consensus that although he had not come of age, it was imperative that the 14-year old, Dom Pedro II should ascend the throne, and he was duly crowned. Administration of the country was centralized again in Rio de Janeiro, the powers of provincial assemblies were curtailed, a national police force set up and the Council of State restored.

It took a couple of years for the balance of power to be worked out between the conservative élites of Rio de Janeiro and the liberal élites of São Paulo and Minas Gerais, but once the interests of different groups had been catered for, the constitutional monarchy worked smoothly for 20 years.

The end of the slave trade

Despite the Anglo-Brazilian Treaty of 1826, the slave trade continued until the British Royal Navy put pressure on Brazilian ships carrying slaves in 1850 and the trade was halted soon afterwards. As slaves in Brazil did not reproduce at a natural rate because of the appalling conditions in which they lived and worked, it was clear that an alternative source of labour would eventually have to be found. Anti-slavery movements gathered strength and in 1871 the first steps towards **abolition** were taken. A new law gave freedom to all children born to slaves from that date and compensation was offered to masters who freed their slaves. During the 1870s, large numbers of European immigrants, mostly from Italy and Portugal, came to work on the coffee plantations, and as technology and transport improved, so the benefits of slavery declined. During the 1880s the abolition movement became unstoppable and, after attempts to introduce compensation for slave owners failed, a law abolishing slavery was immediately passed on 13 May 1888. Some plantation owners went bankrupt, but the large majority survived by paying immigrant workers and newly freed slaves a pittance. Those freed slaves who left the plantations to find employment in the cities were equally exploited and lived in poverty.

Urban development

When the Portuguese royal family fled to Brazil in 1808, the ideas that were brought over from Europe started a major transformation of the city. True, works to beautify and clean up the place had been undertaken when the city acquired viceregal status, but the remodelling which occurred in the early 19th century was on a different scale. The introduction of neo-classicism at this time is discussed in 'Architecture' and 'Fine Art', page 234, but the city also expanded beyond its historical boundaries. It grew north into São Cristóvão and Tijuca and south through Glória, Catete, Flamengo and Botafogo. The prosperous coffee barons and business class built their mansions and the Imperial court was the centre of the nation's attention. The decline of the coffee trade in Rio de Janeiro state and the proclamation of the Republic did not affect the city's dominance as political, economic and cultural heart of Brazil.

Agriculture & industry

The demise of the Minas Gerais gold fields and the expansion of coffee growing in the Paraíba valley at the beginning of the 19th century opened up new routes between the interior and the coast. The crop was taken by mule train to new ports on the Baías de Guanabara, Sepetiba and Ilha Grande, and these roads were the main means of communication until the coming of the railways after 1855. At this point, Rio de Janeiro added to its political importance the trading dominance that came with the rail terminus, first from Petrópolis, then from São Paulo and Minas Gerais. Industrialization soon followed.

In comparison with Rio de Janeiro city's steady growth, other centres rose and fell with the changing economic climate: Paraty was a major port while gold and, later,

The Vaccine Rebellion

At the beginning of 20th century, the appalling state of public health in Rio made it one of the most dangerous cities in the world. Plague, yellow fever and smallpox epidemics were common, especially during the summer months. Thousands of people suffered from these diseases every year – particularly the poor who couldn't afford to spend the summer in pleasant, cool mountain villas in Petrópolis and Teresópolis.

Finally President Rodrigues Alves decided that this was unacceptable for Brazil's capital, and in 1902 he found the right man from the job. **Oswaldo Cruz** *was a young doctor who immediately started to work hard at eradicating these diseases from the city. To deal with the plague, mainly transmitted by rats, he sent government agents to walk the streets buying dead rats for the sum of 300 réis each. To wipe out Yellow fever he dispatched hundreds of public health officials with insecticides to search for contaminated water reservoirs.*

Despite the fantastic results with the death rate from yellow fever falling from 469 in 1903 to only 39 in 1904, the press never missed an opportunity to publish caricatures and jokes about Oswaldo's actions and methods of work. However, the worst came in 1904 when, on Oswaldo Cruz's recommendation, the Government approved a law making vaccination against smallpox compulsory. Rio's population started a revolt against this "violation of their human rights". Trams were set on fire, shops were destroyed and even some military troops mutinied and joined the rebellion. The city of Rio de Janeiro was in chaos and the Federal Government had to call in loyal troops from other states before the rebellion was controlled. As a result, the military rebels were all sent to garrisons in Acre on the border with Bolivia and a few months later smallpox was completely eradicated from Rio.

Fabio Sombra

---

coffee were flowing through it, but fell almost into obscurity after the railways were built. Towns in the coffee zone, such as Vassouras and Valença, lost their importance as the coffee frontier moved.

Republican capital The monarchy did not long survive the end of slavery. The republican movement started in the early 1870s in cities all over Brazil and gradually attracted the support of the military, who also felt under-represented in government, and on **15 November 1889** a bloodless military *coup d'état* deposed the monarchy and instituted a federal system. Despite rivalries between the states, the Republic survived unsuccessful coup attempts by junior army officers in 1922, 1924 and 1926 which saw fighting in Rio de Janeiro.

Growth continued into the 20th century and one of the most significant acts was the construction of a monumental new boulevard through the middle of the commercial district. The 33 m wide **Avenida Central** was driven through the old city's narrow streets in 1904-05 as the principal means of access in Rio; in 1912 it was renamed **Avenida Rio Branco**. Other 20th century modernization schemes included the levelling of the Morro do Castelo in the 1920s, with the earth being used to reclaim land in the bay (known as the *aterro*) for the Santos Dumont airport. Between 1941-44, the **Avenida Presidente Vargas** became another main access when two streets became one as the buildings in between were knocked down. While these great projects were progressing, the city was continuing to expand outwards: north into industrial zones; south around the coast; and inland, up the hills, mainly in the form of the slums known as *favelas*.

The 1930s saw the growth of nationalism as well as the emergence of new political factions and parties such as fascists and communists. In October 1937, the president

Politicians and parties

Throughout most of its history Rio de Janeiro was the centre of the nation's politics. After the move of the capital to Brasília and the removal of its federal privileges the city also lost much of its political influence in the country's decision making. Nonetheless, as the second largest city in Brazil, Rio and the Cariocas have continued to play an important role in current affairs. Many of the current players on the political stage rose to prominence during the resistance to the military regime from the mid-1960s to the early 1980s. Politicians such as **Marcello Alencar** *(who as a lawyer defended political prisoners) and* **Leonel Brizola** *(one of the most radical supporters of President João Goulart, deposed by the 1964 coup) were involved in the return to democracy. To this day they are still important figures, although now often behind the scenes (both have been governor of Rio de Janeiro whilst Brizola was the founder of the PDT).* **Fernando Gabiera's** *autobiography,* O que é isso Companheiro? *is an excellent and critical look at the armed resistance during the late 1960s and early 1970s in which he took part. Today he is a prominent member of the PV (Green Party), founded in Rio de Janeiro in the mid-1980s and finally registered as a separate political party in 1993.*

Political parties are generally transitory homes to a Brazilian politician who will often go wherever he can get most electoral votes. However, the PDT (Democratic Workers Party) and PT (Workers Party) on the left, and the PMDB (Brazilian Democratic Movement Party) and PFL (Liberal Front) on the right all have strong popular support and tend to form the respective oppositions and governments in Rio de Janeiro. When the city and state are governed by different political opinions there are sometimes difficulties between the two. However, today's state governor, the evangelist Anthony Garotinho (PDT) and the current mayor Luiz Paulo Conde (PFL) are collaborating on at least some joint project in the city.

The election campaign for the next mayor of Rio, to be elected in October 2000 is currently in swing with the popular Benedita da Silva (PT) as the left's candidate. Having risen from a favela in Leme to become Brazil's first black female senator, she was recently described as the "Queen of Sheba" by a political opponent who accused her of falling in love with the pomp of power in her current position as vice-governor of the state. Her reply was short but succinct. "Why shouldn't I walk on red carpets? I've washed enough in the past."

Getúlio Vargas declared a state of siege against an alleged communist plot and suspended the constitution which had prevented him being re-elected. Instead, he proclaimed a new constitution and a new dictatorial state, *Estado Novo* which lasted until 1945. Vargas was, however, to be elected again in 1950 with massive popular support but his presidency was beset with problems, rumours of corruption and after his bodyguard was implicated in a plot to kill a journalist, the army issued him with another ultimatum to resign or be ousted. Instead, on 24 August 1954, Vargas shot himself in a room in the Palácio do Catete, leaving a suicide note.

The next president Jucelino Kubitschek finally ended Rio de Janeiro's place as the nation's capital which was transferred to the specially constructed city of **Brasília** in 1960. Rio, as capital of Brazil, had been a federal district in its own right inside the state of Rio de Janeiro, who's capital was at Niterói. After the transfer of the federal district to Brasília, Rio became capital of the newly created **Estado de Guanabara**. The city continued to play an important role on the national stage and was one of the main centres of resistance against the military regime which came to power in 1964 after deposing President João Goulart. The early 1970s saw an increase in

City state

infrastructure projects such as construction of the bridge between Rio and Niterói, as well as new access roads to the west of the city which have helped populate the suburbs of São Conrado and Barra da Tijuca. In 1975 the states of Guanabara and Rio de Janeiro were finally amalgamated into the new Estado do Rio de Janeiro, with its state capital at Rio. The late 1970s and early 1980s were difficult years for the city, after the loss of a sizeable chunk of income from state taxes and the relocation of most government offices to Brasília.

Modern Rio de Janeiro

Government and politics

National Rio de Janeiro is a member state of the República Federativa do Brasil. The 1988 constitution provides for an executive president elected by direct popular vote, balanced by a bicameral legislature (81 seats in the Federal Senate, 513 seats in the Chamber of Deputies) and an independent judiciary. The vote has been extended to 16-year-olds and illiterates. Presidential elections are held every five years, with a second round one month after the first if no candidate wins an outright majority. Congressional elections are held every four years, the deputies being chosen by proportional representation. In 1997, a constitutional amendment was passed allowing the re-election of the president, state governors and mayors.

State Rio de Janeiro has a popularly elected Governor who exercises the executive power from the Palácio Guanabara in Laranjeiras for a four year term. He chooses the members of his government and controls the State's police forces. There is a Legislative Assembly based in the Palácio Tiradentes in Centro, which legislates on all matters affecting provincial administration and provides for state expenses and needs by levying taxes. The state has its own judicial system, except for cases in which states are in dispute with each other or those instances where the national judiciary is required to deliberate on issues which state courts cannot decide.

Local Each municipality has a similar structure, with a mayor (*prefeito*), also popularly elected for a four year term, and a local council (*câmara de vereadores*). The mayor of Rio governs from the Palácio da Cidade in Botafogo and appoints a secretariat who are mainly located in the São Sebastião administrative centre in Cidade Nova. The 42 council members of Rio's municipal council meet in the Palácio Pedro Ernesto in Cinelândia and act as the legislative power by approving the mayor's decisions as well as proposing their own projects.

Economy

Covering 43,653.3 sq km and with a population of 14.4 million (1998), 94.3% of whom lived in metropolitan areas, the Rio de Janeiro state is Brazil's second largest industrial producer. Some of the major privatized enterprises based here are the steel company *Companhia Siderúgica Nacional* and the mining company *Companhia Vale do Rio Doce*. Some of this local industry is defence related, generally situated along the valley of Rio Paraíba do Sul. The city is mainly orientated towards administration and service industry but there are a number of important financial institutions such as BNDES, one of the country's most important investment banks. The strong presence of universities in the city has also contributed greatly to research and development of new technology.

Media & communications

Due to the presence of the influential *Globo* network Rio de Janeiro remains an important media centre in both news and entertainment, with its popular soap operas being exported to many parts of the world. More recently there has been a concentration on information technology especially in software design and about 40% of Brazil's systems and software are developed here. Telecommunications giant *Embratel* and *IBM* both have their Brazilian headquarters in the city

Energy

Offshore of the northeast coast of Rio de Janeiro state are the oil wells of the Campos basin which make up some 70% of the nation's current petroleum production. This has made Rio, the centre of the Brazilian oil industry with *Petrobras*, *Shell* and *Texaco* all having their main offices in the city. A 620 MW nuclear power plant at Angra dos Reis, west of Rio de Janeiro came on stream in 1985, but financial restrictions have slowed its development. A second plant built in the area by *Electronuclear* and due to start operation in June this year was still waiting to conclude final testing.

Tourism

As a world-famous tourist destination, Rio de Janeiro attracts many holidaymakers and has also successfully developed this infrastructure for the hosting of conferences and events. When it was decided several years ago to overhaul Rio's physical and social infrastructure, the authorities also recognized that the tourism sector was suffering from the negative image that the city had gained over the years. Hence the creation of the *Plano Maravilha*, a strategic plan for tourism, which was drawn up in 1997 with Spanish assistance. The plan not only identified the strong and weak points of the city for tourism, but also aimed to contribute to the improvement of life for the citizens of Rio by including them in the sector's development. There were a great number of elements within the plan which was accompanied by a strong campaign to sell the city in the United States and Europe.

Society

Poverty & urban migration

The population of Rio de Janeiro has historically been heavily concentrated along the coastal strip where the original Portuguese settlers could exploit the agricultural wealth such as the coffee plantations in the north of the state. The urban population of Rio increased at rates more than double the overall average rate, until the 1980s. Internal migration, particularly from the northeastern states, because of their poverty, has brought problems of unemployment, housing shortage, and extreme pressure on services; and the shanty towns known as *favelas* are now an integral part of the urban landscape.

However in 1997, the Brazilian Institute of Geography and Statistics (IBGE) stated that the migration of people from one region to another had almost halved between 1991 and 1996, compared with 1986 to 1991. Although the Brazilian population was continuing to become more urban (78.4% living in cities in 1996 against 75.6% in 1991), expansion in the largest metropolises like Rio de Janeiro was slowing.

Health

Rio de Janeiro's system of health care in many ways reflects its society. The rich elite have access to private care with modern technology whilst an inadequate public medical service is all that is on offer for the poor. What financial resources were made available have traditionally been concentrated in the hospital sector and very few doctors and nurses were trained to meet the needs of the wider community. Reform has been underway, however, with responsibility for health being devolved to local authorities. There are now more attempts to concentrate on primary care something in which expertise from NGOs and countries such as Cuba, who have successfully combated specific problems such as HIV infection, has been of great help.

Other improvements during the last few decades have been the decrease in infant mortality, the reduction of infectious and parasitic diseases and the increase in life expectancy at birth. The main causes of death tend to be circulatory system illnesses, homicide and traffic accidents. Recently Dengue fever has become apparent in many urban areas of Rio de Janeiro. Education programs in environmental health have so far made little impact on this problem.

Environment

When, in 1960, the nation's capital was moved from Rio de Janeiro to Brasília, the city went into decline, especially in the commercial centre. The amount of work that God is supposed to have devoted to Rio began to suffer badly from poor urban planning decisions, too many high-rise buildings and a failure to maintain or clean the city adequately. However, in the late 1990s, the mayor of the city, Luiz Paulo Conde, embarked on a massive programme of regenerating the centre through remodelling and attracting residents to neglected districts. As an architect and urbanist he brought a social vision which encompassed the improvement of *favelas* and a plan to clean up the south of the city as far as Leblon.

In December 1997 a new expressway, the **Linha Amarela**, was opened from the Ilha do Fundão, near the international airport, to Barra de Tijuca. It is designed, like the Linha Vermelha which runs around the bay (and this year integrated with the Linha Amarela), to speed traffic across the city, avoiding the horrendous traffic jams on the older access roads. The Linha Amarela is 25 km long, cost US$400m (almost twice the original estimate) and cuts by more than half the journey time to Barra. It goes through the neighbourhoods of Bonsucesso, Meier, Água Santa and Jacarepaguá and includes four tunnels, the longest, Covanca, being 2,180 m. There are tolls and buses run along it.

Land and environment

Geography

One of the main attractions of Rio de Janeiro state is its varied geography. The coast has three large bays, intricately carved with inlets and dotted with islands. Where erosion has deposited soils at the foot of the coastal mountains, lowlands (*baixadas*) have formed a wide belt between the mountains and the sea. In these lowlands there are sand banks, salt marshes (*restingas*) and lakes. Another feature of the coast is the number of fine beaches, some on the open sea and others, which are calmer, in the bays or on the lakes behind the sand bars. Just inland from the Atlantic litoral is the **Serra do Mar**, a range of mountains which includes, among other features, the weird shapes of the **Serra dos Órgãos**. Further inland again is the **Serra da Mantiqueira**, which has the highest mountain in the state, Pico das Agulhas Negras (2,787 m). Between the two ranges runs the **Rio Paraíba do Sul**, the main valley of many in the state. Before the conquest of Brazil by the Portuguese, the entire region was covered in tropical forest, hardly any of which now remains.

Geology

Ancient rock structures, some of the oldest in the world, underlie much of the state of Rio de Janeiro creating resistant plateaux and a rounded hilly landscape. These ancient Pre-Cambrian rocks culminate in the crystalline/granite ranges known as *serras*, which run close to the state's

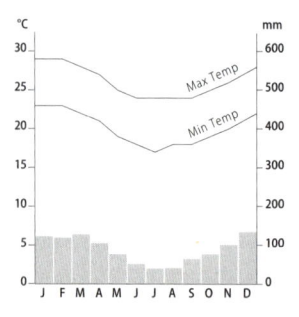

Climate: Rio de Janeiro

coastline. Although not particularly high or wide, the narrowness of the coastal strip has had a profound effect on the history of settlement in the state. Until comparatively recent times, the lack of natural access to the hinterland confined virtually all economic activity to this area, and today most of the major towns and the majority of the population are on or near the coast.

Because of varying erosion over many millions of years, there are a number of interesting natural features in these highlands. The many granite 'peaks' in and around Rio de Janeiro are the resistant remnants of very hard rocks providing spectacular viewpoints, **Pico da Tijuca** (the highest, 1,012 m), **Corcovado** (710 m) and **Pão de Açúcar** (396 m) – the best known. In many places, what rivers there are flowing eastwards necessarily have to lose height quickly so that gorges and waterfalls abound. There are also many kilometres of spectacular coastline and fine beaches.

Climate

In general terms the climate of the state is characterized by a dry season, usually between June and August, with the rest of the year rainy to a greater or lesser degree. Being a tropical zone, temperatures should be high, but the influence of the Serra do Mar affects all aspects of climate, giving the state a wider variation in temperature and rainfall than would otherwise be expected. On the **highest parts of the Serra**, facing the Atlantic, rainfall is the heaviest and temperatures the lowest in the state; there is no dry season to speak of. A little lower on these slopes, for instance at **Petrópolis** and **Teresópolis**, the climate falls somewhere between the extremes of the hot, humid coast and the cool, wet summits, which is why this amenable area was favoured by the Imperial court. In the rain shadow of the Serra do Mar, in the **Rio Paraíba valley**, temperatures are higher and the dry season lasts longer. The heat and humidity of the **central coast** is modified in the west (for example at Paraty) by the closeness of the mountains to the shore, almost eliminating the dry season. In the other direction, **north of Rio**, the dry season is more prolonged as the region suffers less from the prevailing winds off the sea.

Although there are occasional storms causing local damage, for example in the *favelas* (shanties) of Rio, the state is not subject to hurricanes or indeed to other natural disasters common elsewhere in Latin America such as earthquakes, volcanic eruptions or unexpected widespread and catastrophic floods.

The coastal climate is a mixture of tropical and temperate influenced by the South Atlantic anticyclone and southern polar winds. This causes east and northeast winds in summer which are stronger on the north coast past Cabo Frio, on average between 25-30 knots. These are lighter around 15 knots near Rio and Niterói and milder between 5-10 knots on the south coast near Angra dos Reis and Paraty. In winter however these winds are usually very mild. There are also occasional winds from the southwest when cold fronts arrive from the south (generally predictable by meteorological stations). Weak currents about 1.5 knots are mainly from the east but after a few days of winds from the southeast, they normally turn south, occasionally causing a swell. The *Cajú* is a wind from the northeast, named after that district of Rio, which is strong but rarely lasts long.

Sea conditions

Flora and fauna

The Atlantic rainforest used to cover 2.6 million sq km in a coastal strip 160 km wide and 4,200 km long. The coastal rainforest is bounded inland by a series of mountain ranges which contribute to the varied landscape and hence species diversity. It is one of the Earth's biological hotspots. Now critically fragmented and reduced to less than 5% of its original extent, it remains home to a very high proportion of unique

Atlantic rain forest

☞ Rio's beach penguins

Some of the city's most unusual visitors are a strange but popular sight on Rio's beaches during the winter months from June to August. Migrating north from the Straits of Magellan in Southern Argentina to the milder climates further up the coast, penguins occasionally find themselves somewhat off course. Once taken to the city's zoo to receive veterinary care and medication via doctored fish they however quickly adapt to their new home. As long as they have a pool for bathing and an air-conditioned room to cool off in during the summer they are more than happy to become honorary Cariocas. So there's no need to worry if you happen to bump into a couple of our feathered friends on the sands after a lengthy session of drinking ice-cold Antarctica (whose symbol is also a penguin double act) beers at your local beach bar.

species. For example 17 of the 21 primate species found there are unique to that region, and of those, 13 species, including the golden lion tamarin (see box, page 185), are endangered. Populations of South America's largest primate, the woolly spider monkey, locally known as *muriqui*, were decimated by European colonists who first settled along this coastal zone.

Restinga Along the coast, mangroves provide a breeding ground for numerous species of fish including many that are commercially important. Further inland is the *restinga*, a zone of shrub forest, coastal sand dunes, ponds and wetlands. The lush coastal rainforest itself extends to 800 m in elevation and grades into cloud forest between 800 m and 1,700 m. Drenching by mist, fog and rain leads to a profusion of plant growth, trees and shrubs which are covered with a great variety of epiphytes – orchids, mosses lichens and bromeliads. At the highest elevations, the forest gives way to mountain grasslands or *campos de altitude*. In the southern zone of the Atlantic forest there are large stands of monkey puzzle tree, *araucária*, which is characterized by its own parrot community, many of which are also endemic.

National parks

"Ecotourism is the international passion of this decade, but it is also a question of survival. It is modern and urgent to be a conservationist, to respect flora and fauna, not to pollute the beaches or the forests, to respect local populations, to value our cultural heritage, customs and traditions." Guia do Turismo, 10, 1997, page 25.

Different countries have different approaches to the relationship between national parks and tourism. In Brazil, the system which protects areas of outstanding beauty and unique flora and fauna has the dual role of providing centres of scientific research and places which are open to the public as an alternative form of recreation and education. Ibama (Instituto Brasileiro do Meio Ambiente e dos Recursos Naturais Renováveis – the Brazilian Institute for the Environment and Renewable Natural Resources) has in its care 35 national parks (Parques Nacionais, or PARNA). They are by no means the whole picture, though. They form part of a system of protected areas which go under different titles and which have varying degrees of public access. The network comprises, in addition to the national parks: Estações Ecológicas (ecological stations), Reservas Biológicas (biological reserves), Reservas Ecológicas (ecological reserves), Áreas de Relevante Interesse Ecológico (areas of relevant ecological interest), Reservas Particulares do Patrimônio Nacional (private national heritage reserves) and Áreas sob Proteção Especial (areas of special protection). In all these entities, the exploitation of natural resources is completely forbidden. They are for research, education and recreation only. Three other types of entity are designed to allow the sustainable use of natural resources, while still preserving their biodiversity: Florestas Nacionais (national forests), Áreas de Proteção Ambiental (areas of environmental protection) and Reservas Extrativas (extractive reserves). A new initiative is the Projeto Corredores Ecológicos (Ecological Corridors Project), which aims to create avenues of forest between isolated protected areas so that fauna may move over a greater area to breed, thus strengthening the stock of endangered animals which might otherwise suffer the ills effects of inbreeding. An example of this is project to link the Mata Atlântica of Poço das Antas (see page 184) with other pockets of coastal forest to help the survival of the golden lion tamarin.

Ibama was created in 1989, under Law No 7.735 of the 5 October 1988 Constitution. The Institute was formed by uniting four separate bodies, the environmental secretariat (SEMA), the Brazilian Institute of Forest Development (IBDF), and the superintendencies for the development of fishing and rubber (SUDEPE and SUDHEVEA). Brazil has a long history of passing laws to protect natural resources, such as that of 1808 which excluded from international trade the export of *pau-brasil* and other woods. At the same time, though, enforcement of such laws has not been easy. Today, the achievement of Ibama's goals is determined by resources, but funds are insufficient to commit either enough money or staff to the job of protecting the areas that have been designated for preservation. Sad though this is, there are still a large number of parks open to the visitor which can give a good idea of the variety of Brazil's natural resources and the value that they hold for the country.

Visitors should apply directly to the park's office if a permit is needed to visit a specific park or other conservation entity. Be aware that not all have easy access or are designed for tourism.

There are five national parks in the state of Rio de Janeiro of which three are open to visitors. These are **Parque Nacional da Tijuca** located within the city of Rio de Janeiro, **Parque Nacional da Serra dos Órgãos** situated in the northeast of the state between the towns of Petrópolis and Teresópolis, and **Parque Nacional da Itatiaia** in the northwest of the state straddling the border between Rio de Janeiro and Minas Gerais. The other two that are not generally open to casual visitors are **Parque Nacional da Restinga de Jurubatiba** in the southeast of the state near the town of Maca and **Parque Nacional da Serra da Bocaina** in the southwest of the state between Angra dos Reis and Paraty, which crosses the border with São Paulo.

Further information

For more information, contact Ibama at its local addresses, its national headquarters, SAIN, Avenida L-4, bloco "B", Térreo, Edifiço Sede do Ibama, CEP 70.800-200, Brasília DF, T061-2268221/9014, F061-3221058, or at its website, www.ibama.gov.br.

Information can also be obtained from the Ministério do Meio Ambiente (MMA – the environment ministry), Esplanada dos Ministérios, bloco "B", 5-9 andar (5th to 9th floors), CEP 70068-900, Brasília DF, or at its website www.mma.gov.br. See also the book *Parque Nacionais Brasil*, Guias Philips (1999), with a good map, beautiful photographs, sections on history, flora and fauna and tourist services, US$15.

Arts and architecture

Fine art and sculpture

The colonial era: 16th & 17th centuries

No visitor to Brazil should miss visiting a colonial church. During the colonial period in Brazil the Church dominated artistic patronage, with the religious orders vying with each other to produce ever more lavish interiors. In the 17th century the Benedictines included several notable sculptors among their ranks. Much of the magnificent gilded interior of the monastery of São Bento in Rio de Janeiro is by Frei Domingos da Conceição (circa 1643-1718), who worked there during the 1660s.

A distinctive feature of colonial interiors is the incorporation of decorative scenes in blue and white painted tiles, *azulejos*, around the walls. These were imported from Portugal from the earlier 17th century onwards, with subject matter as often secular as religious. Good examples include the church of **Nossa Senhora da Glória** in Rio de Janeiro, which has hunting scenes in the sacristy, Old Testament figures in the choir, and in the nave, astonishingly, scenes of pastoral love loosely based on the Song of Songs.

The 18th century

Although 17th-century church decoration is often lavish there is little warning of the extraordinary theatricality which characterizes the work of the 18th century. Behind their sober façades churches open out like theatres, with the equivalent of balconies and boxes for the privileged, and a stage for the high altar with a proscenium arch and wings of carved and gilded wood. Cherubs whisper to each other or gesticulate from their perches amongst the architectural scrolls; angels, older and more decorous, recline along a cornice or flutter in two dimensions across an illusionistic ceiling. The object of devotion is usually placed high above the altar on a tiered dais, surrounded by a Bernini-esque sunburst of gilded rays. A skilled exponent of this type of design was the sculptor Francisco Xavier de Brito (died 1751), as in **São Francisco de Penitência**.

It is in Rio that sculpture first begins to sober up again as, for example, in the work of the sculptor Valentim de Fonseca e Silva, known as Mestre Valentim (circa 1750-1813) which can be seen in several churches including **São Francisco de Paula** and **Nossa Senhora da Glória**. Valentim also designed the first public gardens in Rio: the **Passeio Público** was inaugurated in 1783 and included walks, seats decorated with *azulejos* and pavilions. A unique series of six painted views of Rio and Guanabara Bay by Leandro Joaquim (1738?-1798?), originally made for one of the pavilions, are now in the Museu Histórico Nacional in Rio.

French influence in Imperial Brazil

After the transfer of the Imperial court to Rio in 1808 João VI made a determined effort to renovate Brazilian culture, and in 1816 the French Artistic Mission – a boatload of painters, sculptors, architects, musicians and craftsmen – arrived from France to found what was to become the Imperial Academy. Two artists were particularly influential: **Nicolas-Antoine Taunay** (1755-1830) and **Jean-Baptiste Debret** (1768-1848). Taunay's luminous landscapes of the area around Rio and Debret's lively street scenes helped to open up new areas of secular Brazilian subject matter, and inspired artists throughout the 19th century. The Academy provided scholarships to send promising young artists to Paris, so reinforcing the French influence, and there are echoes of Delacroix in the work of **Vítor Meireles** (1832-1903) as for example, in his *Battle of the Guararapes* of 1879 in the Museu Nacional de Belas Artes, Rio, and of Ingres in *La Carioca* (1882) of **Pedro Américo** (1843-1905) in the same museum. The influence of Courbet can be seen in the so-called *belle époque* of the first republican years (1889-1922), in particular in the work of Meireles' pupil, **José Ferraz de Almeida Júnior** (1850-1899).

Brazil moved from this essentially academic tradition straight into the radicalism of the early 20th century, and movements such as Cubism, Futurism, Fauvism and Constructivism were quickly translated into distinctively Brazilian idioms. **Lasar Segall** (1891-1957), **Anita Malfatti** (1896-1964) and the sculptor **Vitor Brecheret** (1894-1955) were pioneers of modernism, working in relative isolation before the Semana da Arte Moderna (Modern Art Week) in São Paulo in 1922 drew together a group of artists and intellectuals whose influence on Brazilian culture can still be felt today. They sought to challenge established bourgeois attitudes, to shake off the traditional cultural subservience to Europe, and to draw attention to the cultural diversity and social inequality of contemporary Brazil. **Emilio di Cavalcanti** (1897-1976) mocked the artificiality of middle class socialites. **Tarsila do Amaral** (1886-1973) borrowed her loud colours from popular art while her imagery includes ironic reworkings of European myths about the savage cannabilistic Indians supposed to inhabit the Brazilian jungle. **Cândido Portinari** (1903-1962) used murals to expose the exploitation and injustice suffered by workers and peasants while **Osvaldo Goeldi** (1895-1961) explored similar themes in his powerful wood engravings. Portinari, in an interesting revival of the colonial use of *azulejos*, created murals in blue and white painted tiles for modern building such as the MES building by Costa and Niemeyer of Rio, begun in 1937.

The economic strength of the middle years of the century encouraged state patronage of the arts. President Getúlio Vargas recognized that art and architecture could be used to present an image of Brazil as a modern industrialized nation, with Brasília being the culmination of this vision. Museums of Modern Art were founded in São Paulo and Rio, and in 1951 São Paulo hosted its first Bienal Internacional which attracted abstract artists from Europe and the US and confirmed Abstraction – symbol of progress and technological modernization – as the dominant mode in Brazil during the 1950s. Rivalry between the artistic communities of Rio and São Paulo helped to produce some outstanding avant-garde art. In the 1950s **Waldemar Cordeiro** (1925-1973), leader of the São Paulo Grupo Ruptura, painted what at first sight appeared to be rather simple geometric patterns in bright, contrasting colours, but on closer attention the flat surface seems to break up, suggesting recession, space and restless movement, in some ways prefiguring the British Op Art movement of the 1960s. The Neo-Concrete group of artists of Rio argued for the integration of art into daily life, and experimented with art which makes sensory and emotional demands on the 'spectator' whose participation leads in turn to creation. During the early 1960s Lygia Clark (1920-1988) made *Bichos (Animals)* out of hinged pieces of metal which, as the name implies, are like creatures with a life of their own: they can be rearranged indefinitely but because of their complexity it is impossible to predetermine what shape will result from moving a particular section. Nowadays, unfortunately, they are displayed in museums where touching is not encouraged. Hélio Oiticica (1937-1980) took the idea further, working with people (poor and often black) from the samba schools in the Rio *favelas* to create artistic 'happenings' involving dance, music and flamboyant costumes called *Parangolés (Capes)*. The notion that a key function of art should be to shock the bourgeisie was first voiced by in the 1922 Week of Modern Art. Oiticica often succeeded, and he and other artists of the 1960s also realized another of the aims of the first modernists: to create a Brazilian modern art that was not the poor relation of developments in Europe or the US. A museum of his work has recently opened in Rio. Other important figures of this generation include the neo-concretist painter Ivan Serpa (1923-1973), Sérgio Camargo (1930-1990), who produced textured rhythmic constructions of white on white but because they are made with off-cuts of wood they suggest the tensions between form and material, geometry and nature, and Amílcar de Castro (born 1920) whose deceptively simple sculptures are often cut from one large panel of cast iron.

The military coup of 1964 marked the beginning of a period of political repression and of renewed artistic energy, with figurative tendencies re-emerging. In 1970 Antônio Enrique Amaral (born 1935) took as his theme the banana, so often used in dismissive references to Latin America, and in an extended series of paintings monumentalized it into an extraordinary symbol of power and fruitfulness. In an ironic neo-colonial altarpiece (circa 1966) installed in the Museu de Arte de São Paulo, Nelson Leirner (born 1932) makes the object of devotion the neon-lit head of pop star Roberto Carlos. Conceptual art offers different ways of confronting the dominant ideology. Both Cildo Meireles (born 1948) and Jac Lierner (born 1961) have used, misused or forged banknotes, for example, and both they and Waltercio Caldas (born 1946) and Tunga (born 1952) have created installations which draw attention, directly and indirectly to environmental issues. The painter Siron Franco (born 1947) also often addresses the issue of the destruction of the Amazon rainforest, but his disturbing surreal images explore many other areas – industrial pollution, sexual fantasy, political corruption, national identity – making him one of the most exciting artists in Brazil today.

Architecture

Indian architecture

Before the arrival of the Portuguese in 1500, Brazil was inhabited by the Tupi-Guarani Indians, who had developed forms of art and architecture which appeared very primitive in comparison with that of other precolumbian cultures such as the Incas, the Maya and the Aztecs. In fact, the first colonizers were disappointed with what they found. Instead of rich cities, impressive palaces, temples and massive stone walls, they faced relatively small groups of semi-naked Indians living in houses covered mostly with palm leaves.

The tropical climate and their nomadic way of life did not allow these tribes to develop permanent cities or solid, lasting constructions. They lived in *tabas*, temporary sites formed by a group of *ocas* (collective buildings, made of branches, leaves and vegetable fibres), placed around a main square. After a year or two, they would abandon the *taba* and move to another place, in search of better hunting grounds and new fields for their subsistence agriculture. A few examples of these interesting building techniques can be seen in museums, such as the **Museu do Índio** in Rio de Janeiro.

Brazilian colonial style: houses & civic buildings

The earliest Portuguese colonizers to arrive in Brazil in the 16th century faced many problems in building their houses, forts, churches and other necessary structures. First of all there was a lack of building materials, such as bricks, roof tiles and mortar. Second, there were few trained craftsmen, such as carpenters and bricklayers, in the colony. They therefore had to improvise by developing unusual building techniques and trying different materials. In the hinterland the majority of the houses were built with *taipa de pilão*. This technique consisted in using a wooden form to build thick walls. These forms were filled with a mixture of clay, vegetable fibres, horsehair, ox

A Brazilian colonial house

blood and dung. This paste was then compacted with a pestle and allowed to dry for two to three days before the next layer was added. The roof tiles were often moulded on a female slave's thigh and dried in the sun.

It is quite easy to identify a house in Brazilian colonial style. Their shapes, colours and building techniques remained virtually unchanged for almost three centuries. Firstly, they always had large, visible roofs, made with red clay tiles, finishing in eaves extending beyond the walls. All the buildings were painted in a white wash, with bright colours used only on window and door frames. These were made of wood and had, mostly, elegant arches at the top. In the 19th century, sash windows with squared 10 cm by 10 cm pieces of glass were added in many houses, as can be seen in cities like Paraty.

Urban colonial houses had doors and windows opening directly onto the street. Courtyards were never placed in front of the house, but internally, forming airy patios which protected the privacy of the family. The furniture was extremely simple and rough. Often, the only pieces of furniture in a bedroom would be the bed itself and a leather box to store clothes and personal belongings. In the colonial period, the highest status symbol was to live in a *sobrado* (a house with more than one floor, usually two). The ground floor was normally a commercial business and above it the residence of the owner's family.

Churches, convents & religious buildings: the Baroque in Brazil

Houses, public buildings and other colonial civic edifices were generally unelaborate – all the refinement, style and sophistication in art, architecture and decoration being lavished on churches, convents and monasteries instead. The great religious orders, such as the Jesuits, Franciscans, Carmelites and Benedictines brought to Brazil the latest artistic trends from Europe, mainly the Baroque and Rococo.

Two separate strands in Brazilian religious architecture evolved. In the most important cities, close to the seaboard and more influenced by European culture, the churches and convents were built according to designs brought from Portugal, Italy and Spain. Some were merely copies of Jesuit or Benedictine temples in Europe. Examples of this can be found in the Mosteiro de São Bento and the Convento de Santo Antônio in Rio de Janeiro.

Brazilian Baroque

At the end of the 17th century gold was found in the region of Minas Gerais. One of the first administrative acts of the Portuguese crown in response to this discovery was to banish the traditional European orders from the mining region. The royal administration wanted to control the mining itself, taxation and traffic in gold and, as the friars were regarded as among the most shameless of smugglers of the metal, the orders in this instance were denied the support they were given elsewhere in the Portuguese colonies. Therefore, the majority of the churches in cities like Ouro Preto, Mariana, Congonhas and Sabará were built by local associations, the so-called 'third orders'. These lay orders had the gold and the will to build magnificent temples but, although they wanted their projects to be as European as possible, the original designs were hard to obtain in such out-of-the-way places. So the local artists had to find their own way. Inspired by descriptions and second-hand information, they

A coffee farmhouse with Neo-classic influences

created their own interpretation of the Baroque, thoroughly infused with regional influences and culture. This is the reason why the 'Barroco Mineiro' is so original.

Curved churches & the decline of the Gold Era

At the beginning of the 18th century, when gold was easily found in Minas Gerais, the main attraction was the inside of the church, richly and heavily decorated in carved wood and gold. Many of the churches built in this period will be a total surprise for the visitor. Their façades and exteriors are so simple and yet the naves and altars are highly and artistically decorated. As the mines started to decline, the outside of the buildings became more sophisticated, with curves, round towers and sinuous walls, such as the churches of São Francisco de Assis and Rosário, in Ouro Preto. As the gold for covering walls ran out, it was replaced by paintings and murals.

The 19th century & the Neo-classic style

The beginning of 19th century brought a major change in the history of Brazilian architecture. When Napoleon invaded Portugal in 1808, the Portuguese royal family and some 15,000 nobles and wealthy families fled to Rio de Janeiro, bringing with them their own view of what was sophisticated in the arts. In 1816 the king, Dom João VI, invited a group of French artists (The French Artistic Mission) to Brazil to introduce the most recent European trends in painting, sculpture, decoration and architecture. This was the beginning of the Neo-classic style in Brazil. An Imperial Academy of Fine Arts was created and all the new government buildings were built in Neo-classic style. The great name of this period as the French architect **Grandjean de Montigny**, who planned and built many houses and public buildings throughout the city of Rio de Janeiro.

The rich and famous also wanted their houses in this newly fashionable style, which revolutionized the Brazilian way of building. The large roofs were now hidden by a small wall, the plat band. Windows and doors acquired round arches and walls were painted in ochres and light tones of pink. Public buildings and churches started to look like ancient Greek temples, with triangular pediments and columns. However, this new style was not best suited Brazil's climate: the earlier, large colonial roofs had been much more efficient in dealing with heavy tropical rains and, in consequence, the Neo-classic style never became popular in the countryside.

Even when the coffee planters, in the second half of 19th century, started to become extremely rich and fond of imported fashions, they would build their urban mansions in the Neo-classic style, but still keep their farm houses with large roofs, sometimes adding small Neo-classic details in windows, doors and internal decoration. Good examples of this 19th-century rural architecture can be found very close to Rio de Janeiro, in cities like Vassouras, Valença, Barra do Piraí and Bananal, where some of the old farm houses are open to visitors.

There are many examples of urban Neo-classic building in Rio de Janeiro, such as the Museu Nacional, the Santa Casa da Misericórdia, the Casa de Rui Barbosa and the Instituto Benjamin Constant. Also very close to Rio, in Petrópolis, the Museu Imperial (formerly the Emperor's summer palace) is also a perfect example of the style. This

Eclectic style in Rio de Janeiro

Neo-classic remained popular in Brazil until the end of the 19th century, being also the 'official' style of the First and the Second Brazilian Empires.

After the Republic, in 1889, the Neo-classic style lost favour, having served the king and the emperors for such a long time. A new style, or rather a new harmony of different styles started to gain popularity, also under the influence of Paris and the Belle Époque. There were elements of neo-classic architecture, but also an excess of decoration and adornment on the façades. A broad 'boulevard' was constructed in Rio de Janeiro in 1906, the Avenida Central (today Avenida Rio Branco), with the idea of creating 'a Paris in the Tropics'. There are many examples of buildings in the Eclectic style on this avenue: the Biblioteca Nacional, the Teatro Municipal (Opera House) and the Museu Nacional de Belas Artes, all of them built in the first decade of 20th century. During the first two decades of this century, the Eclectic style remained very popular.

The early 20th century & the Eclectic style

In 1922 a group of artists, painters, poets and architects organized in São Paulo 'A Semana da Arte Moderna' or the Modern Art Week, during which they exhibited their distaste at the extreme influence of foreign standards in Brazilian art. They considered their role to be a continuous quest for a genuine Brazilian form of expression. This search resulted in the rejection of all imported standards and, as far as architecture was concerned, two main currents emerged.

The 'Modern Art Week' of 1922 & national pride

The first movement sought its true Brazilian style in the past, in the colonial period. Architects like **Lúcio Costa**, studied the techniques, materials and designs of the 16th, 17th and 18th centuries, soon producing houses with a colonial look, but also combining elements which were only previously found in Baroque churches. These included pediments and decorated door frames. The style was called Neo-colonial and remained popular until the 1940s, especially in Rio de Janeiro and São Paulo.

The Neo-colonial

In search of greater authenticity, many architects employed original materials brought from demolished old houses. A good example of this can be found in Rio de Janeiro, in the Largo do Boticário (very close to the train station for Corcovado, in Cosme Velho), a small square surrounded by Neo-colonial houses painted in fancy, bright colours.

The other current generated by the Semana da Arte Moderna looked to the future for its inspiration for Brazilian-ness. Architects such as **Oscar Niemeyer**, **Lúcio Costa**, **Affonso Eduardo Reidy**, the landscape designer **Roberto Burle Marx** and many others started to design functional and spacious buildings, with large open areas and *pilotis* (pillars carrying a building, leaving the ground floor open). The use of concrete and glass was intense and the masterpiece of the Brazilian architectural Modernism is Brasília, the capital, planned from scratch in the 1950 by Lúcio Costa and Oscar Niemeyer.

Modernism

Neo-colonial house with a Baroque influence

Many examples of Modernist building can be found in Rio de Janeiro such as the Ministério da Educação e Saúde, the Museu de Arte Moderna, the Catedral Metropolitana, the Petrobrás building (Brazilian State Petrol Company), the BNDES building (National Bank of Social and Economic Development), all in the central area of the city.

Brazilian contemporary architecture The most recent trend is the post-modern. Many business centres, shopping malls and residential buildings are being designed in a style which uses coloured mirror glass, granite and stylized structures reminiscent of classical temples.

Brazilian architects are also famous worldwide for their techniques in designing houses for construction on steeply-inclined hills. In Rio de Janeiro, if you are driving along the coastal road in the neighbourhoods of Barra and São Conrado you can see many of these astonishing projects, homes of the very wealthy.

Literature

The colonial period Some of the major differences between Brazil and Spanish America spring from the history of colonization in the two areas. There were no great empires with large cities like those of the Incas or the Aztecs, and Portuguese exploitation concentrated first on extractive, then on cultivated export products (brazil-wood, then sugar). Although cities like Rio de Janeiro did finally develop, there was, incredible as it may seem, no printing press in Brazil until the flight of the Regent, later King João VI to Rio in 1808. This is not to say that there was no colonial literature, though scholars can still quarrel about how 'Brazilian' it was. When the Portuguese set foot in Brazil in 1500, the letter sent back to King Manuel by Pero Vaz de Caminha, already wondering at the tropical magnificence of the country and the nakedness of the inhabitants, set themes which would recur in many later works. The first plays to be put on in Brazil were religious dramas, staged in three languages, Portuguese, Spanish, and Tupi, by the Jesuit **José de Anchieta** (1543-97).

The 19th century It is helpful to understand Brazilian literature, even long after political independence, as a gradual, and to some extent contradictory, process of emancipation from foreign models. Every European literary movement – Romanticism, Realism, Symbolism, etc – had its Brazilian followers, but in each there was an attempt to adjust the model to local reality. A good example is the first of these, Indianism, which flourished in the mid-19th century, and produced two central figures, the poet **Antônio Gonçalves Dias** (1823-64) (himself partly of Indian descent) and the novelist **José de Alencar** (1829-77). It is a form of Romanticism, idealizing the noble savage, and with plots adapted from Walter Scott, and it happily ignored what was happening to real Indians at the time. However, it does express national aspirations and feelings, if in nothing else in the nostalgia for a kind of tropical Eden expressed in perhaps the most famous Brazilian poem, Gonçalves Dias *Canção do exílio*: "My land has palm-trees/ where the sabiá sings./ The birds that sing here/ don't sing like those back home." Alencar's novels, not all of them about Indians, are a systematic attempt to portray Brazil in its various settings, including the city. *O guarani* (1857), turned into a famous opera by Carlos Gomes, and *Iracema* (1865) are his most popular, the latter perhaps the most complete mythical version of the Portuguese conquest, allegorized as a love affair between a native woman and an early colonist, Martim Soares: Iracema, "the virgin with the honeyed lips" dies in childbirth at the end, but the future lies with their mixed-blood son, Moacir.

After his death, Alencar was succeeded as the chief figure in Brazilian letters by **Joaquim Maria Machado de Assis** (1839-1908). Perhaps Brazil's best writer, and certainly the greatest to appear in Latin America until well into the 20th century, he had to fight against formidable obstacles: he was of relatively poor origins, was mulatto, stammered and in later life was subject to epileptic fits. He wrote nine novels and more than 200 short stories as well as poetry and journalism. He ended his life as an establishment figure, founder of the Brazilian Academy of Letters, but his novels, especially those written after 1880, when he published *Memórias póstumas de Brás Cubas*, and the best of his stories are surprisingly subversive, covert attacks on slavery and on male power, for instance. He avoided detection by not using his own voice, hiding behind quirky, digressive narrators who are not always trustworthy. All the novels and most of the stories are set in Rio, which he hardly left, and give a remarkably varied account of the city and its different social levels. His most famous novel, *Dom Casmurro* (1900) is one of the best-disguised cases of an unreliable narrator in the history of the novel, and still arouses critical polemics.

Machado's atmosphere is predominantly that of the empire, which fell in 1889, a year after the abolition of slavery. In the Republic, a younger generation, more overtly rebellious in their aims, and affected by new scientific ideas from Europe, came to the fore.

The other important prose writer of this period, the novelist **Afonso Lima Barreto** (1881-1922), was mulatto like Machado, but there resemblances end. Much more openly rebellious and less of a conscious artist than Machado, his novels, the most notable of which is *Triste fim de Policarpo Quaresma*, are overt attacks on intellectual mediocrity, and the corruption and despotism into which the Republic soon fell.

The 20th century

In general, the poetry of the turn of the 19th and 20th centuries was imitative and stuffy: renewal did not come until the early 1920s, when a group of intellectuals from São Paulo, led by **Mário de Andrade** (1893-1945) and **Oswald de Andrade** (1890-1954) (unrelated) began the movement known as Modernism. This is conveniently supposed to have begun in 1922, the centenary of political independence, with a Week of Modern Art in São Paulo, but in fact it began earlier, and took until the mid-1920s to spread to the provinces. In great part, Modernism's ideology was nationalist, and though the word spanned the political spectrum, at its best it simply meant the discovery of a real Brazil behind stereotypes: Mário travelled throughout the country, attempting to understand its variety, which he embodied in his major prose work, the comic 'rhapsody' *Macunaíma* (1928), which in its plot and language attempts to construct a unity out of a complex racial and regional mix. Also in 1928, Oswald launched the 'anthropophagist', or cannibalist programme, which proclaimed that Brazilian writers should imitate their native predecessors, and fully digest European culture: a new kind of Indianism, perhaps ...

The most enduring artistic works to have emerged from Modernism, however, are poetic: two of Brazil's major modern poets, **Manuel Bandeira** (1886-1968) and **Carlos Drummond de Andrade** (1902-1987) were early enthusiasts of Modernism, and corresponded at length with Mário. Bandeira, the older man, made a slow transition to the new, freer style: his poems, often short and based on everyday events or images, nevertheless have a power and rhythmic accuracy which are deceptively simple. Drummond's poetry is more self-conscious, and went through a complex intellectual development, including a period of political enthusiasm during the Second World War, followed by disillusionment with the beginning of the Cold War. His themes, including some remarkable love poetry addressed by a 50-year old to a younger woman, and a lifelong attachment to Itabira, the small town in Minas Gerais where he was born, are very varied. Readers without Portuguese can best approach Drummond, widely regarded as Brazil's greatest poet, through an excellent anthology, *Traveling in the Family*.

The 1930s were a crucial decade. With increasing political mobilization, the growth of cities, and of an aspiring middle class, literature began to look to a wider audience. At first, however, it still reflected the dominance of rural life. The realism of this period, which often had a strong regionalist bias, had its *raison d'être* in a society still divided by huge social and/or geographical differences, and indeed played its part in diminishing those differences. Many of the first group came from the economically and socially backward northeast. **José Lins do Rego** (1901-57) is perhaps the most characteristic figure. He was highly influenced by the ideas of **Gilberto Freyre** (1900-1987), whose *Casa grande e senzala* (*The Masters and the Slaves*), published in 1933, one of the most important and readable of Brazilian books. It is a study of the slave-based, sugar-plantation society, and one of the first works to appreciate the contribution made by Blacks to Brazil's culture. It remains, however, very paternalist, and Lins do Rego's fiction, beginning with the semi-autobiographical *Menino de engenho*, reflects that, commenting on the poverty and filth of the (ex-)slave-quarters as if they were totally natural. His 'Sugar-cane cycle' sold in large editions, in part because of its unaffected, simple style.

A greater novelist belonging to the same group is **Graciliano Ramos** (1892-1953). His fiction is much more aggressive, and in later life he became a communist. His masterpiece, turned into an excellent film in the 1960s, is *Vidas secas*, which returns to the impoverished interior of *Os sertões*, but concentrates on an illiterate cowhand and his family, forced from place to place by drought and social injustice: it is a courageous attempt to enter the mental world of such people. *Memórias do cárcere*, published after Ramos's death, is his unflinching account of his imprisonment for a year on Ilha Grande during the Vargas regime.

Gradually, in the 1940s and 1950s, a subtler and more adventurous fiction began to be published alongside the regionalist realism that was the major heritage of the 1930s.

The stories and novels of **Clarice Lispector** (1920-77) now have a considerable audience outside Brazil, as well as a huge one inside it. Her stories, especially those of *Laços de família* (1960), are in general set in middle-class Rio, and usually have women as their central characters: the turbulence, family hatreds, and near-madness hidden beneath routine lives are conveyed in unforgettable ways, with a language and symbolism that is poetic and adventurous without being exactly difficult (she said she fought with the Portuguese language daily). Some of her novels have over-ambitious metaphysical superstructures, and may not be to some readers' tastes – *A paixão segundo G H*, for instance, concerns a housewife's confrontation with a dead cockroach in her maid's room, and her final decision to eat it, seen as a kind of "communion". At her best, in some of her journalism, in her late, deliberately semi-pornographic stories, and above all in the posthumous novel, *A hora da estrela*, which approaches the poor in an utterly unsentimental way, Lispector can stimulate and move like no one else.

The 1964 military coup, and the increasing use of torture and censorship in the late 1960s and early 1970s, had profound effects on literature, especially as they were accompanied by vast economic changes (industrialization, a building boom, huge internal migration, the opening up of the Amazon). At first, censorship was haphazard, and the 1960s liberation movements had their – increasingly desperate – Brazilian equivalents. Protest theatre had a brief boom, with *Arena conta Zumbi*, about a 17th-century rebel slave leader, produced by **Augusto Boal** (born 1931), being one of the most important. The best fictional account of those years can be find in two novels by **Antônio Callado** (born 1917), *Quarup* (1967), set in the northeast and centred on a left-wing priest, and *Bar Don Juan* (1971), whose focus is on the contradictions of a group of middle-class guerrillas. A remarkable documentary account of the period is ex-guerrilla (now leader of the Green Party) **Fernando Gabeira**'s *O que é isso companheiro?* (1982), which chronicles his involvement with the kidnapping of the American ambassador in 1969. Poetry at this time went through a crisis of self-confidence, and it was widely thought that it had emigrated into the (marvellous) lyrics of such popular composers as Chico Buarque de Holanda and Caetano Veloso, who were also the foremost standard-bearers of political protest in the 1970s.

It is impossible in the space available to give more than a few suggestions of some of the best work published in recent decades, concentrating on books which have been translated. **Rubem Fonseca** (born 1925), whose story 'Feliz ano novo' (1973) created a scandal because of its brutal treatment of class differences, has dedicated himself to the writing of hardnosed thrillers like *A grande arte* (1983); **Caio Fernando Abreu** (1948-96) is a short-story writer of considerable talent, dealing with the alienated urban young in such books as *Morangos mofados* and *Os dragões não conhecem o paraíso*.

Essays and books which can be wholeheartedly recommended for those who want more information are: Ray Keenoy, David Treece and Paul Hyland, *The Babel Guide to the Fiction of Portugal, Brazil and Africa in English Translation* (London: Boulevard Books, 1995). Irwin Stern (ed) *Dictionary of Brazilian Literature* (New York: Greenwood Press, 1988). Mike González and David Treece, *The Gathering of Voices* (Verso, 1992) (on 20th-century poetry). Elizabeth Bishop and Emanuel Brasil (eds) *An Anthology of Twentieth-Century Brazilian Poetry* (Wesleyan University Press, 1972). John Gledson, 'Brazilian Fiction: Machado de Assis to the Present', in John King (ed), *Modern Latin American Fiction: A Survey* (Faber, 1987). Many of the essays in Roberto Schwarz, *Misplaced Ideas: Essays on Brazilian Culture* (Verso, 1992), especially those on Machado de Assis, and 'Culture and Politics in Brazil, 1964-69' are very stimulating.

Further reading

Machado de Assis, Joaquim Maria (1839-1908), the classical satirical novelist of the Brazilian 19th century, is one of the most original writers to have emerged from Latin America. *Epitaph of a Small Winner* (London: Hogarth Press, 1985). *Posthumous Memoirs of Bras Cubas* (New York: Oxford University Press, 1997). (The same novel.) *The Heritage of Quincas Borba* (London: WH Allen, 1954). *Philosopher or Dog?* (New York: Avon Books, 1985, also London: Bloomsbury, 1997). (The same novel.) *Dom Casmurro* (New York: Oxford University Press, 1997, also in Penguin Modern Classics, Harmondsworth, 1994). Abreu, João Capistrano de (1853-1929) A fascinating account of the first three centuries of Brazilian history. *Chapters of Colonia History* (New York: Oxford University Press, 1997). Cunha, Euclides da (1866-1909) The 'epic' story of the military campaign to crush the rebellion centred in Canudos in the interior of the State of Bahia. One of the great books about the Brazilian national make-up. *Rebellion in the Backlands (Os sertões)* (Chicago: University of Chicago Press, 1944-) Often reprinted, including London: Picador, 1995. Lima Barreto, Afonso Henriques de (1881-1922) A sharp attack on some of the failings of the Brazilian political and social system, set in the 1890s. *The Patriot* (London: Rex Collings, 1978). Morley, Helena (1882-1970) The diary of a girl's life in Diamantina, in Minas Gerais: translated by the great American poet Elizabeth Bishop, who lived in Brazil for many years. A delightfully intimate and frank portrait of small-town life. *The Diary of Helena Morley* (London: Bloomsbury, 1997). Bandeira, Manuel (1886-1968) The oldest member of the Modernist movement, and one of Brazil's greatest poets, master of the short, intense lyric. *This Earth, that Sky: Poems by Manuel Bandeira* (Berkeley: University of California Press, 1988). Ramos, Graciliano (1892-1953) The greatest of the novelists of the 1930s and 1940s: a harsh realist. *São Bernardo* (London: Peter Owen, 1975). *Anguish* (New York: Knopf, 1972). *Barren Lives* (Austin: University of Texas Press, 1965). Andrade, Mário de (1893-1945) Written in the 1920s: a comic statement in picaresque form about Brazilian nationality, by the leader of Modernism.

Macunaíma (London: Quartet, 1988). Freyre, Gilberto (1900-1987) A central figure, still controversial: this account of racial mixture, and of sugar-plantation society in the northeast of Brazil in colonial times, is very readable. *The Masters and the Slaves* (Berkeley: University of California Press, 1986). Lins do Rego, José (1909-1957) Highly influenced by Gilberto Freyre, this is an evocative account of childhood on a northeastern sugar plantation. *Plantation Boy* (New York: Knopf, 1966). Drummond de Andrade, Carlos (1902-1987) Perhaps Brazil's greatest poet, with a varied, lyrical, somewhat downbeat style. *Travelling in the Family: Selected Poems* (New York: Random House, 1986). Guimareães Rosa, João (1908-1967) The most poetic of

Brazilian Literature in English translation

modern prose-writers, who sets his work in the rural interior: very difficult to translate. *Sagarana* (Austin: University of Texas Press, 1990). Lispector, Clarice (1920-1977) Brazil's greatest woman writer, with a considerable following abroad. *Family Ties* (Manchester: Carcanet, 1986; Austin: University of Texas Press, 1990). *The Foreign Legion* (Manchester: Carcanet, 1986; New York: New Directions, 1992). *The Hour of the Star* (Manchester: Carcanet, 1986; New York: New Directions, 1982). Fonseca, Rubem (1925-) A thriller, set in Rio.

High Art (London: Collins, 1987). *The Lost Manuscript* (London: Bloomsbury, 1997). Ribeiro, João Ubaldo (1940-) A panoramic historical novel, entitled *Long Live the Brazilian People* in the original. *An Invincible Memory* (London: Faber and Faber, 1989; New York: Harper and Row, 1989). Buarque de Holanda, Chico (1944-) Most famous as a pop singer and composer, Chico Buarque has written a short, fast-moving allegory of modern Brazil. *Turbulence* (London: Bloomsbury, 1992). *Benjamin* (London: Bloomsbury, 1997). Ângelo, Ivan (1936-) Much the best novel and about the political, social and economic crisis at the end of the 1960s, the worst period of the military regime. *The Celebration* (New York: Avon Books, 1992). Abreu, Caio Fernando (1948-1996) Short stories: one of the writers most effective in dealing with life in the Latin American megalopolis. *Dragons...* (London: Boulevard Books, 1990). Weishort, Daniel (ed), *Modern Poetry in Translation*, No 6, Brazil (London: King's College, 1994) contains 19 poets, including Mário de Andrade, Oswald de Andrade, Carlos Drummond de Andrade, Manuel Bandeira, João Cabral de Melo Neto.

Culture

People

The name 'Carioca' originally comes from the Tupi-Guarani word for a white-person's house. Today it is used to describe someone who was born in, or who lives in, Rio de Janeiro, and the city's population is descended from a mixture of many different races and traditions. No one knows how many indigenous peoples were living in Rio de Janeiro state when the Portuguese arrived but whatever the exact numbers, the effects of European colonization have been devastating and all the tribes were either wiped out or moved inland. During the 17th and 18th centuries large numbers of slaves were bought from Africa to the port of Rio de Janeiro. They were usually sold at market to work on the coffee fazendas or in the gold mines of nearby Minas Gerais. Many, however, were employed in the city and they performed almost all menial duties as well as many skilled professions. A small but important foreign community were the British who had special trade privileges during the early 19th century.

In the mid to late 19th century there was another wave of European immigration including many from Portugal and Spain who settled in the city. Inland there are also a number of Finnish, Swiss and other northern European communities who preferred the more agreeable climate of the mountainous areas of the state. There is also a small Japanese community in the city as well as a well represented Jewish group. The Lebanese community is also strong, as the presence of the Monte Libano club shows.

Immigration continued in the 20th century but this time mainly from within Brazil. Droughts and the subsequent failure of agriculture in the northeast of Brazil caused many *nordestinos* to head south to try to find work in the city. Today they form a substantial community in many neighbourhoods. *Mineiros* from the nearby state of Minas Gerais also make up another large Brazilian community in the city. Many Argentines and Chileans arrived in the 1970s fleeing persecution from military regimes and today there are many other small foreign communities from French to Scottish all contributing to the mixing pot that is Rio and the Carioca.

Religion

In order to discuss religion in Brazil, it is necessary to consider the three main cultures from which the Brazilian people originated, the Indian, the Portuguese and the African. Each has contributed its own religious traditions and in many cases they have intermingled and influenced each other.

Before the arrival of the Portuguese colonizers, Brazil was inhabited by many tribes of Indians. They had their own animist cults and a very rich, poetic mythology. The most important of their divinities was **Tupan**, the spirit of tempests, fire, lightning and thunder. It was he who had taught their ancestors the secrets of agriculture and hunting. The three other important gods were Jaci, the moon, Guaraci, the sun, and Rudá, love. There were also minor divinities such as Guirapuru, the lord of the birds, Caapora, the guardian of the animals, and Anhanga, the protector of hunters. There were also devils and one of the most feared was the Jurupari, an evil spirit which came in the night to bring nightmares to men. The designations of Tupan and Jurupari as the most important divinities in relation to Good and Evil were made by the Catholic missionaries in colonial times. The Europeans could not deal with the Indians' polytheistic religion, so they condensed the attributes of these spirits into concepts they could comprehend and educate against.

The priests, or shamans, were called **Pagés** and they knew the secrets of plants and magic potions. They would cure people in rituals in which they would invoke the spirits of the forest, their ancestors and certain animals. When faced with the diseases brought by the colonizers, however, the Pagés were almost helpless.

The Indians' religious system was based on many aspects of nature and on situations they had to face in their daily life. Today, the traditional cults of the Brazilian Indians have practically disappeared, not only because of the decrease in the numbers of the Indians themselves, but also because of the persistent work of missionaries (Catholic and Protestant) from the very first moments of European colonization.

With 'a sword in one hand and a cross in the other', one of the principal, official motives for the European colonization of the 'New World' was the necessity to convert the indigenous people to Christianity. Most of the great Catholic religious orders, such as the Benedictines, Carmelites, Franciscans and Jesuits, went to Brazil precisely with this aim. At the beginning of the colonial period, mainly in the 16th and 17th centuries, the religious orders were practically the only institutions providing public education, artistic and academic studies. The Jesuits specifically were dedicated to converting the Indians and they created many missions (*aldeias*).

In the colonial period there was absolutely no tolerance of other religions and many Jewish and Muslim immigrants understood the convenience of converting to the Catholic faith. This practice was also common in Portugal and many of these 'cristãos novos', or newly-converted Christians, acquired Portuguese surnames related to trees and natural elements, such as Pereira (peach tree), Carvalho (oak tree), or Oliveira (olive tree).

At the beginning of the 19th century, when Napoleon invaded Portugal and forced the Portuguese royal family and nobility to move to Brazil, a stronger commercial and diplomatic relationship with the British Empire made the king, Dom João VI, more tolerant of the Protestants. After 1808, many English families and tradesmen emigrated to Rio the Janeiro. Even so, they were only allowed to build a Protestant cemetery in 1811 and their first church in 1819, "as long as it did not have the appearance of a religious temple", according to Dom João VI's decree.

During the Brazilian Empire and up to the creation of the Republic in 1889, Catholicism was the official state religion. After that, as stated in all Brazilian republican constitutions, there is total freedom of religion and no one may suffer

👉 *The Body Beautiful*

A large part of the population of coastal cities like Rio de Janeiro is orientated towards the cult of the body as well as towards female sensuality, attaching great importance to physical appearance. This doesn't mean, of course, that everyone has perfectly sculpted bodies but that everybody (in particular, women) use their sensuality to the best effect regardless of their physical form. Due to this tolerance both the fat and the thin have a certain social permission to show off as they wish without worrying too much about aesthetic harmony. What's most important is to feel good in yourself and no one sees anything strange in walking from their apartment to the beach in a bikini, although a thin wrap called a canga (used to lie on the sand) is often wound around the waist.

Beatrix Boscardin

Catholicism was the official state religion. After that, as stated in all Brazilian republican constitutions, there is total freedom of religion and no one may suffer any kind of religious persecution, under protection of the law. Nevertheless, the influence of the Catholic church remained very important, both economically and politically. At present, the majority of the Brazilian population is still Roman Catholic, although in the last 10 to 15 years many Brazilians, especially in the very poor areas, have converted to Protestantism. Among the traditional Protestant churches, the most important ones in Brazil are the Baptists, the Presbyterians and the Lutherans, particularly in the south, which was mostly colonized by Germans. In many cases, though, the nonconformists are represented by new evangelical sects, such as the Universal Church of God's Kingdom, directed by its 'bishop', Edir Macedo. These new Christian sects, generally called 'evangélicas', have been very successful in attracting new converts for their flocks. They use modern marketing techniques and electronic media, including their own TV channels, radio stations and newspapers. Their pastors use very dramatic speeches, full of examples of miracles, cures and solutions for all possible material and spiritual problems. In some cases, scandals have been widely reported in the press and the financial operations of certain churches have been subject to investigation.

Afro-Brazilian religions When the Portuguese colonizers started to plant sugar cane on the northeast coast of Brazil, they soon realized that they would need a large, strong workforce to carry out the labour. The first option was to use the local indigenous population as slaves, but the Indians (those who did not die of European diseases) regarded that kind of work as demeaning, they soon became exhausted, frequently escaped, or simply refused to co-operate. Portugal, therefore, had to bring in black slaves. These people came from different regions of Africa and belonged to many different tribes, such as the Bantu, the Sudanese, the Angolans and the Hotentots. After the rigours of transatlantic shipment, they suffered further trauma on arrival at the Brazilian ports. They were often sold in groups which were segregated to avoid slaves from the same family or speaking the same language being together. By breaking all cultural and sentimental ties, the Portuguese hoped to eradicate ethnic pride and rebellions on the estates. Of course, these people brought their own religions, but the point is that none of their cults remained pure in Brazil. Taking, for example, the region of what is now Nigeria, there were different groups of people, each with its own divinity or Orixá (pronounced *Orisha*). These Orixás were normally the spirit of a distinguished ancestor or a legendary hero and they were worshipped only in a particular region. As the slaves went to Brazilian estates in groups made up of people from different African regions, they soon started to worship all the Orixás, instead of just one. This was the origin of Candomblé and Umbanda, Afro-Brazilian

Naturally, the Catholic Portuguese did not allow the slaves to maintain their own beliefs. So the Africans ingeniously began to associate their own gods with the Catholic saints who had more or less the same characteristics. For example, when the masters thought the slaves were praying to Saint George, the warrior saint, they were, in fact, praying to Ogun, the Orixá representing war and battles. This association is called religious syncretism and is one of the defining characteristics of the Afro-Brazilian religions.

Religious syncretism

In Candomblé, the figure of God, the Creator is called **Olorum**. But this figure is almost never mentioned. To some degree, this is because Olorum is too busy to care about mankind's small problems. These are taken care of by the Orixás, the spiritual guides responsible for all sorts of matters concerning our lives. According to Candomblé, from the moment of birth, every person has one or two Orixás to act as protector and tutor. The personality and the temperament of everyone is directly influenced by his or her Orixá. For example, a son or daughter of Ogun (the Orixá of war) is likely to be an impulsive and combative person, while the sons and daughters of Oxun (the Orixá of waterfalls and love) tend to be charming and coquettish.

The cult of the Orixás

To discover who your protector Orixá is, you must go to a Pai de Santo (male priest) or a Mãe de Santo (woman priest) and ask him or her to use the *Jogo de Buzios*. This is an oracle using 16 sea shells by which the priests can predict the future and answer questions related to material or spiritual matters. It is also very common to make offerings to the Orixás, consisting of special foods (every Orixá has his or her own preferences), alcoholic beverages, cigars, flowers, pop-corn, candles, toys and even ritually sacrificed animals such as cockerels, goats and pigeons. These offerings are delivered in different places, according to the Orixá. For example, offerings to Oxossi, the hunter, are delivered in a forest or a bush, and so on. The offerings are always associated with a wish being made, or by way of thanks to the Orixá for a favour received.

The religious ceremonies take place in *terreiros*, with much singing and drumming. The Pais de Santo and Mães de Santo enter into a trance and each is possessed by his or her protector Orixá, being able to communicate with humans, answer questions, give advice and predict the future.

It is very difficult to estimate the exact number of Brazilians who follow Candomblé and Umbanda. One of the main reasons is that many of their followers also profess to be Catholic. For many years the Afro-Brazilian religions were officially forbidden and only recently are people becoming more open in admitting their beliefs in public. Rio de Janeiro is one of the cities where the greatest influence of Candomblé and Umbanda is to be found. Many writers, academic and otherwise, have written on the subject, notably the novelist Jorge Amado, himself a member of the Candomblé cult (see his book, *The War of the Saints*, 1993).

Mãe de Santo & the Buzios Oracle   *An offering to Exu*

Some of the most important Orixás

Exu (pronounced Eshoo) is considered the messenger between people and the Orixás. Sometimes associated with the Christian Devil, Exu is always represented with a trident and his colours are black and red. Offerings to this Orixá are always made at crossroads and normally consist of cigars, cachaça and red and black candles. His day is Monday.

Ogum the Orixá of war, thunder, lightning and iron. His colour is deep blue and he is always represented with an iron sword. The sons and daughters of Ogum are very combative and impulsive. His day is Tuesday.

Oxossi (pronounced Oshossee) is the hunter and protector of wild animals. This Orixá lives in the forest and is represented with a bow, arrows and a leather hat. His colour is green and sometimes blue. His day is Thursday and all his offerings, including raw tobacco and fruits, must be made in wooded places. People protected by this Orixá are normally very independent and solitary.

Xangô (pronounced Shango) is the Orixá of truth and justice. His colours are red and white and his day is Wednesday. He is represented with a double-headed axe, the African symbol of justice.

Oxum (pronounced Oshoon) is a feminine Orixá, associated with love and the family, found in waterfalls and whitewater. Pretty and extremely coquettish, she is sometimes represented as a siren with a golden mirror. Her colour is yellow and offerings to her should be delivered close to a waterfall. Her sons and daughters are very dedicated to the family. Her day is Saturday.

Yemanjá, the mother of the seas and salt water. Her principal day is 31 December, New Year's Eve, and on this day people offer her white flowers, champagne and small boats full of candles and gifts placed in the sea. Her colour is light blue.

Iansã (pronounced Iansan) is a female Orixá related to tempests and storms. Very impulsive, Iansã is the only Orixá who can command the **Eguns**, the spirits of the dead. She wears red and her day is Wednesday.

Omolu, a strange Orixá who never shows his face (severely disfigured by smallpox), is always invoked in cases of disease and illness as he has the power to cure. Often referred as the 'doctor of the poor', he is represented as a strong man covered by a straw coat and holding a straw box full of herbs and medicines.

Oxum   *Omolu*

NB Two other terms are sometimes used in relation to Afro-Brazilian religions: Macumba used to be employed, mainly in Rio de Janeiro, as a generic term to describe all Afro-Brazilian cults. It was a popular expression at the beginning of the 20th century, but has become a derogatory term, not very politically correct. To call someone a 'macumbeiro/a' is offensive. The other term is Quimbanda. This is the dark side of Afro-Brazilian religion. It is associated with black magic and sorcery. A 'trabalho de quimbanda' is a ritual designed to hurt someone through offerings or sacrifices. Perhaps performed in cemeteries or at crossroads, these 'trabalhos' may use wax models of the intended victim (like in voodoo), or may involve imaginative and weird practices such as writing the enemy's name on a piece of paper, putting it in a frog's mouth, then sewing up the mouth. The victim is supposed to die a death as slow and painful as the frog's. Quimbanda is a taboo subject and no one will profess to being involved with it.

Spiritism (*espiritismo*) is a philosophical and religious doctrine founded by the French scientist Allan Kardec (1804-1869), in his famous *The Book of the Spirits*. Spiritists believe in reincarnation and in the possibility of contact between men and spirits. Life is a necessary experience for spiritual progress and death is just the beginning of another stage in the spirit's evolution. Brazil is said to be the country with the greatest number of spiritists in the world and many spiritist mediums have become internationally famous. A good example is Rubens Faria in Rio de Janeiro who performs thousands of mediumistic surgeries every day. Many influential people and artists have been operated on by him. Sadly, his mystique was called into question in 1999 when police investigated him for murder, charlatanism, tax evasion and money laundering.

Other important religions in Rio de Janeiro

Music and dance

Rio de Janeiro has an envious musical reputation even though most people outside of Brazil would be hard placed to name any song other than the 'Girl from Ipanema' or a composer other than Tom Jobim. But things have moved on somewhat since those heady days of the Sixties and although no longer the recording capital it once was, a wide variety of excellent music can still be heard in the city. Some styles like samba and choro are homegrown, others like rock and rave have been imported but all are played with a distinctive Carioca flair. Below is a brief guide to the musical treasure chest that waits in store for you. Those wishing to delve deeper into the complex and diverse Brazilian music scene are strongly recommended to consult some of the excellent books on the subject mentioned in 'Further reading' on page 84.

Meaning the new spirit, trend or feeling, *Bossa Nova* was born in the white middle class neighbourhoods of Rio's Zona Sul towards the end of the Fifties and lasted until the end of innocence in 1964 with the military coup. Its most famous exponents were Vinícius de Moraes and Tom Jobim although Baden Powell, Toquinho and João Gilberto were just as important. It was, however, Stan Getz, the American jazz saxophonist, who performed on Astrud Gilberto's recording of 'Girl from Ipanema', that projected the genre onto the world stage. Today although most of the pioneers are no longer with us, the songs are still extremely popular and can be heard in clubs all over the city but especially in Ipanema and Lagoa.

Bossa Nova

Towards the end of the 19th century a new instrumental style of music emerged in Rio which came to be known as *choro* (crying). It featured a solo instrument such as a flute which competed with the accompanying instruments which could be guitars, cavaquinhos (four string ukulele) or others. Although more closely linked with samba, the flautist and composer Pixinguinha with his group Os Oito Batutas,

Choro

also played this style throughout Europe and South America in the 1920s. Despite the later prevailing fashions of foxtrot, maxixe and tango, it continued in popularity throughout the 20th century, with many samba or jazz musicians also playing choro. Today it can still be heard in many of the samba clubs in Centro and Zona Norte as well as being popular in cultural centres and some cafés and restaurants.

Dance For many years links between the London and Rio club scenes have been growing steadily. In Copacabana clubs these days you are likely to hear far more techno, drum'n'bass and trance than you are samba or bossa nova. The beach party has become the beach rave for at least some of Rio's youth and is attracting more and more foreign partygoers to the scene as well as top DJs to the clubs. As well as the clubs of Zona Sul, the area around Lapa in central Rio is a good area for cheaper clubbing with a much wider social range of young Cariocas.

Forró It was during the Forties that an immigrant to Rio de Janeiro, Luiz Gonzaga created a new sound called *Baião* from the rhythms of his native state Pernambuco in the Northeast of Brazil. With his distinctive nasal vocals and accordion he recorded songs such as 'Asa Branca' the unofficial hymn of the *nordestino* still forced by drought to find work in Rio today. Forró is what their music and simple yet sensual dance is now called. Musicians from the Northeast such as Alceu Valença, Geraldo Azevedo, Zé and Elba Ramalho mixed it with MPB and rock during the 1970s whilst today popular groups for dancing are Banda Magníficos and Mastruz com Leite. It can be heard at the Feira do Nordeste as well as clubs all over the city and a few years ago even enjoyed popularity with young Cariocas who briefly adopted it before mostly moving on to the next fashion.

Funk A new musical import to the city's poorer districts, Rio funk is a mix of American hip hop with Brazilian cultural influences such as *capoeira*. Indeed it was the Brazilian community in New York who were the main instigators behind that city's break dancing craze which became popular at the beginning of the 1980s. Funk parties were mainly held in favelas usually sponsored by local drug traffickers who would pay for a DJ and sound team as a form of community relations. They have since spread to residential districts such as Campo Grande in Zona Oeste and are still extremely popular with younger and usually poorer Cariocas. Recently, however, they have gained a bad reputation due to violence between rival gangs of fans. Artists who have had commercial success with this genre are Gabriel O Pensador and Claudinho & Buchecha.

Jazz North American Jazz has benefited immensely from the participation of Brazilian musicians and in return the influence of the United States has also become closely interwoven with many forms of composition in Brazil. The records of Miles Davies, Herbie Hancock, Pat Metheny, Weather Report, Paul Winter and many others feature Brazilian musicians such as percussionists Airto Moreira, Naná Vasconcelos or singer Flora Purim. Other important Brazilian jazz musicians are saxophonist Moacir Santos, pianist Eliane Elias and the influential arranger Sérgio Mendes. There are many good jazz clubs in Zona Sul and it can be heard in the city's many piano bars as well.

MPB It was in the late Sixties and early Seventies that Bossa Nova and the newer sounds of 'Tropicalismo' began to be labelled together under the new catch all title of MPB (Música Popular Brasileira). Milton Nascimento and Chico Buarque, who had written protest songs like 'A Banda' against the military regime joined with the Great Bahians as they became known: Gilberto Gil, Gal Costa, Caetano Veloso and his sister Maria Bethânia to form the new Brazilian musical elite. Later arrivals included Djavan with his classic song 'Flor de Lis' and in the nineties Marisa Monte. Today the term is used to describe any form of easy listening music with usually a singer accompanied by a guitar or piano performing the songs that everyone knows. The stars usually perform in Canecão, the MPB temple but this is also the music you will often hear in bars and restaurants and a very pleasant accompaniment it is too.

Samba is still popular today outside of Carnival although mainly in the form of informal meetings of musicians known as *Rodas de samba* or *Pagodes de mesa* held in bars or botequins. The popular commercial recordings heard on the radio and seen on the television these days are now also known as *pagode*. Today's stars are often handsome male singers such as Alexandre Pires of Só Pra Contrariar, who resemble American soul groups in appearance. Although recording their fair share of ballads the music however is usually lively for dancing with irreverent lyrics and that distinctive samba rhythm. Many of these younger stars such as Grupo Molejo also still play their part in the traditional samba schools. Expect to find *pagode* anywhere from a Zona Sul beach bar to a *gafiera* dance hall in Centro.

Pagode

The roots of Brazilian rock were in the Jovem Guarda television show from 1965 to 1968 which launched the career of Roberto Carlos, who became the country's most popular recording artist in the seventies with his romantic ballads. Although often considered somewhat underground, stars such as Rita Lee and Ney Matogrosso also gained success in the 1970s with their mixture of American and Brazilian musical genres. It was however in the eighties that rock achieved its greatest popularity with groups like Blitz, Barão Vermelho and Paralamas do Sucesso playing on the bill of the 1985 *Rock in Rio* festival along with famous international acts. Many solo careers were formed in these groups producing singers such as the late Cazuza, Lobão and Fernanda Abreu. Although as much a part of the MTV generation as any country today there are still many local groups producing diverse rock music with a tropical twist.

Rock
The third Rock in Rio festival is scheduled to be held in Jacarepaguá during January 2001 with Cidade Negra, Jota Quest, Kid Abelha, O Rappa & other national & international acts

Samba was born around the turn of the century in the most African part of Rio around the old Praça XI. Musicians like Pixinguino and Sinhô mixed in other styles such as marcha and maxixe but the first song generally recognized as a samba was Donga's 'Pelo Telefone' in 1917. The Estácio district of the city was the cradle of the early *sambistas* such as Ismael Silva and Nilton Bastos who in 1928 formed the first escola de samba known as Deixa Falar. It was composers like Ary Barroso and Noel Rosa who made samba respectable but Carmen Miranda, made it world famous by taking it to Hollywood. By the 1950s the middle class however had turned to bossa nova and samba returned to the *morros* performed by figures such as Cartola, Nelson Cavaquinho, Zé Keti and the singer Elza Soares. The revival came during the 1970s and was later transformed by Beth Carvalho, Zeca Pagodinho and others into what became known as *pagode*. Today traditional samba clubs can be found in Centro and throughout Zona Norte but this is something you can hear anywhere in the city performed in the street and bars by amateur yet excellent musicians.

Samba

The following list is only a suggestion of the names and some recordings of the most famous exponents of the various musical styles covered above. A good place to start for the beginner to Brazilian music are the excellent *Cores do Brasil* (Music Collection International, 1991) compilations by Rick Glanville which have a good selection of artists and songs from bossa nova, choro, jazz, MPB and samba. David Bryne's *Brazil Classics* (Sire Records, 1989-1991) compilations covering Forró, MPB and Samba are also highly recommended.

Discography

Bossa Nova Astrud Gilberto, *The Astrud Gilberto Album* (Verve, 1965). João Gilberto, *Chega de Suadade* (EMI, 1959). Antônio Carlos Jobim, *Tom Jobim e Convidados* (Philips, 1985). Nara Leão, *Meus Sonhos Dourados* (Philips 1988). Baden Powell, *Afro Sambas* (Philips, 1966). Toquinho & Vinícius, *Dez anos de…* (Philips, 1979).

Choro Egberto Gismonti, *Solo* (ECM, 1979). Paulo Moura, *Confusão Urbana, Suburbana e Rural* (Braziloid, 1976). Hermeto Pascoal, *Slaves Mass* (WEA, 1977). Bola Sete, *Autêntico* (Fantasy, 1987 reprint).

Dance Marina Lima, *1 Noite e ½ - Remixes* (Polydor, 1999). M4J, *Brazil - Electronic Experience* (Trama, 1998).

Forró Luiz Gonzaga, *O Melhor de Luiz Gonzaga* (RCA, 1989). Banda Magníficos, *Me Usa* (Sony, 1997). Mastruz com Leite, *Ao Vivo* (Som Zoom, 1997). Jackson do Pandeiro, *Sua Majestade - O Rei do Ritmo*, (EMI, 1954). Elba Ramalho, *Flor da Paraíba* (BMG, 1998). Zé Ramalho, *Nação Nordestina* (BMG, 2000). Alceu Valença, *Sol e Chuva* (Som Livre, 1997).

Funk Claudinho & Buchecha, *A Forma* (1998). Gabriel O Pensador, *Quebra Cabeça* (1997).

Jazz Stan Getz with Luiz Bonfá, *Jazz Samba* (Verve, 1962). Ivan Lins, *Amar Assim* (Philips, 1988). Sérgio Mendes, *Sérgio Mendes & Brasil '66* (A&M, 1966). Airto Moreira, *Identity* (Arista, 1975). Tutty Moreno, Pirulito (and others), *Brasil* (Soul Jazz Records, 1994). Good percussion and other rhythms recorded in Rio. Flora Purim, *500 Miles High* (Milestone 1976). Uakati, *Mapa* (Philips, 1992). Naná Vasconcelos, *Rain Dance* (Island, 1989).

MPB Jorge Ben, *Jorge Ben* (Polygram, 1969). One of the liveliest and most infectious performers from Rio. Maria Bethânia, *Memória da Pele* (Philips, 1989). João Bosco, *Bosco* (CBS, 1989). Chico Buarque, *Construção* (Universal, 1971). Gal Costa, *Gal Costa* (Polygram, 1969). Djavan, *Luz* (CBS, 1982). Gilberto Gil, *Em Concerto* (WEA, 1987). Marisa Monte, *Verde Anil Amarelo Cor de Rosa e Carvão* (EMI, 1994). A more modern style by this good singer. Ed Motta, *Manual Práctico para Festas, Bailes e Afins - Vol 1* (Universal, 1997). Many different influences in this singer's style including his uncle Tim Maia. Elis Regina, *Essa Mulher* (WEA, 1979). One of Brazil's best female singers who died tragically in 1982. Caetano Veloso, *Caetano Veloso* (Philips, 1968).

Pagode Molejo, *Não Quero Saber de Ti Ti Ti* (Continental, 1996). Negritude Junior, *Gente da Gente* (EMI, 1995). Raça Negra, *Coleção Raça Negra* (Globo, 1998). Só Pra Contrariar, *Só Pra Contrariar* (BMG, 1997). Zeca Pagodinho, *Samba Pras Moças* (Universal, 1995).

Rock Roberto Carlos, *Em Ritmo de Aventura* (Sony, 1967). Cazuza, *Exagerado* (Gala, 1998). Good compilation of songs by the controversial Eighties singer. Engenheiros do Hawaii, *10,000 Destinos - Ao Vivo* (Universal, 2000). Rita Lee, *Rita Lee* (Som Livre, 1979). Paralamas do Sucesso, *Bora Bora* (Capitol, 1989). Planet Hemp, *Invasão do Sagaz Homem Fumaça* (Sony, 2000). Lulu Santos, *Amor à Arte* (RCA, 1988). Ney Mattogrosso, *Ney Mattogrosso Ao Vivo* (CBA, 1989).

Samba Alcione, *Fruto e Raiz* (RCA, 1986). Strong female singer from the Mangueira samba school. Beth Carvalho, *Alma do Brasil* (Philips, 1988). Clara Nunes, *O Canto da Guerreira* (EMI, 1989). Nélson Sargento, *Encanto da Paisagem* (Kuarup, 1986). Bezerra da Silva, *Justiça Social* (RCA, 1987). Sambas about life in Rio's favelas. Martinho da Vila, *Coração Malandro* (RCA, 1987). Consistently smiling singer from the Vila Isabel samba school. Paulinho da Viola, *Eu Canto Samba* (RCA, 1989). Traditional composer associated with the Portela samba school. Velha Guarda da Portela, *Tudo Azul* (Phonomotor, 2000).

The Business Side of the Othon Hotels Group.

The Othon Palace Hotels are the first class properties whithin the Othon Chain of Hotels in Brazil. Newly renovated rooms, a variety of restaurants, a full complement of banquet facilities, are some special features of Othon Palace Hotels. Now we are introducing the Othon Business Service, with even greater confort for your business needs, with these exclusive facilities:

OTHON *Palace*

- Rooms with mini bar, mini safe, datapoint for personal computer
- Complete Business Centre
- Complimentary airport transfer and advanced check in for Varig Airlines flights at Rio Othon Palace

To book Othon Palace call your travel agent, fax to 55 21 522-1697, or available under the SRS chain in all air line GDS.

www.srs-worldhotels.com
www.hoteis-othon.com.br
e-mail: srorio@othon.com.br

Othon Palace Hotels - Brazil
Whether You're ready for business or leisure, we are available for You.
Rio Othon Palace • Bahia Othon Palace • Belo Horizonte Othon Palace • Imperial Othon Palace

WORLD HOTELS

Useful words & phrases — see also Language in Essentials, page 24 and Food and drink, page 63

Greetings & courtesies

hello	oi	How are you?	*Como vai você?/ tudo bem?/tudo bom?*
good morning	*bom dia*		
good afternoon	*boa tarde*	I am fine	*vou bem/tudo bem*
good evening/ good night	*boa noite*	pleased to meet you	*um prazer*
		yes	*sim*
goodbye	*adeus/tchau*	no	*não*
see you later	*até logo*	excuse me/ I beg your pardon	*com licença*
please	*por favor/faz favor*		
thank you	*obrigado* (if a man is speaking)/*obrigada* (if a woman is speaking)	I do not understand	*não entendo*
		please speak slowly	*fale devagar por favor*
		What is your name?	*Qual é seu nome?*
thank you very much	*muito obrigado/ muito obrigada*	my name is_	*O meu nome é_*
		Go away!	*Vai embora!*

In conversation, most people refer to **you** as "você", although in the south and in Pará "tu" is more common. To be more polite, use "O Senhor/A Senhora". For **us**, "a gente" (people, folks) is very common when it includes **you** too.

Basic questions

Where is_?	*Onde está?/onde fica?*	Why?	*Por que?*
How much does it cost?	*Quanto custa?*	What for?	*Para que?*
How much is it?	*Quanto é?*	How do I get to_?	*Para chegar a_?*
When?	*Quando?*	I want to go to_	*Quero ir para_*
When does the bus leave?/arrive?	*A que hora sai/chega o ônibus?*	Is this the way to the church?	*Aquí é o caminho para a igreja?*

Basics

bathroom/toilet	*banheiro*	notes/coins	*notas/moedas*
police (policeman)	*a polícia (o polícia)*	travellers' cheques	*os travelers/os cheques de viagem*
hotel	*o hotel (a pensão, a hospedaria)*	cash	*dinheiro*
restaurant	*o restaurante (o lanchonete)*	breakfast	*o café de manh*
		lunch	*o almoço*
post office	*o correio*	dinner/supper	*o jantar*
telephone office	*(central) telefônica*	meal	*a refeição*
supermarket	*o supermercado*	drink	*a bebida*
market	*o mercado*	mineral water	*a água mineral*
green grocery shop	*a sacolão*	soft fizzy drink	*o refrigerante*
bank	*o banco*	beer	*a cerveja*
exchange house	*a casa de câmbio*	without sugar	*sem açúcar*
exchange rate	*a taxa de câmbio*	without meat	*sem carne*

Getting around

on the left/right	*à esquerda/à direita*	bus	*o ônibus*
straight on	*direito*	train	*o trem*
second street on the right	*a segunda rua à direita*	airport	*o aeroporto*
		aeroplane/airplane	*o avião*
to walk	*caminhar*	flight	*o vôo*
bus station	*a rodoviária*	first/second class	*primeira/segunda clase*
train station	*a ferroviária*	ticket	*o passagem/o bilhete*
combined bus & train station	*a rodoferroviária*	ticket office	*a bilheteria*
		bus stop	*a parada*

Accommodation

room	*quarto*	hot/cold water	*água quente/fria*
noisy	*barulhento*	to make up/clean	*limpar*
single/double room	*(quarto de) solteiro/ (quarto para) casal*	sheet(s)	*o lençol (os lençóis)*
room with two beds	*quarto com duas camas*	blankets	*as mantas*
		pillow	*o travesseiro*
with private bathroom	*quarto com banheiro privado*	clean/dirty towels	*as toalhas limpas/ sujas*
		toilet paper	*o papel higiênico*

Health

chemist	*a farmacia*	contraceptive (pill)	*anticoncepcional (a pílula)*
(for) pain	*(para) dor*		
stomach	*o estômago (a barriga)*	period	*a menstruação/ a regra*
head	*a cabeça*	sanitary towels	*toalhas absorventes/ higiênicas*
fever/sweat	*a febre/o suor*		
diarrhoea	*o diarréia*	tampons	*absorventes internos*
blood	*o sangue*	contact lenses	*lentes de contacto*
doctor	*o doutor/a doutora*	aspirin	*a aspirina*
condoms	*as camisinhas/ os preservativos*		

Time

at one o'clock	*a uma hora (da manhã/da tarde)*	it's twenty past six/ six twenty	*são seis e vinte*
at half past two/ two thirty	*as dois e meia*	it's five to nine	*são cinco para as nove*
at a quarter to three	*quinze para as três*	in ten minutes	*em dez minutos*
it's one o'clock	*é uma*	five hours	*cinco horas*
it's seven o'clock	*são sete horas*	Does it take long?	*Dura muito?*

Days

Monday	*segunda feira*	Thursday	*quinta feira*	Sunday	*domingo*
Tuesday	*terça feira*	Friday	*sexta feira*		
Wednesday	*quarta feira*	Saturday	*sábado*		

Months

January	*janeiro*	May	*maio*	September	*setembro*
February	*fevereiro*	June	*junho*	October	*outubro*
March	*março*	July	*julho*	November	*novembro*
April	*abril*	August	*agosto*	December	*dezembro*

Numbers

1	*um/uma*	7	*sete*	19	*dezenove*
2	*dois/duas*	8	*oito*	20	*vinte*
3	*três*	9	*nove*	21	*vinte e um*
4	*quatro*	10	*dez*	30	*trinta*
5	*cinco*	11	*onze*	40	*cuarenta*
6	*seis*	12	*doze*	50	*cinqüenta*
		13	*treze*	60	*sessenta*
		14	*catorze*	70	*setenta*
		15	*quinze*	80	*oitenta*
		16	*dezesseis*	90	*noventa*
		17	*dezessete*	100	*cem, cento*
		18	*dezoito*	1000	*mil*

(note also that *"meia"* - half - is frequently used for number 6, ie half-dozen)

Index

A

Abreu,
  Caio Fernando 239
accommodation 47
  see also *'sleeping'*
adventure sports 68
Agulhas Negras 205
AIDS 82
air travel 31
  domestic 50
airport information 37
  getting there 31
airline companies 31, 35
  domestic 50
aldeias 241
Alencar, José de 236
Amado, Jorge 243
Amaral, Antonio Enrique 232
Amaral, Tarsila do 231
Américo, Pedro 230
Anchieta, José de 236
Andrade, de Mário 237
Andrade, de Oswald 237
Angra dos Reis 207
Araruama 176
Archer, Manuel Gomes 158
architecture 230, 232
Arraial do Cabo 177
art galleries
  Arte Contemporanea 168
  Arte Moderna 119
  Arte Naif 129
  central Rio 108
  Belas Artes 103
  Palácio Capanema 103
ATMs 29
Autódromo 157
Avenida Presidente Vargas 99
Avenida Rio Branco 102
azulejos 230

B

Bandeira, Manuel 237
Barra da Tijuca 157
Barra de Guaratiba 163
Barra do Piraí 200
Barra Mansa 201
bars 65
  see also individual area
  Essentials sections
Benjamin Constant 126
Bienal Internacional 231
Biological Reserve of
  Poço das Antas 184

birdwatching 71
Bishop, Elizabeth 239
blocos 15
Boal, Augusto 238
boats to Rio 36
Bonaparte, Napoleon 220
Bosque da Barra 158
bossa nova 245
Botafogo 131
Brazilian literature 239
Brecheret, Vitor 231
Buarque, Chico 238
Burle Marx, Roberto 163, 235
buses 36, 53
  see also individual areas'
  transport section
business hours 38
Búzios 180

C

Cabo Frio 178
Caldas, Waltercio 232
Callado, Antônio 238
Camargo, Sérgio 231
camping 49
Campo Grande 164
Campos 184
candomblé 242
canoeing 69
car hire 56
cargo ships 36
Carioca 240
Carnaval 10, 108
  museum 111
cash machines 30
Castro, Amilcar de 231
Catete 118
Cathedral, Metropolitan 102
Cathedral, (New) 102
Catholicism 241
caving 69
Centro Cultural Laurinda
  Santos Lobo 126
Chácara do Céu 125
children 40
  health 77
  travelling with 40
Choro 245
Cinelândia 104
cinema 65
  see individual areas' Essentials
  section under 'Entertainment'
Clark, Lygia 231
climate 227
  when to go 22

climbing 68
clothing
  climate 22
  etiquette 42
Coffee Zone 196
colonization 219
Conde, Luiz Paulo 226
Conservatória 201
consulates,
  Brazilian worldwide 26
  foreign in Rio 46
Convento de
  Santo Antônio 102
Convento do Carmo 97
Copacabana 136
Corcovado 129, 227
Cordeiro, Waldemar 231
Cosme Velho 129
cost of living 31
Costa do Sol 174
Costa Verde 206
Costa, Lúcio 235
credit cards 29
  emergency numbers 30
Criadouro Zoobotânico da
  Pedra Branca 164
cultural tourism 71
currency 29
customs regulations 28
cycling 58

D

da Conceiço,
  Frei Domingos 230
dance 245
de Almeida Júnior,
  José Ferraz 230
de Brito, Francisco Xavier 230
de Moraes, Vinícius 245
Debret, Jean-Baptiste 230
departure tax 38
di Cavalcanti, Emilio 231
diarrhoea 79
Dias, Antônio Gonçalves 236
disabled travel 40
discography 247
diving 72
drink 64
drugs 46
Drummond, de Andrade 237
duty free allowance 28

E

eating 62
  Barra da Tijuca 160
  central Rio 106
  Copacabana 141
  Gloria, Catete and
  Flamengo 123
  Ipanema 148
  Leblon 148
  Leme 141
  Niteroi 169
  Northern Rio 115
  Santa Teresa 126
economy 224
ecotourism 43, 72
email 59
embassies
  Brazilian worldwide 26
  foreign in Rio 46
Engenheiro Passos 205
environment 226
Estácio de Sá 219
exchange rate 29

F

fauna 227
favelas 71, 156
fax services 61
Fazendas 196
festivals 67
  when to go 22
fishing 73
Flamengo 118
flora 227
Fonseca, Rubem 239
food 62
football 73
Forró 246
Fortaleza de Santa Cruz 168
Forte de Copacabana 137
Forte do Vigia 137
Forte Duque de Caxias 137
Franco, Siron 232
Freyre, Gilberto 238
fruit 64
fuel 55
Fundação Eva Klabin
  Rapaport 153

G

Gabeira, Fernando 238
Gávea 152
gay travel 40
　bars 134
geography 226
geology 226
Getz, Stan 245
Gilbertom, João 245
Glória 118
Goeldi, Osvaldo 231
golf 73
government 224
Guanabara Bay 165

H

hang gliding 70
health 76, 225
　AIDS 82
　children 77
　hepatitis 82
　intestinal upsets 79
　medical facilities 77
　rabies 82
　vaccinations 77
　what to take 77
hepatitis 82
　vaccinations 78
history 219
hitchhiking 59
holidays 67
horse racing 74
horse riding 69
hotel price guide 48
hotels 47

I

Ibama 228
Igreja da Ordem Terceira
　do Carmo 97
Ilha de Guaritiba 163
Ilha de Paquetá 166
Ilha Grande 209
Imperial Palace 97
indigenous peoples
　history 219
inoculations 28, 77
Instituto Moreira Salles 154
insurance
　car 56
　medical 76
internet 59
　useful websites 86
Ipanema 146
Itacuruçá 206
Itaipava 190
Itatiaia 204
Itatiaia National Park 204

J

Jacuecanga 208
Jardim Botânico 152
jazz 246
Joaquim, Leandro 230
Jobim, Tom 245

K

Kardec, Allan 245

L

Lagoa 152
Lagos Fluminenses 174
language 24
Largo da Carioca 101
Leblon 146
Leirner, Nelson 232
Leme 136
lesbian travel 40
library, National 103
Lierner, Jac 232
Lima Barreto, Afonso 237
Lispector, Clarice 238
literature 236

M

Macaé 183
Machado de Assis,
　Joaquim Maria 236
magazines 61
Malfatti, Anita 231
Mangaratiba 207
maps 39
Maracanã Stadium 111
Maricá 174
Marina da Glória 118
Maringá 203
Maromba 203
media 61
medical facilities 77
Meireles, Cildo 232
Meireles, Vítor 230
Mestre Valemtim 230
metrô 52
Miguel Pereira 197
Minas Gerais 221
Miranda, Carmen 95, 247
Mirantão 203
mobile phones 61
money 29
Montigny, Grandjean de 234
Morro da Conceição 101
motor sport 74
motorcycling 57
motoring 54
　car insurance 56
mountain biking 70
Muriqui 206

Museu do Bonde 126
music 245
　central Rio 108

N

National Museum 113
National Observatory 113
national parks 228
newspapers 61
Niemeyer, Oscar 235
nightclubs, 107
　see also individual areas'
　Essentials sections
Niterói 167
Northern Rio 111
Nova Friburgo 194

O

Oiticica, Hélio 231
Olorum 243
Oratório de Nossa Senhora do
　Cabo da Boa Esperança 97
orixá 242
Orixás 243

P

Pagode 247
Pão de Açúcar 131, 132, 227
parapenting 70
Paraty 211
Paraty Mirim 213
Parque Arruda Câmara 158
Parque Carlos Lacerda 152
Parque da Chacrinha 138
Parque da Cidade 153
Parque das Ruínas 125
Parque do Flamengo 118
Parque Ecológico Municipal
　Chico Mendes 158
Parque Estadual da
　Pedra Branca 164
Parque Guinle 122
Parque Laje 153
Parque Nacional Restinga
　de Jurubatiba 183
Parque Tom Jobim 152
Pati do Alferes 197
Pedra Bonita 156
Pedra da Gávea 156
Pedra de Guaritiba 163
Penedo 202
people 240
Petrópolis 186
Pico de Tijuca 227
Planetarium 153
police 46
　tourist 93
Poliomyelitis
　vaccination 78
politics 224
Portinari, Candido 231

Portugese 24
postal services 59
Praça da República 105
Praça Marechal Âncora 99
Praça Mauá 100
prohibitions 43

Q

Quinta da Boa Vista 112

R

rabies 82
radio 61
rain forest 227
Ramos, Graciliano 238
Rego, José Lins do 238
Reidy, Affonso Eduardo 235
religion 241
Resende 202
restaurants 62
　see also 'Eating' and
　in individual areas'
　Essentials sections
restinga 228
Rio Bonito 183
Rio das Flores 200
Rio das Ostras 182
Rio Water Planet 158
road travel 36
Rua da Gamboa 111
Rua Pinheiro Machado 122

S

safety 90
sailing 76
samba 247
samba schools 10
Sambódromo 111
Santa Cruz 164
Santa Teresa 125
Santo Antônio de Pádua 184
Santos Dumont airport 37
São Conrado 155
São Cristóvão 113
São Pedro da Aldeia 177
Saquarema 175
sculpture 230
security 45
Segall, Lasar 231
self-catering 49
Semana da
　Arte Moderna 231, 235, 237
Serpa, Ivan 231
Serra da Bocaína 211
Serra da Bocaina,
　Parque Nacional 216
Serra dos Órgãos 193
shopping 66
Sítio Roberto Burle Marx 163
slave trade 221

sleeping
  Barra da Tijuca 159
  Botafogo, Urca 134
  central Rio 105
  children 41
  Copacabana 138
  Gloria, Catete and
    Flamengo 122
  Ipanema 147
  Jardim Botanico 154
  Leblon 147
  Leme 138
  Niteroi 169
  Northern Rio 115
  Santa Teresa 126
  Sao Conrado 156
  Western Rio 165
Southern Rio 118
Spiritism 245
sport
  adventure sports 68
  diving 72
  fishing 73
  surfing 74
  squash 75
  swimming 75
student travel 40
Sugar Loaf Mountain 131, 132
surfing 74

T

taipa de pilão 232
tamarin 185
tap water 79
Taunay, Nicolas-Antoine 230
taxis 54
taxis from airport 37
Teatro Municipal 102
telephones 60
  mobile 61
television 61
tennis 75
Teresópolis 191
Terra Encantada 158
Tetanus 78
theatre
  see individual areas'
  Essentials sections
  under 'Entertainment'
Tijuca National Park 158
time 38
tipping 43
Toca de Vinicius 147
tour operators 22
tourism 225
tourist information 24, 38
train travel 51
trams, Santa Teresa 52
transport
  air 31
  airport information 37
  boat 36
  car hire 56
  car insurance 56
  cycling 58

getting there 31
hitchhiking 59
motorcycling 57
motoring 54
travellers' cheques 29
trekking 69
Tunga 232
Tupan 241
Typhoid
  vaccination 78

U

Umbanda 242
Urca 131

V

vaccinations 28, 77
Valença 200
Vassouras 197
vegetarians 63
Veloso, Caetano 238
Vidigal 155
Vila do Abraão 209
Vila Riso 156
visas 25
Visconde de Mauá 203
Volta Redonda 201
voltage 38

W

water 79
websites 86
weights 38
Western Rio 163
Wet'nWild Rio 158
whitewater rafting 71
windsurfing 76
women travellers 41

Y

yachting 76
Yellow Fever 78
youth hostels 49

Z

Zoological Garden 113

Maps

149	Arpoador	112	Northern Rio: west of centre
160	Barra da Tijuca and National Park	214	Paraty
138	Copacabana	187	Petrópolis
174	Costa do Sol	96	Praça 15 de Novembro
206	Costa Verde	94	Rio de Janeiro centre
50	Domestic air routes	52	Rio de Janeiro orientation
120	Glória, Santa Teresa, Catete, Flamengo	90	Rio de Janeiro Metrô
209	Ilha Grande	11	Sambódromo
146	Ipanema, Leblon	193	Serra dos Órgãos
204	Itatiaia	132	Urca, Botafogo, Cosme Velho
104	Lapa	196	Vale do Rio Paraíba do Sul
167	Niterói		

Will you help us?

We try as hard as we can to make each Footprint Handbook as up-to-date and accurate as possible but, of course, things always change. Many people write to us - with corrections, new information, or simply comments.

If you want to let us know about an experience or adventure - hair-raising or mundane, good or bad, exciting or boring or simply something special - we would be delighted to hear from you. Please give us as precise information as possible, quoting the edition number (you'll find it on the front cover) and page number of the Handbook you are using.

Your help will be greatly appreciated, especially by other travellers. In return we will send you details about our special guidebook offer.

Write to Elizabeth Taylor
Footprint Handbooks
6 Riverside Court
Lower Bristol Road
Bath
BA2 3DZ
England
or email: rio1_online@footprintbooks.com

RIO. INCOMPARÁVEL

More than just a city, Rio is an incomparable place to visit.
It has natural beauty, friendly and spirited people -
the Cariocas - and an abundance of things to do
and places to visit, beaches, superb food and music
to be enjoyed all year round.

For information or a suggested itinerary contact:
Rio Tourist Office
Tel: 020 7431 0303
Fax: 020 7431 7920
Email: destinations@axissm.com
Web: www.rio.rj.gov.br/riotur

Acknowledgements

I would like to thank the following for their help in the preparation of this Handbook and/or for their hospitality in the city and state during my visits in February, June and August of this year. **Ben Box**, who has seen the Rio de Janeiro text grow from the South American Handbook to the Brazil Handbook and finally to its very own Handbook. Thank you indeed for all your assistance over the past three years. **Fábio Sombra** for his illustrations, paintings and expert knowledge as well as for showing me parts of the city I'd never seen. **Beatrix Boscardin** for her detailed research in the city and articles on Brazil from a woman's point of view. **Cristina Monteiro** and all the staff at *Riotur* for their excellent information on the city. **Faud Atala** of *TurisRio* for information on the state. The **Rio Convention & Visitors Bureau** for information on conferences and the city. **Denise Werneck** of *Rio Hiking* for her perceptive notes on Santa Teresa and Rio's youth. **Luiz Felipe Amaral** of *Rio Life* for his enjoyable company and for showing me where Cariocas like to spend their evenings. **Marcelo Armstrong** of *Favela Tour* for a very interesting visit to Rocinha and Vila Canoas. **Paulo Celani** of *Just Fly* for his information on hang gliding. **Professor Carlos Roquette** of *Cultural Rio* for his information on cultural tourism in the city. **Marcia Leão Bonnet** (University of Essex) for her informed advice on everything from Rio's churches to its restaurants. Many thanks to **Debbie Wylde** for her assistance with my flights, hotels and for sharing her memories of Rio and Paraty with me. Also thank you to **Tim Murray-Walker** of *Journey Latin America* and **Renata Pires** of *Varig Brazilian Airlines* in London as well as Tomás Ramos of Othon Hotels and all the staff of the Savoy Othon in Copacabana. And a special thank you to Martin Morgan who first encouraged me to try and write a book on the city to carry on from the cult Insider's Guide to Rio by Christopher Pickard (who also gave me valuable advice). Thanks once again to the team at Footprint for all their efforts and for putting up with me through yet another book this year!

Fábio Sombra

Fábio Sombra was born in Rio de Janeiro, Brazil. Besides his work as a painter and illustrator, he teaches and researches History of Art, Brazilian Folklore and other subjects related to Brazilian Culture. Since 1994 he has been in the tourism business, acting as a consultant and coordinating projects on Cultural Tourism. Fábio has provided many illustrations for this Handbook, including the painting on the back cover, as well as articles on Búzios, Vassouras, Paraty, Religion and Architecture.

Beatrix Boscardin

Born in Curitiba, Southern Brazil, Beatrix first started travelling the world as an airhostess for Lufthansa. Later after working in tourism in the Amazon and Iguaçu Falls, she lived in Rio de Janeiro for eight years and was a partner in a travel agency there. She currently works as a freelance photojournalist and her articles on Brazil have appeared in several Portuguese magazines.

Specialist contributors

Peter Pollard, Geography and Climate; Dr Nigel Dunstone (University of Durham), Flora and Fauna; Professor John Gledson (University of Liverpool), Literature; Dr Valerie Fraser (University of Essex), Fine Art and Sculpture; Dr David Snashall, Health;

Piet Hein Snel, Surfing; Mark Eckstein, Responsible Tourism; Richard Robinson, Worldwide Radio; Lucy Davies and Mo Fini (Tumi) who allowed us to use material from Arts and Crafts in Latin America.

Many thanks also to all the members of the Footprint family and friends: the travellers and residents who wrote in with their comments, corrections and further information on Rio de Janeiro: Michaela Braunreiter, Wien, Austria; Caroline Brown and Brett Howat, Gymea, Australia; Kevin Casey; D Cohn; Alex D. Halbach, Rio de Janeiro, Brazil; Andreas Isler and Sandra Pfister, Pfäffikon, Switzerland; C.G. McKensie, London, England; Katharina Gsaenger; Alfred Lauener, Switzerland; Sam Solow, Netanya, Israel; Tim Shaw, Wotton-Under-Edge, England; Fanie and Lené Smit, South Africa; Andreas Staubli and Judith Zanini, Oberwit-Leili, Switzerland; Åshild Talland, Oslo, Norway; Don and Ruth Waterhouse, Honiton, England (and Arraial do Cabo, Brazil); Janine and Tim, Pilbara, Australia.

Ben Box and Mick Day

Mick Day

Since 1990, Mick has lived, travelled and worked throughout Central and South America from the Yucatan to Port Stanley. After graduating from the University of Essex in Modern Languages and Linguistics he became a consultant on Latin America and the Caribbean. His first visit to Rio de Janeiro was in 1995 when he saw the New Year in on Copacabana beach. Since then he's returned to the 'Cidade Maravilhosa' many times, including in 1998 for Carnival, and greatly enjoys running his virtual office from a shady Ipanema beach bar. He currently writes the Brazil Handbook and Venezuela Handbook for Footprint, and is a regular contributor to the legendary South American Handbook.

Ben Box

As a freelance writer Ben has contributed to newspapers, magazines and learned tomes, usually on the subject of travel, and became editor of the South American Handbook in 1989. For Footprint, he has also been involved in the Mexico & Central American Handbook, Caribbean Islands Handbook and Brazil Handbook since their inception. Having a doctorate in Spanish and Portuguese studies from London University, Ben maintains a strong interest in Latin American literature. He lives in a 16th-century farmhouse with his family and assorted four-legged and feathered friends and, when not travelling, he indulges in the very un-Brazilian pastime of village cricket.